Selling Mrs. Consumer

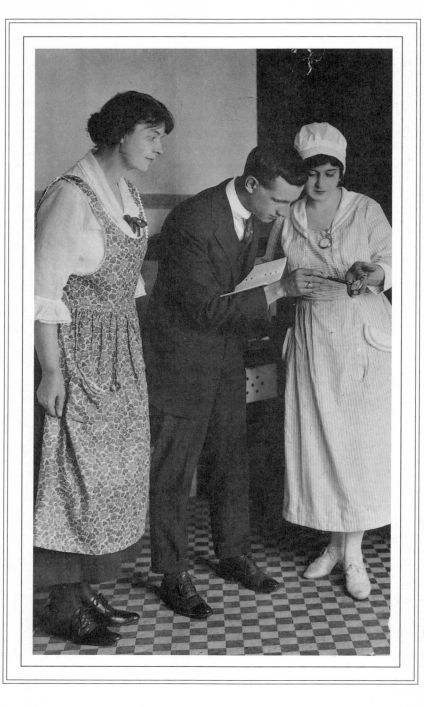

Selling
Mrs. Consumer

CHRISTINE FREDERICK
& the Rise of
Household Efficiency

Janice Williams Rutherford

The University of Georgia Press
Athens & London

© 2003 by the University of Georgia Press
Athens, Georgia 30602
All rights reserved

Designed by Sandra Strother Hudson
Set in Goudy Oldstyle with Kennerly Oldstyle display
by Graphic Composition, Inc.
Printed and bound by Maple-Vail
The paper in this book meets the guidelines for permanence
and durability of the Committee on Production Guidelines
for Book Longevity of the Council on Library Resources.

Printed in the United States of America
06 05 04 03 02 C 5 4 3 2 1

Library of Congress Cataloging-in-Publication Data
Rutherford, Janice Williams, 1942–
Selling Mrs. Consumer : Christine Frederick and
the rise of household efficiency /
Janice Williams Rutherford
p.   cm.
Includes bibliographical references and index.
ISBN 0-8203-2449-3 (hardcover : alk. paper) —
ISBN 0-8203-2480-9 (pbk. : alk. paper)
1. Frederick, Christine, b. 1883—Biography.
2. Home economics. I. Title.
TX140.F74 R88 2003
640—dc21   2002011210

British Library Cataloging-in-Publication Data available

FOR FRANK

Contents

Preface

WHEN I FIRST DISCOVERED Christine Frederick and began to focus on her work as a possible dissertation topic, I found her interesting because I did not like her. At the time, I was earnestly absorbing the revelations I found in feminist women's history, and I condemned Christine harshly for duping early-twentieth-century women into thinking that they were participating in modernity by becoming more efficient housewives. By contrast, she was enjoying the exhilaration and rewards of a career in the public sphere. It seemed to me that the modernity she sold to other women was compromised by the old ideology that confined women to the private sphere. It was gendered modernity.

The longer I have worked on Christine Frederick's life and career, the more I have come to understand that I am intrigued by her contradictions because I am bound by them. Nineteenth-century ideology was alive and well in the 1950s when I was learning how to be a woman. I was reared to be a good homemaker, and I happily became one. What's more, I enjoyed the role enormously during the years when my children were young and our magnificent old Queen Anne house required much of my attention. I still find as much satisfaction in turning out a perfect loaf of whole-wheat bread as I do in developing an argument for a conference paper. Somewhere in my psyche or my DNA—pick your theory—I revel in my own affinity for "woman's work." Since I also value women's—and men's—right to reject natural affinity for assigned gender roles, however, I continue to be both fascinated and appalled by Christine Frederick's insistence that all women would be happier if only they learned to be content in their homes. If contradiction is evident in my own assessment of the contradictions I examine here, I offer this acknowledgment of my own duality.

I have struggled mightily with another feminist dilemma and must explain here a convention I have adopted reluctantly. I have used my subject's first name throughout the book. I aver that the use of a first name suggests diminution of the subject and, when that subject is female, further suggests diminution of women. But much of this history is the history of Christine's relationship with her husband, J. George Frederick. In chapters in which both Fredericks figure prominently, it has simply been clearer to refer to both of them by their first names. For the sake of consistency, I have continued the practice in chapters in which J. George does not appear.

From the first inspiration to the final publication of this book, I have received support and assistance from mentors, colleagues, friends, and loved ones. Since the project was conceived as a doctoral dissertation, my first expression of gratitude must go to my committee at Louisiana State University: Burl L. Noggle, Robert A. Becker, Gaines M. Foster, Emily Toth, and Charles J. Shindo. I am also grateful to the late Sarah Hunter Graham for encouraging me to pursue women's history.

I wish to thank the Arthur and Elizabeth Schlesinger Library on the History of Women in America for a dissertation grant, Louise Dougher and the volunteers at the Greenlawn-Centerport Historical Association, and Patrick M. Quinn, archivist at Northwestern University. I owe special thanks to Kathryn K. Conoly, who handles interlibrary borrowing at Atlanta-Fulton Public Library. I am grateful to Washington State University for two Completion Grants and to my colleagues there; Richard Hume read an early version of the manuscript, and Susan Armitage offered the advice of an eminent and seasoned women's historian. The comments of Elizabeth Fox-Genovese, Emory University, and Natalie A. Naylor, Hofstra University, have done much to shape the final document. I am especially grateful to Professor Naylor for the care with which she examined different versions of the manuscript.

Many informants shared their memories of Christine Frederick and her family. They are all listed in the back of this book as sources, but I must express my special debt to Christine's daughter, the late Jean Joyce, without whose impeccable memory and tolerance for probing questions this work would lack the humanity her stories give it.

I owe the endurance required to finish this project to my mother, Margaret M. Williams, who taught me that to be happy, one must love one's work. My daughter, Melissa Rutherford, and my son, Wayne Rutherford, whose achievements have always cheered me, inspired me, in turn, to expand my own. Finally, I would have neither begun nor finished this book without the support and encouragement of Frank Steffes.

PORTIONS OF THE TEXT were previously published as "A Foot in Each Sphere: Christine Frederick and Early-Twentieth-Century Advertising," *The Historian* 63, no. 1 (fall 2000): 67–86. Portions of the text were previously published as "Christine Frederick: Barometer of Conflict" in *Long Island Women: Activists and Innovators,* ed. Natalie A. Naylor and Maureen O. Murphy (Interlaken, N.Y.: Empire State Books, 1998), 217–26, and appear here courtesy of Hofstra University, Long Island Studies Institute. Excerpts from Advertising Women of New York, Inc., Records, Beecher-Stowe Family Papers, Bureau of Vocational Information Records, Dorothy Dignam Papers, Christine MacGaffey Frederick Papers, and Records of the Women's Educational and Industrial Union are used courtesy of the Schlesinger Library, Radcliffe Institute, Harvard University. Excerpts from the Atlanta Woman's Club Papers are used courtesy of the Atlanta History Center. Excerpts from the Alumni Biographical Files of Northwestern University are used courtesy of Northwestern University. Excerpts from the Calbreath Family Collection are used courtesy Special Collections and Archives, University of Oregon.

Prologue

Woman's true position is in her home. It is here that her
highest development is attained; here is her greatest field of usefulness.
Her relation to the world is as important as man's.
CHRISTINE MacGAFFEY (FREDERICK), "The Genius of Woman," [1902?]

She who is the mother and housekeeper in a large family is the sovereign
of an empire, demanding more varied cares, and involving more difficult duties,
than are really exacted of her who wears a crown and professedly regulates
the interests of the greatest nation on earth.
CATHARINE BEECHER, *Treatise on Domestic Economy*, 1869

CHRISTINE MACGAFFEY FREDERICK wanted early-twentieth-century American women to embrace modernization. But she adhered to the basic premise of an ideology constructed in the previous century, the century into which she was born. To understand this dichotomy, one must understand the nineteenth-century view of women. A fitting protagonist of that view was a woman who lived with a similar dichotomy, a woman whose work shaped some of Christine Frederick's ideas.

Catharine Esther Beecher was born in 1800, the eldest child of the prominent nineteenth-century Calvinist religious leader Lyman Beecher.[1] Although she remained single all of her life, Catharine Beecher defined the American woman's primary role as wife, mother, and homemaker more fully than anyone else in her time. Her remarkable career serves as prologue to the equally re-markable career of her twentieth-century successor, Christine Frederick.

The Beechers, though prominent, were often short of funds, and at the age of twenty-three, Catharine opened the Hartford Female Seminary as a means to earn money. This step marked the beginning of her lifelong work in educational reform. Nine years later, in 1832, Catharine accompanied her father to Cincinnati, where he became president of Lane Theological Seminary. There, within a year of her arrival, she established the Western Female Institute. Its failure in 1837 did not deter Catharine from her mission to establish schools throughout the West and to recruit young women to teach in them. For the next three decades she was an indefatigable traveler and promoter. She engaged female teachers, established an organization to facilitate their training, and spoke to scores of groups to raise money.[2] She also wrote voluminously about education, morality, and religion. All of her writings revealed her strong belief that woman should wield influence from the home, and it is this aspect of her work that presaged Christine Frederick's course a generation after Beecher's death.

Beecher was born at the dawn of the century that "knew the differences between the sexes and that these differences were total and innate."[3] As the century advanced, American social commentators identified the virtues of "true womanhood": piety, purity, submissiveness, and domesticity.[4] A woman demonstrated these virtues to the fullest by marrying and presiding over a home. As wife and mother, she was expected to offer emotional support to her husband as he pursued his work in the larger world, to oversee the religious and moral training of her family, and to manage the labor necessary to operate a home.[5]

The rapid progress of the Industrial Revolution during the nineteenth century precipitated the separation of spheres by gender. People perceived a decline in morality in the public arena, where industrialization and commerce prevailed; but the home, protected from the competition and materialism of the business world, could preserve virtue. Women would eschew the outside world to ensure that the values threatened by industrialization would survive.[6]

Catharine Beecher's work reflected the view that the public sphere was so besmirched by competition, greed, and hostility that women should not enter it, but rather provide a countervailing force to it. In 1837, for example, she wrote that politics was so riddled with "falsehood, anger, pride, malice, revenge and every evil word and work" that women, who were the "appointed ministers of all the gentler charities of life," should "relinquish the attitude of a partisan" and mediate as "advocate[s] of peace" among men.[7] Beecher understood that women had struck a bargain, according to her biographer. If they would "limit their participation in the society as a whole . . . then they could ascend to total hegemony over the domestic sphere."[8] Beecher articulated this understanding in 1851 when she wrote that when women are properly trained to be educators in the home, "every woman will be so profitably and so honorably employed in the appropriate duties of her peculiar profession, that the folly of enticing her into masculine employments will be deemed . . . ridiculous."[9]

Nor should men undertake feminine employment. As eldest daughter,

Beecher accepted without question that it fell to her to tend to her brothers' domestic needs. Edward Beecher wrote to her from Yale, "I wish the striped pantaloons I send to be lengthened as the other pair was," and, "P. S. I wish a watch pocket to be made in each pair of pantaloons immediately." Not only did his sister mend his clothes, she also laundered them. "There was no towel among my clothes so that I am obliged to use a pillow case—I wish two to be sent next week," he complained two months after requesting the alterations.[10] Catharine wrote in both her *Treatise on Domestic Economy*, 1841, and *The American Woman's Home*, 1869, "Few things are in worse taste, than for a man needlessly to busy himself in women's work," a view in which Christine Frederick emphatically concurred fifty-nine years later.[11]

For Beecher, woman "dignified her own profession" in the home. Within "the domestic and social circle" she could do her moral duty and instill Christian values without the risk of facing the conflict man encountered "in the boundaries of his sphere." If she emerged from the domestic circle, woman would not only lose influence, but also "the sacred protection of religion."[12] Beecher explained this view in 1841:

[N]o domestic, civil, or political, institution, is right, that sacrifices [woman's] interest to promote that of the other sex. But in order to secure her the more firmly in all these privileges, it is decided, that . . . in civil and political concerns, her interest be intrusted to the other sex, without her taking any part in voting, or in making and administering laws.[13]

Woman, then, had "a superior influence" in matters of education, religion, and morals. Of course she was also responsible for the physical maintenance of the home. In this capacity, the wife and mother should "meet [her] daily crosses with . . . a cheerful temper."[14] Housekeeping duties were so well fitted to woman's nature, Beecher believed, that the proper performance of them benefited her health: "God made woman so that her health and comfort are best promoted by doing the work she is appointed to perform. The tending of children, the house-work of a family, duly combined with its sedentary pursuits, all tend to strengthen and develop those central muscles of the body that hold its most important organs in their place."[15]

Beecher promoted the field of education as an appropriate extension of the domestic sphere for women who did not marry and rear children, but she never lost sight of the basic assumption that women's ordained work was domestic.

Even single women should form families, she suggested. In a plan she outlined for women's universities, for example, she wrote that the principal and associate principal of the elementary section could "establish a family, consisting of the two, who would take the place of parents to several adopted orphans and to several pay-pupils whose parents . . . would relinquish the care of their children." Beecher suggested in many of her writings that single women could make homes by adopting orphans.[16]

Marriage, however, was woman's preferred state. At the age of seventy, Beecher wrote an urgent letter to Elizabeth Cady Stanton, trying to dissuade Stanton from speaking out in favor of dissolution in the wake of a sensational divorce case. The "family state," she told Stanton, was being undermined and laws that "sustain" it should be upheld at all costs. Beecher believed that proven adultery was the only valid ground for divorce. She begged Stanton to be "very cautious and guarded" regarding this matter in an upcoming lecture.[17]

Like most nineteenth-century writers, Beecher portrayed domestic life as serene and blissful. While staying at her sister Harriet's home in 1837, she wrote a description of the happy scene to friends:

> I wish you could just step across our garden into [Harriet's] little box & go up stairs into a little upper verandah & there you will see a little swing cradle suspended and at one end sits little Harriet playing, who looks up with bright blue eyes & an ever ready smile—a fat, easy, plump, quiet little puss. At the other end lies little Elisa—smaller, more delicate, & quietly sucking her thumb. . . . Harriet sits by darning stockings & looking rather thin & worn. Mr. Stowe is in his little study busy with his books. Anne—the mainstay is in the kitchen alternate nurse, cook & chambermaid. They live very snugly & have but little work to do compared with most families, & have as great a share of domestic enjoyment as ordinarily falls to the lot of married people who are entirely satisfied with each other.[18]

The ideal notwithstanding, Beecher had to create a role within a role for the single woman. "Generally speaking there seems to be no very extensive sphere of usefulness for a single woman but that which can be found in the limits of a school-room," she wrote to her father after her own plans to marry were dashed by her fiancé's death.[19] Her argument that it was woman's peculiar moral duty to educate children allowed her to include the school in the domestic sphere.

In Catharine Beecher's early educational programs at the Hartford Female

Seminary, housekeeping was incorporated into school life.[20] Later she decided that domestic training should be taught in girls' schools as part of the curriculum, too. "[M]any young ladies, who can tell how to make oxygen and hydrogen, and discuss questions of Philosophy or Political Economy, do not know how to properly make a bed and sweep a room," she wrote disapprovingly. Girls would respect domestic economy as an important field of learning, she argued, if it were taught properly in the schools.[21]

Beecher feared that woman's sacred duty was being dishonored because so many young women did not know how to manage a home, and the servants available after the onset of the Industrial Revolution were primarily immigrants who did not know how to keep house by American standards.[22] "It is generally assumed. . . ," she wrote, "that a housekeeper's business and cares are contracted and trivial; and that the proper discharge of her duties demands far less expansion of mind and vigor of intellect than the pursuits of the other sex."[23] Beecher wanted to correct this assumption by elevating homemaking. If women's work were "elevated to an honorable and remunerative science and profession, by the same methods that men have taken to elevate their various professions," she believed, American women would be much happier.[24] "[A] woman who has charge of a large household should regard her duties as dignified, important and difficult," she wrote. Christine Frederick would borrow this argument in 1913 when she wrote that training in scientific management would improve the reluctant homemaker's attitude about domestic labors.[25]

For Beecher, then, American education should "raise the science and practice of domestic economy to its appropriate place, as a regular study in female seminaries."[26] Housekeeping was as worthy of professors, lectureships, and "scientific treatment" as any occupation held by men.[27] When society does not value homemaking, she said, women are drawn away from it. Men were leaving their "comfortless," uncared-for homes to go to men's clubs. Thus deserted, she cautioned, women would seek clubs, too. Furthermore, competent servants were not available because American girls preferred factory work to domestic service, which they perceived as less respectable.[28] Christine Frederick would update these views to address twentieth-century ambivalence over the value of domestic labor half a century later.

Her biographer notes that Catharine Beecher exerted a strong influence on American households through her housekeeping manuals, *A Treatise on Domestic Economy* and *The American Woman's Home*. After publishing *Treatise* in

1841, she became a recognized authority on the home. Wherever she went, she was hailed "as the heroine who had simplified and made understandable the mysterious arts of household maintenance, child rearing, gardening, cooking, cleaning, doctoring, and the dozen other responsibilities middle class women assumed to keep their children and husbands alive and well."[29] Before Beecher organized the information contained in her homemaking books, there had been no attempt to systemize "that body of knowledge needed to run and care for a household."[30] She offered advice on a wide variety of subjects in which she felt the American housewife should be competent: laundry, cleaning, nutrition, social intercourse, etiquette, and spiritual obligations. In the later volume, Beecher emphasized a woman's responsibility to create a Christian home and a Christian family, but in both books, much of the information had to do with the proper care of a household.

Beecher was one of the first to advise American women to develop the "habit of system and order" in caring for their homes, or to practice efficiency, as a later era would label it. She suggested a weekly schedule: Monday should be set aside for planning, Tuesday for laundry, Wednesday for ironing, and so on. Not only did Beecher advise the homemaker to manage her time, she also suggested ways to organize space. She advised that a special closet be designated for laundry supplies, a compartmentalized trunk for sewing and mending, particular nooks in the kitchen for each implement.[31] Christine Frederick's 1913 efficiency manual would also instruct the homemaker in methods of putting her household in order.

Beecher provided detailed instructions for all manner of household work. She carefully described the process of washing dishes properly, for example, listing the necessary tools (swab, cloths, towels, tin tubs, draining waiter, soap dish, and soap) and then enumerating each step (scraping, mixing soap, washing dishes in a particular order, rinsing, draining, wiping, and putting away). She detailed in similar fashion the minutiae of setting the table, doing the laundry, starching, ironing, and cleaning the house. Her books gave clear instruction on laying wall-to-wall carpet, varnishing furniture, and carving meat. Beecher also offered interior decorating advice, suggesting types and colors of floor coverings, wallpapers, and upholstery and commenting on fashions in furnishings.[32]

Acknowledging the fact that it was becoming more and more difficult to hire servants, Beecher provided plans for small houses in which the housewife could do all her own work, and in the 1869 volume, she featured a plan of her own design.[33] She advocated simplicity, commenting that she "hoped, that, as the science of domestic economy improves in this Country, much less money will be laid out in parlors, verandas, porticos, and entries; and the money thus saved, be employed in increasing the conveniences of the kitchen, and the healthfulness and comfort of those parts of the house most used by the family."[34] Christine Frederick would argue for women's right to household conveniences decades later.

Foreshadowing the redefinition of the female role as consumer, Beecher assumed that the wife purchased the household goods, and offered sensible advice on choosing products. She suggested a budget system, advising women to divide their expenditures into categories. Young girls, she wrote, should be taught how to purchase necessities economically, since "so many young ladies take charge of a husband's establishment, without having had either instruction or experience in the leading duty of their station."[35]

Catharine Beecher's advice revealed a profound respect for usefulness and a stern bias against wasting time. Turning to leisure, she counseled that "the only legitimate object of amusement is to prepare mind and body for the proper discharge of duty, the protracting of such as interfere with regular employments, or induce excessive fatigue, or weary the mind, or invade the proper hours for repose, must be sinful."[36] She frowned on attending the theater, dancing, or novel reading for the young because these activities were too exciting and might promote ill health. Instead, young girls should pursue gardening, music, collecting shells and rocks, and doll making.[37]

Catharine Beecher's life stood in sharp contrast to the ideology she espoused. "By 1847," her biographer has written, "her life was a bundle of contradictions. She was an expert on domestic economy, but had no home of her own; she was a writer on the moral education of children, but had no children herself; she was a competent religious writer, but had never experienced conversion; and she urged young women to become teachers, but was herself not willing to teach."[38] Gender was the cause of this conflict. Beecher espoused the doctrine of separate spheres, yet she sought the power and influence available only to men under the terms of that doctrine.

Beecher's story illustrates a dilemma for middle-class women that began in the nineteenth century and dominated much of women's experience during the early decades of the twentieth. It was during Beecher's mature years that a movement for women's rights was conceived, and it was during those same years that she herself helped to crystallize woman's role as guardian of the home. Beecher preached that women should remain cloistered from the world of politics, commerce, and business, yet she was a fund-raiser nonpareil, daring to write aggressive letters to prominent men of influence in pursuit of her educational aims.[39] She "traveled like a candidate for political office, moving quickly from one city to another, thereby promoting a large amount of newspaper coverage of her arrivals and departures."[40] And she exhibited vigorous entrepreneurial energy in promoting her own works.[41] She was caught in the contradiction that was inherent in an ideology that perceived women as subordinate to men, for she herself was ambitious, talented, and driven to exert power and influence.

But Catharine Beecher's legacy to her twentieth-century sisters was the belief that woman's primary sphere of influence was in the home. The woman movement of her generation threatened, she feared, to render female education "anti-domestic." The care of the home was more important than any other activity women might consider.[42] This belief still shaped the lives of most middle-class American women five years after Catharine Beecher's death when Christine Isobel Campbell (Frederick) was born.

Selling Mrs. Consumer

Introduction

DURING CHRISTINE MACGAFFEY FREDERICK'S LIFETIME, significant forces that would shape twentieth-century society intersected to create the modern consumer culture. Relationships between government and society, capital and labor, manufacturers and consumers, men and women underwent upheaval and change. Conflict and contradiction were inherent to all these transitions.

White middle-class American women considered new possibilities for expanding their sphere, and as Christine came of age and began her career in 1912, educated women of her class faced a conflict of values. The first wave of feminism intersected with the emergence of a fully industrialized society that would depend on the development of large consumer markets. Both were linked to Progressive reform: feminism as an aspect of the social justice movements and industrialization as the target of reformers who hoped to curb the excesses of late-nineteenth-century capitalism. The efficiency movement that accompanied the emergence of scientific management, the development of modern advertising as a means to create markets, and the efforts on the part of big business to maintain control of distribution were all historical developments in which Christine Frederick would participate. In doing so, she would embody a contradiction by encouraging newly liberated women to remain in their homes—the traditional domestic sphere—to become professional consumers.

Early in the twentieth century, some feminists sought change far more dramatic and controversial than mere equal suffrage; they sought to alter the organization of the home, sacred locus of the nuclear family. But the window of opportunity that they opened by beginning a public discourse about cooperative ways to arrange domestic life was closed when Americans settled into the conservative climate of the prosperous, postwar 1920s, the decade during which business had clearly become "the chief business of the American people."[1] After the brief period before World War I during which a few educated, middle-class, white women tried to expand their world by changing the role assigned to them in the nineteenth century, many retreated in the face of conservative reaction. Although the numbers of women in the workforce continued to grow, few feminist voices were heard again for nearly half a century.

This inquiry into Christine Frederick's role in these historical forces and into the way that she reflected them began with the idea that the home itself should yield clues to society's, indeed women's, resistance to the radical changes proposed by the early-twentieth-century advocates of collective housekeeping. Some writers had raised questions about the single-family house: Did it promote inequality? Was it really a mechanism that provided a haven for men but imposed isolation and a circumscribed role on women? Literature on the American home revealed an intriguing clue to the inability of early feminists to bring about significant change in the gender roles that had been fashioned in the nineteenth century.

Among the women who had enjoyed increased access to education and at least partial entrée into the public sphere, there were some who used their newfound emancipation to reinforce the *old* ideas about women's and men's places in a changing society. Christine Frederick was one of these: a home efficiency expert, an advertising consultant, and a consumer advocate, who eagerly embraced the modernization that occurred in the wake of rapid industrialization yet steadfastly preached the ideology of the home that had been developed in the previous century. The historian June Sochen concluded in 1972 that Americans resist reform if it seriously threatens the "fundamental structure of society."[2] This pattern applies to feminism, for some have feared that the ultimate goal of total equality would threaten the existing order.

A disciple of the engineers and entrepreneurs who made America hum with efficiency and bustle with commerce, Christine Frederick did not join those women of her class, education, and ability who wanted equality in the public sphere. Instead she was with the forces that reinforced the old ideas; she devoted her energies to making the home an efficient and well-appointed workplace where women would be relieved of drudgery but would nevertheless continue to be primarily housekeepers. By founding a career on advising other women to find happiness in the efficient management of their homes, Christine illustrated the conflict many women of her class faced, for nineteenth-century ideology prevailed even as new opportunities enabled women to become something other than traditional homemakers. Christine entered fully into the public sphere as an advertising consultant to manufacturers and advertisers who sold products to women and thus helped to define a new function for the homemaker. Women gained importance in the economy as America's primary consumers, but most middle-class married women continued to center their lives on the private home.[3]

Historians who tell women's stories have noted that "when both the subject and the biographer are women 'gender moves to the center of the analysis.'"[4] This work is no exception. The central thesis of this book is that Christine Frederick's life and work illustrate the dilemma facing educated women of the early twentieth century: whether to seek professional gratification on the one hand or to adhere to the nineteenth-century ideal on the other. Christine chose to resolve the conflict by fashioning a career for herself that encouraged other women to remain homemakers. She was the product of new forces. Educated and talented, she took great interest in the traditionally male world of industry, commerce, and business. But because she was a woman who had been reared with nineteenth-century views that separated—at least ideally—women's and men's spheres, she applied her skills and interests to serving the home. In doing so, she assumed that most women she advised would stay home while she went out in public to spread the gospel of efficiency and consumerism. The inconsistency between what she did and what she said was the result of being caught in the crossfire between persisting old and emerging new visions for women. In trying to serve both, she conceived a gendered modernity. Historian Alan Dawley points out that Christine's contemporaries who worked in the settlement house movement exemplified the public-private dilemma in much the same way: they "violated the canons of 'true womanhood'" in their work while accepting "the prevailing family ideology."[5]

Christine Frederick's name appears in several histories of technology, the home, and domesticity. These usually cast her as either an innovative promoter of scientific management in the home or an accomplice in the selling of consumerism to the American housewife. Siegfried Giedion, the historian of mechanization, "discovered" Christine in 1948 and considered her the prototype of a group of women who applied scientific management, a system developed by Frederick Taylor to improve industrial efficiency, to the home. Nearly twenty years later, in his study of scientific management as Progressive reform, Samuel Haber referred to Christine as one of the "feminists" who used Taylor's ideas.[6] During the 1970s, several writers noted Christine's role in the efficiency movement. In *Captains of Consciousness*, a critique of advertising and consumerism, Stuart Ewen credited Christine with promoting the "ideology of the industrialized home" to reconcile traditional nineteenth-century values with new industrial ones. The architectural historian Gwendolyn Wright identified Christine as the "foremost evangelist of the domestic science ideology," who taught millions of other women how to manage their homes with assembly-line precision. In *The American Home*, the social historian David Handlin considered Christine's contribution to scientific management in the home important because it professionalized homemaking, but he recognized the conflict between her work and life, which demonstrated "ambivalence between old and new values."[7]

Among these scholars who wrote during the decade of "women's liberation," only Barbara Ehrenreich and Deirdre English noticed that the scientific management techniques Christine promoted might not free women at all. Christine preached "the full managerial revolution in the home," they wrote, but since the solitary homemaker had to fill multiple roles—planner, thinker, and worker—the new scheme might actually create more work for her. Ehrenreich and English placed Christine among the Progressive era's experts who attempted to standardize home life and child rearing.[8] The English professor Martha Banta's more recent history of the disciples of scientific management identified Christine as one of the "forceful theorizers" of her time whose work placed "Taylorism" "front and center" in the discourse about improving—and saving—the home. Banta, like Handlin, recognized Christine's ambivalence, pointing out that she portrayed herself as a traditional practitioner of domesticity on the one hand and an efficient scientific manager on the other. She wrote that although Christine Frederick's homemaker replaced nineteenth-century sentiment with twentieth-century efficiency, her housekeeping was done under the influence of the same ideology as that of the Victorian women who preceded her.[9]

Among the many historians, sociologists, and feminists who took part in the new debate about women's place in society during the 1970s and 1980s, several examined women's relationship to consumerism and uncovered Christine Frederick's part in creating the female consumer. Most accounts were unflattering. Gwendolyn Wright called Christine a "double agent" because she helped advertisers appeal to women. The architectural historian Dolores Hayden considered her "anti-feminist" because she was "pro-consumption," noting that her advice to advertisers included tips on appealing to female suggestibility, passivity, and feelings of inferiority. The historian Susan Strasser found

Christine to be disingenuous in her support of manufacturers who wished to fix prices of consumer goods during the second and third decades of the twentieth century, arguing that her advocacy of business was not in the consumer's interest. In his 1985 history of advertising, Roland Marchand detected Christine's inconsistency; although she posed as the female consumer's advocate, he wrote, she expressed disparaging opinions about the average American woman. Glenna Matthews, a historian of domesticity, cited Christine Frederick as an example of how easily corporate America "bought" professional female home experts as spokespersons for its products.[10]

More recent assessments of Christine's role in the rise of consumerism have not been sympathetic either. In an essay about the home economists who worked in industry during the 1920s and 1930s, the historian Carolyn Goldstein reported that professionally trained women resented Christine Frederick because she was not trained in a home economics program. Home economists who were themselves helping manufacturers sell their wares to women feared that Christine's lack of specialized training led her to exploit women rather than to help them.[11] Jennifer Scanlon, in her recent study of the *Ladies' Home Journal,* joined the scientific management historians who saw Christine as the "foremost spokesperson for the professionalization of housekeeping through more scientific approaches." But Scanlon also noted that Christine's efficiency advice quickly moved into work with manufacturers.[12]

Christine Frederick's work merits closer examination than historians have heretofore given it. Her significance to American history transcends her work as home efficiency expert, her promotion of consumerism, or even her embodiment of the contradiction with which many influential early-twentieth-century women lived. She reflected the many currents of her time and the way they interacted to change American society. She enthusiastically embraced and promoted technology, scientific management, modernization, and consumerism. Yet she limited the ways members of her own sex could benefit from that modernization because she labored under the nineteenth-century assumption that a woman's work should be located in the home. Christine Frederick has a place alongside Catharine Beecher and Charlotte Perkins Gilman in the history of the American home and woman's role in managing it. Beecher, from 1841 until the 1870s, did much to promote the idea that women should stay at home, but that in executing their domestic duties they should be trained, competent, professional workers. Gilman, on the other hand, led a campaign to broaden women's opportunities by releasing them from the solitary caretaking of individual homes from the 1880s to the 1930s. Christine Frederick, whose most important work was done between 1910 and 1930, represented a reaction to the feminists of Gilman's stripe, and in some ways a return to Beecher's views, and her career helps explain why most women did not embrace the ideas of early-twentieth-century feminists. But Christine also deserves a place among the "apostles of modernity" identified by Roland Marchand.[13] Her early work was an important influence in the creation and promotion of the modern, twentieth-century consumer culture, and her late-life career extended that influence into the post–World War II housing boom in California.

Christine MacGaffey Frederick's willingness to endorse the middle-class, nineteenth-century belief that women were responsible for the management of the home helped to perpetuate a conflict with which many American women still struggle. She embodies, as I have tried to make clear throughout this book, a contradiction that was not and is not uncommon to educated women who still feel the effects of time-honored ideology that endows a domestic role for women with considerable value. The fact that she embodies a conflict that seems to me to be so universal is precisely what makes her important. That is not to say that her life was typical. It was far from it. But she wrote for and in support of the woman whose life *was* typical, at least of the middle class. And she encouraged that woman to find satisfaction by using modernization to perpetuate those old values. That was important because the typical woman was, herself, in conflict.

This study is about the experiences of one who represents a particular group. The lives of Christine Frederick's audiences did not reflect the lives of all American women. Omitted here are the experiences of early-twentieth-century working-class women—many of them immigrants—who had to work to live and so could not remain at home; of African American women who labored under racial and economic barriers that made full-time housekeeping in their own homes impossible for most; of Native American women, most of whom lived at the margins of American society; and of the many other minority groups who lived in Christine Frederick's America. Neither does this work address the experiences of lesbians who could not comply with the domestic ideal that recognized only heterosexual unions.

Christine Frederick's exclusivity was not singular. In the nineteenth century, the pioneering educator Mary Lyon wrote: "To this class in society would

I devote, directly, all the remainder of my strength (God permitting)—not to the higher classes, not to the poor classes. This middle class contains the main springs, and main wheels, which are to move the world."[14] Glenna Matthews observed that the nineteenth-century "ideology of domesticity arose in the middle class and may well have been one of the principal means by which the middle class assumed a self-conscious identity."[15] Although historians now properly include in broader surveys groups who did not often appear in the political histories that dominated the field before 1960, it is still fair to say that at least until recently the white middle class, rightly or wrongly, has defined the common values of American society. Warren Susman wrote in 1984 that the "story of American culture remains largely the story of [the] middle class."[16] Christine Frederick identified herself as a member of the middle class, and she spoke only to white, middle-class women who shared her background, experience, prejudices, and values. She and they are my subjects.

I · *"Only a Girl"*

It was a bleak, chill morning on that Tuesday, February 6th, in Boston. Nevertheless, some light cast its weak illumination around the old Roxbury house in
that early dawn. A man . . . held his old turnip-shaped watch in his hand to
check the hour his first son and legal heir for whom he had waited so long would
be born. . . .

In a few moments the nurse brought in the baby and the man eagerly
stretched out his arms for the bundle. The nurse paused a moment, then folded
back the blanket. "Horrors!" he cried out in disgust. "Why, it's only a girl!"[1]

So BEGINS the unfinished autobiography that Christine Isobel MacGaffey
Frederick began to write in the last year of her eighty-seven-year-long life.[2] The
knowledge of her natural father's disappointment that February morning in
1883 when he learned that his firstborn child was a girl, coupled with the memory of her mother's subsequent trials as an untrained Victorian gentlewoman
who needed to support herself, had a profound impact on Christine's life. As
a female child of the nineteenth century, she was reared to understand, as
Catharine Beecher had taught, that woman's place in life was confined to a domestic sphere. As a young adult during the first years of the twentieth century,
she was to witness the enlarging and eventual breaching of that sphere. Her
Victorian roots, her mother's terrifying experience, and her modern youth were
to shape her life around the conflict posed by these different perspectives.

Uncommon Genesis

THE AGING CHRISTINE recounted an exotic family history. Her maternal
grandfather, Robert Scott, had emigrated from Scotland to Missouri sometime
before the Civil War. His bride-to-be, Christine Brands, had joined him in the
early 1860s. Scott, a handsome young man of whom the Brands family did not
approve, had captured Christine's heart years before in the Lowlands of Scotland where she and her three sisters, Isobel, Mimie, and Elizabeth, were reared.
In their youth they spent time with "Robbie" and his brothers, handsome blond
Highlanders. According to her admiring granddaughter, recalling the tales her
mother had told her, Christine Brands was a dark-eyed beauty, the object of all

the Scott brothers' affections. But she cared only for Robbie, the brother whose wanderlust had taken him across the sea. When she was twenty-eight years old, Christine followed Robbie to America, where he had established himself in Saint Louis as the partner in a flourishing livery business. She packed her belongings and sailed for New Orleans, where she took passage on a steamboat and traveled upriver to Saint Louis. Robbie met her at the wharf and they were married then and there by the boat's captain.[3]

The Scotts succeeded in the New World. Robbie's business provided comfort enough that Christine could be driven about Saint Louis in a victoria by Sam, their black butler, and shop for delicacies in the French market. Her granddaughter remembered accompanying her on these excursions and delighting in the wares—especially the "great, luscious watermelons"—that Sam brought from the market stalls to the carriage for their inspection.[4] She also recalled the ritual her grandfather's well-appointed appearance required: "I remember my beloved grandmother putting out my grandfather's Sunday clothes. As a little girl, I used to watch the solemn rite. There, on the big bed, she spread one article after the other—his pleated shirt, his white cravat, his waistcoat and suit. Then she put special jeweled studs in the sleeves and buttons in the vest; she laid the shoes ready, and the underwear and the hat and the cane and the gloves."[5] By 1880, when the Scotts' daughter, Mimie, was a young woman, they were able to clothe her in the best satins, velvets, and laces. By the standards of the day, they were quite well-to-do. A circuit court judge would write of them in 1888 that their "standing in the community here is of the very best."[6]

To demonstrate Robbie's success to the family that had discouraged their marriage, Christine took nineteen-year-old Mimie, decked in finery, to visit Scotland. En route, they met a struggling young preacher from Boston who had recently graduated from Andover Theological Seminary and was just then awaiting his first call to the ministry.[7] To twenty-five-year-old William R. Campbell, the handsomely dressed Mimie presented an enticing picture. His father, also a man of the cloth, had eked out a meager living on a rocky Vermont homestead and had provided but poorly for his family. William's sister, Mary, remembered years later that poverty combined with fervent religious beliefs had made their childhood quite bleak. They were not allowed to go to the circus, she recalled, but might be given a penny to see the animals on display outside, since this would instruct them in the wonders of God's creation.[8]

William Campbell asked Mimie Scott to marry him while they were still aboard ship. She accepted, and he followed her home to Saint Louis, where he formally asked Robbie Scott for his daughter's hand. But Mimie soon began to have second thoughts about marrying the cool minister from New England and, during his second trip to Missouri, told him as much. Her father, who had consented to the marriage on Campbell's previous visit and who seemed to his great-granddaughter to be a "tyrannical old Scot," told Mimie that she had given her word to a "man of the kirk" and could not take it back. By the time of their marriage, William had secured a position as pastor of the Highland Congregational Church in Boston.[9] Thus Mimie married unwillingly and with heavy heart accompanied her new husband to Boston, where she conceived and bore him the unwelcome female child eleven months later.[10]

The painful birth, during which Mimie was denied any medication that might have eased her agony, and her growing aversion to the man who showed such disdain for their little daughter, steeled the young mother's determination to leave Boston as soon as she was able. "Nothing but nothing," her daughter wrote nearly ninety years later, "would make her return to her green-eyed husband whom she had never liked and bear Henry or Paul, or any other children which her husband envisioned."[11] Christine Frederick's description of this episode, written a lifetime after she had first heard it told, conveys the resentment she still felt for her mother's ordeal and her own rejection. The room in which she was born, she writes, was "hideous." The floor was a "dirty yellow." Her mother, "emaciated," had "agonized and almost died." Most telling is her description of her father as a man with "green snaky eyes," a phrase she must have repeated many times to her children. Her daughter described William Campbell, whom she met many years later, as a lustful man whose "green eyes" awakened deep distrust.[12] The memory of this story galvanized Christine Frederick's determination to learn how to make a living and to ensure that her daughters did as well.

Mimie and Christine spent much of the next two years, from 1883 through 1885, in Saint Louis, and, on one occasion, they took a trip to Michigan. During the protracted visits with her parents, Mimie learned to do accounting work while helping her father. She spent enough time in Saint Louis to meet the man with whom she would unite in a second marriage ten years later. Mother and child left Boston for the last time in January 1885, when Christine was just twenty-three months old.[13] Mimie appealed to her parents to help her extricate herself from her unhappy marriage, but Robbie Scott was not yet willing to help his daughter leave her husband permanently. Although Mimie's mother was more sympathetic, she, too, was against a divorce. Nevertheless, she arranged for Mimie to leave the country and work as a governess in Russia, and in August 1885, Mimie took little Christine to Moscow.[14]

While Christine Brands Scott had traveled west to shape a new life in the United States, her sisters had traveled east from their home in Scotland to become governesses in czarist Russia.[15] It was to these aunts that young Mimie Scott Campbell fled, seeking refuge from her unhappy marriage. Her mother had prevailed upon her sisters to find Mimie a position, and with only her two-year-old daughter as company, she made the long journey to Moscow by ship and train.[16]

Aunts Elizabeth and Isobel had arranged for Mimie to serve as governess to the five-year-old daughter of a wealthy Russian family, the Gilinskys, whose country estate lay outside Moscow. Little Christine, however, was sent to live with Aunt Elizabeth, who served as a governess in a beautiful apartment on the fashionable Névsky Prospékt in Saint Petersburg. The gray rock apartment building stood in a "row of palaces and new apartments." Eighty years later, Christine could describe the double-paned windows under which she played with small toys, the high ceilings, the cream walls, and the elegant glazed tile stove. She did not attend school; a tutor who had been engaged for Aunt Elizabeth's employer's children instructed them all at home in reading, writing, French, and dance.[17]

During Christine's sojourn in Saint Petersburg, she was exposed to Russian society as her Aunt Elizabeth's small companion. They would go shopping in the family's carriage or "drosky" along the market streets where the stalls and shops yielded up delights such as wrapped chocolates and small toys. They made frequent visits to a family named Bibekoff whose daughters became Christine's friends and whose maid liked to brush the child's long black hair. One memorable Christmas, Christine attended a party at the Bibekoffs' home where a dwarf dressed in gold dazzled her as he distributed gifts from beneath a candle-lighted golden tree. Once she played at the home of a banker whose daughter had a troupe of dancing white mice. She recalled trips to Moscow, too. Sometimes she and her mother and aunts would go into the woods outside the city for picnics, and they would pick mushrooms at Sparrow Hill.[18]

Easter was the most exciting time in Russia during Christine's early childhood there. Feasts, carnivals, and celebrations marked the holy days in Saint

Petersburg. Christine colored boiled eggs, made paper flowers, and enjoyed frolicking on the still-frozen Neva River during the Easter holidays. The little girl especially liked the rich puddings and cakes.[19] Sometimes she would receive gifts hidden in the mysterious interiors of the beautiful china eggs set about the apartment: perfumes, dolls, and delicate workbaskets.[20] The vivid memories of this three-year Russian interlude had a great impact on young Christine and led her, in later years, to claim a much longer sojourn. In 1919, she professed to have spent eight years in Russia, and in the autobiographical notes, she stretched it to ten.[21]

Family lore holds that Mimie's leaving William Campbell was a great scandal in Boston and that his family regarded her as a scarlet woman for many years thereafter. Court records of a bitter custody battle in the Circuit Court of the City of St. Louis during the fall and winter of 1888 reveal the animosity in the Campbell marriage. Mimie was forced to bring Christine back to the United States to play out a distressing drama three years after she had fled to Russia.[22] The late-nineteenth-century confusion surrounding the awarding of child custody had undoubtedly served as a powerful incentive for Mimie to leave the country. Although the courts had begun to reject the ancient notion that children belonged to their father and were awarding custody to the mother more and more often, it was by no means a certainty that a woman who had left a marriage would keep her children. The issue was decided by a judge in almost all states, and the decisions varied.[23]

On 15 November 1888, William Campbell filed suit for divorce and for custody of his daughter in the superior court in Suffolk County, Massachusetts. Thirteen days later, he was granted temporary custody "during the pendency of" the case.[24] Mimie was served with papers in Saint Petersburg and, accompanied by one of her aunts, brought Christine to New York. Leaving the child there, Mimie and her father, who had traveled from Saint Louis to be with her, went on to Boston and appeared in court. William had the matter postponed until Mimie could be forced to produce Christine. Upon advice from counsel, Mimie and Robert Scott left Boston, fearing that the court might force them to hand over the child. Back in the Scott home in Saint Louis, Mimie received a copy of the order granting temporary custody of Christine to her husband. When she ignored it, William filed a petition for a writ of habeas corpus in the Circuit Court of the City of St. Louis on 7 December, and a trial ensued.[25] William had not seen his daughter for three years.

Mimie responded to his petition by accusing him of an "ungovernable temper" and "crued [*sic*] and barbarous treatment" to both her and their daughter. She said that he had struck her, that she feared for her life, and that on one occasion, he had bound Christine, ill with a rash, to the slats of her crib, bruising and injuring her. William denied these charges, explaining that, on the advice of a physician, he had restrained the child's arms to prevent her from scratching lesions during an eczema attack. Each parent claimed that the other was an unfit guardian. Mimie objected to surrendering Christine's care to William's mother, who was now his housekeeper, claiming that the older woman was physically and mentally infirm. William countered that Mimie's charges were untrue. She had deserted him, he said, and had denied him access to his child, even refusing his offers of monetary assistance.[26]

The trial, held on 18 December 1888, was well attended even if no one but the twenty-six subpoenaed witnesses appeared in the courtroom. Among those called was a Miss Brand [*sic*], whose address was the same as that of Mr. and Mrs. Robert R. Scott, also subpoenaed as witnesses. This was the aunt, probably either Elizabeth or Isobel, who had accompanied Mimie and Christine on the trip from Russia.[27] The Honorable George W. Lubke held that both Mimie and William were fit parents, but that since the child was young and female, she would need her mother for some time to come. Invoking the "tender years" doctrine, he awarded custody to Mimie, granting generous visitation privileges to William, visitation that would prove impracticable since William lived twelve hundred miles away.[28]

The judge's decision suggests a close relationship between Mimie and her six-year-old daughter and reveals something of Mimie's character. Judge Lubke noted that she was "a refined christian woman; that she is passionately fond of the child; that she has cared for it with a watchful eye." But he dismissed her charges that William was cruel, unfeeling, or ungenerous, giving credibility to William's testimony, too.[29]

Christine Frederick remembered her father's visits to the Scott home at the time of this trial. When Campbell came to claim her, Grandfather Robbie rode shotgun at the top of the stairs, presumably to prevent Campbell from forcibly taking her away, while her father plied her with gifts. There were also tales of attempted kidnappings through bribes to servants.[30]

Exactly eighteen months after the Missouri trial ended, the divorce that was finally granted to William Campbell by the superior court in Suffolk County,

Massachusetts, became absolute. After attempting to serve Mimie with notice to appear throughout the spring and summer of 1889, the court finally granted Campbell a divorce on grounds of desertion and gave him custody of Christine in December. The decree stipulated that Mimie could have the child for three months out of every year, provided she keep her in the state of Massachusetts.[31] In fact, Mimie Scott Campbell never complied with the decree.

Into a Business-Dominated World

WHEN CHRISTINE CAMPBELL WAS BORN, changes that would define her adult years were already well under way. Industrial production grew tremendously during the second half of the nineteenth century. Technology provided new machines, sources of power, and communication systems. Railroads that traversed the continent by the 1880s provided the transportation for moving goods. And finance capitalism provided the resources to fund the growth of large industrial corporations.[32]

Public waterworks had been a feature of the American city since the Civil War. Thomas Edison established the first commercial electric power plant, the Edison Electric Illuminating Company's Pearl Street power station in New York City, in 1882.[33] The cultural gap between city and country that would become critical by the third decade of the twentieth century was already evident. Manufacturing aimed at nonlocal markets had fueled urbanization after the Civil War, and growing cities were assuming control over areas of life once governed by local custom and authority. In 1820, there had been fifty-six towns with populations between 2,500 and 25,000 and only five with populations between 27,000 and 152,000 in the United States. A mere 7 percent of Americans had lived in these population centers. But by 1870, 25 percent of the nation's people lived in urban areas. By 1920, more than half of the American people would live in towns and cities.[34] Thus Christine Frederick had entered a world rapidly changing through technology, industry, and urbanization.

These three phenomena served as handmaidens to the rise of big business at the turn of the century. Politics served as a fourth. The election of Republican presidential candidate William McKinley in 1896 marked the beginning of a long period of government-assisted business growth in the United States. Large chain stores like Woolworth's, Grand Union, and Kroger Grocery and Baking Company emerged in the 1880s and 1890s. In 1900 the American Economic

Association "agreed that business competition in the old sense had practically disappeared," and it supported the combinations that it believed would provide more goods and higher wages.[35] Antitrust legislation, passed to protect people from the abuses of big business, was not scrupulously enforced. Twelve years after Christine Frederick's birth, government stepped in to assist George Pullman in putting down a strike.[36]

Institutions other than government served the cause of business, too. Emily Fogg Mead, business educator and author of *The Place of Advertising in Modern Business*, was urging "business men to penetrate the home, break down the resistance of ordinary housewives, and 'forget the past' in their pursuit of profits" as early as 1901. The Harvard School of Business opened in 1908 and, in 1911, established its Bureau of Business Research. Even museums promoted business, offering special exhibits to manufacturers who might glean design ideas from historic textiles or American Indian artifacts.[37]

The Home: A Gendered Sphere

WHEN MIMIE'S HUSBAND voiced his disappointment at siring a girl in that dismal Boston bedroom in the winter of 1883, he was expressing hopes and desires based upon the moral and social values of America's Gilded Age. The infant Christine had entered a world in which most influential people still believed, as Catharine Beecher had argued, that the sexes' spheres should be separate. William Campbell had wanted a child who would carry on his name and his work. A girl, he believed, could do neither.

In fact, the spheres of late-nineteenth-century men and women were not as separate as Campbell believed them to be.[38] Large numbers of women joined the industrial workforce at the onset of America's industrial revolution in the early nineteenth century, even as Beecher was advising women to remain in the home.[39] Still, the doctrine of two spheres was the ideal to which most middle-class white women and men subscribed when Christine was born. During the decade of her birth, for example, the editor of the *Popular Science Monthly* wrote that "women may make transient diversions from the sphere of activity for which they are constituted, but they are nevertheless formed and designed for maternity, the care of children, and the affairs of domestic life."[40]

Catharine Beecher was only the most prominent among several purveyors of middle-class values who defined the domestic sphere in the nineteenth century.

Many others echoed her advice. For example, the editor of *Godey's Lady's Book*, Sarah Josepha Hale, though an outspoken advocate for women's property rights and access to professional education, believed that women were nevertheless responsible for the sanctity of the home.[41]

Nineteenth-century medical theories, based on Darwinism, provided the rationale for keeping women at home. In 1870 one physician wrote, "It was as if the Almighty in creating the female sex, had taken the uterus and built us a woman around it."[42] Three years later, Dr. Edward Clarke of Boston University argued that too much education and mental exercise would damage girls' reproductive systems. Countering these assertions in 1875, Antoinette Brown Blackwell wrote *The Sexes throughout Nature* in which she argued that both males and females contributed to the progress of the human being and should therefore be educated equally. Nonetheless, Clarke's theories prevailed among the general public and promoted the notion that a woman's worth lay in her reproductive organs.[43]

Yet Christine would grow to adulthood during a time when she would be forced to straddle the dividing line between full acceptance of the "woman's sphere" and the view that women could enjoy a public professional life. By the time of her childhood, there was a mature, consolidated movement for female suffrage.[44]

There were other signs that white middle-class women were beginning to expand the boundaries of their world when Christine Campbell was born. For one thing, growing numbers of them were seeking and attaining higher education. In 1865, Vassar College had opened to offer a full liberal arts curriculum to women.[45] Ellen Swallow (later Richards) became the first woman admitted to a scientific school when she was enrolled as a "special student" in chemistry at the Massachusetts Institute of Technology in 1870. Eight years later, women were admitted to MIT as regular students.[46] In 1885, when Bryn Mawr was established, its founding dean, M. Carey Thomas, insisted on giving women the same rigorous scholarship the best colleges of the nation offered to men, a policy she continued as the institution's second president.[47]

There were also signs of sexual polarization at the end of the nineteenth century. Temperance reformers and suffragists often held that male behavior was bad while female behavior was good. In 1890, Basil March, the fictional magazine editor in William Dean Howells's novel, *A Hazard of New Fortunes*, explained the behavior of the magazine's manager to his virtuous wife as follows:

"Fulkerson's standards are low; they're merely business standards; and the good that's in him is incidental and something quite apart from his morals and methods. He's naturally a generous and right-minded creature, but life has taught him to truckle and trick, like the rest of us."[48] On the other side, books like the Peck's Bad Boy series of the 1870s and 1880s often portrayed women as foolish and lacking in authority.[49]

This polarization was associated with a deep division in the underlying arguments used to further women's position within the ranks of female activists themselves. Some women turned Catharine Beecher's argument to keep women out of politics on its head, reasoning that *because* they were different from men, *because* they were the moral guardians of civilization, *because* they were superior in religious fervor, they should be allowed to participate in public decisions. Others, basing their arguments on natural rights thinking, asserted women's rights on the basis of equality, arguing that there were no differences between the sexes that were not culturally induced.[50]

Nevertheless, when Christine was born, a "gendered concept of the home" had emerged, as the historian Sarah Stage has pointed out.[51] And since women took on the responsibility for maintaining moral rectitude in the nineteenth century, the home itself acquired moral value. Most mid-nineteenth-century, middle-class Americans disapproved of living arrangements other than the single-family home. Communitarian experiments like Transcendentalist Brook Farm at Concord, Massachusetts, were seen as threatening to the institution of the family.[52] Catharine Beecher had argued that even unmarried women should form single-family units. Young men were advised that their primary role was to earn income enough to provide a good house for their families.[53] Late in the century, Mark Twain wrote that his house in Hartford "had a heart, and a soul, and eyes to see us with; and approvals, and solicitudes and deep sympathies; it was of us, and we were in its confidence, and lived in its grace and in the peace of its benediction."[54] Still, by Christine's seventh birthday, most Americans could not realize the ideal. Workers could not afford a home that typically cost between twenty-four hundred and thirty-one hundred dollars.[55] In 1890, fewer than half of American families owned their own homes.[56]

During Christine's childhood, most homemakers still did a good bit more hard work than the ideology implied. It was not until the beginning of the twentieth century that precooked or prepared foods were available to the American housewife. Until then, urban and farm women alike had to pluck

poultry, sift impurities out of flour, soak hams, and roast and grind their own coffee beans.[57] For the affluent middle class, there was still hired domestic help,
and Christine's grandparents employed six servants in their Saint Louis
home.[58] But servants were not available to all; in 1880, there were 188 servants
per one thousand families in New York City. By 1900, that number had been
reduced to 141 servants per one thousand families.[59]

Since not every American family could afford a private home in the 1880s
and 1890s, most city dwellers lived in apartments or tenements. Yet even in
metropolitan areas such as New York, where middle-class apartment dwelling
was largely a function of limited space, it was roundly criticized by the promoters of the single-family home. Attacks targeted women because women were
expected to be the keepers of the home. In 1903, a contributor to the *Architectural Record* complained that apartments would not have been so popular "without the acquiescence of large numbers of women; and it is devoutly to be hoped
that many more women will not be foolish enough to follow this example,
thereby sacrificing the dignity of their own lives and their effective influence
over their husbands and children."[60]

Notwithstanding the rhetoric, many Americans did not, and could not, find
succor in their homes. In 1893, Stephen Crane wrote of a tenement home in
New York's "Rum Alley" where the alcoholic mother "vented drunken fury
upon" the furniture and her children, where the walls were "grimey," and where
"disorder and dirt" prevailed.[61] The social reformer and photographer Jacob
August Riis revealed to Americans how bleak life in the homes of countless urban immigrants could be in his photographic essay, *How the Other Half Lives*,
first published in 1890.[62] The idealized home, the seat of the calm, loving, and
morally upright domestic sphere, was simply not available to all classes of
Americans. It remained an ideal.

Growing Up in Conflict

AFTER THE CUSTODY TRIAL, Christine and her mother lived in Saint Louis
with the Scotts.[63] Life there was pleasant, at least for Christine. Not only was
the little girl treated to shopping excursions with her grandmother, but
Grandpa Robbie took her on buying trips, too. The merchants with whom he
traded would give her treats, and she could listen to the music box in the jewelry store. Sometimes Grandpa Robbie would take Christine to his big iron safe,

open it, and take out a wooden box full of gold pieces. These, he told her, would pay for her college education.[64] Mimie kept accounts for her father and also did much of the fancy cooking for her parents' guests.[65]

Mimie had already met Wyatt MacGaffey before she took Christine to Russia. MacGaffey, who lived in Chicago, had been in Saint Louis working for Robbie Scott when Mimie came home with her baby from Boston. He had fallen in love with her, and they had exchanged affectionate letters during the years she was abroad with Christine.[66] Mimie Scott Campbell married Wyatt MacGaffey in Saint Louis on 7 August 1894, when Christine was eleven years and seven months of age.[67] The new family of three repaired to Chicago and made their home on Humboldt Avenue.[68] Christine came to love her kind, amusing stepfather, and before she entered high school, she took his name as her own. When she was in her teens, her parents presented her with two little half-brothers, Wyatt and Crichton.[69]

Christine achieved an admirable record at Northwestern Division High School in Chicago, where she excelled in oratory. She won first place in a competition in her third year, receiving the highest marks in all categories from all three judges for her speech, "The Consolidations of To-Day." The school newspaper reported that she had delivered "the most logical oration of the evening," and she was "complimented upon the easy way in which she treated the subject."[70] Her accomplishment made headlines in the *Chicago American*, which reported that her oration "was a somewhat remarkable production considering the youth of the writer."[71] Christine made outstanding high school grades, and both Northwestern University and the University of Chicago offered her partial scholarships. She chose Northwestern because it also offered a part-time student work program. With two additional children at home, the family could not stretch Wyatt's salary to pay Christine's college expenses; and since Grandpa Robbie's death, the mysterious box of gold pieces that were to have paid for her education had disappeared.[72] Even before enrolling as a full-time student, she was admitted into J. Scott Clark's English literature class. She was thrilled to study with a professor who had taught so many notable writers, she later wrote in her autobiography.[73]

Christine was to tell her own daughters many times that a woman must acquire an education in order to take care of herself. The memory of her mother, the timid and frightened Mimie, crying in an upstairs bedroom in Grandpa Robbie's house because she had to depend on her father for her living and enlist his help in freeing herself from a disastrous marriage, aroused the girl's determination to go to college and to prepare herself for a career.[74]

In September 1902, Christine entered Northwestern as a full-time student enrolled in the "scientific course" in the College of Liberal Arts.[75] She was able to reduce her tuition by working an hour a day at cleaning, dishwashing, and maid's work. She also worked as a tutor. To advertise, she distributed calling cards on which she added in her own hand, "Private Instruction in Science, English, and Mathematics, 3/9 Humboldt Avenue."[76] In addition, the university's Vocational Bureau found her jobs with "the rich ladies of the community," serving tea on their cooks' Thursday afternoons off. She was sometimes called upon to prepare fancy foods for the ladies and sixty years later remembered specific recipes. This work was probably the nearest thing to home economics training that Christine had while in college.[77]

The scientific course at Northwestern was the alternative to the "classical course."[78] Christine concentrated on courses that used the talents she had already discovered in high school. She took elocution, rhetoric, narration, and a course titled "Masterpieces in Eloquence." After oratory, her second emphasis was on literature and writing: editorial writing, prose masterpieces, paragraphing, and a variety of literature courses. She studied both German and French, took some biology, and had a smattering of history, philosophy, and math.[79]

Christine studied under some very well known professors at Northwestern. She took oratory from Robert McClean Cumnock, who had established the Cumnock School of Oratory, predecessor to Northwestern's prestigious School of Speech. J. Scott Clark instructed her in writing and literature, and she enrolled in three courses taught by Walter Dill Scott, the early theorist on advertising.[80] These men had a profound influence; Christine would make public speaking and writing central to her career, and she would play an important role in the development of modern advertising. Years later, she playfully called Professor Scott "Walter Dill 'Pickle' Scott" in conversations with her children.[81] She told of an encouraging encounter with Professor Cumnock in her autobiography. Cumnock, she wrote, called to her across campus one day and said: "Miss MacGaffey, why do you waste your time with all this school stuff? I have heard you recite and speak, and that is what you should be doing—training that voice of yours which, with your unusual poise and stage presence, could make you a tremendous success just as a lecturer." She replied that teaching offered steadier employment, but Cumnock disagreed. According to her story, he gave her the key to a luggage room on the top floor of one of the college buildings and advised her to "go up there and yell [her] head off." She followed his advice, and when she practiced in the huge storage room with only trunks for an audience, she would visualize before her a rapt multitude. Christine did not pretend modesty—then or later in life—and she added, characteristically, "[W]hen I became a world wide lecturer, I realized that old Cumstock [sic] was right in his prognostication."[82]

By the time she entered Northwestern, Christine had begun to develop the sense of purpose and the capacity for hard work that would assure her later success. Besides working at three outside jobs, she participated in college life to the fullest. During her sophomore year, she was treasurer of Le Cercle Français and an honorary member of a mysterious group called the Top Heavy Club. The following year, she served as president of Le Cercle Français, sat on the literary board committee of the yearbook, joined the Alethenai Literary Society and the YWCA, and directed the junior class play, She Stoops to Conquer, in which she also played the roll of Miss Neville. During her senior year, she was an officer (the "critic") in the all-woman Alethenai Literary Society.[83]

Christine exhibited a sense of obligation to a task undertaken, a healthy disregard for Victorian propriety, and confidence in her own judgment during her theatrical experience as director of the junior play. When the dean asked her to remove one of the leading men from the cast because a young woman had been seen leaving his room during the wee hours of the morning, Christine resisted, asking the dean what that had to do with the play. The dean implied that there might, after all, be a baby, to which Christine retorted, "But, Dean Holgate, the play is scheduled to open in six weeks. I may be stupid, but I do know it takes nine months for a baby to be born, so I cannot understand your attitude." The dean's response to Christine's rather shocking pragmatism is not recorded, but the young man was removed from the play and she was forced to coach a new actor in a very short time.[84]

This incident may be apocryphal, but it is only one indication that Christine possessed bearing and self-assurance even at this early stage. She was known to have a sense of humor and fun as well. At the end of her sophomore year, she was accorded the dubious honor of having her name appear in a "resolution" to "bawl . . . out" certain students who "have acquired the habit of asking foolish questions and of talking most of the time in the class rooms" and who "exceedingly tire the rest of the class with their talk under the pretext of being seekers after truth while in fact they are only after 'grand stand' plays." She was included in this list of grandstanders for her performance in Professor Cumnock's English B class: hence the professor's knowledge of her speaking ability. Her fellow students found her interesting; the brief description of personality that appeared under her picture in the 1906 yearbook reads, "Her infinite variety."[85]

Christine had become a tall, graceful, statuesque young woman blessed with an abundance of thick, dark hair that she drew softly up off her face in the Gibson girl fashion with a full, cascading chignon on her neck. She had inherited Grandmother Christine's dark eyes, and they were set under black, arching brows in a clear, oval face. Her gaze was steady and serious, but her face could break into a sunburst of laughter at a good joke.[86]

Christine was tapped for Phi Beta Kappa on 25 May 1906, an honor she cherished all of her life.[87] Like many young women who were graduating from college during this period, Christine assumed, as she had indicated to Professor Cumnock, that her education had groomed her for teaching. As a tutor during the years at Northwestern, she had discovered that she was a "'born' teacher of the first water." Her professors agreed. Several wrote glowing letters of recommendation commending her teaching abilities in any number of subjects. Her French teacher considered her "the strongest student in her class." Two English professors, one of them J. Scott Clark, recommended her highly for teaching English. And an official from the Garrett Biblical Institute in Evanston, with whom she had apparently boarded for a time, wrote that she could perform admirably in "any position she may accept." Walter Dill Scott remembered twenty-three years later that Christine "was one of the best students I ever had in my class."[88]

What we know of Christine's college career suggests that she was one of the growing number of young women who wished to free themselves from the confines of the domestic sphere, to learn how to perform in the world outside the home, and to exercise talents heretofore demonstrated only by men. She aggressively pursued a higher education, she worked for her school expenses, she tested her abilities against men's in the classroom, she engaged in spirited debate with male professors, and she envisioned herself as a commanding orator. Yet after her marriage, Christine was to fashion a career that would use that aggressiveness and talent to urge other women to stay in their homes and be happy as homemakers. Like most educated women during this period of rapid change, she faced conflict. Women were breaking out of the confining isolation of the domestic sphere, yet they were still counseled to hold fast to the notion that their special realm was the home. Christine exhibited thorough indoctrination in this ideology of separate spheres in a paper she wrote as a student.

In "The Genius of Woman," the young Christine—seeking to please her instructor, perhaps—wrote that woman, in her capacity as keeper of the home, "guided and shaped the progress of the world." But alas, woman had achieved a place in man's world during the past century, and the world was "now witnessing a condition weighed with grave possibilities." While some of this achievement might be hailed as progress, she wrote, it had gone too far. The position of the club woman and the business woman had been "glorified by the noisy and thoughtless as great triumphs," but in fact these women were merely trying to "gain public notice or escape [their] plain duty." They were "out of [their] place" and a "dead weight on human progress."[89] She seemed to affirm the consequences of which Catharine Beecher warned thirty-two years earlier when she predicted that women might follow men into clubs if homes were not properly tended. Christine warned:

> Endless columns of women have entered into competition with man. They have toiled and struggled; they have worked and striven. And what has it availed? Reckon the two or three successful few against the countless hordes who have turned their backs on their homes and labored in vain. Some have done this urged on by a genuine love for their work; and many to earn their living. But there can be not [sic] doubt that the great majority were influenced by an unhealthy craving for public applause and public work, and by the desire to get away from the cares of domestic life.[90]

Changes had "tempted [the American woman] to give up for this new occupation of money-making, her own true work of home-maker." "What Woman's Club," she asked, "can watch the home made beautiful and sacred for husband and children?"[91]

Christine specifically articulated the doctrine of two spheres when she wrote that although men and women are equal, "their spheres are different; that of the man, public life; that of the woman the home. Man represents the force of nature; woman its beauty." Men, she wrote, will always struggle, fighting wars and engaging in strife, while women can influence them to subdue these tendencies and strive for nobility instead.

> It is the sweet home-making woman, the wife, the mother, who has been the inspiration of the highest ideals of painting, the best efforts of song, the greatest

achievements of history, the most glorious deeds of war. She has stretched out her hand to struggling man, has built his character and led him on to careers of distinction and fame; she has lifted a savage and barbarous condition into the resplendent civilization of to-day.

But woman must stay in the home, serving as helper to her husband, who will accomplish great deeds. "Woman's true position is in her home. It is here that her highest development is attained; here is her greatest field of usefulness."[92] Although Christine's views on this subject broadened to accommodate her own ambitions as she matured, the impact of the ideology expressed in this youthful polemic would be evident throughout her career.

2 · "Drudgifying Housework"

I was constantly struggling to obtain a little "higher life" for my individuality
and independence; and on the other hand I was forced to give up this
individuality to my babies and drudgifying housework.

CHRISTINE FREDERICK, *New Housekeeping*, 1914

IN 1906, baccalaureate degree and Phi Beta Kappa key in hand, Christine
MacGaffey accepted a position teaching biology in the small town of Ishpeming, Michigan, far to the north, only twenty-five miles from the southern shore
of Lake Superior. A small hamlet nearly four hundred miles from Chicago, Ishpeming was bitterly cold in the winter, and Christine learned to navigate the
snowy landscape on skis. She would stay for only one year; when she left in
1907, she would never again think of school teaching as a career.[1]

Before leaving Chicago, Christine had met a charming young "Pennsylvania
Dutchman" who was rapidly working his way up the ladder in the newly bur-
geoning field of advertising. Justus George Frederick, "J. George" to his friends,
was working for the J. Walter Thompson Company in Chicago when he attended a college function at Northwestern and was smitten by the tall, dark-
eyed young woman who appeared so lively and interesting. She seemed to be a
"go-getter," he remembered later, and he fell for her "right off the bat." He
determined to get to know her better, and during the ensuing year he convinced
her to come back to Chicago and marry him.[2]

Christine Isobel MacGaffey and Justus George Frederick were married at
Irving Park, Chicago, on 29 June 1907. By the time the wedding took place,
J. George had already relocated to New York City, and an apartment at 1008
Simpson Street in the Bronx awaited the young couple. J. George was twenty-
five years old, and Christine was twenty-four.[3]

J. George's Star Ascends

THE BRONX WAS "a good middle-class suburb," Christine told her daughter
years later.[4] The Fredericks' Simpson Street flat was located in a ten-family

apartment house.[5] When the newlyweds settled into their new home in October, Christine became a full-time homemaker. She could not have resumed her fledgling teaching career even if she had wished to do so. The New York City Board of Education, like many other public school governing boards of the early twentieth century, did not hire married female teachers.[6]

In September 1908, nine months after the Fredericks moved into their Bronx apartment, their first child, David Mansfield, was born. A daughter, Jean Olive, joined the family two years later.[7] Sometime before 1911, the Fredericks moved to another, nearby apartment at 830 Manida Street.[8] Christine left only passing references to apartment life in the Bronx, but J. George gave the readers of a novel he wrote in 1924 a glimpse of what it might have been like. The three-room, third-floor front apartment in which the fictitious Phyllis found herself upon marriage "was one of the multitudinous brownstone residences of an age long since outgrown—a veritable deserted village of homes now peopled with wholly different human beings from their original occupants."[9]

More telling, perhaps, are the passages in which he described the frustrations suffered by this young woman, an aspiring journalist. She felt "entombed," he wrote. Even though she was at home all day, there seemed to be no end to the housework that needed doing. This distracted her from working on articles she had hoped to write. By late afternoon, Phyllis's day seemed "increasingly leaden and gray," and she hated thinking of herself as "one of the colorless, innumerable army of women who are the valets of the home, with the petty responsibilities of a chambermaid."[10] For Christine, the sudden change from the life of an independent young woman who was just beginning to develop her considerable talent for pedagogy to the confined and laborious existence of a young housewife and mother was going to require the creative application of her skills.

J. George, on the other hand, was on the move in the exhilarating new field of advertising. The dichotomy was striking; he might have been reflecting his own feelings when he had his fictional character's admirer say: "She came from another world than mine—she had a college education and I hadn't; she came from cultivated, artistic people and I came from a farm where six or seven books were thought to be about all anybody ought to fritter away time reading. She was all that I wasn't."[11]

J. George had grown up among Germans who were known as the "Pennsylvania Dutch" in Reading, eldest son among the ten living children his parents reared. Many of his relatives still used the characteristic dialect. As a boy, he worked on his grandmother's farm during the summer, often stirring huge pots of apple butter for her. The young man's ticket out of Reading was the knowledge and inspiration he received as a printer's devil for the local newspaper. He later wrote that his scholastic ability had been "mediocre" and that the printer's devil job fascinated him because of the physical aspects of setting type. But it was during this experience that he was "bitten by writing and publishing." As he put it, he "was wanted for more important work" and would go on to put "thought into words" rather than "words into type."[12]

His early successes came by way of advertising, an adjunct to the business world that was just then beginning to come into its own as a recognized field of specialization. William Dean Howells's character, Fulkerson, had declared a decade and a half earlier, "The advertising department is the heart and soul of every business."[13] Mass production required larger markets, and advertising was a way to expand those markets.[14] J. George Frederick understood this well: *"Advertising is the only efficient tool available to accomplish the much-needed purpose of raising the buying power and consumption standards of the world to the level of the rapidly mounting capacity for production"* (Frederick's italics).[15]

Public announcement of new products' availability had always been a part of American commerce; in the mid-nineteenth century, advertising agencies bought large blocks of space in newspapers and resold them to manufacturers. But sophisticated techniques such as jingle writing and special type were used by only a few until late in the century. At that time, advertisers began to establish professional organizations; the prestigious Sphinx Club in New York and the Agate Club in Chicago were early examples. The end of the century also saw the emergence of advertising journals. *Printers' Ink,* launched in 1888 as a house organ for George P. Rowell, an advertising agent and dealer in ink, taught advertisers how to write copy, how to analyze businesses and markets, and how to apply the new science of psychology to advertising.[16]

By the time J. George entered the field, more advertisers were forming associations. He was in Chicago in 1905 when the new Chicago Advertising Associates hosted the first meeting of the Associated Advertising Clubs of America. By 1907, the year that the Fredericks married, seventeen local advertising clubs had joined this national group.[17]

Professional advertisers were beginning to tap the expertise available from the new fields of psychology and market research. In Chicago, Walter Dill Scott, Christine's professor of psychology and logic, first spoke on the use of psychology in advertising to the Agate Club in 1901. In 1903, he published *The Theory and Practice of Advertising*, the subtitle of which was *A Simple Exposition of the Principles of Psychology in their Relation to Successful Advertising*. He revised it later and called it simply *The Psychology of Advertising*.[18] Scott said that the element of choice in purchasing indicated that advertising should appeal to reason, and he counseled advertisers to write "reason-why" advertising copy.[19]

Popular magazines such as the *Ladies' Home Journal* became mass circulation periodicals thanks to increased revenue from selling advertising space. In 1904, the *Journal* charged four thousand dollars for a single one-page advertisement and its readership had risen to nearly one million.[20] In 1911, the *Journal*'s publisher, Curtis Publishing, hired a market researcher who looked at national markets and distribution systems in order to choose and court advertisers more profitably. The large advertising agencies began to do market research at about the same time, establishing research departments within their operations by 1915. And it was during the early years of the twentieth century that manufacturers, with the help of advertising agencies, began to develop planned advertising strategies, campaigns based on market research.[21] The growth of advertising meant that manufacturers were now spending large sums of money to get their messages to the buying public. Walter Dill Scott claimed that advertising spending reached six hundred million dollars in 1904.[22] Twenty years later, J. George used that figure for 1910 spending.[23] Whatever the figure, by 1910 the advertising industry had become big business.

J. George, who had begun a writing career at the age of twenty-two, was working for J. Walter Thompson, a major advertising agency with offices in both Chicago and New York, and editing the Chicago trade journal *Judicious Advertising* when he met Christine. At the time of their marriage, he was transferred to the New York office.[24] This farm-bred Pennsylvania Dutch printer's devil from Reading had become sophisticated and urbane by the time he married Christine. Through the years, his writings would reflect easy conversance with a wide variety of literature, philosophy, and science.[25] From an early age, he was open to ideas and interested in current intellectual discourse. Later there would always be books and magazines "galore" in the Fredericks' home.[26]

In 1909, J. George was made managing editor of *Printers' Ink*. While there, he later claimed, he helped George Rowell educate businesses about the value of good copy.[27] He was instrumental in changing the journal's policy to meet the modern challenges of twentieth-century selling, advocating market research, a new aspect of the field in which he took great interest.[28] He remained at *Printers' Ink* until 1911 and wrote for it often afterward.[29] Drawing upon Walter Dill Scott's ideas, perhaps, he helped revolutionize advertising techniques with "reason why" copy.[30]

J. George was confident enough of his own abilities by 1910 to leave J. Walter Thompson and establish his own market research and publishing house, the Business Bourse. His first office was located at 347 Fifth Avenue, quarters he would occupy until the early 1920s.[31] But he continued to work in the field of advertising, and he was active in the Advertising Men's League of New York City, serving on a committee organized in 1911 to promote "'practical' truth in advertising work."[32] J. George also maintained his association with advertising trade journals and served as editor of *Advertising and Selling* from 1911 to 1915.[33]

His work in advertising gave J. George entrée into the related field of management, another rapidly expanding specialization within the world of American business. He founded the New York Salesmanager's Club and, several years after opening the Business Bourse, wrote a manual on the subject.[34]

Thus, while Christine labored with the babies at home, J. George quickly became involved with the exciting intellectual life in New York City. Through his interest in market research, he worked with Columbia's Professor Harry Hollingworth, a market researcher who, like Walter Dill Scott, promoted the use of psychology in advertising. Associations like this led J. George to found the Psychology Roundtable, forerunner of the Economic Psychology Association of which he became president.[35] Stimulated by new ideas and people with experiences different from his own, J. George wrote affectionately about the kaleidoscope that was Manhattan. Its "sheer colors, line, mass and human character" delighted one of his fictional characters.[36] With J. George, the latest thought on all sorts of topics "kept washing into the house."[37]

His stimulating life in the city presented J. George with temptations, too. Christine was not a joiner by nature, but even if she had wanted to participate in J. George's activities, she was confined by her domestic duties. J. George's office, which would later double as a studio apartment, allowed him the freedom to pursue liaisons with the exciting women he met, and he began to conduct extramarital affairs, a weakness he would indulge for the rest of his life.[38]

During the first three years of his marriage to Christine, J. George Frederick had served as an editor to two important advertising periodicals, written articles for other magazines, participated in the founding of organizations that would influence the development of modern American business practices, and started his own business in a promising new field. He seemed destined for a stellar career.

Dilemma and Opportunity

IN THE FIRST FEW MONTHS of marriage, Christine, like J. George's character Phyllis, came face to face with the realities of homemaking. For a young woman of her talents and aspirations, the new life seemed isolating, frustrating, and boring. She was proud of her college degree, proud of the Phi Beta Kappa key for which she had worked so hard. Yet here she was, confined in a small apartment, faced with the arduous chores that she later described so often as "drudgery."[39] "[I]t was a daily struggle to 'get ahead' of household drudgery," she wrote of this period. "And between it all, I knew I was not doing justice to myself."[40]

Christine had chosen to marry and to bear children, decisions that launched a traditional life modeled upon Catharine Beecher's injunction that a woman's highest duty was to care for home and children. However, she had grown to womanhood during a period when women were attending college, entering professions, and seeking positions in the wider world. She had been an ambitious student whose scholastic achievements and developing talents made her long for a way to put her speaking and writing abilities to use. But the nineteenth-century ideology was still a powerful influence in American life, and the majority of Americans, men and women alike, subscribed to it in 1910.[41] Christine was caught between Catharine Beecher's ideal and an emerging feminism that would demand a place for women outside the home, the most radical element of which questioned the value of the home itself.

This dilemma was clear to Christine's husband. In his 1924 novel, the character Phyllis found that housekeeping interfered with writing:

> The house demanded attention more imperiously now that she was at home than when she was working. At cleaning alone she spent many hours and discovered to her own grim amusement, that the seeds latent of a fussy housewife in her were unquestionably sprouting. She would seat herself at her typewriter at 2 or 3 o'clock in the afternoon, with a sigh of satisfied expectation. Words then not coming readily, she would gaze about the narrow confines of her domicile, and shortly observe that the picture mouldings were scandalously dusty. . . . Up she would rise, and an hour was gone before she returned again.[42]

Christine wrote that during her *own* first years of married life, housework and cooking consumed every hour of every day and that she had no time for a "higher life," no way to express her "individuality and independence." She was "forced to give up this individuality" to "babies and drudgifying housework." There was no time to read, write, or even take care of personal grooming, she wrote.[43] Even though she and J. George were able to hire a nursemaid to help with the babies, Christine worked hard on housekeeping chores.[44]

As she struggled to cope with the life of a homemaker, doors for women to enter the public sphere were opening ever wider. One historian has written, "The years 1870–1920 may be the high-water mark of women's public influence: through voluntary organizations, lobbying, trade unions, professional education, and professional activity."[45] In 1910, 10 percent of all doctoral degrees conferred by American universities were granted to women. By 1920, that figure had risen to 15 percent.[46] Many middle-class women used their educations to work in reform movements. Those who worked in the settlement house movement developed the field of social work and successfully urged the creation of the Children's Bureau in 1912.[47] Other women sought reform activity outside their homes through clubs. In 1912, the General Federation of Women's Clubs claimed one million members.[48]

The array of opportunities available to women by 1911 is suggested in the brochures published by the Women's Educational and Industrial Union of Boston (weiu): probation work, publishing house work, real estate, industrial chemistry, and bacteriological work, for example.[49] Many of these fields had previously been open only to men. Colleges offered vocational conferences for women after 1910, and these conferences optimistically encouraged young women to pursue a wide variety of careers.[50]

Nevertheless, most middle-class women did not seek paid jobs outside of the home, and those who did were often criticized. The secretary of Christine Frederick's contemporary, Jessie Daniel Ames, recalled that in 1914, when Jessie and her mother operated the local telephone company in Georgetown, Texas, "most of the men just thought it was terrible that she was trying to wear the pants."[51] In 1915, the *Ladies' Home Journal* suggested that marriage was far more fulfilling than a career could be. One article told the *Journal*'s readers that women could achieve the satisfaction of being needed only through marriage and motherhood.[52] As in the nineteenth century, however, women of the working class worked outside the home out of necessity. At the turn of the century,

20 percent of all American women over sixteen years of age worked for pay, though most of them did not make enough to support themselves.[53]

As Christine labored in her Bronx apartment, the women's movement to gain the vote was moving into its final decade. In 1910, three years after her marriage, the Women's Political Union of New York began marching in suffrage parades.[54] When the New York legislature decided to submit the question of woman suffrage to the voters, the *New York Times* ran an editorial urging that it be voted down.[55] The question sparked a volley of responses, and the next week the *Times* devoted a seven-page section to the question, "Should Women Vote in New York State?"[56] Edward Bok of the *Ladies' Home Journal,* who had been against suffrage, warned his readers in 1914 that, like it or not, the American woman should prepare for the inevitable and "open her eyes to the big world."[57] Christine Frederick surely read these articles.[58] Several neighbor women were active suffragists, and Christine later claimed that she had marched with the "suffragettes," but her daughter has no recollection of her mother taking any part in the suffrage movement. Christine skirted the subject in her writings.[59]

The word "feminism" was beginning to appear in the New York papers soon after Christine married.[60] The feminist leader Marie Jenney Howe conducted two mass meetings at Cooper Union in February 1914 on the topics "What Is Feminism?" and "Breaking into the Human Race."[61] According to one observer, Howe was "thoroughly impregnated with the feeling that there was a conspiracy of men against women . . . a feeling characteristic of that time."[62] The members of a luncheon group called Heterodoxy that Howe organized in 1912 certainly embraced feminist ideas.[63] They hosted speakers such as Margaret Sanger on birth control and Emma Goldman on the Russian revolution.

Presumably, Christine kept abreast of all this through the many publications to which the Fredericks subscribed. At least one of her acquaintances, Leta Hollingworth, was a member of Heterodoxy.[64] It is reasonable to assume, then, that Christine was aware of the public discourse on women's place in early-twentieth-century America.

Consolidating household tasks into cooperative ventures was an idea that attracted attention during this period, too. The *Journal of Home Economics,* reporting on a successful cooperative community kitchen delivery service, noted that there was "a surprising number of community kitchens" operating in the United States in 1915.[65] Charlotte Perkins Gilman and Henrietta Rodman, both early members of Heterodoxy, hired the architect Max G. Heidelberg to design the "Feminist Apartment House" to be built near Greenwich Village in New York City in 1914. The apartments would have no kitchens, food preparation and housekeeping would be done centrally by domestic science students, and there would be a collective nursery facility. But Gilman, Rodman, and their associates failed to raise the necessary capital and the apartments were never built. Two years later, a radical innovation planned by the architect Alice Constance Austin featured a "garden city of kitchenless houses" in the proposed socialist city of Llana del Rio, California, but it, too, failed for lack of funds. In a four-year experiment in Carthage, Missouri, suffragists busy with the voting rights campaign ran a cooperative kitchen using their own servants collectively.[66] Christine was aware of these ideas, but she did not explore them as a way out of her own dilemma. By 1919, in fact, she would soundly denounce them.[67] Like many other Americans, she supported the single-family home.[68]

All of these trends—professional opportunities for women, the suffrage movement, feminism, and suggestions for cooperative living—fueled the fear that had surfaced in the late nineteenth century that the home was threatened. By 1910, many social observers believed that in the wake of full industrialization, the home had lost its primary purpose. The household no longer had "social value" as a center of production, but was now the "centre of consumption," wrote the Chicago educators Marion Talbot and Sophonisba Breckinridge in 1912. Now, they argued, the housewife's role was to "administer incomes" and consume efficiently.[69] "We may as well face the fact cheerfully that industry in the home is doomed," advised the home economist Martha Bruère. Like Talbot and Breckinridge, she urged women to exchange outdated tasks that could now be done by industry for municipal housekeeping, or the caretaking of the community.[70]

Still, Talbot and Breckinridge saw the woman as the "heart of things" at home, the person who must bring up children to form good habits. In fact, the well-brought-up child was now the home's ultimate product.[71] These professional women espoused a traditional position—that woman should manage the home—from which to propose a new and radical suggestion—that as a homemaker, she was not only justified but compelled to take action in the public sphere.

The home and Catharine Beecher's view of woman within it were fiercely defended during this period of feminist expansion and turmoil. "It is the distinct and essential function of the home to furnish privacy and repose, and it is the distinct business of women to see to it that the home performs this function," stated the leaders of the Atlanta Woman's Club in 1909.[72] The president of the National Association Opposed to Woman Suffrage wrote in 1915 that her group was "asking for a division of labor for the sexes in the State and in the home." She argued that government was business, the province of the male sex.[73] Edward Bok of the *Ladies' Home Journal* told his readers that a "normal" wife should be "at the side of man as the worker."[74] Even modern women like Talbot and Breckinridge, who counseled women to embrace modernization, agreed that they should also fill the traditional role of mother. True homemaking, they wrote, perpetuated the home feeling, the spirit of home.[75] The problem was articulated by the president of the Woman's Department of the Southeastern Fair Association in 1916. She wondered "how woman can be helped to meet these new responsibilities which civilization demands of her, and at the same time not fail in her first and most essential duty as the home maker and home keeper."[76]

The middle-class American housewife, then, was in a quandary in 1910. Was she to remain within her sphere and manage a home as Catharine Beecher had urged? Should she enter the public work world? Should she work for suffrage so that she could tend to municipal housekeeping as so many writers of the day urged her to do? The writer Margaret Deland noticed a "prevailing discontent among women." She wrote that housewives who appeared outwardly to be perfectly happy might "confide in you that they are bored to death."[77] Christine Frederick might have been one of them in 1910. She wrote that prior to her discovery of a way to make it efficient, housekeeping represented "the most dreary shackles of which [women] have ever complained."[78]

But Christine accepted the validity of the ideology developed by Catharine Beecher, the ideology that she herself—influenced by the expectations of her class—had affirmed as a student when she had written "The Genius of Woman." Yet for her, the old ideology would, paradoxically, join with full acceptance of the modern age. She would employ the new ideas and practices that the male world of business was developing to increase the nation's productivity and distribution of goods, and she would embrace enthusiastically the technology that was creating labor-saving devices for the private home and developing the power sources to operate them.

Christine recognized that in spite of the debate, most Americans did not want radical change; they wanted to preserve the traditional home. And she responded to the solution offered by the new fields of home economics and scientific management, which drew from the current Progressive trends toward specialization and expertise. If the home suffered because it must perform a new function, if women could not manage it because the tasks were now different, the solution was to bring expert knowledge to bear upon the problem. "I believe that many a home . . . is not what it ought to be, not because the woman is not trying to do her part, but because she does not know how," wrote the president of the Woman's Department of the Southeastern Fair Association.[79] The hope that the home could be saved by experts would provide Christine Frederick with a career. Her solution to the educated American woman's dilemma was not to encourage her to leave the home. Nor did she propose to reorganize it into a cooperative institution. Rather, she would invite the public sphere into it. Ironically, the acceptance of the old assumption provided Christine Frederick with a way out of drudgery and inspired a public career. She would have the support of the majority of the middle class as she encouraged women to enjoy their roles as homemakers; she would also be able to enter into a very public life of her own as she spread the gospel of home modernization.

3 · The Rise of Home Economics and Scientific Management

Those who can make the home all it should be will get nearer the
foundations of life than even the teachers, ministers and educators.
First Annual Report, Lake Placid Conference on Home Economics, 1899

I suppose you smart men and efficiency experts will soon try to tell me
and all the other women that washing dishes can be "standardized". . .
or that we could save a million dollars if we would run
our homes on "scientific management"!
CHRISTINE FREDERICK, 1914

CHRISTINE MACGAFFEY'S SCIENTIFIC COURSE at Northwestern did not,
in fact, include very much science. Her emphasis was on speech, English, and
writing. The only science courses she took during her four years of college
were biology, problems in plant life, geology, and psychology.[1] Chemistry is conspicuous by its absence, in view of the fact that Christine's later career would
focus on women's work in the home. Many early home economists began their
training in chemistry.[2]

While home economics had made its way into thirty-six land grant colleges,
primarily in the West and Midwest, by 1905, Northwestern did not offer such a
course, and it is doubtful that Christine would have elected to take it even if it
had been available.[3] There is no evidence that she had any inclination in that
direction at this point in her life. But while she was honing her skills in oratory
and writing as she prepared herself to teach school, other women were making
of the home arts a new female profession they called home economics. It would
prove to be a significant development for Christine's future.[4]

Home Economics Is Professionalized

THERE HAD BEEN INTEREST in the home arts all through the latter half of
the nineteenth century; Catharine Beecher, as we have seen, had promoted the

36

idea that women should be trained to be homemakers. During the 1870s, cooking schools had appeared in several northeastern cities because, according to Ellen Swallow Richards, "the standard of the family table seemed to be deteriorating."[5] Middle-class women's groups also instituted housekeeping classes such as the School of Housekeeping established by the Women's Education and Industrial Union (WEIU) of Boston in 1897.[6] The school's brochures bolster the argument that the emergence of home economics coincided with the spreading fear that the home was threatened. One leaflet suggests that training in the home arts and sciences might save it:

> The aim of the School of Housekeeping is a scientific study of the Home, to save what is of permanent good, to discard what is useless, and to bring it into line with present industrial tendencies and scientific facts, social and physical, that it shall work not against, but for progress. This study is not to the end that the homes of any one class may be bettered, but that the standard of living and life may be raised, in all homes, in the belief that this would make for better citizenship, for a greater country, for a nobler race.[7]

The school's administrators, then, were joining with other early theorists to promote the idea that homemakers needed professional education. As Catharine Beecher had argued half a century earlier, proper training would elevate homemaking and preserve the home. Now the medical profession agreed: in 1899 the American Medical Association praised the study of domestic science on the grounds that it would reduce "infant mortality, contagious diseases, intemperance (in eating and drinking), divorce, insanity, pauperism, competition of labor between the sexes, men's and women's clubs, etc."[8]

Home economics was not recognized as an academic discipline until the Columbian Exposition in Chicago displayed several household exhibits in 1893. It was at the exposition that the National Household Economics Association was founded by the Women's Congress under the auspices of the General Federation of Women's Clubs.[9] Six years after the Columbian Exposition, the first of a series of ten conferences on home economics was held in Lake Placid, New York. Ellen Swallow Richards led the move to organize this convocation, which was attended by ten women and one man. One of this group's major goals was to put home economics into school curricula.[10] In 1900, the second Lake Placid Conference resolved to urge the National Education Association to create a Department of Home Economics and to call upon women's clubs to promote this objective.[11] In 1909, the American Home Economics Association was founded at the tenth Lake Placid Conference, a move that coordinated the efforts of developing and perfecting a science of housekeeping.[12] The next year, Ellen Richards defined "home economics" as "the preservation of the home and the economics of living."[13]

The Massachusetts State Board of Education began offering "domestic training" courses in 1912.[14] Two years later, the Atlanta Woman's Club heard a paper "on the relation of the study of Home Economics to the future success in home making."[15] But it was the land grant colleges that were established under the Morrill Land Grant Act of 1862 that first offered home economics courses in institutions of higher education. Early home economics students were required to work in the kitchens and dining rooms—not to earn money, as Christine MacGaffey was forced to do at Northwestern—but as a part of their course of study as Catharine Beecher's seminary students had done. By 1905, the year that Christine entered her senior year, thirty-six land grant institutions in the West and Midwest offered home economics courses. Public schools also began home economics instruction at the end of the nineteenth century.[16]

In light of dual sphere ideology, home economics became a more and more complicated subject. It incorporated the scientific advances and expert training acquired in the public sphere of educational institutions while it trained young women to keep the traditional domestic sphere. The application of scientific methods to housekeeping had the potential of destroying domesticity, the "home feeling" so prized in the nineteenth century, the "haven in a heartless world." Indeed, professionalizing homemaking might bring the heartless world into the home.[17] As a matter of fact, the study of home economics blurred the division between the private and public spheres. Scientific training would now be necessary to manage a home, and this would require the penetration of the domestic sphere by outside experts. A WEIU School of Housekeeping official wrote, "No home, however isolated, can escape the social obligation that rests on it, i. e., responsibility for the quality, fineness, and strength of the men and women who are its output."[18] The home, then, became a factory with "output" as its goal.

For some, the home economics movement was a way to assure women the right to college educations. Chemistry was required of the college students who entered the "young college women" track of the WEIU of Boston's school, but if an applicant did not have chemistry training, the school offered twelve lessons.[19] In 1899, Ellen Swallow Richards was on the faculty, which included professors from Wellesley, Harvard, and the Massachusetts Institute of Technology as well.[20] This professionalization of the training posed a dilemma: was home economics a new profession for women who wished to work outside the home or was it training to perfect in housewives the art of homemaking?

As home economics entered college and university curricula, academic home economists began to see themselves as professional women. Few married and those who did usually did not have children. Ellen Swallow Richards, for example, married at the age of thirty-three and remained childless. Henrietta Goodrich of the WEIU of Boston's School of Housekeeping envisioned a full curriculum elevating home economics to a science, culminating in a Ph.D. This compounded the paradox. Among these professionally trained experts, there was "confusion about the housewife's place."[21] The president of the National Household Economics Association told the 1902 Lake Placid Conference, "Fortunately there are a few thinking, progressive persons in the world besides ourselves and they are just as firm as we are in the belief that homemaking is the most natural and therefore the most desirable vocation for women."[22] Adopting this view, Christine Frederick would, within eight years, begin to extol the virtues of the woman who kept house. In doing so, she would often leave her own home to speak out as an expert in the public sphere.

The Home under Siege

THE FEAR among some home economists that the home was threatened was not without foundation. The ideal of a domestic sphere characterized by the ideology of the private home notwithstanding, resistance to the isolated woman's sphere had appeared even as Beecher and Stowe were publishing *The American Woman's Home*. As early as 1869, the middle-class housewife Melusina Peirce had proposed a cooperative housekeeping experiment in Boston, arguing that cooperative cooking, laundry, and sewing would free women to pursue professional lives if they wished.[23] Several cooperative housekeeping experiments were attempted throughout the remainder of the nineteenth century, indicating that at least a few Americans sought an alternative to the doctrine of two spheres. The Boston Cooking School delivered meals to working-class homes in the 1880s, the Twentieth Century Food Company distributed cooked meals in New Haven in 1900, and several other groups tried to centralize cooking, dining, and laundry. Americans were reading Edward Bellamy's bestseller *Looking Backward* in 1888, and many were eager to try his ideas for a cooperative, utopian system he called "Nationalism."[24] One of his disciples, Charlotte Perkins Gilman, offered the most radical alternative to traditional domestic arrangements.

In 1903, Gilman—socialist, evolutionary theoretician, feminist, and social commentator—wrote *The Home*, a scathing critique of the single-family dwelling as archaic and wasteful. The home, according to Gilman, had not progressed in evolutionary terms, and it arrested woman's proper development. "Traditional sentiments connected with home," she wrote, caused "positive injury to the life of to-day."[25] To Gilman, the domestic ideology of the nineteenth century had damaged woman's evolutionary progress and inhibited her ability to achieve full personhood. Gilman drew upon Darwinian principles to fashion a theory about gender roles. She believed that woman's development had been stunted by oppression and that one path to freeing her was a complete revolution of the home.[26] "By the end of 1890, Charlotte had produced a rather impressive array of subversive writings on the fraudulence of love and marriage myths," writes her biographer.[27]

Born into the extended Beecher family in Connecticut in 1860, Gilman grew up among people who devoted their lives to social issues. She lived with her divorced mother, but both parents encouraged her to excel intellectually.[28] Her talents were legion: she drew and painted; she wrote poetry, essays, and stories; and she developed ideas. Writing to a friend about her work on an autobiography late in life, she confessed that it did not interest her much. "My real interest," she reminded him, "is in ideas, as you know."[29]

As an adult, Gilman defied convention. After a divorce, she remained on very good terms with her first husband, Charles Walter Stetson, who later married her best friend and sometime collaborator, Grace Ellery Channing. The three shared the care of Charlotte's and Charles's daughter, Katharine. For several years thereafter, Gilman did not have a permanent address, but traveled across the country, speaking and staying with friends.[30]

Gilman wrote prolifically and lectured widely. She was associated with many women's organizations, the Women's Press Association, the Woman's Alliance, and the Parents Association, to name a few. She was also a member of Marie Jenney Howe's Heterodoxy group. After her divorce, she had been a close associate, indeed a housemate, of Helen Campbell, who had helped found the

National Household Economics Association. With Campbell, Gilman founded the Chicago branch of this organization, a group that formed committees on cooperative housekeeping. She responded enthusiastically to ideas such as Bellamy's that promoted collectivism and equality between the sexes. Her association with the sociologist Lester Ward influenced the writing of her first theoretical study of women, *Women and Economics*, in 1898. In this work, she examined the adverse effects of women's economic dependence upon men.[31]

In *The Home*, Gilman attacked nineteenth-century "mythology." The home, she wrote, was neither private nor sanctified. Furthermore, it did not promote economy. It was wasteful of time, energy, and woman's talent. Shockingly, she dismissed the idea that there was such a thing as maternal instinct. Mothers, she dared to write, did not know any better than others how to care for the young. Society was laboring under a myth she called "matriolatry."[32] Therefore, home was not really a "little heaven," but rather a "bunch of ill-assorted trades, wherein everything costs more than it ought to cost, and nothing is done as it should be done." Isolated in her home, woman labored for her family twelve hours a day and neglected the very purpose of the home, that is, caring for her children. This situation had resulted from the mistaken notion that housework was sex-specific. Americans had exalted this state of affairs, when actually it was wasteful and inefficient.[33]

Gilman proposed that advances in science and management be utilized to consolidate the tasks that had traditionally been done on a small scale in the home. A city block of two hundred homes housing perhaps one thousand people was traditionally fed by the labors of two hundred cooks, she wrote. How much better and more efficiently, she asked, might these two thousand souls be fed by a staff of thirty professional cooks? Like the home economists who argued that there was a need for training and expertise in managing the home, Gilman believed that most housewives were ignorant about their work. "Ignorance . . . is an essential condition of home-cooking," she noted sarcastically.[34]

Gilman saved her most vitriolic language for affluent women of leisure, women who entertained lavishly in their homes to give their otherwise useless lives purpose. This lifestyle, she argued, was hard on marriages. Men must bear the costs, and "to the expense of maintaining a useless woman is added the expense of entertaining her useless friends." Not only did the private home visit economic hardship upon the male, it also perverted his view of human relations by teaching him that "women were made for service . . . and that his own particular tastes and preferences are of enormous importance." "The woman is narrowed by the home," she wrote, "and the man is narrowed by the woman."[35]

Gilman did not argue for the destruction of the home so much as she urged change. Her proposal was to free women, to allow them to become economically independent. In Gilman's view, that was the greatest damage the home had done; it had made woman dependent. Instead, she should be allowed to enlarge her world, to become a competent mother in the way that men became competent fathers—by entering and working in the public sphere. Staying in the domestic sphere, in the home, had made women into "social idiots" and denied them progress. Change would come, Gilman predicted, through the woman's movement. Women would lead a campaign to shrink domestic industries and to socialize them, collectivize them, so that wives and mothers need not stay at home. There would be nurseries and eating houses. The home should consume but a small part of a woman's—or man's—attention. While the home would continue to be the "base and background of our lives," all humans, men and women alike, could live in the broader world.[36] Gilman advocated alternatives to the isolated, single-family home. She wrote of kitchenless apartments with cooperative eating facilities for working women with families and kitchenless suburban homes connected to a cooperative eating house.[37]

Gilman's influence was significant. *Women and Economics* was translated into seven languages and used as a text at colleges like Vassar. It inspired women's groups throughout the country to establish community kitchens and cooked-food delivery services in an attempt to free women from full-time home duties.[38] The breadth of Gilman's activities made it possible for even rural women to hear her message. Irene Calbraith, a Yamhill County, Oregon, physician's wife who belonged to the Pacific Coast Women's Press Association from 1891 until the early 1900s, during which time Gilman served as its president, heard Gilman speak at an annual meeting in San Francisco in April 1891.[39] In Dolores Hayden's words, Gilman reached "small-town suffragists, metropolitan planners, and specialists in the higher education of women."[40] Even so, promoters of ideas such as hers remained a small minority.

As Gilman was denouncing the "domestic mythology" of the nineteenth century and writing that "nothing in the work of the house . . . requires . . . maternal affection,"[41] the young Christine MacGaffey was earnestly giving vent to a very different, more traditional sentiment: "Woman's . . . relation to the world is as important as man's. To her belongs the education of the young. Since so much depends on that early training, woman's immense advantage in moral opportunity is clearly perceived. It also shows the incalculable wrong and loss if her work has been neglected or poorly done. A good woman will make a good home and will send out into the world sons taught in lessons of integrity and uprightness."[42] Like Gilman, who was twenty-three years older, Christine would write thousands of words, deliver scores of speeches, and reach countless women. But her message would be quite different. Christine would adhere to the mythology, even as her own life would belie it.

Reformers like Gilman who wanted to see fundamental changes in the home looked to technology and industrialization. Advanced expertise, efficient production, and wider distribution of goods might mean that innovations like commercial laundries, bakeries, and food processors would take over the tasks that had traditionally fallen to the housewife. Women, then, would be free to pursue other interests and talents. Industrialization was, indeed, to have a significant impact on the home, but not in the way these reformers imagined.

Scientific Management to the Rescue

SCIENTIFIC MANAGEMENT was a response to the desire for increased production. It promised to utilize the worker to maximum capacity. When the efficiency engineer Harrington Emerson showed that streamlined innovations could save the railroads one million dollars a day during the Eastern Rate Case of 1910, the terms "efficiency" and "scientific management" became household words.[43] Frederick Taylor, the leader of the movement, had conducted experiments to increase the production of pig-iron handlers at Bethlehem Steel Company and shovelers at Midvale Steel during the last quarter of the nineteenth century. He explained his revolutionary method of systemizing work in the influential book *Principles of Scientific Management*. Using stopwatches to determine the minimum time required to perform these tasks, he was able to raise output considerably, leading to the "standardization" of each task. Plans could be drawn up that would detail the movements required, the tools necessary, and the "routing" of the process. Planners would generate work assignments, giving each worker precise instructions for the task of the day. The four principles Taylor developed to implement scientific management were development of the "science of the task" through careful timing and analysis of required motion; selection and training of workers suited to that task; careful supervision of workers coupled with a reward or "bonus" when they increased production; and strict division of labor between workers and management so that management made all decisions about tasks.[44]

Taylor's system became a movement. The Taylor Society, the Efficiency Society of New York, and the *Efficiency Magazine* all promulgated his ideas. The Taylor Society quickly grew to include not only engineers, but businessmen and industry managers as well. Many nonmembers attended meetings, Secretary of War Felix Frankfurter and the muckraking journalist Ida Tarbell among them.[45]

One of the most prominent of Taylor's early disciples was Frank Bunker Gilbreth. Gilbreth's work augmented Taylor's by adding the element of motion study to the stopwatch analyses. He used the new medium of the motion picture to identify sixteen elementary motions the human hand could perform. By cataloging these motions, Gilbreth claimed to be able to standardize all human labor.[46] Gilbreth's widely publicized study of bricklaying seized the imagination of those interested in efficiency and increased production. By first studying the motions of bricklayers, then sorting bricks and changing the height of the pallet from which they worked, Gilbreth increased the single bricklayer's output from 120 bricks per hour to 350, according to Taylor, or, in another account, from 1000 to 2700 per day.[47] Gilbreth, working with his wife, Lillian, sought to find the "one best way" to do work.[48]

The *Ladies' Home Journal* hailed scientific management as a boon to the housewife. The next step, the editor wrote, was to send the expert into the home. There should be "visiting housekeeper[s]" to help desperate women "feed and clothe a family on a meager income" efficiently. Utilizing the principles of scientific management in the home had opened to women "an enormous field."[49] The *Journal* was selling over one million copies annually by the dawn of the twentieth century, so its influence was widespread.[50] If scientific management could help save the home, women's magazines such as the *Journal* would do their part to bring the expertise of its practitioners to the American housewife.

Other periodicals, too, promoted the idea of applying scientific management to the home. In 1910 the *Journal of Home Economics* suggested that housewives should imitate factory and commercial laundry managers and calculate their hours.[51] The next year, Ellen Swallow Richards advised homemakers to become "engineers" and learn to keep their homes "under modern conditions."[52] In 1911 and 1912, *Outlook* ran a series of articles on homemaking, many of them urging the application of scientific management. One included a discussion of the standardization of dishwashing.[53] Marion Talbot and Sophonisba Breckinridge observed in *The Modern Household* that everyone was talking about scientific management in 1912.[54] The message was clear. Homemaking could be changed from drudgery to humming efficiency through scientific management, but only if housewives were properly trained by experts.

By the beginning of the twentieth century, then, as Christine MacGaffey was enjoying a measure of the equality claimed by women of her generation while paying lip service to the inequality accepted by her mother's, the future of the traditional home seemed to hang in the balance. Two new fields of study, home economics and scientific management, emerged as ways to stabilize and preserve it. Home economics would train women to become proficient (and satisfied) homemakers, and scientific management would make them efficient managers.

4 · *Conceiving a Career*

I came to earnestly believe that scientific management could, and must,
solve housework problems as it had already solved other work problems. . . .
Formerly I had been doing my work in a dead, mechanical way, but now
every little task was a new and interesting problem. I found that housework
was just as interesting and more so than many other tasks of business.

CHRISTINE FREDERICK, *Household Engineering,* 1919

AMONG THE PURVEYORS of modern culture that J. George Frederick brought
home to the Bronx apartment that he and Christine rented in the first years of
their marriage were advocates of scientific management.[1] Hearing these men
talk of the time saved by the efficiency of this system, Christine "had an intu-
ition that perhaps in this new idea was the life-preserver" that would save her
from her sea of drudgery.[2] Harrington Emerson, who had testified in the rate
case, was one of those who discussed scientific management with her.[3]

Becoming an Expert

CHRISTINE HAD TWO BABIES and "was struggling with young and inexperienced help" when she first began listening to her husband and his friends.[4]
J. George's fortuitous conversations furnished her with the first of many modern ideas that would make her life as a homemaker come alive with purpose.
"For once I found a use for some of the college training I had despaired of ever
putting into practice," she later wrote. Fundamental to her pleasure in discov-
ering this possibility was the belief that applying scientific management to
housework would make it just as interesting and worthwhile as the "business
and industrial world which men tackle with zest and results."[5]

Christine listened with great interest to an account of Frank Gilbreth's experiments with bricklayers and wondered if similar methods could be applied to
housekeeping, an occupation that involved so many different tasks. When
Emerson gave her a copy of his book, *The Twelve Principles of Efficiency,* she

asked him how his ideas might be applied to the home.[6] "It seemed to me," she wrote, "that this was exactly what my aim was in my own home."[7] "Do you know that I am going to work out those principles here in our home!" she exclaimed to J. George. "I'm going to find out how these experts conduct investigations, and all about it, and then apply it to *my* factory, *my* business, *my* home."[8]

The experts suggested to Christine that housewives might avail themselves of "competent counsel," a tactic suggested in Emerson's twelve efficiency principles, by reading government bulletins, women's magazines, and manufacturers' brochures, and she applied herself to the study of these sources with energy.[9] To any reader of his book, *Principles of Scientific Management*, Frederick Taylor had made a standing offer of tours of the firms in Philadelphia where his system had been installed.[10] Christine may have taken him up on his offer, for she later wrote of visiting several facilities while she was making her study of scientific management. She studied the advantages of grouping tools in a cash register factory, she observed labor-saving devices that counted pills in a chemist's shop, and she witnessed the improved efficiency that resulted from decreasing the number of cuts made in the manufacture of envelopes.[11]

Christine took full advantage of the currency and intersection of two modern ideas: that scientific management could improve any work process and that expertise would save the home. Catharine Beecher had sought to convince women that their duties in the home were as important as any on earth for moral reasons; woman's primary role in her domestic sphere was a moral one. Christine Frederick would share her newfound knowledge of home efficiency with other women and show them that homemaking was a fulfilling and satisfying profession; Christine's new homemaker would concentrate on operating the home efficiently. She joined a housekeeping reform that significantly modified the old ideology. The historian T. J. Jackson Lears has observed that there was a general "shift from a Protestant ethos of salvation through self-denial toward a therapeutic ethos stressing self-realization in this world" when Christine was formulating a new ethic of housekeeping.[12]

Early in 1912, Christine sent a series of four articles on efficiency in the home to Edward Bok's *Ladies' Home Journal*. She had chosen a conservative, middle-class audience. A typical reader of the *Journal* was white, married, operating a home without a servant, and had means enough to sample the many products the magazine advertised. The *Journal's* readers believed in the traditional values of the nuclear family home and upheld the notion that women should be the keepers of those values.[13] Christine had undoubtedly read the magazine as a new bride and understood its appeal for other women. Her series was titled "The New Housekeeping," and Karl Harriman, the *Journal's* literary editor, liked it very much. He asked Christine to come to the *Journal's* offices in the new Curtis Building on Independence Square in Philadelphia to discuss her articles with Bok. Bok not only agreed to run "The New Housekeeping" series, but he also offered Christine a position answering letters to the magazine under a department called "How Can I Run My House More Easily?"[14] Bok recognized the public appeal of scientific management, and Christine's interpretation of it had been a major selling point for her articles. At the annual conference of Curtis Publishing's advertising department that year, Bok had told the group that he intended to push scientific management "just as far as the freight will carry it."[15]

Bok offered Christine $600.00 for the four articles and $15.00 for every one hundred letters answered. The magazine would begin listing her in its directory, "Whatever You Want to Know Ask the Ladies' Home Journal," in the July issue. When Christine held out for a larger sum for the articles, the *Journal*, wanting her to "feel justly compensated," raised the fee to $750.00.[16] Christine demonstrated remarkable self-confidence in this early negotiation for her first real professional fee. She also demonstrated that she already had plans for a larger writing career. She asked Harriman if the *Journal* would object to her peddling similar articles to other magazines, but he asked her to wait until after the pieces had run in the *Journal*.[17] In June, a supply of *Ladies' Home Journal* stationery arrived at the country home Christine and J. George had purchased on Long Island the year before, and she became the magazine's new housekeeping expert.[18]

Encouraged and motivated by her immediate success, Christine produced another article about the reorganization of the kitchen in the old house on Long Island and sold it to the *Journal* for one hundred dollars. It was published in July 1913.[19] Pursuing publication with great energy, Christine decided to expand her housekeeping articles into a book and offered to send chapters to Harriman for spring issues even as the *Journal* was running the first articles.[20] A piece drawn from the new material was published in the November issue.[21]

Bok was pleased with Christine's work. He ran six more of her articles during

1913 and 1914, and after a test of her letter-answering skills in which he sent her a dummy letter (a practice he employed with other contributing editors as well), he commended her on the "prompt answer" that was "full and comprehensive." He was pleased that she was courteous and demonstrated personal interest in the writer.[22]

Christine worked continuously, sometimes jotting down ideas for new articles on the backs of envelopes. She conscientiously typed up lists of readers' problems and summarized her responses.[23] By now it was clear that she could not produce work at this rate and perform all the duties of the full-time housewife and mother that she represented herself to be; so a housekeeper became a permanent part of the Frederick household when the family moved to Long Island.[24]

Sometime before Bok accepted her articles for publication, Christine joined an organization called the Associated Clubs of Domestic Science, and she may have attended meetings every other Thursday.[25] This membership provided her with credentials as the "competent counsel" that the efficiency engineers recommended, for she included under her name, "National Secretary of the Associated Clubs of Domestic Science."[26] As such, she joined the ranks of the home economists who argued that professional training in domestic science would preserve the home. Christine believed that she could demonstrate to other women that through modernization, housekeeping could be made more pleasant than office work. "Certainly, baking a cake or bathing a baby is not a whit as much 'drudgery' as monotonously addressing envelopes or pounding a typewriter," she wrote.[27]

Each of "The New Housekeeping" articles was prefaced by the story of Frank Gilbreth's improvement of bricklaying.[28] The first was reminiscent of Catharine Beecher's instructions on washing dishes. It included a detailed description of how Christine had standardized dishwashing, analyzing and reducing the number of motions necessary to complete the job, thus cutting the time necessary. Following the example of the efficiency engineers she had studied, she broke dishwashing into three separate operations: scraping and stacking, washing, and drying and putting away. No element of the minutiae of this task escaped her analysis. "My first step was: pots and pans filled with water," she wrote. "Note, please, that my drainer is at my *left* and the dishes are stacked up to the *right*" (Frederick's italics). She demonstrated the time saved by her analyses with charts. She also suggested a formula for adjusting the height of the kitchen sink, a suggestion that would later prompt her to tell audiences that she would be remembered for "raising the kitchen sink."[29]

Not only did Christine adopt the methods of the efficiency experts, but she also used their lexicon. The housekeeper who washed the dishes, served the meals, and cleaned the rooms was the "worker." Tasks were "standardized," and the work components were divided to create "specialization." Tools should be grouped, supplies inventoried.[30] She exemplified the historian Victoria de Grazia's observation that scientific management encouraged homemakers to imitate the factory.[31]

Christine's second and third articles, again reminiscent of Catharine Beecher, dealt with scheduling and record keeping. While Christine told her readers that she disliked "'system' as much as any woman," she revealed a penchant for extremely detailed organization. The sample schedule, her own, set exact times for bathing the baby, working the bread, making the salad dressing, and cleaning the bathroom. Her record system involved a card file of one thousand three-inch by five-inch cards on which she recorded everything from clothing sizes to financial records to jokes and quotations. The last stood her in good stead at parties, she wrote. She once brought out the quotation file and provided "entertainment by card system."[32]

In the fourth article of this first series, Christine discussed the "servant problem" at length, arguing that its solution lay in treating domestic help like workers in any other industry. She advocated definite hours, hourly wages, work plans, and regular days off.[33]

Christine was not the only Frederick who was writing articles about efficiency in 1912. Although his focus was on advertising, J. George was also interested in scientific management and what it could do for the production efficiency of manufacturing. In an article that was intended to be the first in a series for *Harper's Weekly*, he identified efficiency as the third major improvement in modern industry, the first and second being invention and organization. Efficiency could cut the administrative costs of selling by 20 percent, he claimed. J. George believed, as did Frederick Taylor, that scientific management promoted the most humane treatment of the workforce, primarily because it offered bonuses for goals met. Revealing a natural bias for one who earned his living writing about advertising and management, he wrote that the efficiency movement "automatically shattered the coercive effects of the labor-unions."[34]

The promised series did not materialize, and J. George did not write any further efficiency articles for *Harper's* that year.

Life at Applecroft

WHEN, AFTER NEARLY THREE YEARS in New York City, the Fredericks had decided that they would prefer to rear their children in the country, they bought a house on over an acre and a half of property forty miles out on Long Island in the rural community of Greenlawn.[35] The family temporarily moved across the East River to Port Washington on the other side of Long Island Sound while the old house, situated in a long-neglected apple orchard, was renovated. By the time Christine wrote the *Journal* articles in 1912, they had moved into the house she christened "Applecroft," honoring, perhaps, her Scottish heritage.[36]

Greenlawn was a small town of about four hundred inhabitants when the Fredericks moved to Applecroft. The station where J. George caught the train to the city every morning was a mile and a half away over farm roads. The nearest market town was Huntington, five miles distant. Widely scattered farms dotted that portion of Suffolk County, a few of them owned by immigrants. German and Swedish neighbors grew cabbage and cucumbers that they sold to the pickling works near the Greenlawn station. They kept dairy cows and hogs, fed in winter by homegrown corn silage.[37]

By the time the Fredericks moved to Greenlawn, Christine was solidly launched as a household writer, busy enough to require an office of her own. The roof on the old garage at Applecroft was raised to accommodate a light, spacious loft that was furnished with desk, typewriter, file cabinets, Morris chair, and pot-bellied stove. Christine hired a secretary to help her with the large volume of letters and the continuous flow of articles.[38] Her writing suggested that she did her own housework, and for a time she did much of it. Certainly, she conducted the time study experiments and operated the equipment she acquired. Her daughter remembered that her mother was an "excellent housekeeper" and that "especially in the early years," Christine "did a good bit of cooking."[39] Still, the volume of her writing and the need for staff suggest that, in her own home, she delegated and supervised much of the work she urged other women to find fulfilling.

Christine's renovated kitchen at Applecroft reflected the twentieth-century transition to power-operated kitchen appliances. In the early years she cooked on a three-burner kerosene stove supplemented by a "fireless cooker," one of her favorite labor-saving devices.[40] Though the Fredericks soon installed an electric generator in their basement, Christine conducted her early efficiency experiments without the benefit of electricity "to show what could be done in a kitchen in which electric current and city conveniences were not possible."[41] She made her kitchen efficient, though: countertop and sink height were adjusted to her five-foot, six-inch frame; furniture and appliances were arranged for the proper "routing" of food preparation and cleanup; and drain board and serving surfaces were covered with galvanized iron for easy cleaning. She also installed an elevator icebox, which operated "on pulleys and counterweights" that could be "easily raised and lowered through the kitchen floor into a cold storage closet" in the basement.[42] Christine repainted her twelve-by-fourteen-foot kitchen in light cream with white woodwork to enhance the light provided by large casement windows, mindful, perhaps, of Catharine Beecher's advice to provide "a neat and cheerful kitchen" and "to promote a neat look and pure air."[43] A pressed cork floor afforded comfort during periods of standing, and all shelves were open for easy access.[44]

Life at Applecroft was happy for Christine's children. They played in the orchard, occasionally getting shooed from beneath the office window by their busy mother, who needed peace to concentrate on her writing. When they reached school age, they walked to the two-room Elwood Elementary School, about a mile and a half from the house. They played with the neighboring farm children; helped to tramp the pungent, fermenting silage as it was blown into the top of the silo; watched, wide eyed, as pigs were killed and butchered for German sausage; helped with farm chores; and enjoyed the rewards of warm strudel and coffee.[45]

The Fredericks owned a car, always a used one, from the time they moved to Applecroft. J. George would start its motor with the crank every morning before breakfast and Christine would drive him to the station after they had eaten.[46] "In the author's home, five miles from fresh supplies, and 40 miles from a city, meat and perishables are bought once a week; monthly a large grocery order is sent to a city dealer," Christine wrote of shopping.[47] She hated to crank the car and she did not really like to make the drive to Huntington, but country living required it. The family used the car to drive to the nearby shore or to a picnic, too. Not everyone on Long Island in those early years owned a car. A woman who sewed for the family from time to time drove to Applecroft by horse and buggy, a familiar sight in Greenlawn when the children were small.[48]

Christine wrote much of her housekeeping advice for women who did not hire help, and often claimed that she did all her own work. But as her writing and lecturing commitments increased, she required the assistance of at least part-time help not only for child care but also for laundry, sewing, and cleaning. The Frederick family saw many nursemaids come and go, but the nursemaid-housekeeper who stayed the longest was a Norwegian woman who had a daughter of her own.[49] Christine tried to hire mothers with the understanding that they could keep their children with them at Applecroft. This made the somewhat remote country life more attractive, and she trusted mature women to be more capable than young single women. Women with children, she wrote, provided the most dependable and permanent help, especially for those who lived in the suburbs.[50] Christine did not address the inconsistency that this situation revealed. While she advised other middle-class women to be happy in their own homes, she hired women who had to work for a living away from theirs.

The children called the Norwegian housekeeper "Nursie," and Christine's daughter remembered her as "a delightful woman, motherly and clean."[51] Christine mentioned "the dearly beloved 'nursie'-housekeeper" in her second book, describing how she was given Fridays off but was always welcome to join the family for dinner on those evenings.[52] Nursie did not meet all of Christine's requirements, however. "The author confesses, regretfully, that in her own home an excellent ironing machine, gas iron, fireless cooker, dishwasher and washing machine stand unused by any save herself—more than one worker (and that, too, of education, and more than 15 years' experience in managing homes of their own) refusing to be 'bothered' with 'new-fangled' ideas," she wrote. Apparently Nursie and other household help did not share her enthusiasm for technology.[53]

When J. George and Christine moved to Applecroft, Christine was thirty-one years old. A journalist described her two years later: "[Y]ou would think she was a young college girl, keen and intelligent, but carefree and full of the joy of living." Her manner was "placid," her face "unlined."[54] Another interviewer wrote that she "contrives somehow to look like a healthy and happy girl."[55] She was still slim and lively. Unlike her contemporary dress reformers, Christine still wore corsets and continued to wear them well into her old age. She believed that corsets were essential to health because they promoted erect posture and did not allow the abdomen to relax. "[S]ome form of corset or abdominal belt or supporter should always be worn when doing the manual tasks of housework, especially by women who have had children," she wrote.[56] She believed in dressing for the evening, after the day's work was done and before J. George returned home from the city. She would always put on a "clean waist" in the late afternoon, she wrote in 1912.[57] She planned her day so that she would have to "spend only a minimum of time in the kitchen at night when she [was] dressed for the evening."[58] The housekeepers doubtless made this possible by doing part of the work.

Home life was pleasant enough. Though she claimed to have a tin ear, Christine played the piano a bit, and J. George sang. The entire family gathered round the piano for "family sings" from time to time.[59] J. George tinkered with do-it-yourself projects around the place. Since his printer's devil days he had enjoyed working with his hands, and he had developed an interest in home projects like gardening, plumbing, paperhanging, and painting when he and Christine were apartment dwellers in the Bronx.[60] At Applecroft, he and his young son, David, built a poured concrete picnic table and benches in the old orchard.[61] The family also played tennis on their own concrete tennis court.[62]

Sometime after the move to Long Island and before the birth of the Fredericks' third child, Phyllis, in the spring of 1915, Christine gave birth to a stillborn baby boy. Though she recovered fully, and rarely mentioned it, she thought of it more often as she aged. Four years before she died, she told an audience that she had borne five children, and on her deathbed, she lamented that there should have been another son.[63] In 1917, the family was made complete with the arrival of the fourth child and third daughter, Carol, who was born on 22 August of that year.[64]

Christine's most creative, most active career years coincided with the rearing of the four children at Applecroft. Although she wrote less about child rearing than other homemaking activities, she occasionally revealed progressive beliefs on the subject. Children, she believed, had rights. In her second book, she advised mothers to avoid using their children as personal servants, but to encourage them to do chores according to efficiency principles. In the Fredericks' bathroom, for example, each child had a personal hook placed at a convenient height on which to hang his or her own towel and washcloth. The linens were marked with each name in different colors of thread.[65] The Fredericks made sure their children's health was monitored: their bouts with childhood diseases were carefully recorded, they were vaccinated for smallpox, had their eyes checked, and made regular trips to the dentist.[66] The children addressed their mother by the familiar term "Muzz," an endearment they used all her life.[67]

The atmosphere was always stimulating. J. George believed that children should be taught to question and challenge. He often tossed out topics at the dinner table and encouraged the children to argue with him. His daughter remembered hearing "trial marriages" discussed, a subject explored in Elsie Clews Parsons's 1906 work, *The Family.* No doubt, J. George and Christine were familiar with her arguments.[68] Many magazines found their way into the Frederick home. Both J. George and Christine mentioned periodicals such as the *Atlantic,* the *North American Review,* the *Review of Reviews,* the *New Republic,* and the *Bookman.* Their daughter remembers reading *Harper's* and the *Literary Digest.*[69] And although they lived a considerable distance from the city and J. George's contacts, there was often company.

Encouraged by her early success as a home efficiency writer, Christine worked to expand her career not only because it was exciting and enjoyable, but because the money mattered, too. Though J. George's career had shown early promise, the truth was that he was an impractical visionary who "just held on to paying his office rent to the Business Bourse." One of his daughters' childhood friends recalled that he had been considered something of a dilettante in some quarters; according to her, his books had a very limited audience and did not sell well.[70] The family needed Christine's earnings. Even though she hired help to keep the household running while she wrote and traveled to speaking engagements, she had to be frugal. A seamstress made all the children's clothes while they were small, and Christine bought cloth in bulk to save money.[71]

Middle-class families that lived comfortably in 1912 did so on incomes of between one thousand and thirty-five hundred dollars a year.[72] In 1919, Christine used a model income of fifteen hundred dollars as the basis of her typical family budget.[73] That may suggest the Fredericks' income bracket at the time. To help keep it at that level, Christine had to maintain a prodigious work schedule.

She was undoubtedly the primary breadwinner as the children were growing up at Applecroft. Her daughter recalled that Christine was "carrying a heavy load. . . . [S]he earned money and he [J. George] didn't."[74] The need to make money was surely part of the motivation for Christine's ever more aggressive pursuit of work. Understanding that syndication greatly expanded the earning power of single articles, for example, she urged that material she wrote for the *Philadelphia Ledger* (a publication briefly controlled by Cyrus Curtis) be syndicated in 1913.[75] Later, when testing household appliances would become a large part of her work, manufacturers and publishers alike paid her for her analyses of products. And as she moved into the lecture circuit, she charged for her appearances.[76]

A Gendered Career

HER BOOK, *The New Housekeeping*, set forth the principles on which Christine Frederick would base a career for the next three decades. She quoted from Catharine Beecher's *Treatise* to support her argument that housekeeping could be transformed into a stimulating and satisfying occupation for all women: "When young ladies are taught rightly to appreciate and learn the most convenient and economical modes of performing all family duties, and of employing time and money; when they perceive the true estimate accorded these things by teachers and friends, the grand cause of this evil [of poor housekeeping] will be removed."[77] Christine blamed discontent among housewives on poor outlook. Too many women let housework weigh them down by focusing on the physical aspects of the work, she wrote. Others lacked confidence or were inept. Too many merely tolerated housework and felt contempt for it, wishing they could do something else instead. All these attitudes, she argued, were "*poisonous and antagonistic to either efficiency or the highest personal happiness.*" If women would shake off these destructive attitudes, they would then find that "*far from being dull drudgery, homemaking in all its details is fascinating and stimulating if a woman applies to it her best intelligence and culture*" (Frederick's italics).[78] She failed to acknowledge that she had overcome similar negative attitudes not through housework, but through writing.

Christine seemed unaware that much of the elaborate timing, planning, and record keeping she suggested might actually result in more work for the housewife. Her mentor, Harrington Emerson, recognized the problem, however. He cautioned the readers of her second household manual that simply because Christine's efficient methods made "tasks as formerly done much easier," they should "not take on a great deal more 'unessential' work."[79] Expanding the time spent on household chores would make it even harder to find time for activities outside the home. Christine held housewives to the new, higher standards of cleanliness that the advent of appliances inspired, too.[80] "Increasingly high standards of sanitation in the home have made cleaning one of the most important divisions of housework," she wrote in 1919.[81] She recommended that bathrooms be cleaned and floors mopped daily. She even suggested that cleanliness was more important than minimizing labor: "the vacuum cleaner, oil dusters and small removable rugs are important not so much as labor-savers as because they minimize the number of impurities and disease germs." But she also told the woman who did not hire a servant that she should avoid making her schedule too elaborate or raising her standards of cleanliness too high. "It is quite possible to keep the house *too* clean," she wrote. "*Housekeeping should never be an end in itself*" (Frederick's italics).[82] She failed to realize that following her prescription might make it just that.[83]

Christine believed that women should continue to do most housekeeping tasks at home. In 1914, she assured the homemaker that "*no matter how difficult and trying are the household tasks and burdens she finds placed upon her, there positively are ways to meet and conquer them efficiently — if she approaches these problems vigorously, hopefully, and patiently*"[84] (Frederick's italics). She reported that she had spent hours working out her "scientifically" performed tasks, analyzing the steps she took to make a cake, for example. She provided charts that showed time saved by converting to "standardized" methods.[85] This process, she believed, would make housework interesting and thus help save the home; women would be happier staying at home if they made it efficient. But by offering her own experience as a model, Christine ignored the fact that her typical reader would not be able to parlay housekeeping experiments into the exciting writing and speaking career that she had created for herself. Like the home economists who did not always make it clear whether their training would produce homemakers or teachers, Christine delivered a conflicted message. Sometimes she claimed that scientific management would make the woman content to stay home; at other times, she acknowledged many women's desire to enter the outside world. The "new home-making," she acknowledged, would provide a "life for woman freed from demeaning house drudgery—the opportunity to give thought and care to the wider range of interests which it is now certain will be woman's future sphere."[86] The point of standardizing housework, she wrote in the *Journal of Home Economics*, was to have time for other activities.[87] Yet a model schedule she developed in 1919 offered a full day of housekeeping chores with rest periods, but no time for venturing into the public sphere. When she did allow time out of the home, it was not for paid employment. A woman who prepared her dinner during lunch cleanup, for example, would have "*more definite 'off time' in the afternoon for calling, club meetings, or rest*" (Frederick's italics).[88]

Despite the enthusiasm with which Christine and other writers embraced the scientific management model for housekeeping, its principles were misplaced in a home operated by a lone woman. Christine unintentionally acknowledged the problem herself: "It is the great misfortune of women as homemakers that each one of them must stand alone as the directing head of a separate establishment, without any trained, efficient mind to guide and direct them," she wrote. Men in the workplace, conversely, had foremen and overseers and "the social stimulus of working among other men in competition."[89] Taylor had used teachers, toolroom men, planning clerks, and, of course, the workers in factories.[90] One of his four main principles was to choose the right worker for a given task. He wrote that his system worked well only when "the best man suited" to the work was "carefully selected." His planners were specialists. "One . . . is a specialist on the proper speeds and cutting tools to be used. . . . Another man analyzes the best and quickest motions to be made by the workman. . . . Still a third . . . makes out a timetable."[91] Christine ignored Taylor's careful division of labor when she suggested that any woman could be happy keeping house by scientific management, juggling alone all planning, scheduling, and working.

In making scientific management the focus of housekeeping, Christine had departed from Catharine Beecher's injunction that women's primary task was to provide moral authority in the home. She replaced it with the canon of efficiency. Not all middle-class women were willing to make that exchange, however. One home economist protested in 1914 that the home was still an expression of "the law of God," the place where people are nurtured. "I hope," she entreated, "we shall not change for the thing called efficiency the real treasures of our home life."[92] "[A]ssailed of late by experts in domestic science," a reader of the *New York Times* wrote that she did not think she was as ignorant and wasteful as the home efficiency engineers would have her believe. She could "give chapter and verse" on how she operated her home and did not need to be taught scientific management.[93] Nevertheless, the currency of scientific management gave Christine's articles and books great authority. Through her self-taught expertise in efficiency, Christine had launched an important career teaching other women how to make work in the home a fulfilling occupation. Her expert advice, of course, would keep her followers in their homes.

5 · Promoting Industry to Save the Home

We have never thought of the economic waste of the labor of the woman
in the home. . . . It is not possible for mothers to rightly fulfill their work while
they practice at the same time that combined and chaotic group of industries
which goes on inside the sacred circle of the home.
CHARLOTTE PERKINS GILMAN "Women and Vocations," 1915

I believe that the individual home is going to last. . . . That is why I say that
home making as a profession has a bigger future than any other single occupation.
CHRISTINE FREDERICK "Household Economics," 1916

CHRISTINE FREDERICK and Charlotte Perkins Gilman both lectured for a
course titled "Women in Industry: Her Opportunities in Business Today," sponsored by New York's Intercollegiate Bureau of Occupations during the winter
of 1915–16. The School of Commerce at New York University hosted the
seven-month-long course. The school's dean, when introducing Gilman as the
first lecturer, told the attendees that "woman's greatest need is the ability and
the opportunity to earn a living independently of men."[1] Four months later,
Christine tailored her own comments to this audience of profession-seeking
women by listing several paid occupations that training in homemaking might
qualify them to pursue: dietitian, home economics teacher, restaurant manager,
child care provider, or household engineer.[2] But the tenor of Christine's message contrasted sharply with that of Gilman's. Gilman's lecture drew from her
well-developed criticism of the traditional home; Christine's was a defense of
it. Some twenty months earlier she had declared to an audience of home economists, "Our greatest enemy is the woman with the career."[3]

Keeping Housework at Home

THE STRIKING DISPARITY in the views of these two prominent women re-
flects, of course, the divide between dual sphere thinking and the feminist

argument for full gender equity in the public sphere. But it also brings the struggle of those who tried to straddle that divide into sharp relief. An inherent paradox lay in the development of an industrialized consumer culture dependent on large female markets. On the one hand, modernization would make housekeeping easier by the mass production of labor-saving appliances designed for the home, where women would remain to use them. On the other hand, the full industrialization of household tasks might have relieved women of doing them at all. Obviously, industrializing baking, canning, sewing, and laundry would allow homemakers much more free time. Nevertheless, in the spring of 1914, when Christine, as the "high priestess of the gospel of home efficiency," was invited to set up an efficiently arranged kitchen for the Efficiency Exposition and Conference at the Grand Central Palace in New York, she re-created Applecroft with stove, sink, and worktable arranged properly. "It is not so much that she wants to spend less time in dishwashing and more in running for alderman," reported the New York Tribune, "but that she feels it is a moral disgrace to waste her energy."[4]

When the Fredericks moved into the remodeled house at Greenlawn in 1912, Christine had inaugurated the Applecroft Experiment Station, an idea that Edward Bok had proposed to her.[5] There were already two established household experiment stations nearby, and, like Applecroft, they were inspired by the popularity of scientific management.

Charles and Mary Barnard operated a home experiment station just across Long Island Sound in Darien, Connecticut. In 1908, the Barnards had built a country home on the outskirts of Darien, where they hoped to conduct a "simple servantless life" on "the principles of scientific management that rule the business world." They, too, had been impressed by Gilbreth's bricklaying experiment and sought to apply motion-saving techniques to housekeeping. They operated their home without benefit of either gas or electricity, using a coal stove in the basement to heat water, an alcohol-burning range to cook food, and a fireless cooker that could be preheated for slow-cooking meals. The Barnards' experiments and bulletins were designed to help women who were too "isolated to work out their own salvation" from drudgery. Charles Barnard claimed to have received and answered four thousand letters from housewives by 1910.[6]

Another nearby experiment station had been established in 1909 under the auspices of the New Jersey Federation of Women's Clubs. Mary Pattison, the president of the Federation, described the station as "an attempt to standardize the demands at least of the club women of New Jersey for labor-saving devices and pure economical foods." Unlike the Barnards, the New Jersey women sought to achieve efficiency by fully modernizing housekeeping. Their purpose, in fact, was to test new products. They equipped their station with four types of cookstoves, but Pattison declared that "the future belongs to electricity." An electric motor operated a coffee mill, a polisher, a washing machine, and a chopper. Club members were enthusiastically in favor of appliances that saved housewives' labor, and Pattison thought that once women knew about all the new devices on the market, they would "joyfully buy them." She also believed such devices would eventually do away with the need for servants.[7]

Christine acknowledged that there were "many excellent domestic science laboratories" operating when she created her "Applecroft Efficiency Kitchen," as she initially called it.[8] But Applecroft, she believed, was "the first to emphasize methods and the personal attitude of a woman toward her work, rather than mere tools and machinery"; it was a place where she could standardize household tasks by running time and motion studies in an efficiently planned kitchen.[9] Like the New Jersey Federation, she would also test new devices and appliances. At Applecroft, Christine developed a multifaceted business that demonstrated her skills as an entrepreneur.

An early letterhead for "Applecroft Experiment Station" advertised several services: "The Efficiency Kitchen," "Household and Pure Food Information Service," "The Applecroft Press Publishers," and "The New Womanhood Magazine."[10] Describing her operation as a publishing house was an exaggeration.[11] Applecroft publications amounted to little more than a short-lived series of bulletins Christine called the *New Womanhood Magazine*, brochures promoting her own services, and household charts that she sold by mail. Her first bulletin, titled "Dishwashing Number," was a time and motion analysis of hand dishwashing compared to the performances of four models of mechanical dishwashers, all of which she roundly criticized. In another, the "Cleaning Number," she analyzed various methods of cleaning. Christine used these bulletins to advertise her book, *The New Housekeeping,* and a food chart that she had devised. In addition to developing written materials on housekeeping, she also offered her services to individual housewives and, on occasion, helped plan kitchens.[12]

Christine occasionally claimed to promote efficiency because it could free women to work outside the home, but her usual argument was that it made housework itself more satisfying. Most of her work assumed that domestic tasks would remain in the home. Her vacillating advice about laundry over the years revealed a conflict over liberating women further through industrializing housework.

Laundry was one of several household chores that might have moved out of the home and freed housekeepers from arduous work. In 1912, Martha Bruère suggested that laundry was becoming a "public utility" since so many families sent their soiled clothes out to commercial establishments.[13] Christine once prepared a kitchen calendar for a commercial laundry that claimed a woman who sent her clothes out could save seven weeks a year to read, relax, "keep radiantly young," and be a "real partner" to her husband.[14] But the combined forces of technology, business, and consumerism kept laundry a staple of housework, and Christine changed her view.[15] In 1915, she offered her readers detailed advice on how to do the laundry at home. The chapter on laundry in her second book resembles Catharine Beecher's long discussion on the subject. Christine explained nearly a dozen separate washday processes, including boiling, stain removing, starching, and sprinkling. Like Beecher, she discussed the processing of chemicals and the use of garment stretchers, assuring the reader that laundry was easily standardized because it is "one set of tasks which can be planned and followed year after year after the same identical method, once that method is established." But she still assumed in 1919 that men's shirts and collars would be sent out.[16]

In 1922, however, Christine wrote (in a booklet prepared for the Hurley Machine Company) that sending laundry out was far more costly than investing in a washer.[17] But five years later she advised British housewives against purchasing washing machines for "very small families. It is more economical," she said, "to send the work to a laundry."[18] Back home in 1931, she told the National Electric Light Association that American manufacturers were making too many washing machines because women could send their clothes to good community laundries.[19] The inconsistency over the years reflected the requirements of the commercial interests she had come to serve, of course, but it also revealed a conflict between advocating that household work be kept at home and embracing the industrialization that might allow women to participate in the public sphere.

In 1916, Christine turned to a new medium to promote her views on housework and produced a motion picture on housekeeping at Applecroft. Movies were relatively new in 1916. Companies that manufactured projectors for the home advertised film exchanges that operated like lending libraries. They also provided rental machines in outlets such as Wanamaker's department store.[20] Corporations saw films as a way to test markets and used film as a medium of advertising.[21] Christine seized upon this idea and set about making her own commercial film to promote scientific management in the home. Her script told the story of a housewife who had lost her servant and found that she was incapable of keeping house by herself. Her home was delivered from chaos by a visiting housekeeper who showed her not only the "one best way" to do things, but also demonstrated all kinds of labor-saving devices. Christine's intention was to sell her film to home economics educators and women's clubs.[22] She also approached the *Ladies' Home Journal* about the project, but Karl Harriman was not interested in "the story as such" although he suggested that he might use still photographs from the film.[23] If Christine's movie was distributed, there is no evidence that it was a success, but the alacrity with which she attempted to utilize this new technology to promote her own ends illustrated her keen sense of coming trends.

Christine began her career at the time when the new household technology was just emerging, and her housekeeping experiments in efficiency fostered enthusiasm for new labor-saving devices. In her first *Ladies' Home Journal* article, she noted that most household laundry was still done "without a washing-machine and with only a common boiler" and that "thousands of women" could not afford vacuum cleaners and did not have hot water piped into their kitchens.[24] She wanted to show these women that stretching their budgets to include the purchase of new appliances could lighten their work. One of her main functions, she wrote, was to keep a file on every manufacturer of every piece of equipment that she used so that she could serve as a "clearing house between the manufacturer and the homemaker." In this way, she served both consumer and manufacturer: "Manufacturers, too, often care to have a practical test of their devices before they are put on the market; already, several have received helpful criticism of their products."[25] Christine's assessments also appeared in advertising pamphlets.[26]

In the 1912 *Outlook* series on housekeeping, the home economist Martha Bruère reported that families with incomes of three thousand to four thousand dollars a year were buying vacuum cleaners, washing machines, electric irons, gas ranges, fireless cookers, and many other home appliances just then becoming available. The use of these machines was the modern way to administer a home, she wrote. She believed that home appliances would replace the servant and relieve the housewife from concern about the fatigue, hunger, or health of her employees. Bruère rejoiced in the freedom from "moral responsibility" for another human being that this change would bring, a clear expression of the shift from Catharine Beecher's thinking about the home's moral function.[27]

Christine Frederick told the housewife of lesser means who could not afford a full-time servant that she, too, could justify the outlay of money for "every device she can afford." Dishwashers, bread mixers, and electric washing machines would save the family the wages of "'temporary' or day service." Tacitly averring that the housewife's time had no monetary value, Christine told her readers that "there is no question of the economy in replacing the human by the mechanical servant." The investment in equipment would average out to half of the six hundred dollars a year a servant might cost, she wrote.[28] She missed the opportunity to comment upon the fact that the "very bedrock" of family economy was "women's unpaid household labor."[29] And her endorsement of home appliances affirmed her preference for keeping industrialized work at home.

Public enthusiasm for home appliances reflected the convergence of several early-twentieth-century phenomena: advances in technology, increased production, the need for new markets, and the effort to preserve the home as an agent of consumption. Power companies brought gas and electricity into more and more American homes during this period, and as electricity edged gas out of the lighting business, gas companies began promoting the home heating capability of their product. The American Gas Association subsidized work on the improvement of gas stoves, hot water heaters, and hot air furnaces. By 1930, more Americans cooked with gas than with any other fuel. In the meantime, the trade associations formed by electric companies, the National Electric Light Association and the National Electrical Manufacturers Association, had put America on standard alternating current, and by 1910, electricity routinely entered American homes at 120 volts. This advancement enabled manufacturers to produce small electrical household appliances at a profit. When Christine Frederick began to test products for the home, the fuel companies actually gave away appliances such as sewing machines, vacuum cleaners, and refrigerators in order to sell power.[30] Christine played a role in creating the home market for these power sources by using their appliances and writing about their labor-saving qualities.

Like Mary Pattison and the New Jersey club women, Christine recognized the future of electricity. She, too, promoted the small, home electric motor that could operate home appliances; she featured a photograph of a sewing machine operated by a Western Electric Company motor in her 1919 housekeeping manual. But she recommended a gas engine for operating the pump, washing machine, and ironer in her ideal laundry room.[31]

Christine began passing along information about new household products in her earliest magazine articles. In 1913 she recommended several improved kitchen utensils.[32] Some of the equipment at Applecroft, she confessed, was "fairly expensive," but she was trying "to see if the labour saved justif[ied] the expense." One kitchen cabinet she tested, for example, provided a complete pantry and saved the steps that would be necessary if pantry items were kept in a separate room.[33] She collaborated with her efficiency mentor, Harrington Emerson, to conduct time and motion studies of meal preparation using the Nepanee Dutch Kitchenet.[34] Her model kitchen in the New York Efficiency Exposition of 1914 featured equipment such as the Hoosier kitchen cabinet furnished by the department store owner John Wanamaker.[35] By 1919, Christine claimed to be testing "new tools" at Applecroft every month.[36] Throughout her second housekeeping manual she mentioned specific brand names: Kitchencraft kitchen cabinets, Simplex ironers, and Walker Electric dishwashers, for example. She featured at least one product—a Sentinel automatic fireless gas range—for which she wrote a promotional pamphlet.[37] And she often casually mentioned specific cleaning products by their brand names: Ivory soap, Bon Ami, Brillo pads, and Parson's ammonia.[38]

The commercial nature of her work notwithstanding, Christine's early advocacy of modern equipment probably reflected a sincere effort to make housework less arduous. In the first years of her career, she did not see herself as primarily a spokesperson for manufacturers, but rather as "competent counsel" to housewives. In her second book, for example, she included a thorough discussion of modern fuels, revealing both the benefits and the drawbacks of each. Although she included photographs of specific cookstoves—Westinghouse, Hughes, and Perfection were three—she did not promote any of them in the text. Many of the household devices that Christine recommended to her readers really did save labor. Hot water heaters eliminated the heavy and un-comfortable work of heating large boiling pots full of water on the cookstove, washing machines lessened the time spent laundering each week, and vacuum cleaners made carpet cleaning easier. Her manuals provided important infor-mation about these products. Her discussion of washing machines, for example, included an informed description of how the various types worked and the pro-cesses by which they cleaned.[39]

In these early years, Christine also dispensed sound buying advice. Believing that women should understand the mechanical principles upon which their equipment operated, she counseled housewives to learn everything they could about an appliance before purchasing it. A particular purée strainer, for ex-ample, was impractical because it took too long to clean its many parts, she wrote. In 1919, she was advising against purchasing anything the family did not really need.[40]

Most of the labor-saving devices Christine tested at Applecroft were new on the market, and she was introducing them to the American housewife. In 1916, for example, she wrote an informative article about the new electric toaster, percolator, and chafing dish. These appliances modernized simple kitchen tasks by reducing the number of steps required to perform them.[41] Some of the items tested did not last to become standard equipment in the modern kitchen—the electric kitchen table with a warming compartment is an example—and some, like the early mechanical dishwashers, were far from perfected.[42] A commen-tator who wrote about Christine's work years later reported that many of the products she tested were redesigned according to her specifications.[43] By 1938, Christine claimed to "have tested some 10,000 devices, appliances, and food products."[44]

Christine was ahead of her time in soliciting products for testing. American manufacturers were only beginning to realize the importance that testing, in-struction, and endorsements would have in marketing their new products. Eventually, most developed in-house laboratories where they tested their new appliances and devices before putting them on the market. This practice opened up a whole new field for women who were trained as home economists, and Christine's offer to provide testing services to manufacturers by contract was on its cutting edge. The New York Edison Company had established a Home Economics Department as early as 1915, but Sears, Roebuck did not in-stall a testing laboratory in its textile division until 1919. After 1920, testing by the industries became more scientific. The Household Refrigeration Bureau of the National Association of Ice Industries, for example, hired the chemist and bacteriologist Mary Engle Pennington as its head in 1923. During the 1920s, utilities companies such as General Electric and Westinghouse began hiring home economists to advise them on appliance design. In 1936, Elizabeth Weirick, head of Sears's textile testing lab, drafted a company policy that required Sears to seek accurate, scientific, and unbiased information about its products, a move that would require the services of personnel formally trained in chemistry and physics.[45] This professionalization of product testing eventually closed the field to women who were not academically trained, but Christine tested products and enjoyed a brisk business writing advertising pamphlets through the 1920s.

Taking Up Advertising

FROM THE BEGINNING, Christine had been interested in J. George's work in advertising. In 1910, at his request, she had written a series of articles for *Printers' Ink* on the prevalence of trademarked goods in New York department stores. Apparently she had not yet been fully committed to the pursuit of a public career, for she wrote these first articles under her great aunt's name, Isobel Brands.[46] J. George believed that there was no "fundamental difference" between the writer and the advertiser. Both wished to sell something to the public.[47]

Booklets offering information about manufactured products were widespread by 1905; many were offered by mail through magazines. This tactic also provided a crude sort of market research: companies counted pamphlets sold and set production schedules accordingly.[48] In 1914, when Christine and Emerson were photographed with the Nepanee Dutch Cabinet, she wrote a pamphlet promoting a competitor, the Hoosier cabinet, which she had demonstrated in her model kitchen at the Efficiency Conference in the Grand Central Palace that spring.[49] The next year, she produced a booklet that described the advantages of owning a fireless cooker manufactured by Sentinel. During the following three decades, she would write the copy for pamphlets promoting a wide variety of manufactured and processed goods: washing machines, chocolate, frankfurters, and enamel ware. She wrote promotional copy for the Florida Citrus Exchange, the International Nickel Company, and the League of

Advertising Women. Some of these booklets were published by magazines and covered an entire genre of goods.[50]

Those who promoted careers for women outside the home were just then recognizing advertising as a potential field for women. In 1911, the Women's Educational and Industrial Union of Boston offered a booklet titled "Advertising As a Vocation for Women" that suggested department store or advertising agency work.[51] A woman advertiser told the attendees at the Women in Industry course for which Christine and Charlotte Perkins Gilman lectured that advertising was a natural choice for women since "ninety-five per cent of the purchasing power of the world is in women."[52] A vocational conference held at Vassar College in 1917 offered two lectures on salesmanship titled "Opportunities for the College Graduate in Department Store Education" and "The College Woman and the Magazine Game."[53] Two years later, the University of Pittsburgh included a presentation on advertising in its vocational conference for women.[54] During World War I, women got jobs in the advertising field partly because there was a shortage of men. And war's end saw a host of new products designed to enhance women's sex appeal enter the market. Many thought that women copywriters were better able to promote these products.[55] By 1919, J. Walter Thompson assigned "all material of interest to women" to female copywriters and everything else to men. "The J. Walter Thompson Co. has a very large per cent of women in responsible positions," wrote an interviewer for the Intercollegiate Bureau of Occupations. She added, however, that Thompson was "quite the exception among other companies doing the same kind of work."[56] Although women were breaking into the field of advertising during Christine's early career, their numbers were still few and there was an immutable division of labor according to gender. Women were not allowed to attend the meetings of the Advertising Men's League of New York, and the discrimination led Christine to become involved in the organization of a professional association for women advertisers.

Women still encountered discrimination in most fields that had heretofore been dominated by men. One of the most widely used mechanisms of exclusion was to establish employment standards through professional associations from which women were barred. As a result, women formed a number of their own professional organizations between 1910 and 1930.[57] By 1919, ten states had organizations for women in advertising.[58] Christine played a role in establishing the group in New York City.

Early in 1912, Marie Bronson, the advertising manager of Macy's department store, asked J. George Frederick if she could attend a meeting of the Advertising Men's League. "No," he told her, "but why don't you advertising women of New York have your own club?" Bronson refused to initiate such a move, but J. George enlisted Christine's help in organizing a meeting for that purpose. The Fredericks invited all the advertising women they knew to a dinner at Reisenweber's restaurant on Eighth Avenue on 11 March, and more than forty women attended. The group christened itself the League of Advertising Women, and J. George, serving as chairperson, appointed an organizing committee headed by Claudia Q. Murphy. The inclusion of one of J. George's employees caused a ripple of dissension that suggested class consciousness among the professional women. "When Anna Rosenblatt came on the scene as Mr. Frederick's secretary," a club historian wrote later, "and when she became a member of the club, Miss Pomeroy resigned as stenographers were not allowed." J. George later recalled that Rosenblatt, who was "with the Business Bourse," was one of the organizers of the league.[59]

Christine, who was not working in the advertising industry either, never became a dues-paying member of the league she helped to establish. She would later explain, "I was not much of a joiner—just a crusader."[60] But she attended meetings frequently, spoke to the group on occasion, and was made an honorary member. In the 1930s, she was the group's honorary vice president, and the league named a scholarship for her in 1952. When it celebrated its golden anniversary ten years later, she was honored as its cofounder.[61] At her death, she left the league a bequest of five hundred dollars.[62]

Christine spoke before other advertising groups, too. In 1914, she was the principal speaker at the annual women's dinner and fashion exhibit sponsored by the Advertising Men's League (the same group that barred women from its regular meetings). Her topic was "advertising from the consumer's viewpoint."[63] Nine months later, she participated in a Pure Food Show put on by the Lancaster, Pennsylvania, Advertisers' Club, joining other prominent speakers who discussed the Pure Food and Drug Act from the advertisers' perspective.[64] In 1916, she enjoyed the company of a large group of Connecticut advertisers at the Charter Oak Advertising Club's formal "Ladies' Night" banquet in Hartford.[65]

Christine agreed with her husband that advertising provided an invaluable service to the consumer. It cost no more than old-fashioned traveling salesmen, and it generated far more sales. To criticisms that advertising exploited a gullible public, J. George responded in 1925 that the public's willingness to buy manufactured goods had made the U.S. economy boom.[66] Christine echoed these sentiments:

> Modern advertising in periodicals, on billboards, cards, etc., is another means of bringing goods of all kinds to the consumer's attention. The costs of advertising must be included in the general cost of distribution of an article, and do not add any more to the price of an article than any other means of display, such as store window exhibits, circular letters, and the older forms of traveling salesmen which were practiced in the days before periodical publication made modern advertising methods possible.[67]

She argued that advertising was in the consumer's interest because "our daily papers and periodicals would be impossible if it were not that the advertising they carry pays largely for their printing."[68]

But even as the Fredericks hailed the maturing of modern advertising as boon to producer and consumer alike, it was raising doubts in certain quarters. At the same time that Christine's fourth efficiency article was being published in the *Ladies' Home Journal*, Charlotte Perkins Gilman wrote in her own magazine, the *Forerunner*, that advertising was the "ceaseless, desperate effort to compel patronage." She blamed it for making "our cities hideous with signs and posters" and for defiling "the face of Nature with huge, begging, boards." If industries were socialized, she wrote, advertising would be unnecessary.[69]

Advertisers themselves were ambivalent about the ethics of promoting consumption. Some were concerned about the moral implications of manipulating the public. Walter F. Albert, a window dresser at Macy's from 1907 until 1916, sometimes worried about tempting people to want what they could not afford.[70] In a series of articles on advertising in the *Atlantic Monthly*, Charles Mulford Robinson, like Gilman, objected to billboards that infringed upon the "public's aesthetic rights." Tacks used to affix bills killed trees, advertisements posted on church walls showed disrespect for religion, and advertising in general blighted scenery, he wrote. Robinson's solution, however, was not to eliminate advertising, which he thought useful, but to regulate it.[71] J. George Frederick was a leading participant in organizations established to monitor the industry from within, an effort that the historian T. J. Jackson Lears sees as evidence of "unease in a consumer culture where all values—including truth itself—seemed in constant flux."[72]

Christine Frederick seemed to share none of these doubts. She believed that advertising helped make life better. In 1919, she wrote, "Because [advertising] has brought so many thousand articles of furnishing, comfort, and luxury before the consumer, it has, naturally, tended to raise the standard of living."[73] Lears argues that early-twentieth-century advertisers were among those who believed that partaking in abundance was therapeutic. Their "reason why" copy was actually calculated to show consumers how a new product "would transform" their lives. The copy did not really inform about the product itself, but presented its therapeutic value instead.[74]

Christine Frederick had told the "Women in Industry" students that homemaking was "the one occupation . . . which offers more opportunities to women than any other," because the new labor-saving devices would "make possible in the home conditions of work similar to those in business."[75] Charlotte Perkins Gilman thought that women should be allowed to use their talents in the *real* world of business. "[F]or all kinds of women to practice the same trade at home," she suggested to the students, was "amateurish," inefficient, and "primitive."[76] Christine argued that when industry came into the home, the home became an efficient, fulfilling workplace. Gilman, on the other hand, argued that most industry should leave the home and that most women should go with it, specializing, as men did, in their individual aptitudes. Both women were responding to the circumstances that challenged traditional thinking about sex roles. As the scholar Richard Ohmann has written, modern women at the turn of the twentieth century were "knowledgeable about the public sphere, . . . not . . . homebound angels softly guarding a haven from the heartless marketplace."[77] Christine wanted women to invite the marketplace into the home and trade guardianship for efficiency. Gilman wanted women to be free to leave the haven to the care of others and go forth into the marketplace as equal participants.

6 · Expounding the Business Ethic

[L]ooking over my world as I first did in about 1906, I thought . . .
the distribution of merchandise inadequate and based on a false premise. . . .
So I started to write . . . to the public.
CHRISTINE FREDERICK, Laguna Library Book Day Speech, 1966

BY 1917, Christine Frederick had developed a rather distinguished career as household efficiency expert and, by extension, adviser to advertisers and consumers alike. She achieved recognition in the beginning largely through the written word.

The Housekeeping Manuals

CHRISTINE FREDERICK'S FIRST BOOK, *The New Housekeeping*, was reviewed widely, went through several printings, and was translated into several foreign languages.[1] The *Journal of Home Economics* praised Christine for making "a strong stand for educating the housewife to demand good quality" and suggested that *The New Housekeeping* was a good supplement to books written by professional home economists.[2] The *Bookman* ran a portrait of Christine and reported her claim that household efficiency could save the nation one million dollars a day.[3] Several newspapers ran columns praising the book. One claimed, "Any person who can lessen the drudgery of housekeeping, thereby saving time for intellectual gratification should be considered a benefactor of the most useful character."[4] Another found the book "packed as full of commonsense as a nut is of meat."[5] But the most noteworthy of these early reviews was the full-page article with photographs that appeared in the Sunday *New York Times*, 6 July 1913.

Shown in her kitchen at Applecroft, Christine was touted as the woman who had most completely imitated the male model of "systemized 'business efficiency.'" The *Times* reviewed her basic scientific management premises and claimed that the book could serve as a substitute for an efficiency engineer for the housewife. Praise for Christine was effusive: "[T]o this young woman belongs the distinction of finding perhaps the most practical and at the same time the most scientific solution of the household problem." Although the piece repeated Christine's contention that she had once done her own work in a flat, the reporter noted that she had since transferred her system to a country home where "she must necessarily have the assistance of servants."[6]

Christine took pride in this first book's success for the rest of her life. In 1929, she claimed that *The New Housekeeping* "was largely instrumental in interesting women in this new and more scientific attitude toward their households," and eight years before her death, she reminded the Advertising Women's League historian that her first book had "initiated widespread changes in the home and its equipment."[7]

In *The New Housekeeping,* Christine had praised the land grant colleges for giving "the greatest possible stimulus to the teaching of home economics." They were teaching women applied science, not to run tractors but to operate the kitchen stove, she wrote.[8] She had read the current literature, citing facts about the movement available in works by home economics leaders such as Ellen Swallow Richards, Isabel Bevier, and Susannah Usher.[9] The growing interest in home economics education created a brisk market for textbooks on the subject. In 1903, the Department of Agriculture reported, "Satisfactory textbooks on food and nutrition (important branches of home economics) are not available, and at present a large proportion of the teachers depend on Department publications to supply their place."[10] By 1912, when *The New Housekeeping* was published, several home economics textbooks were available, but the demand was growing.[11] The American School, a Chicago correspondence school that had been established in 1897, organized a separate department, the American School of Home Economics. Its textbooks were widely used in university home economics programs and were well publicized.[12]

Christine was surely aware of this growing market when she contacted the American School of Home Economics about publishing a second book. In 1919, the school issued a greatly expanded version of an earlier 109-page bulletin titled *Household Engineering: Scientific Management in the Home.* This second housekeeping manual was a home-study program divided into twelve parts, each of which included a list of study questions.[13] Widely read, it eventually appeared in seven editions, the last titled *Efficient Housekeeping: Or, Household Engineering, Scientific Management in the Home* in 1925.[14]

Three male mentors figured prominently in the production of *Household*

Engineering. Christine dedicated the 1919 edition to Edward Bok, "to whose encouragement and progressive leadership in reaching the mass of American homemakers with the gospel of home efficiency," she wrote, "I owe much inspiration."[15] Frank Gilbreth wrote a brief preface praising Christine for eliminating "from housework that monotony that comes from doing uninteresting and repetitive work without an incentive."[16] And Harrington Emerson contributed a foreword that commended Christine for "specializing and standardizing the tools and methods for the many ever changing occupations of the home."[17]

These male advisers suggest a key to understanding Christine's concept of women's work. "[M]en and women have parted company industrially," Emerson wrote in his foreword. "Man may be at fault because he rushed impetuously ahead, woman may be at fault because she has held too long to the old."[18] Though her mission was to change women's work, Christine rarely sought advice from other women, and she rejected the ideas of feminists such as Charlotte Perkins Gilman. Her models were men, and the workplace she sought to emulate was the predominately male factory.

Household Engineering, Christine told her readers, included "in greater detail everything given in my book 'The New Housekeeping,' and all the help and suggestions gathered from constant study during the five years which have elapsed since its publication."[19] The laundry chapter was a new, modernized guide to the use of labor-saving equipment. She added a chapter on "The Servantless Household" and expanded her theories on employing servants in "Management of Houseworkers." The chapter "Health and Personal Efficiency" included new information about personal hygiene, and she wrote entirely new chapters on planning food for the family and on home design. Like the home economics educators, Christine relied heavily on U.S. Department of Agriculture bulletins for her research.[20] Her lack of formal home economics training did not deter her from offering herself as "competent counsel." She told her readers that her expertise derived from "studying, visiting plants and factories, and getting in touch more widely with the movement." She also gleaned information, she said, from the experiences of friends.[21]

The book offered much useful information that most housewives needed to know if they were to operate modern homes with the new powered appliances. One reviewer described the book as "a complete manual on the economics of up-do-date housekeeping and home-making."[22] Christine wrote authoritatively about electricity, for example, explaining watts, volts, amperes, and the importance of understanding the difference between alternating and direct current. She also gave examples of figuring the cost of electricity per kilowatt hour. Like Catharine Beecher, she provided instruction on cleaning the different surfaces one might find in the modern home: varnished wood, enameled woodwork, linoleum, and cork. In her updated laundry chapter, she discussed the effects of temperature, water chemistry, and types of soap on different fibers.[23] And like Beecher, who had written an extensive chapter on health in her 1841 *Treatise*, Christine took on the role of health reformer. *Household Engineering* discussed the importance of fresh air, sleeping conditions, nutrition, posture, clothing, exercise, and mental health. But Christine believed that health was the "basis for personal efficiency," while Beecher held that good health was necessary because women were in charge of their family's health and morality.[24]

In *Household Engineering*, Christine also ventured more deeply into interior decoration than she had before. Embracing modernity, she advised against buying suites of period furniture and counseled women to eliminate Victoriana from their homes to create modern, efficient households. Kitchens should be light, she warned. "Ugly green" and "hideous blue" were to be banished. If possible, a housewife should match her cookware and utensils to the overall decorating scheme. Even the laundry room could be attractive, she wrote, and she promoted the use of Monel metal, a highly polished, rustproof sheet metal used for work surfaces.[25]

Household Engineering was an even greater success than *The New Housekeeping*. Reviewers praised Christine for lightening "the burden of [housewives'] labours" and for giving them "release from the tyranny of the household 'general.'" The book would, one reviewer claimed, "enable any woman, unless her household is especially large, to cope singly, or at most, with one non-resident servant, with every house duty . . . and yet to have time for self-development, for practical sympathy in her husband's interests, and for 'outside' interests of her own."[26] The book served not only as a correspondence course in housekeeping, but was also adopted by home economics educators. "[W]hen I was young in the vineyard," one Cornell research associate wrote to Christine in 1947, "you were a most inspiring leader and I learned at your feet (or from your printed pages). For many years at the University of Chicago your advanced ideas were spoon fed to my charges."[27] The ideas in *Household Engineering* were disseminated even more widely than this letter suggested. Thirty-two years after the book's publication, an admirer wrote to Christine, "In the 1920s your book: 'Work in Household Efficiency' [*sic*] was standard equipment for every progressive architect in Europe."[28]

Finally, *Household Engineering* foreshadowed Christine's later role as an outspoken commentator on the subject of consumerism. In this book, she thoroughly expounded a position favoring trademarked merchandise and what contemporary business leaders called "price maintenance" on manufactured goods. A reviewer sensed the importance of the business aspect of Christine's work:

> Mrs. Frederick is as much a business woman as a "household engineer"; has enjoyed a rich and varied experience in many fields, notably advertising and publicity. . . . I am of opinion that husbands as well as wives, business men as well as business women, will dip repeatedly, and with equal profit and pleasure, into the pages of a book that is the triumphant efficiency-record of an uncommonly accomplished woman.[29]

In the Press

CHRISTINE WROTE ARTICLES for the *Ladies' Home Journal*'s competitors from the beginning, occasionally under the pen name Isobel Brands.[30] *The New Country Life*, for example, ran an article she wrote about J. George's concrete picnic table in the apple orchard.[31] And in 1915, she reached a European audience for the first time when the French journal *Revue de Metallurgie* published a translation of extracts from *The New Housekeeping*.[32]

Early in her career Christine discovered that newspaper syndication could provide a larger readership than magazines could. In 1913, not only did she write for the *Philadelphia Public Ledger*, but she also contributed a column to the short-lived Wheeler Syndicate in New York.[33] Her most important newspaper assignment began when she landed the job of contributing household editor for William Randolph Hearst's giant newspaper chain. From 1917 until 1944, she wrote a column for Hearst's Sunday supplement, *American Weekly*.[34] When Christine first began writing for Hearst, he had papers in San Francisco, Los Angeles, New York, Boston, Atlanta, and Washington, D.C. By the early 1920s, he had added Milwaukee, Seattle, and Detroit to his empire.[35] Thus, within a decade after she first began writing about household efficiency, Christine's columns were reaching people across the country.

Christine continued to write and answer housekeeping letters for the *Ladies' Home Journal* until the 1920s. The volume of mail received by all departments of the *Journal* was impressive; one account reports that when Christine's first articles ran, the magazine was receiving over 28,000 letters a month.[36] Christine's portion was modest by comparison; she billed the *Journal* for 478 letters during the month of November 1914.[37] Still, letters from people all over the country came in to thank her for introducing them to the "new housekeeping."[38]

Occasionally the *Journal's* staff had to mediate misunderstandings that arose between Christine and her readers: it was suggested that she might have "exploited" another's work on one occasion.[39] And advertisers sometimes took issue with her advice if it ignored their products. The manufacturers of Valspar varnish complained that her advice regarding oils and finishes was inaccurate, for example, and the California Packing Corporation objected when an article on fruit consumption did not promote canned goods. As Christine noted in her response to the packers, it was impossible "for every article to cover all interests."[40]

This dilemma was compounded by the fact that the *Journal* sometimes blatantly used Christine's work to court advertisers. In 1915, Harriman asked her to recommend the Whirlpool dishwasher in her responses to letters. The household editor who corresponded with Christine in 1918 asked her to suggest new labor-saving equipment, noting, "I know you are in close touch with the manufacturers."[41] Christine, too, used the relationship to sell. In the early years, the following preface preceded Christine's *Journal* articles: "Mrs. Frederick is an expert in helping women solve the problems of housekeeping. Her 'Applecroft Experiment Station' is a real home, where she tests appliances and new materials."[42] This notice surely boosted her product-testing business. After Harriman asked her to include her *New Womanhood* bulletins in her responses to mail, she sent him her revolving food chart for inclusion in the magazine. The four hundred dollars she asked for the chart was too steep for the *Journal*, and after Bok had seen it, Christine was offered three hundred dollars. Two years after that exchange, another editor suggested that she keep the charts at home. Inquiries would be forwarded to her so that she could "send them out directly."[43] Christine's work for the *Journal* was beginning to reveal the difficulties inherent in fusing advertising with journalism.

Until 1916, Christine's name had appeared as editor of the regular column "The New Housekeeping," the title of which had been inspired by her first articles.[44] But that year another editor took the column, and the magazine printed only two of Christine's articles. In March, her name ceased to appear as the correspondent for "How Can I Run My Home More Easily?"[45] Anna East, a home economist who had worked for the New York Edison Company, took over as household editor in January. Perhaps feeling insecure about her position with the magazine, Christine had invited East to visit Applecroft in the fall. A month after East assumed her post, she responded to a "moving" letter from Christine, assuring her that she was "indellibly [sic] connected with The Journal."[46] East stayed only a year, and her replacement only six months. In 1918, Theresa Wolcott, who had handled Christine's articles prior to East's arrival, resumed as head of the household department.[47] Though Christine visited the *Journal*'s offices in June 1917 and the magazine published four of her articles that year, Wolcott rejected as many.[48] When Christine proposed an article on the family, Harriman quashed the idea, writing her that "it would hardly be typical."[49] Two years later, Wolcott sent Christine four pages of suggested changes when she submitted an article on the eight-hour day for house workers and suggested that another article could be reduced to a chart.[50] Christine's relationship with the *Journal* was clearly strained.

In 1919, the *Journal* confronted the conflict of interests that resulted when editorial columns mentioned advertisers' products. Christine wrote to tell Theresa Wolcott that she had been asked to promote a product in an article. Wolcott replied that she and the managing editor believed that complying with the request would damage Christine's reputation and that if she proceeded with the idea, the *Journal* would not want to use her work again. "I think the time is coming," Wolcott wrote, "when there will have to be a destinction [sic] between the editorial and advertising domestic science and household writers." Christine had apparently accompanied her suggestion with the names of two other household writers who had advertised products. "I think the two women, whom you mention in your letter," Wolcott responded, "have already greatly injured themselves by doing this very thing that is asked of you."[51]

Wolcott also took Christine to task for claiming to be the magazine's "household editor." After receiving letters for Christine that were obviously generated by articles in other publications, Wolcott cautioned her to use an accurate title when referring to her connection with the *Ladies' Home Journal*. Wolcott suggested "'contributor to the Ladies' Home Journal' . . . eliminating the idea of permanent association."[52] Nevertheless, Christine and Theresa Wolcott remained friends; Wolcott visited Applecroft, and they exchanged gifts and cards throughout 1919 and 1920. When the managing editor and eight of his staff quit the *Journal*, Wolcott stayed on for a time and attempted to serve Christine's interests. But after a trying two years, she, too, finally left the *Journal* "because of changed conditions" in October 1920.[53] The turmoil at the *Journal* resulted in Christine's removal as the household correspondent and in the rejection of many of her proposed articles. Nonetheless, the magazine published several of her pieces through 1920.[54] By this time, her work was appearing in many other publications as well.

Brand Names, Price Maintenance, and the Consumer

CONVINCED that the home had been transformed from a place of production to an agent of consumption, Christine assumed the role of consumer advocate for the American housewife. Many others were advising women on buying, too, for it was clear that women were becoming important consumers. "As newspapers and magazines are both particularly eager to please women, who are the principal purchasers and therefore the most important readers of advertisements," wrote a journalist in 1915, "the woman's point of view ought to be expressed as adequately as possible in almost all publications."[55] Purchasing, wrote John Guernsey in his 1912 piece on scientific management in the home, was so important in industry that it warranted a separate department. The housewife should consider it important, too, for it was an area in which she could economize.[56]

Most authorities agreed. The home economist Ellen Swallow Richards told women that they should learn "the new science, the economics of consumption." In fact, since consumption included "the ethics of spending," Richards thought it should "have a place in our higher education."[57] Talbot and Breckinridge recommended that housekeepers be "trained in the technique of spending," and suggested books and articles that would assist woman in her new role as consumer.[58] Christine recognized very early that women consumers would be the target of manufacturers, advertisers, and retailers, and she understood that this gave women power: "The hand that rocks the cradle also rocks most of the world's industries, and that life in the cradle will be as deeply affected by the manner in which we, as women, rock the world's industries, through the influence we wield as purchasers, as the manner in which we rock the cradle."[59]

Recent inquiries into the nature of the emerging consumer culture that Christine Frederick helped to shape have suggested that perhaps women were *not* empowered by their new role. The historian Susan Porter Benson points out that although women made household purchases, they "had little authority over the economic context that shaped their families." Poor women were excluded from the culture of consumption altogether both because they could not indulge in the strict division of labor by gender modeled by the middle class and because they had little discretionary income. T. J. Jackson Lears has argued that the rise of the consumer culture provided much-needed therapy or "self-realization" against the loss of selfhood as the interdependent society of industrialization expanded.[60] Indeed, Christine Frederick's advice suggested that modernized homemaking with the use of labor-saving purchases could provide therapy for the housewife overcome by "drudgery," but she would never have admitted that "Mrs. Consumer" lacked power. She told women that they could exercise a great deal of it in the struggle between manufacturers and retailers over the issue then known as "price maintenance."

In *The New Housekeeping,* Christine had supported the use of brand names and what she originally called "single pricing," that is, maintaining manufacturers' suggested prices in retail stores. Manufacturers' right to set prices was a volatile issue at the time, and by speaking out on the matter, Christine jumped into the middle of a long-standing battle between manufacturers and retailers. She argued that most manufacturers were hardworking and motivated by the desire to produce quality products. They could not maintain quality, she insisted, if retailers cut their suggested prices. Christine believed that retailers and jobbers, not manufacturers, caused prices to be too high in the first place. She counseled buyers to insist on brand-name products and to refuse to buy the imitations that dealers might try to sell instead. She suggested that retailers would not want to mark items up so high if they knew these items would move; and she believed that prices would come down if consumers consistently asked for quality products. The "one-price idea," wrote Christine, would enable the customer to depend on "standardized branded articles." She argued that consumers should not succumb to the reduced price of a named brand—what modern retailers might call a "loss leader"—because the retailer only wanted to get the consumer into the store to sell other items. This technique injured the manufacturer of the superior product whose price had been cut, she maintained, because his good name had been "stolen."[61]

Christine believed that when dealers engaged in price wars, selling brand-name articles below cost, they would eventually quit carrying those items because they could not make a profit on them. And so she urged consumers not to buy at discounted prices. Christine wanted an orderly market in which everyone—manufacturer, retailer, and consumer—received fair value. If everyone supported fair prices, she believed, the manufacturer could keep costs down and make a fair profit, the retailer would realize reasonable returns, and the consumer would enjoy quality merchandise. She assumed that such a market would result if all parties acted out of concern for the whole. Retailers should sell the items for a fair price, and the consumer should pay what an item was worth. Christine also wrote that the small dealer should not have to pay more for wholesale goods than did large stores that bought in quantity, and she told housewives to patronize the small retailers in their neighborhoods. "It is not fair to buy locally sugar and other articles on which there is little or no profit and then go downtown for other articles," she admonished.[62] Christine's position suggested an unrealistic view of consumer behavior in a free market.

In spite of her claim to be the housewife's representative, Christine took a stance on price maintenance that put her squarely in the manufacturers' camp, as did her argument against buying products that were cheaper imitations of the brand-name commodities. When a consumer bought such an imitation, Christine wrote, she was "harming the distribution of the good article, and lessening its sales, thereby decreasing the possibility of the continuance of the good article in the market." She added that buying substitutes "destroys the judgment of the purchaser." She seemed to blame women for business practices that injured the consumer. Apparently, when housewives patronized price-cutting dealers, they became responsible for the questionable behavior of those dealers.[63]

Christine repeated this argument often. It was the focus of the article she gleaned from her first book for the *Ladies' Home Journal* in the fall of 1913,[64] and she polished and expanded it for *Household Engineering* six years later. In the chapter titled "Efficient Household Purchasing," Christine told the housewife that as the "purchasing agent" of the family, she should understand the distribution system and how it works. Christine traced the product from manufacturer to jobber to retailer to consumer, explaining that the consumer needed the retailer "*to give us service in providing necessities and perishables*" (Frederick's italics). She argued that the consumer had a duty to keep the retailer in business by buying more costly items from him (rather than using parcel post or buying cooperatively) because the cost of distribution "*includes the risk* taken by each one of the distributors *that the consumer will actually buy this product*" (Frederick's italics).[65]

While it was quite proper for the consumer to pay for delivery, service, and convenience, these costs should not be excessive. For that reason, Christine departed from her usual support of a free market to advocate regulatory legislation, though she did not suggest specific measures. In *Household Engineering*, she again argued for buying brand-name or "trademarked" brands exclusively: "The one means of protection the consumer can rely on is the 'trademark' on the package or product she buys."[66] If the consumer purchased products packaged for a handler, Christine explained, she could not track down the packer should there be a complaint. "In every case, the trademarked brand carries more integrity or guarantee," she wrote.[67]

Christine called price cutting "bait" and told the reader that this kind of buying was "demoralizing" because it "trap[ped] women into buying" things they did not need, and it gave "them a false idea of the price which they should pay for the article." The cut price, Christine believed, lulled the customer into assigning false values to goods and prompted her to "demand 'bargains.'"[68] This argument, of course, ignored the fact that most consumers preferred bargains to helping maintain Christine's notion of a fair market system. It ignored evidence that the free market would respond to supply and demand.

Christine was helping to further the process that transferred consumers' loyalty and trust from local merchants to national manufacturers. She was undoubtedly influenced by discussions with J. George, who had written an article defending price maintenance for patented goods while she was putting the finishing touches on her articles for the *Ladies' Home Journal* in the summer of 1912. Inspired by legislation before the U.S. House of Representatives that sought to repeal a law that allowed producers of patented goods to set prices, J. George wrote that fixing retail prices had been universally supported by manufacturers and that most dealers favored it, too. Sellers of patented goods had to develop a market at great expense, he wrote, and to pay for this, they needed fair prices for the goods. J. George argued that a maintained price was not necessarily a high price, but a stable price. As Christine would subsequently do, he argued that price maintenance (that is, price fixing by manufacturers) meant quality products: "If the public desires to get a good article of uniform quality and responsible guarantee, which will stay in the market, it is necessary that the public should agree to the doctrine of a standard price." Price cutting, he wrote, had caused many well-intentioned manufacturers to either lower the quality of their goods or lower the weight or volume of units to meet the cut prices offered by retailers.[69]

In fact, manufacturers did sometimes withhold their products from stores that cut the suggested prices. On their side, wholesalers might refuse to carry brand names if they did not like the manufacturer's terms. After 1913, when A & P started a chain of economy stores, cash and carry operators discovered that they could profitably cut prices, even on brand-name, trademarked goods, by eliminating services such as delivery, phone orders, and credit. Manufacturers of brand-name goods thereupon began the campaign in which Christine enlisted: they demanded the legal right to set retail prices. Between 1909 and 1914, there were several bills before Congress on the subject of price maintenance. In 1912, the Supreme Court upheld price fixing by the makers of patented products, but it reversed itself two years later. In one of the first lawsuits on this issue in 1915, Cream of Wheat charged A & P with selling its cereal three cents under the regular price and refused to fill A & P's orders. A & P sued Cream of Wheat. Both the federal district court and the circuit court of appeals held that Cream of Wheat had the right to refuse sales to A & P because it could not enforce its fixed prices, and refusing to sell was its only legal recourse.[70]

In 1914, Christine testified in favor of price maintenance before the House Judiciary Committee.[71] A test of the Kellogg Toasted Corn Flake Company's right to set the wholesale and retail prices of its product was before the committee.[72] Christine testified on behalf of the Housewives' League, a group founded in 1911 for the purpose of protecting the housewives' interest on consumer issues.[73] She told the committee that one consistent price for a particular item saved the housewife time, for she would not have to test a new product each time she went shopping if she could rely on one she knew. She did not adequately explain why the same price was required, but she argued that it would maintain a "standard." As a consumer, she said, she was in favor of uniformly maintained prices, for they guaranteed quality. A consistent price, regardless of where a product was purchased, protected the consumer, she argued, and it assisted the housewife in preparing her budget and staying within it. Furthermore, discounted prices were nothing more than bait used to attract customers to items that were not trademarked. "I wish I could compel every manufacturer to mark every package at its price," Christine told the committee, "and let me take it or leave it at that price, and not have it offered to me at all kinds of prices!"[74]

Christine admitted that she was defending not only the housewife's interests; cutting prices was also hard on small businesses. They could not compete with the lower prices offered by the "downtown" stores. Nor did she hesitate to align herself with the manufacturers. The manufacturer, she argued, not retailers, bore the costs of all the advertising; retailers who cut prices "tr[ied] to rob him." Christine concluded by asking that Congress pass legislation assuring price maintenance, for by doing so, she said, it would be giving "permission to manufacturers to protect their prices for my benefit."[75] Both the *Baltimore Star* and the *New York Times* covered Christine's testimony. The *Times* reported that it "aroused intense interest," primarily because she criticized housewives who chased down bargains.[76]

Christine traveled to the nation's capital to testify in favor of price maintenance on two more occasions in 1917. When Congressman Dan Voorhees Stephens of Nebraska introduced a new price maintenance bill in April of that year, Christine reiterated her position before the Interstate and Foreign Commerce Committee of the U.S. House of Representatives. She claimed to be speaking "purely in the interest of the consumer" and said this time that she did not care about "the rights or wrongs of retailer or manufacturer except as they affect the consumer." Before the Federal Trade Commission in October, she recited the statistics that demonstrated women's purchasing power. In both hearings, she argued again that the trademark on goods allowed the purchaser to identify value and to save time and money.[77]

Christine's testimony was well received. A newspaper reporter who witnessed the FTC hearing wrote, "Perhaps the advocate who above all others received the large measure of friendly interest from the commissioners and others at the hearing on price maintenance before the Federal Trade Commission, last week, was Mrs. Christine Frederick."[78] A year after Christine appeared, the FTC recommended to Congress that producers "be protected in their . . . good will" but be denied "unlimited power" in fixing and maintaining prices.[79]

Almost from the beginning, then, Christine portrayed herself as a spokesperson for and adviser to the female consumer. But underlying her arguments was a strong faith in American business, and she believed that it had an unfailingly beneficial impact on the American home. She seemed unaware of the contradictions in her discussion of price maintenance. She evidently did not understand that lower prices could lead to greater sales or that retailers, when faced with requests for certain goods, would eventually respond to customer demands. But these issues were relatively new in 1914 when Christine began her crusade, and consumers in markets driven by advertising were an untried constituency. In any case, the assertion that she cared only for the housewife belied the bulk of Christine's argument, which, to the modern observer, seems clearly in the interests of business and against the interests of the consumer.[80]

Christine's involvement in consumerism helped her accomplish several of her missions. She could act as expert "competent counsel" for the manager of the new consumer household, she could promote the technology that she believed would relieve the housewife's burden, and she could help preserve the home by showing how the use of that technology to promote efficiency would make the American woman happier in her traditional role as homemaker.

Whether the message was consumer education, labor-saving technology, or household efficiency, Christine Frederick disseminated it through the printed page. From a simple contract for four articles with the *Ladies' Home Journal*, she had moved to writing for other periodicals, to the publication of two widely recognized housekeeping manuals, and, finally, to syndication with the biggest newspaper chain in the country. In seven years, she had become a major writer on the subject of modernized homemaking.

7 · *Accommodating Progressivism*

[T]he new homemaking . . . [offers] . . . the opportunity to give thought
and care to the wider range of interests which it is now certain
will be woman's future sphere.

CHRISTINE FREDERICK, "Putting the American Woman
and Her Home on a Business Basis," 1914

CHRISTINE FREDERICK'S EARLY CAREER as a home expert coincided with
the Progressive movements that dominated American society for the first two
decades of the twentieth century. Regulatory legislation, woman suffrage, municipal housekeeping, and feminism were but a few manifestations of Progressivism. Many of the movements' leaders (although there were vastly different
reform programs promoted by very different people) were, like Christine and
J. George Frederick, white, middle-class, native-born, educated Protestants.
And like many Progressives, the Fredericks adhered to old values regarding the
family while believing that science, technology, organization, and management—in a word, modernization—would hasten society along the road to perfection.[1] Christine's causes, efficiency and modernized housekeeping, reson-
ated with the rhetoric of reform.[2] She joined other Progressive campaigns as
well, notably the attempt to solve "the servant problem."

Progressivism was inspired by a complex of historical developments: widespread unease associated with the excesses of the "Gilded Age," the countervailing infusion of new ideas, and the continuing belief that humankind was
naturally progressing toward a better civilization. An important aspect of Progressive reform was the need for expertise that the process of modernization
generated. Many Progressives believed that expert advice and professional
guidance could benefit all levels of society. Popular magazines now brought
new scientific theories to millions of Americans, and new disciplines such as
psychology encouraged people to believe that even day-to-day life required
expert advice.[3]

The Progressive Reformer

PROGRESSIVE REFORM influenced both of the Fredericks. J. George's participation in movements toward organization, efficiency, and management was an

expression of the Progressive impulse.[4] Similarly, Christine's interest in scientific management was a response to Progressive ideas. The optimistic view that scientific discoveries would lead to a better life informed her celebration of technology, for example. She praised an audience of farmers in Illinois for modernizing: "The modern farmer of to-day is willing to experiment, to try new methods, and to take the advice of scientific agriculturalists."[5]

In 1911, an article in the *Journal of Home Economics* had blamed a perceived exodus of women from the home on the failure of the home to modernize. While men had access to machines and labor-saving devices, their wives wasted the best years of their lives "in a round of mechanical drudgeries."[6] Christine, too, preached the Progressive idea that technology would lighten housework and thus improve the housewife's lot. She believed that farm women, in particular, could benefit from technology. "With the conditions improved, and better tools and equipment, the farm woman will have time not only for recreation and the higher family interests, but she will also have the *longed-for leisure to study books and courses on advanced home-making*" (Italics mine).[7] Although Christine often mentioned leisure time as one of the benefits of technology, this last statement underscores her failure to propose that labor-saving devices might enable women to pursue work outside the home. She implied that the farm woman's leisure time should be spent acquiring more expertise in housekeeping.

When Christine took her expertise in home efficiency to farm women, she was participating in yet another Progressive reform crusade, the Country Life Movement. Concern over the decreasing farm population and what appeared to be the diminished status of agriculture in a nation still loyal to the Jeffersonian tradition of the yeoman farmer moved urban Americans to search for ways to keep rural Americans on the land. In 1908, President Theodore Roosevelt had appointed a Country Life Commission to investigate the deficiencies in rural life and to recommend solutions. The commission's report recommended, among other measures, that the land grant colleges undertake extension programs. Subsequent reports confirmed the need for vocational training in agricultural communities, and legislation eventually followed. The Smith-Lever Act of 1914 and the Smith-Hughes Act of 1917 provided for rural extension education in both agriculture and home economics. Programs were designed to teach farm women to manage their homes efficiently, thus "improving the general conditions of country life." Agents sought to teach farm women how to "properly" prepare "wholesome food," how to care for "the family linen and

wardrobe," even how to care for and manage their children. The home economists wanted the farmwife to gain "time for reading, self-development, child
teaching, social life, and recreation." The U.S. Department of Agriculture told
the readers of the *Journal of Home Economics* that city women could help
"through greater social intercourse with farm women."[8]

These reformers implied that farm women needed to be taught proper values. Although Christine was not a home economist, she shared their vision of
how the Smith-Lever Act could promote middle-class values. She suggested
that the extension program include "Rural Social Advisors" who might "stim-
ulate country dwellers in the formation of distinctive ideas of living, in dress
and furnishings, and recreation." Farmers should instill in their daughters
"ideals about country living," "honesty," and "simple right living."[9] As her 1916
housekeeping movie had demonstrated, Christine was especially enthusiastic
about the extension program's visiting housekeepers whom she dubbed "professional grandmothers." She praised them for helping young wives with family
budgets, ignoring the potential for intrusion.[10] Christine subscribed to the
middle-class values that characterized the Progressive movement, and, like the
home economists who were dedicated to bringing expertise to homemaking,
her counsel reinforced these values.

In two addresses before the Farmers' Institute, Christine seemed to embrace
yet another Progressive reform, municipal housekeeping. In 1916 she told the
audience that if the farmwife's kitchen were modernized, she would have time
for "community housekeeping": schools, sanitation, and pure food.[11] The following year, she praised the efforts of visiting housekeepers to encourage country wives to join in "united effort toward schools of better standard, in improved
roads and in neighborliness."[12] She apparently took cues from other writers who
were encouraging women to get involved in broader reforms of municipal
housekeeping. In 1912, Marion Talbot and Sophonisba Breckinridge exhorted
the consumer housewife to ask how merchandise was made before purchasing
it in an effort to discourage the exploitation of workers.[13] The following year,
Christine argued in *The New Housekeeping* that if women were lured by cut
prices, they were helping to lower the wages of workers and deprive them of sanitary, healthful working conditions. Women could "prevent social injustice" by
paying "the needed price" for merchandise, she wrote.[14] Thus she used the
social justice reform campaign to argue against price cutting. And as the first
presidential election after the ratification of the Nineteenth Amendment ap-

proached, she toyed with the idea of writing an article titled "The Housewife and the Vote" in which she would demonstrate how homemaking reached "out into national housekeeping."[15]

Christine admonished the readers of *Household Engineering* to familiarize themselves with the Pure Food and Drug Act and then to help enforce it. "It is a large share of the modern consumer's work and training to detect . . . frauds, boycott them and bring them to the attention of the proper inspectors," she wrote.[16] A Huntington women's group to which Christine belonged, inspired by an exposé in *Collier's* magazine, organized a pure food show in 1913. The group joined with the local chapter of the Women's Christian Temperance Union, the local historical society, and several reluctant food retailers to expose food and drug adulteration and deceptive weighing methods. Their exhibit, Christine wrote, actually "boost[ed] the dealers, dairymen, bakeries, etc." of Huntington whose practices "were up to standard." In fact, it boosted her efforts at Applecroft, too, for she demonstrated equipment such as the fireless cooker, the gasoline iron, and various electric appliances from her kitchen.[17]

Christine carried the pure food and drug message into rural America, too. She chided Illinois farmers in 1916 for using ineffective and impure medications:

> [I]t is a known fact that the patent medicine industry in this country is sup-
> ported by the farmer. Doan's kidney pills, Swamp-root, stomach bitters and
> Peruna have long ago been expelled from the good metropolitan newspapers
> and national weeklies. But where do they still thrive? On the pages of the best
> country weeklies. . . . I want you to use your influence to get honest advertising
> in your country papers.[18]

Christine's admonition was patronizing, as much of the Country Life Movement was, but it might have been well placed. Before doctors or drugstores were available on the frontier, nineteenth-century Americans had become accustomed to the patent medicines sold by traveling salesmen.[19]

Christine admitted that her Progressive expertise in scientific management was useful primarily to middle-class women. Wealthy women, she wrote, could hire servants while others, deferring marriage, lived in apartments or boarding-houses. She dismissed poor women because their housekeeping was not complex, and, in any event, settlement workers could teach them at no charge. She felt that society expected much of middle-class women, however. They were "refined, educated women, many with a college or business training," she wrote, and they must keep up the "fair standard of appearances obligatory on the middle class."[20] Other Progressive reformers imposed middle-class standards not only on white working-class women, but also women of non–western European groups. Ellen Richards developed a syllabus for use in domestic science education in 1900 that suggested that the social development of the Anglo-Saxon home life was superior to all others. Subtopics in the syllabus included "The psychology of the races—expression of the home idea in races other than the Anglo-Saxon" and "The home life of the Anglo-Saxon vs. The Communistic family system."[21]

In fact, black Americans were taking it upon themselves to teach home and community values in institutions of their own. In the South, both Tuskegee and the Hampton Institute provided courses in home economics and nursing.[22] These programs trained teachers, visiting rural nurses, and extension agents.[23] The home was important to these young black women, wrote one home economist, because they had not had real homes before 1865. Training for home life, she wrote, was "the most essential part" of a girl's training. Like many white Progressive reformers, she believed that home economics training would provide instruction in "right living."[24] The majority of these black students, however, were not destined to manage middle-class homes of their own. A telling statement about the training at the Hampton Institute in 1925 revealed that "the prospective teacher is trained to wait on table and to serve large numbers." Food preparation and serving was one of the primary subjects taught at Tuskegee.[25] Many would eventually use their home economics training as domestic servants.

The Servant Question

DOMESTIC SERVICE was the subject of a lively public discourse among Progressive reformers, and Christine Frederick had a great deal to say about it. In fact, her position on servants was probably her best-developed Progressive reform thinking. Servants had been a "problem" for middle-class homemakers since Catharine Beecher wrote her *Treatise* in 1841. "They ought ever to be looked upon, not as the mere ministers to our comfort and convenience," Beecher wrote, "but as the humbler and more neglected children of our Heavenly Father, whom he has sent to claim our sympathy and aid."[26] Beecher believed that the woman of the house had a moral responsibility to her employees. By 1869, she had decided that servants should be accorded the same respect shown to dressmakers or milliners. A servant should receive "courteous treatment from all whom [the mistress's] roof shelters," she wrote in her second housekeeping manual. And she advised that employers refrain from interfering in their servants' activities during their free hours.[27]

The servant problem had become critical by the time Christine began her career. An official from the U.S. Department of Commerce wrote in 1911 that servants in American homes labored under "antiquated labor contracts" that amounted to "social discrimination." Young women who had previously worked in homes were now moving into factories and offices. He agreed with the promoters of scientific management who maintained that its adoption by homemakers would eliminate the necessity for servants, but in the meantime he urged that they be given decent wages and working conditions. This theme recurred in many commentaries prior to World War I.[28] Yet servants were still usually treated as social inferiors.[29] In 1913, Charlotte Perkins Gilman decried the bargaining position of the servant: "The domestic servant is still expected to take part wage in barter, food and shelter being given instead of the full price in money; to live in the house of the employing family, to show . . . humility, loyalty, faithfulness."[30] In 1913, J. George Frederick's Business Bourse found that only 8 percent of American families employed servants.[31] Still, many middle-class families wanted "intelligent and skilled service within the home."[32] Willing domestic workers who met these requirements were difficult to find.

One proposed solution was to employ servants for regular hours at wages generous enough to allow them to live in their own lodgings. As early as 1907, the Women's Educational and Industrial Union of Boston promoted "fair conditions" spelled out in a formal contract for domestic service.[33] In 1912, Talbot and Breckinridge, recognizing that social barriers were exacerbated when servants lived in the home, suggested standardizing hours so that they could live away from their employers.[34]

Christine Frederick first expanded upon this idea in the fourth article of her original *Ladies' Home Journal* series, in which she argued that scientific management could help solve the servant problem. She framed her ideas within a conversational format. A "friend" told her that her maid, "Katy," by using the new, efficient methods of housekeeping, accomplished more in less time than she had formerly. Yet the friend had not increased the maid's wages, nor had she

given her extra time off. Christine commented, "Katy is still in the same bar-
baric state of vassalage which was once common in all industries."[35] Christine's
friend eventually changed her policy, dropping "the dictatorial idea of ordering
[Katy] around" as a "subordinate." Under scientific management she was able
to promote "team work" and to change her own attitude about homemaking.
Christine's suggestion that the friend consult the manager of a shop yielded
these happy results, for she discovered that when an employer "assumes the responsibility of enabling the employee to work under the best conditions . . . the
worker cannot fail."

Christine's story revealed her complete faith in the efficiency engineers' system and her belief that it improved the lot of the worker. The friend confided:
"My plans must be carried out; she must feel the responsibility of her work and
not shirk it. When she understands my plans, based on the best way to do her
work, she must accept this program and carry it through." This strategy took all
initiative away from the servant, of course, but Christine believed that set hours
and time off made it somehow less "dictatorial" than the less-regimented system her friend had abandoned. Like the shop manager, Christine's friend "standardized" her maid's hours and pay, setting an hourly wage, a uniform eleven-
hour day, and regular days off. Although this early article was designed to
promote scientific management, Christine's ideas about regular hours and
wages that enabled "Katy" to live in her own flat and the even more radical suggestion that servants be given two weeks of paid vacation after a full year's employment were informed by Progressivism.[36]

Edward Bok liked Christine's first article on servants and, in the spring of
1914, asked her to supply another, suggesting the title "Suppose Our Servants
Didn't Live with Us?"[37] That article appeared the following October. Here,
Christine cited the views of the prominent Progressive activists Jane Addams
and Grace Abbott, who believed that servants were vulnerable to immoral in-
fluences, to argue that servant girls who lived away from their employers' homes
were less likely to lead "an immoral life." "More girls 'go wrong' and become in-
sane, from the servant class," she wrote, because of indefinite hours and the
"feudal relationship" between mistress and maid. She again advised that
women convert their household routines to the scientific management model
and added that the installation of "labor-saving equipment" would help standardize the servant's work.[38]

Christine blamed unstandardized conditions and a poor psychological atmosphere for young women's resistance to domestic work. She argued that the work itself did not deter applicants. Given "standardized" work and provided with enough money to live in their own quarters, young women would find the servant's position "as dignified, independent and professional as the factory worker, the telephone girl or the shopgirl." To objections that the wages she suggested were too high, Christine responded with a list of the overhead costs involved in housing a servant: food, fuel for heat and light, and plumbing, for example. Christine suggested a contract that clarified terms of employment, including hours, wages, and a severance notice.[39] Like Catharine Beecher, who had written that a mistress had "no more right to interfere with [her servants] in the disposal of their time than with any mechanic whom [she] employ[ed]," Christine argued that a contract would prevent a mistress from attempting to "'regulate' a girl's personal life." Nonetheless, Christine's middle-class bias was revealed by the suggestion that a mistress would be well within her rights to insist that the maid bathe during her "off-time."[40]

Christine's third article on servants appeared in the *Ladies' Home Journal* in October 1915. She revisited the advantages of employing servants on a contractual basis, providing them with certain benefits, and paying them enough to rent their own living quarters. Again, she promoted scientific management, or "standardized housework," but in this piece, she emphasized training for house workers, suggesting an elaborate plan for "domestic centers" where young women would not only be trained as house workers, but also would be given room and board during their course. Citing an operating example in an unnamed western city, she suggested that potential employers cooperate to buy and furnish a house, hire a matron, and deduct the costs from future wages. Reflecting both her humanity and her biases, Christine wrote, "I believe 'standardized' work and sleeping out of the home will dignify housework and attract a better class of girls." She suggested that the more businesslike arrangement would improve the mistress, as well: "[W]hen we are able to treat workers in the home on the same plane as we treat intelligent coequal human beings, I think it will be much better for the woman herself. It will develop and broaden her."[41]

In *Household Engineering*, Christine included a chapter titled "Management of Houseworkers" that further defined her Progressive views on servants. She scolded women's clubs for ignoring the matter: "It seems futile for women's clubs to discuss 'Browning' and the 'early Aztec pottery,' while they neglect to solve or make any progress in the great problem of woman as an employer of labor in the home."[42] She urged more democratic ways of treating employees, suggesting that the term "houseworker" be used instead of "servant" or "maid" and that domestic workers be addressed as "Miss" or "Mrs."[43] But at the same time, she wrote, "It is generally unsafe to trust the common grade of household worker with the costly and delicate apparatus of electric cooking, or expect her to understand and use it economically." Christine, then, did not treat all house workers with equal respect, but she believed that there was "no reason why a high grade worker should not take at least the noon meal of informal luncheon with her employer. It is a little thing, but its psychological influence is great."[44] Despite her campaign to raise the status of house workers, she held tightly to the paternalism of middle-class propriety.

Still, Christine seemed sincere in her wish to see reform. She pointed out that her ideas would give the mistress more privacy, provide incentive to the servant to work extra hours when asked, place the relationship on the level of a business transaction rather than "emotional loyalty," and provide the servant with the means to live as "independent and thoroughly human a life as is possible."[45] Her program for elevating the status of house workers was consistent with the views of other Progressive reformers. The same year she published *Household Engineering,* the Committee on Home Assistants, a division of the U.S. Employment Service, brought employers and nonresident house workers together under a contract that would stipulate eight-hour days and overtime pay. This experiment was funded for only seven weeks, but its promoters were convinced that a businesslike arrangement similar to the one Christine had first proposed in 1912 would solve the "domestic problem." Other experiments in several northeastern cities placed eight-hour-a-day house workers for several years after World War I.[46]

Christine's work on the servant question reflected the tensions between more radical Progressive ideas such as feminism and her traditional view of women as primarily homemakers. In the years prior to World War I, her readership broadened considerably, and in 1914 she reiterated her views on scientific housekeeping for the *American Review of Reviews.* The inherent conflict in her message resonates in this article, for she frankly admitted that housekeeping was "distasteful to . . . the livest [*sic*] and most intelligent portion of housekeepers, and is only endured in a dull way by the masses of women." But efficiency could do for women what it had done for men, she wrote, and in fact would help the sexes to join "their spheres . . . toward the real American ideal of comradeship." If women would apply "the modern ideas of efficiency" to their own minds, homemaking could become "the most all-satisfying, broadening and stimulating career open to any woman, and one which offers her widest talents their most varied scope."[47] Blaming women who failed to make this leap for their own unhappiness, Christine once again ignored the fact that her own solution to the problem was to step often outside her home in the pursuit of a public career.

8 · "A World Wide Lecturer"

[S]tanding up in that huge, vast empty room . . . at least three or four times
a week . . . I visualized before me a mighty, enthusiastic and attentive audience.
Later . . . I became a world wide lecturer.
CHRISTINE FREDERICK, "Only a Girl," 1969

IN JUNE 1913, just after Christine had published *The New Housekeeping,* she
was invited to speak before the annual meeting of the American Home Economics Association at Cornell University. Her topic was "The Best Way Yet," "a
discussion of housekeeping equipment and methods."[1] Excerpts from this
speech were printed a year later as "Points in Efficiency" in the association's
journal. It was in this early speech that Christine, having launched an extremely promising career herself, proclaimed, "Our greatest enemy is the
woman with the career."[2] She also hinted in this speech that the cultural activities of the club woman and the charitable work of the reformer were as detri-
mental to homemaking (and by extension, the home) as work for pay. Let the
reformer "find it just as interesting to care for her own children as it is to go
down on the east side and take care of Annie Bolowski," she advised.[3] Never
more clearly than in this early speech did Christine reveal the conflict between
private and public domains that her own life embodied.

On the Lecture Circuit

THUS, SOON AFTER she had established herself as a home efficiency writer,
Christine Frederick began to speak about the "new housekeeping" on the lecture circuit. An early brochure declared: "Mrs. Frederick is a lecturer of trained
and proven ability and attractiveness, specializing on subjects upon which
she is a recognized authority and on which she has had first-hand practical
experience—home efficiency, dietetics, purchasing, the consumer viewpoint
and other phases of woman's work." Produced for the purpose of promoting her
talks, this leaflet praised her "Ability to Draw and Hold Audiences" and listed
fourteen groups, as diverse as the U.S. Congress, Columbia University, and

the National Cash Register employees, to whom she had spoken. The list of topics in which she claimed expertise included efficiency, purchasing, food, country life, and civic issues. She even advertised a lecture titled "The Home Efficiency Basis for Suffrage." An early brochure listed her lecture fees as twenty-five dollars plus expenses for women's clubs and colleges, and fifty dollars plus expenses for business and civic organizations. Another suggested that prospective clients write for "constructive suggestions for making her lectures pay best."[4]

Her speaking career soon began to keep pace with her writing. In 1914 she appeared before the Efficiency Society in Lake Placid and the Advertising Men's League in New York City. She also testified before the House Judiciary Committee that year.[5] Her two oldest children, David and Jean, were then four and six years old, and when their mother was traveling, Nursie cared for them.[6] Christine's speaking schedule for 1915 slowed when her third child, Phyllis, was born in May, but three months before her confinement, she spoke before the Lancaster Advertising group.[7]

During the first three months of 1916, Christine traveled in the Midwest for several weeks, addressing groups in Iowa, Indiana, and Illinois, where she spoke before the Farmers' Institute. The promotional material for the third annual convention of the Indiana Home Economics Association at Purdue University heralded Christine's address, "Women, Home Making and Careers," by urging, "Those who are familiar with Mrs. Frederick's brilliant contributions to the leading journals should appreciate this opportunity to see and hear one of her ability and reputation."[8] By her own account, Christine eventually spoke in "almost every state in the country."[9]

It was during her midwestern tour that she hurried back to New York to deliver the lecture on household economics for the Intercollegiate Bureau of Occupations. If Christine's earlier 1913 speech to the home economists had revealed her own inner conflicts, her 1916 lecture for the IBO's course exposed her differences with contemporary feminists. Gilman had said in the first lecture of the course that women should be changing their "industrial relation to the world" by entering fields other than homemaking.[10] Other speakers in the series included Frances Perkins, who lectured on civil service work; Ida Tarbell, on journalism; Mary Beard, on work in the community; and Fay Kellogg, on architecture.[11] Christine countered the thrust of the course by arguing that professions that took women out of the home were becoming overcrowded.

"I often say that the woman with the career is my greatest enemy," she admitted, but she quickly added, "[S]he is not tonight in this particular address."[12]

The members of the Illinois Farmers' Institute apparently welcomed Christine's views and were so impressed by her 1916 address to them that they asked her back to their meeting in 1917. She spoke before the Institute in Streator, Illinois, that February, capitalizing on her Long Island experience to claim expertise in country living. Later in the year, Christine spoke in Louisville, Kentucky, and twice she traveled to the nation's capital to testify on price maintenance.[13] Her fourth child, Carol, had been born in August.

Christine was a popular speaker because she had seized upon trends that appealed to modern early-twentieth-century Americans: efficiency, streamlined management, technology, and consumerism. She also addressed the middle-class fear that the home was under siege. While she encouraged American families to modernize, she reassured them that change need not disturb the traditional structure of the family because women could modernize while staying home. But Christine was also in demand because of the considerable talent as a speaker that she had discovered and developed as a student at Northwestern.

"Mrs. Frederick has a remarkable platform presence," reported the *Louisville Herald*. She had "a wonderful speaking voice, and magnetism."[14] Her style was brisk; a reporter who covered a lecture in Rochester, New York, wrote that Christine delivered a "succession of rapid fire ideas."[15] She often relieved her practical and efficient demeanor with a playful sense of humor. In 1917, she teased the Illinois farmers: "You all know I made an unfortunate marriage and married a farmboy from Pennsylvania!" She good-naturedly chided them with comic exaggeration for their diets of "pickled this and pickled that," "three-story cakes," and "seven kinds of pies and fourteen other kinds of sweets."[16] But Christine often flattered her male audiences, too. "You are the man of the hour," she told the 1916 gathering of the Farmers' Institute, "with your 12,000,000,000 bushels you are feeding the world."[17] The flattery sometimes became a bit flirtatious. Explaining the percentages of goods that women buy, she would tell a male audience: "Therefore, I say that of the handsome members of the institute before me this evening, 34% of them are wearing clothing chosen for them by women!"[18]

Although Christine's message was ostensibly aimed at women, she often spoke to men. "You see," she told the Illinois farmers, "I speak to so very many groups of gentlemen. I spoke to about 700 in Toledo the other afternoon." In

1921, when asked to list her hobbies for a pamphlet about women in advertising, she wrote that after her "hubby," the four children, and clam digging, her favorite hobby was "addressing 3000 men." In fact, she added, "I'm sure it's this last hobby I love best."[19] She often chastened male advertisers for using young, glamorous women, "pretty girls," in the promotional material they developed to sell household goods. "'You have the wrong feminine psychology when you show a picture of the goods being used by a prettier woman than I am,'" she would tell them.[20] In 1923, she repeated that theme in a speech before the Springfield Publicity Club in Massachusetts.[21] By speaking so often to men, Christine could promote modernization of the home to those who had an interest in encouraging women to remain there.

Christine had a flair for drama and often used stage props. Before the Federal Trade Commission, she exhibited products to illustrate the difference between trademarked and independently labeled goods.[22] On several occasions, especially if she were addressing a group of men, she produced a pail and scrub brush. In evening dress, she dropped to the floor on hands and knees to illustrate the drudgery of housekeeping before technology, asking the gentlemen if this was how they wished their wives to labor.[23] This theatrical gimmick bore such suspiciously close resemblance to two *American Weekly* illustrations of the gowned and bejeweled May Yohe (the former Lady Frances Hope) scrubbing a floor that it suggests either Christine or the author of the Yohe articles purloined the other's idea.[24]

In 1924, she used her showmanship to publicize aluminum at the New York Advertising Club Ball dressed as "Miss Aluminum." Decked out in aluminum kitchen utensils from head to toe, a kettle on her head and pots and pans hanging from her belt, she won first prize for best costume.[25] Disregarding accusations that aluminum was held hostage by unfair business practices, Christine staged this walking advertisement just one month after the Federal Trade Commission charged that the Aluminum Company of America, virtually the only source of the metal in the country, and its subsidiary, the Aluminum Goods Manufacturing Company, had a monopoly on aluminum and aluminum kitchen utensils. The Aluminum Company refused to fill orders from independent utensil manufacturers. The company, coincidentally, was "active in maintaining retail prices," one of Christine's favorite causes.[26]

In the early years, Christine's appearance added to her charm as a speaker. An observer at the Rochester, New York, lecture described her as "a charming

young woman in a modish green gown with a big bunch of daisies at her belt."
On her head, she wore a "bandeau hat with a velvet chin strap."

Christine liked fine clothes; as a mature woman, she often lectured in a long, black lace gown worn over an apricot-colored satin slip.[27] Flair, humor, compelling delivery, and a modern message that could be tailored to meet wartime imperatives made Christine a natural choice for the entertainment and cultural phenomenon of the period: in 1918, she joined a Chautauqua show that traveled through five states from Michigan to Kentucky.[28]

On the Road

CHAUTAUQUA had a long and distinguished history by the time Christine Frederick joined the Redpath-Chicago Chautauqua circuit during the second year of U.S. involvement in World War I.[29] From its inception in the 1880s until its decline in the late 1920s, Chautauqua brought a variety of programs to more than eight thousand cities and towns. In 1918, the Redpath-Chicago circuit concentrated on the states of Illinois, Indiana, Ohio, Michigan, and Kentucky. The troupe presented seven-day shows in each town, lecturers and performers for the first day traveling to the next city as soon as they had finished. Chautauqua's educational function was considered important enough that President Wilson eased the restrictions that reserved trains for troop movement, and Chautauquans were allowed train passage. They were also exempted from the draft.[30] Talent was paid quite well; top performers drew salaries as high as fifteen hundred dollars per week.[31] The first year that Redpath-Chicago operated, it engaged William Jennings Bryan to deliver his famous lecture, "Prince of Peace," from Tennessee to Michigan. He sometimes drew crowds of five thousand people to the enormous, brown Chautauqua tent emblazoned with four-foot-high letters.[32]

Both instructive programs and elocution were popular with Chautauqua audiences, so Christine seemed well suited for the circuit. It is true that one testy Chautauqua manager proclaimed the most dangerous subject for the tents was housekeeping because it was a subject "more thickly covered with a concrete mixture of prejudice and ignorance than any other." Nonetheless, Christine was hired by an agent who had heard her speak in Waltham, Massachusetts.[33]

Christine traveled for several months from spring to fall in 1918, speaking to audiences of two and three thousand people in ten states from South Carolina to Illinois.[34] In tents where the temperature sometimes reached 117 degrees, she delivered a speech titled "Keeping House for Uncle Sam" during which she enlisted women as "'kitchen soldiers' to help win this great war for democracy."[35] Christine's wartime Chautauqua troupe was led by British newspaper correspondent John Foster Fraser, whose lecture, "The Checkerboard of Europe," was thought by some to be a political argument in favor of war.[36] Musical offerings included the light opera *The Chocolate Soldier*; Dunbar's Revue, which featured "The Parade of the Allies"; a Croatian orchestra; and the opera singer Margery Maxwell.[37]

Christine was very proud of her Chautauqua tour. She recalled that she gave "Wm. Jennings Bryan and his curls and his 'Cross of Gold' a run for his money."[38] She told an interviewer many years later that, while with Chautauqua, she had started canning clubs, baby welfare programs, and municipal markets in several towns.[39] And she was warmly received; an Arkansas reporter called her performance "one of the best features of the Chautauqua."[40]

Her lecture drew from her previous work. She concentrated on household efficiency and labor-saving devices. Incorporating efficiency and technology into homemaking, she told her audiences, would further the war effort by conserving food, time, and energy. She exhorted women to create good homes for the returning veterans, to use fewer foods at each meal, to be good homemakers. Though she added the obligatory list of municipal housekeeping projects—pure food, child welfare, better schools, Red Cross service—she told her audiences that German women backed their soldiers by being good homemakers.[41] She had harsh words for American women who participated in the "band playing, flag-flying stage of war." They were "unmindful of the great responsibilities that [were] theirs," she said. Women who expressed their patriotism through benefits, teas, and dances for servicemen, or who donned "trouserettes" to sit on "an attractive tractor" so that their pictures would "appear in some Sunday feature page" were ignoring their real job as "food producer[s]." Christine told them to awaken to "the dignity of household labor."[42] "I'd rather wear a kitchen apron and help win the war for President Wilson than wear the trained robes of a Queen of England," she told a Louisville, Kentucky, group.[43] Christine, of course, was spending several months away from her own husband and four small children.

The Chautauqua experience was an invigorating one for Christine. There were hardships, of course. The tents were oppressively hot. One had to sleep in lumpy beds and eat "wretched" hotel meals.[44] Christine "longed for food that was crisp and refreshing" instead of the restaurant fare of canned vegetables and "greasy fried meats."[45] Performers had to carry their own luggage, and personal grooming was sometimes difficult.[46] But there were also adventures. Christine was occasionally stranded, for example.[47] She once hitched a ride with a Coca Cola truck in South Carolina. On another occasion, deciding to take an alternate route from the rest of the group, she visited Horse's Neck, Alabama, on the manager's recommendation. Detraining at a lonely stop where only a platform and a water tank betrayed any sign of civilization, Christine spent five hours watching dusk fall and the moon rise. Later she wrote, "I was not afraid because I am not a scary woman."[48]

Neither was Christine afraid of people. Although the Eighteenth Amendment banning the nationwide sale of alcohol had not yet been ratified, many of the towns through which the Chautauqua train passed prohibited its sale or consumption.[49] But Christine's fellow performer, John Foster Fraser, liked his whiskey. Christine knocked on his door one afternoon after she had heard him complain of feeling ill that morning. "He was sunk on his pillows," she wrote, "and declared that . . . all he wanted was brandy or whiskey." Christine had the temerity to ask the president of the local women's club (who had approached to congratulate her after her talk that same afternoon) if she could procure a bottle of brandy, explaining that it was for the evening speaker. Unfortunately, the woman's son, she informed Christine, was the local "Revenue Agent." Nevertheless, a bottle appeared in due course, and Christine took her gift to Fraser. The evening lecture proceeded successfully.[50]

Hidden Conflict

CHRISTINE'S CHAUTAUQUA EXPERIENCE marked the culmination of the first phase of her career. By war's end, she had established herself as a writer and speaker of considerable stature. She had applied her talents to the modern trends of her time, and she had capitalized upon the countervailing fears bred by those trends. As she responded to exciting developments in the public sphere—efficiency, technology, consumerism—she echoed Catharine Beecher and advised other women that their highest duty was housekeeping. She suggested that she had found homemaking satisfying by applying scientific management principles, the substitute, perhaps, for Beecher's religious and moral fulfillment. But she did not address the disparity between what she was saying and what she was doing. Christine was, in fact, a career woman, one of those she called her "greatest enemies." She tried to free women from sheer drudgery, but she did not want to free them from confinement to the home. She did not, perhaps could not, join with those who suggested that married women should be free to choose other occupations. Although she occasionally mentioned municipal housekeeping, or briefly recognized that some women *did* work outside the home for pay, she always returned to the theme that housekeeping was woman's primary role and duty.

Christine reinforced the traditional attitude that the novelist Ruth Suckow found in the midwestern farm wife. The mother of her fictional Iowan farm family "always had the feeling that she must be responsible for all that was done in the house."[51] Apparently many real American women had the same feeling. They were happy to adopt Christine's suggestions and ease their household chores because they assumed that they were, after all, "responsible for all that was done in the house." When the *Ladies' Home Journal* hired Christine, it tapped the strong desire of many women to improve, but not eliminate, housekeeping. From Minnesota, South Dakota, Illinois, and Arkansas came responses to her articles. "[T]he freedom from the old drudgery of dishwashing," wrote one, was her "greatest delight." Another wrote in praise of Christine's record-keeping system: "I follow Mrs. Frederick's system of division and grouping quite exactly." A Minnesota woman claimed that Christine's suggestions saved her two thousand dollars per year. The new appliances that a South Dakota housewife acquired at Christine's suggestion made "the 'New House-keeping' a pleasure," she wrote. New appliances allowed another to dispense with the "hired girl."[52] Christine was speaking to a large majority of American women who had no intention of either leaving the home or of changing it radically.

Christine knew that her readers believed that the private, single-family home was the best living arrangement. Because she subscribed to the argument that it was in danger, she defended woman's traditional place in it. When asked early in her career if she advocated the community schemes that Gilman and others had proposed to lighten individual housework, she answered, "I do not! . . . I don't believe in giving up the home as an impossible proposition. . . . Women are trying to escape from the kitchen because they don't understand how to manage the kitchen."[53] In *Household Engineering*, she specifically addressed the apartment hotel that Gilman had planned with Henrietta Rodman. She argued that the advocates of apartment hotels *"entirely leave out of account the cost of managing any cooperative plan"* (Frederick's italics). She maintained that families with moderate incomes could not afford to pay the managers of these institutions. This, of course, was a tacit admission that managers of homes, housewives, worked without pay. Secondly, she argued that apartment living was not ideal for children or family life. She and J. George had acted upon that belief when they moved from the Bronx to Greenlawn. But perhaps her most perceptive argument against cooperative or group living of any kind was this:

> [F]amilies are, and prefer to be, individual in their taste and living habits. Co-operation would be very easy if every one of us is willing to become "standardized"—that is, eat just what the rest do, be served the same way without preference, choice, or personal taste. . . . The truth is . . . that most of us still prefer inefficiency in service and management to being deprived of our love of privacy, individual preference and choice—this is the real reason why cooperation has, and possibly will always continue to fail.[54]

Christine understood how highly most Americans prized individualism. Soon after writing the above critique of cooperation, she told an interviewer, "I'm afraid I am an individualist. . . . Personally, I would rather continue the individual home with all its drawbacks than eat and sleep and launder my family along with fifty others!"[55] But Christine did not acknowledge that requiring all women to be happy as homemakers denied them that very individualism. "[M]arriage excluded women from individualism," Elizabeth Fox-Genovese has written, but "it also offered them important benefits in return."[56] Christine's prescription for other women ignored the first part of this argument.

Not only did Christine reinforce women's feelings of responsibility for the home, but, like her predecessor Catharine Beecher, she also excused men from assuming any part of it: "If the father works hard and faithfully at his task of earning money during his work day, it is not more fair to ask him to turn chore-man as soon as he comes home, than it would be to ask the woman who has cooked and cleaned all day to turn around and do office or business work after five o'clock." Conversely, a man's responsibility was to earn the family's income: "[H]is hours at home should be hours of recuperation, or so that he can study *his own work*, become more proficient, and thus secure advancement or a better economic position" (Frederick's italics).[57]

Christine did not agree with feminists who believed that gender differences were socially constructed. Because women, she believed, were more emotional than men, they had "not lifted their sphere of labour out of the hard physical drudgery era" as men had "lifted [the] office and shop, by scientific management and invention."[58] And because women mismanaged their households, she implied, they impaired their husband's ability to succeed. In her second book, she told a cautionary tale of a man who was forced to do household chores at home and therefore failed to advance at the office "because of his wife's poor management."[59] She seemed to blame women for the drudgery from which she hoped to free them. Christine's public view of marriage, that the woman manage an efficient home and be a "fit companion" to her husband, who should be "progressing," belied the fact that, in the Frederick household, she was making a respectable income while J. George's earnings had stagnated.[60]

The contradictions of Christine Frederick's life might suggest opportunism, hypocrisy, even duplicity. In fact, Christine was deceiving herself. She was caught between the ideology of the nineteenth century and the modern reality of the twentieth. Awakened to her own capabilities by a college education, drawn to new ideas, stimulated by progress and modernization, she was nevertheless held fast by the prescriptive ideas of her Victorian upbringing. When she first began experimenting with scientific management, the stimulation of research and the joy of discovery made her own work in the home far more enjoyable than it had been. She wrote in *The New Housekeeping* that treating housekeeping like a science was "a fine antidote against the unnatural craving for 'careers.'"[61] She may have felt—and suppressed—guilt over her initial dislike of housekeeping in the Bronx apartment. That she quickly became involved in other, gainful employments did not diminish her conviction that her discoveries changed her attitude toward homemaking. She believed she was helping to elevate what had been drudgery into a modern, satisfying occupation.

Christine's writings did help to improve the daily routines and lighten the heavy tasks of women who wished to be—or who had no choice but to be—housewives. But she never acknowledged that her life and work were no longer typical of middle-class American homemaking. When she contrasted housework to work in the public sphere, she used office work as the measure, and she could write with complete conviction, "Look at the tasks of the woman who works in an office in unaesthetic surroundings filing, keeping books, writing letters about a business in which she has no particular interest—often no knowledge even. Would she not be infinitely happier and would she not be more mentally active in applying those same instincts to the business of home-making?"[62] She did not compare housekeeping to writing and speaking. When she told audiences that career women were her greatest enemies, she could ignore the fact that she herself had a career because she was working in the interest of the home. She also ignored the economic implications of her position.

One of Charlotte Perkins Gilman's arguments for allowing women access to the public sphere was that women needed to be economically independent of men to develop fully. She observed that in the United States, housework was "not regarded as labor, in any economic sense, but as a sex-function proper to woman."[63] Christine, conversely, argued that homemaking compensated the woman economically because it saved the wages of domestic workers: "I always feel that the time I put into any task has an actual money value. For instance, I know that the time spent in sewing has actual cash value if it is done by a seamstress, and I consider my time also has this value when I do the sewing myself. . . . [T]he time I spend on these tasks represents money which I would have to give some other person if I did not do these things myself."[64]

While dismissing the housewife's economic dependence, Christine assigned her power in the marketplace and blamed her for conditions over which she clearly had no control. When arguing for price maintenance, Christine wrote, "[B]usiness will never be more moral than we women . . . will allow it to be by our own actions." If Christine hoped to be a liaison between the woman consumer and business, she betrayed a confused sense of loyalty when she wrote, "No transaction can be moral which is based on deception, baiting, injury to manufacturers, loss to dealers, unfairness to competitors, or eventual throwing out of work of factory laborers, or on sweatshop methods, underpay, bad working conditions, etc. Yet millions of housewives' boasts of 'bargains' have cost all these things."[65]

By the time that Christine Frederick completed the Chautauqua circuit, the armistice that ended the fighting of World War I was only weeks away. The war had drawn women into the public sphere on a greater scale than even the feminists could have imagined. Women's numbers in civil service climbed from 5 percent before the war to 20 during the fighting. Women lawyers served on various boards and commissions and women physicians and nurses joined the military effort by the thousands. By war's end, twenty thousand women were working in banks on Wall Street. Women also filled such traditionally male jobs as streetcar conductor and steel mill worker. The increase of women in the workforce prompted the creation of the Women's Bureau of the U.S. Department of Labor in 1920. Yet in 1917, Christine urged women to help the war effort by staying "in the kitchen of the farm where" they were "so badly needed."[66]

Christine had had ample opportunity to read and understand feminist ideas; her rejection of them was certainly a conscious choice. In 1912, Charlotte Perkins Gilman had written that woman's very "shame" was "that she [had] no other business" and made "her living by 'Being a Woman.'"[67] That same year, Christine advised *Ladies' Home Journal* readers to improve their attitudes toward housekeeping. When Gilman wrote that woman's "political activities, rightly fulfilled, will decrease her other cares and labors," Christine believed that most women "knew or cared little" about politics.[68]

At times, Christine's words betrayed the conflict in her own choices. "No one need suppose," she wrote, that she was "sitting in an office writing these articles out of pure theory." She managed "a lovely country home," and she was "the mother of four children 'on the side,' as it were." She believed that "housekeeping can be so simplified that a woman has time for it and children—and to keep young and pretty, too."[69] Suggesting that she was rearing her children "on the side" implied, after all, that she was in the "enemy's" camp. The contradiction in Christine Frederick's life was underscored by her determination to instill independence in her own daughters. "It was just taken for granted with my mother's milk that a woman had a career," one of her daughters remembered. "I [was] brought up by a career woman."[70]

9 · Reframing Women's Role in the Twenties

I am . . . an incurable realist on woman topics. . . . I think the average man
is his wife's . . . intellectual superior, no matter if she has acquired a prattle
about Ibsen and Browning. . . . [S]he needs, and the greater success of her marriage
calls for, a more intimate understanding of her husband's business
and career, since it is their joint career.
CHRISTINE FREDERICK, "The Modern Wife Faces a Problem," 1924

CHRISTINE FREDERICK'S VIEWS about gender roles were squarely in the
mainstream after World War I. The radical feminism that had sought to change
the fundamental role of women lost ground in the twenties. Leta Hollingworth
blamed biology for women's failure to achieve equality and gave men credit for
the progress women had made up to that time: "Men of science, inventors and
philosophers were the real makers of the New Woman," she wrote. Martha
Bruère, who had been encouraged about women's progress under the efficiency
movement, wrote that even though women no longer judged their worth by
their quilts or their piecrusts, their sphere was "the sphere of the human female
still." Bruère's work to promote female proficiency in consumerism lends cre-
dence to the "therapeutic consumption" argument posed by the historian T. J.
Jackson Lears: "Feminist political claims were deflected into quests for psychic
satisfaction through high-style consumption."[1]

Still, a few feminist voices kept the crusade to achieve full equality alive
during the twenties. Alice Beal Parsons's *Woman's Dilemma* and Suzanne La Follette's *Concerning Women*, for example, drew from natural rights arguments
found in the works of the eighteenth-century writer Mary Wollstonecraft and
the nineteenth-century philosopher John Stuart Mill. Parsons examined ob-
vious differences between the sexes to illustrate that they need not impose
limitations on women, and La Follette argued that the established social and
economic order was not in women's best interests, comparing the wife to the
prostitute since both were dependent upon pleasing men for their livelihood.

Both rejected the idea that all women were suited for homemaking.[2] In 1931, the historian Mary Beard criticized her male colleagues for eliminating women from history. She pointed out that H. G. Wells's popular *Outline of History*, the *Encyclopaedia Brittanica*, and the *Biographical Dictionary of American Men of Science* had all failed to mention women. "According to [H. G.] Wells," she wrote, "man even raised the curtain on culture as the farmer, cook and artisan."[3] Parsons, La Follette, and Beard were among the few remaining voices of revolt.

Closing Feminism's Window

AFTER THE NINETEENTH AMENDMENT granted women the franchise in 1920, the early feminist movement lost impetus, although there was a campaign led by Alice Paul of the National Woman's Party to add an Equal Rights Amendment to the Constitution. Immediately after the war, the outspoken critic of the home Charlotte Perkins Gilman still lectured in favor of changing the home and woman's role, but within a few years her advertisements stated that she disliked to be called a feminist because her interest was in humanity. Her passionate appeals to change women's status gave way to other interests after 1923, and in a symposium for *Current History* in 1927, she took a relatively positive view of women's achievements since they had won the vote.[4]

Many of the Progressive era's revolutionary feminists expressed disillusionment in the twenties. A contributor to the *Ladies' Home Journal* scoffed at her own "radical" college days when she foresaw complete economic independence. After marriage, she found that sharing expenses with a better-paid husband left her with little spending money, while he spent his larger surplus on clothes and entertainment for himself. She now envied her conventional friends who lived in nice houses, drove fine automobiles, and were "spoiled" by their husbands.[5] Another disillusioned feminist writing in 1929 contrasted her own generation of feminists with those earlier women who chose career over marriage: "We were determined to have both," she wrote. But they had advocated a marriage of equals, following Charlotte Perkins Gilman's "blueprint," and now many had found that complete honesty between partners could be painful while promises to share housekeeping had proven false. The world was still arranged "primarily for man's technic and convenience," she lamented, and she had begun to question her feminist belief that gender differences were merely cultural.[6]

Most women did not vote in the 1920 election, and only one of the seven women candidates won a Congressional seat that year.[7] A woman commentator claimed that women reformers did not want "feminism in politics," or status as a "separate class." Many of those who had worked for suffrage retreated from the movement to pursue their own careers.[8] There was wide division among those still working for women's political rights. Some were champions of the Equal Rights Amendment and some wanted to enact a broad program of reforms. Peace, prohibition, and protective legislation for women workers were other issues over which women were badly split.[9] While some social reforms were adopted during the decade—the Sheppard-Towner Act, which provided health education for mothers and infants, and the Married Women's Independent Citizenship Act were examples—there were also failures such as the defeat of the proposed child labor amendment. The failures were due in part to a growing conservatism in the United States. A female state representative in Connecticut remonstrated, "Women should be more concerned over the breaking down of homes than over the breaking down of the jury system."[10] This was but the tip of a reactionary iceberg.

A Boston cardinal told his followers that "sinister feminism" would have "disastrous results for humanity." Another Catholic official wrote that it was "quite impossible for a woman to engage successfully in business and politics and at the same time create a happy home." Union pressure had forced women to leave their wartime jobs as streetcar conductors. By 1931, Mary Beard believed that women had become scapegoats, and by then it was fascism, she warned, that held that women should return to kitchen, children, and church.[11]

Perhaps the most frightening aspect of the reaction to feminism during the twenties was the growing conviction among right-wing patriots that many women's organizations were the agents of Communism. Early in the decade the Massachusetts Civics Alliance sent a protest to President Harding that called the Sheppard-Towner Act the "beginning of Communism in Medicine." When the head of the War Department denounced the Women's International League for Peace and Freedom as a threat to the social order, Brigadier General Amos Fries of the Army's Chemical Warfare Service issued the infamous Spider-Web Chart, which showed linkages among fifteen women's organizations and labeled them "Part of International Socialism" in 1922. The American Home Economics Association, the General Federation of Women's Clubs, the League of Women Voters, the National Consumers' League, the American Association of University Women, the National Federation of Business and Professional Women, and the National Council of Jewish Women were among the accused. In 1924, the adjutant general of the National Military Order of the World War told the New York Women's Republican Club that these organizations were "a menace to the present Government by reason of their subversive teaching or their affiliation with radical groups."[12] By mid-decade, several conservative women's groups, the Daughters of the American Revolution and the American Legion Auxiliary among them, had joined the military establishment's attack on women's organizations that participated in social reform or peace efforts. Carrie Chapman Catt, who had successfully organized the final push for woman suffrage, was blacklisted by the Daughters of the American Revolution in 1925 for attempting to bring women's groups together for a peace conference.[13]

But women were entering the workforce in ever greater numbers throughout the decade, and debate continued over whether women could work for pay and at the same time maintain a home. In 1927 the American Association of University Women undertook a study of "the effects on the home of . . . work of women and consequent fear for family life." Christine Frederick, reflecting her own situation while maintaining her opposition to careers for women, wrote that a marriage in which the wife continued to work outside the home was "fraught with psychological dangers . . . because of the lessening of man's traditional sense of economic responsibility." The "two-earner standard," she wrote, was not "a generally feasible solution." In one instance she was roundly criticized for maintaining that wives should not work; a critic responded that he hoped Mrs. Frederick was not married "lest her husband raise hell" when she received "her check for the article" in which she had made the argument.[14] Christine took part in the conservative movement to encourage married women to stay at home. So did most of the magazines for which she wrote.

One writer criticized women's magazines for doing nothing "to adapt women to a changing world." "[M]illions of American women, although the vote is won," wrote another critic, "are still inside the four walls of their houses. . . . And 'their' magazines continue to tell them in honeyed words to stay there." Advertisers now recognized an enormous market in the American homemaker, and their business determined the magazines' policies. Most women were content to stay home; an opinion poll conducted at a Young Women's Christian Association (YWCA) family conference in 1925 revealed that 70 percent of the participants believed that women were happiest and best fulfilled through home, husband, and children.[15]

Christine Frederick was among those who continued to use nineteenth-century ideology to keep women at home. Many young unmarried women read parents' magazines, she contended, because they were unconsciously "dreaming of a home and children." In 1927 she announced, "There is a universal, international housewife's face!" Women the world over were more "natural" when involved in their home, she said. "The moment women step out of their innate home-loving character and become this, that, or the other pretentious, artificial type, they seem to don masks."[16] Women had been made to hate their kitchens by presuffrage, feminist literature such as Alice Duer's *Come Out of the Kitchen*, Christine claimed. But "Mrs. Consumer" of the 1920s "went *into* the kitchen, not out of it." She loved managing her home.[17]

Back to the Home

MEANWHILE, THE HOME had become a symbol of American prosperity and superiority. In 1922, Herbert Hoover had served as president of "Better Homes in America, Inc.," a cooperative effort between government and private interests to urge home ownership and home improvement as a way to build American character. Throughout the decade, real estate associations promoted "Own Your Home" and "Build Your Home" campaigns. In 1928, Hoover used the home as a campaign issue, with the slogan "Hoover, Home and Happiness," and as president, he launched his 1931 Conference on Home Building and Home Ownership with a speech confirming the goal of universal home ownership: "I am confident that the sentiment for home ownership is so embedded in the American heart that the millions of people who dwell in tenements, apartments, and rented rows of solid brick have the aspiration for wider opportunity in ownership of their own homes. To possess one's own home is the hope and ambition of almost every individual in our country, whether he lives in hotel, apartment, or tenement."[18]

For advertisers, the field of home economics served as something of a bridge between the nineteenth-century and twentieth-century views of women. By the mid-1920s, home economics curricula included consumption, family budgets, standards of living, economics of housekeeping, and labor-saving devices, all topics that would prepare women for professional opportunities in business while training them to teach others how to operate a home.[19] Even academically elite women's colleges were beginning to respond to the conservative shift of the twenties by incorporating home economics. Vassar, which had opened in 1865 with the intention of offering courses identical to those of men's colleges, offered "euthenics," or home economics, for the first time in 1923.[20]

Home economists usually promoted their discipline as a means to educate homemakers, teachers of home economics, and professional women in related fields. But by mid-decade, there was a growing demand for women trained in "the economics of consumption" and schooled in the art of writing advertising copy. Home economists went to work for appliance manufacturers and utilities companies.[21] So many home economists were entering business that the American Home Economics Association established a special arm, the Home Economics in Business section, and by 1925 it listed ninety-one members. Like Christine Frederick, many home economists who worked for businesses believed that the interests of consumers and manufacturers were the same. Though some were ambivalent about their relationship with business, most saw themselves as mediators and educators helping American business train the housewife to better use the technological advances of the twentieth century. Still, there was no escaping the connection between the business home economists and advertisers. In 1925, representatives from the Home Economics Association of Greater New York told the city's female advertisers that 18 percent of their members were connected with business.[22]

The Emergence of Sex Appeal

WOMEN WERE ENCOURAGED to seek marriage and home instead of careers not only by the builders of homes and the manufacturers of home appliances, but also by the advertisers who promoted an ideal of youth and beauty during the 1920s. The relaxing of Victorian sexual restraints meant that young women were far more interested in and informed about sex; participants in the YWCA's 1925 family conference exhibited a great deal of curiosity and eagerness to learn about the subject. This trend encouraged women to find fulfillment through male approval. "It does not matter how clever or independent you may be," cautioned a perfume advertisement, "if you fail to influence the men you meet . . . you are not fulfilling your fundamental duty as a woman." The behaviorist-turned-advertiser John B. Watson told women that the business world would "rob" them of their "feminine qualities." If a woman became self-sufficient, he warned, she would not be able to "yield to love," and no man would want to "possess her permanently."[23]

The feminist Alice Parsons criticized the work of the psychologist Havelock Ellis because she believed that by urging women to cultivate satisfactory sex lives he had relegated their newly found independence to secondary importance. Sexual freedom was accompanied by the breaching of other Victorian norms. Some women, particularly college students, now smoked cigarettes, drank alcohol, went dancing, and engaged in petting. Such freedom, however, was in part the freedom to appeal to men more blatantly, not the freedom to pursue independence.[24]

Manufacturers of cosmetics and clothing exploited the new sexual freedom and promoted youthful standards of beauty to sell their products. "To strengthen woman's awareness of sex in relation to herself, to other women, and to man, the advertiser of toiletries relies on both the picture and the printed word," wrote the author of an advertising manual in 1928. Even a shoe company might appeal to this standard: "'Thousands of women have been made to look much older than they are because of the shoes they wear.'" American girls, wrote a commentator in the early twenties, were now "conforming to our new ideals of beauty." They trained "down to a type" by staying slim, plucked their eyebrows, blackened their eyelids, and rouged their cheeks and lips. The historian Mary Beard noted that the "creators and distributors of women's wear, cosmetics, and perfumes" had determined the "tastes and modes of females."[25]

Reflecting the Decade's Contradictions

CHRISTINE FREDERICK was not among the right-wing accusers who tried to portray feminism as a national threat, but she recognized and affirmed the reactionary mood that resisted women's involvement in the public sphere:

> It seems that many "feminists" of today are somewhat disillusioned over working. There is something profound to be said of the relative effects on man of the creative . . . types of women. It is a philosophical problem as to whether . . . we wish a civilization in which women work and create, or one in which women

merely consume. In my own opinion this depends on how well women solve their work and personal problems; how well they are able to maintain the male sex tension by working. If we fail in this, we may move toward the more savage standard where only women work.[26]

This confused observation illustrates Christine's own conflict over the "woman question."

It is small wonder that Christine developed a conflicted view of her own sex while she was building her reputation among male advertisers as an expert on female consumers. Rejecting feminist thought, she subscribed to the belief that men and women were not equal. Although she sometimes wrote as if she believed that women as a whole were practical, reasonable, and competent, much of her rhetoric reflected disdain for women, portraying them as shallow and petty. Speaking to a group of men about women's view of the "Pretty Girl" in advertising, Christine said, "Like the cats we are, we say to ourselves that if this impossible French doll were to tuck up her clothes and actually use the device upon which she is leering she would lose her frozen smile."[27]

Christine sometimes implied that women were unable to understand complexity. "[T]he average woman," she told the New York advertisers in 1920, "does not understand machinery any more than she understands her husband or her watch." In her 1922 laundry booklet, she advised, "[L]et your husband read over this chapter with you, because men are more familiar with the technical construction of machinery."[28] She sometimes portrayed women as childish in the extreme. In an article about the use of color in advertising, she wrote that "women jump at a colored article the way a child grabs at pink ice cream."[29] Or she might impugn their mental stability as she did in 1931 when she wrote that Mrs. Consumer was in "a neurotic state" over electricity.[30] Yet Christine could also boast that the war "showed that woman could run machinery as well as man." In 1925, she asserted that "there is no sex difference in the use of tools and machinery."[31]

In a series for the *World* in 1922, Christine castigated "Housewives Who Fail." One article, "The 'Scourer,'" blamed small-town women who nag and make "the entire family . . . miserable" by insisting on perfection in housekeeping for "man's frequent relinquishment of the home living room in favor of his club or the pool parlor." The "slacker," who refused to do her own mending, make her own potato salad, or sew any of her children's clothes, did not please her husband either. "It is . . . not surprising that one out of every twelve marriages ends in divorce," Christine wrote, "when we know that at least one out of every twelve women is a 'slacker housewife.'" Apparently husbands bore no responsibility for failures in marriage.[32]

Christine remained a strong advocate for maintaining the domestic sphere during the twenties, even when pretending to sympathize with career women. Early in the decade, she told her *American Weekly* readers in an article titled "Keeping Men Fit" that women needed to make things at home "all O.K." for their husbands. Wives' own "petty stuff should be corked up tight just as hubby opens the door," she warned. Meals should be based on "hubby's" work: more starch and fat should be served to active breadwinners, for example. But in the same article she admitted advising a convention of salesmen to marry women who had been "working or business women" for a time, but only because they would have more sympathy for their husbands' career pressures.[33]

In a 1922 response to the Swedish home economist Ellen Key's contention that women could not be good homemakers and have careers too, Christine stated that women could indeed do both, but only if they could make enough money to pay competent employees to replace them. The competent help, in Christine's view, would include "a servant, a nursemaid, a business manager and an evangelist!" Most, she went on, could not hire replacements, for even college graduates made only twelve to fifteen dollars per week. Women's duty, she concluded, was to manage the home, and if she could not pay several assistants out of her own salary, she should do the job herself.[34]

Christine encouraged young college women to find satisfaction in homemaking. Her protagonist in a 1919 article, a graduate who was about to marry, debated with an older woman who questioned her wisdom in wasting four years on a degree. Homemaking was a "real vocation," the young woman exclaimed. And college courses were excellent training for it because household tasks, after all, were just like trigonometry problems. While in college she had learned to concentrate amidst noise and to keep her things in order, important skills for the housekeeper. Her science courses had given her the right attitude of mind, she said. She would "investigate" and keep notes on her findings. She had learned to be so organized that she would have time for other activities, too. And to the charge that homemaking was drudgery, she claimed that efficiency and the status housewives had gained during the war gave it "standing."[35]

"Married or unmarried, old-fashioned or new-fangled, domestic or followers of a career," wrote Christine in 1927, "it is all one—women do not truly express the best that is in them unless they are in a home setting." Christine understood that most middle-class American women were content to remain within the domestic sphere. She once wrote that only 15 percent of American women were "truly interested in careers" outside the home.[36] Good housewives, according to Christine, supported their husbands, who were doing *their* work in the public sphere. "[I]f nine-tenths of women are going to make wifehood their career, as they are," she wrote in 1928, "we have got to develop in America a wifehood which will count in man's life more than a 'neck to hang pearls on.'"[37]

Twice during the decade, Christine published pieces blaming women for men's business failures. Men, she wrote, need to put their ideas across. Wives' duty was to support this masculine urge, but "too few wives" were willing to share "inspired penury" while their husbands rose in the world. Many women, in fact, were "a problem as wives." Christine specifically rejected equality feminism when she wrote that women "with tortoise-shell glasses" who called for change in men's attitudes were preaching "twaddle." Instead of dispensing "prattle about Ibsen and Browning," she advised, women should be acquiring an understanding of their husbands' careers.[38]

Citing novels by Sherwood Anderson, Scott Fitzgerald, and Theodore Dreiser as evidence that the "companionate marriage" was a sham, Christine portrayed men as victims of feminism. They were expected to earn the family's living and at the same time participate in their wives' "garden of leisurely interests." She warned that, instead, the "American wife had better follow [her husband's] soul into man's work, or realize quite clearly that their souls" were "apart." "American wifehood" should "hang its head" when reminded that great men like Mark Twain and Abraham Lincoln were held back by their wives. Christine reached a misogynistic nadir when she recounted the story of a young wife who refused to relocate when her husband wanted to move west. Remaining where he was to please her, the young man failed to prosper and the wife died of overwork, "a true but not a palatable poetic justice," Christine concluded.[39]

Christine Frederick wanted women to remain in the home, but she suggested that complete separation of spheres was unfair to men. Women should use their talents and education to help their husbands advance, become their husbands' "aide-de-camp[s]."[40] This was Christine's new solution to twentieth-century woman's dilemma: women should forgo careers for themselves in favor of helping their husbands fully realize their potential. In this way, women could seem to step out of the nineteenth-century domestic sphere, but they would enter the public sphere only as their husbands' helpers. She encouraged women to understand the business world, but not to join it independent of men. She had written at the beginning of the decade that "the average man's ideal" was a woman "who openly and avowedly loves housekeeping." Wives were still expected to be "responsible for the operation and management of" the home.[41] But now Christine offered a taste of the public sphere through woman's duty to her husband's career. Her harsh judgment of women who did not support their husbands was surely a manifestation of Christine's own conflict. She had, indeed, taken an interest in J. George's work, but she had appropriated it for a career that was very much her own.

Pragmatist that she was, Christine acknowledged the large numbers of women who worked outside the home when it suited her purpose. Contradicting her own advice, she once told a reporter, "Any woman of intelligence can have both babies and a career." On another occasion she qualified the assertion: "if she only simplifies her housekeeping." Paradoxically, she had no intention of allowing her own daughters to grow up unprepared to earn a living: "I am the last person who shall say that every woman should run a home. If any one of my three daughters wishes to be a plumber or a lawyer or a woman doctor, she may do so."[42] In 1922, she wrote a letter to the editor of the *New York Times* praising a piece on twelve great American women because, she wrote, it illustrated how many "lines of work" women can do and "the great progress of women as a group within the last half century." She wished to add home economist Mary Harland's name to the list, however, because Harland had worked to improve the home.[43]

Christine recognized the trend toward smaller families and "the decline of complete concentration of feminine energies on the home." She reminded advertisers in 1929 that many women who worked for pay had changed their eating habits and wanted packaged food.[44] "Where formerly a woman's place was settled upon as being in the home, now it is more and more the case that women are choosing a business career," she wrote.[45] Apparently Christine did not wish to alienate feminist career women, no matter how harsh her rhetoric at times. Sometimes she claimed to be one of them. "Feminist that I may be," she said in 1938, "I have no desire to throw added fuel to the flames. But . . . I believe it is necessary to place women on the boards of large corporations." This proclamation, however, did not signal an attempt to raise women's status in the business world, although that would certainly have resulted from her suggestion. Christine's purpose was to help boards of directors understand the woman consumer.[46]

Christine had always advocated more leisure time for women. Creating leisure had been one of the main purposes of making housekeeping efficient. The war, she wrote at the beginning of the decade, had shown women that they could afford to spend a few hours away from their homes. Now they could use that time for educational and spiritual growth. She suggested several Progressive reforms such as schools, sanitation, peace, and even "standardizing divorce laws" in 1919. Ten years later, she acknowledged that many women spent time on charity, politics, child welfare, or women's clubs.[47] Still, she did not suggest gainful employment.

Christine did not believe that women who chose to work for pay had a real need to do so: "Everybody knows that the great bulk of women in factory and office are there to add to their dress allowance, get away a little from home discipline, and have more opportunity to meet beaux!" Yet the Women's Bureau refuted the "pin money" theory when, after the first World War, women were forced to leave their wartime jobs: "Back to the home was a slogan all too easily and indiscriminately flung at the wage-earning woman by those who had little conception of the causes which forced her into wage-earning pursuits." A feminist contemporary of Christine wrote that "the woman in industry" was "not merely working for pin-money, as thoughtless people assume[d]," but that she was either supporting herself or dependents or helping the family make ends meet. By 1930, 30 percent of the women in the labor force were married, and Women's Bureau investigations suggested that most worked because they had to.[48] Christine's attitude on this issue was only one indication that, despite the occasional reference to her own independence, she was not in sympathy with feminist thinking that sought equal opportunity for women in the workplace.[49]

During the twenties, Christine Frederick also began to pander to those who promoted the notion that most women's dearest wish was to attract men. She wrote in 1929, "As a 'feminist' I hate to say it, but the bare truth is that woman's chief business in life still appears to be to charm and hold a man, and . . . women rely heavily upon cosmetics for success." Despite her harsh criticism of "pretty girl" advertising, Christine agreed that to "charm and hold a man," women needed the help of beautifying preparations. Since a woman held her place "in man's affections" by her "physical charms," she would spend great sums on creams, powders, perfumes, and rouges as she grew older, Christine told advertisers. "[O]ne of the marked characteristics of Mrs. Consumer," she wrote, was that she insisted "on being somewhat girlish even until past 35."[50] The advertising consultant Helen Woodward advised cosmetic manufacturers, "Remember that what we are selling . . . is youth." John B. Watson reinforced fears of aging, too. "A woman is at her best between 19 and 28," he wrote. "After that her wrinkles begin."[51] Christine's accommodation to the cosmetics industry conflicted with her contention that women objected to sexually attractive female images in advertising. Indeed, she seemed to agree that they wanted to emulate the "pretty girl." Reframing women's role to suit twentieth-century progress while continuing to espouse the doctrine of two spheres, Christine Frederick was something of a standard-bearer for the contradictory twenties.

At graduation from Northwestern in 1906, Christine was coiffed in the
Gibson Girl mode. *Schlesinger Library, Radcliffe Institute, Harvard University.*

Christine applies scientific management principles to dishwashing in her own kitchen. *Schlesinger Library, Radcliffe Institute, Harvard University.*

Applecroft after remodeling in 1912. *Schlesinger Library, Radcliffe Institute, Harvard University.*

Christine tests the fireless cooker for which she wrote an advertising booklet in 1915.
Schlesinger Library, Radcliffe Institute, Harvard University.

Christine oils the home electric generator the Fredericks installed to operate the labor-saving devices she tested. *Schlesinger Library, Radcliffe Institute, Harvard University.*

Cleaning in the company of a radio. *Schlesinger Library, Radcliffe Institute, Harvard University.*

ABOVE: Christine's Applecroft Experiment Station served as a test kitchen for the time and motion studies inspired by scientific management. *Schlesinger Library, Radcliffe Institute, Harvard University.*

LEFT: Christine at the podium in Germany in her black lace dress. *Schlesinger Library, Radcliffe Institute, Harvard University.*

J. George and David amuse themselves with the radio set while camping. *Schlesinger Library, Radcliffe Institute, Harvard University.*

Christine (seated) at the 1927 meeting in France. Paulette Bernège is on the right. *Schlesinger Library, Radcliffe Institute, Harvard University.*

Christine (center) poses with Benito Mussolini (third from right) while attending the Rome Home Economics Congress, 1927. *Schlesinger Library, Radcliffe Institute, Harvard University.*

Christine dictating to her secretary in the home office over the garage at Applecroft.
Schlesinger Library, Radcliffe Institute, Harvard University.

Around 1930, Christine modernized the Applecroft kitchen with Monel metal in the "streamline" fashion of the day. *Schlesinger Library, Radcliffe Institute, Harvard University.*

In 1962, the Advertising Women of New York honored Christine as their cofounder at their golden anniversary celebration. She shared celebrity at the head table with the television journalist Mike Wallace (standing). *Schlesinger Library, Radcliffe Institute, Harvard University.*

10 · Becoming Mrs. Consumer

[T]he American woman has accomplished something which no other
women [sic] in any other civilization appears to have done. She has struck up
a closer entente cordial and co-partnership with industry and trade (even if it is
so largely unconscious), than has ever before been known in the history
of trading. . . . [S]he has developed a "consumer acceptance" spirit,—
a readiness to follow where she is led, that has had an immense bearing
upon American industrial prosperity and standards of living.
CHRISTINE FREDERICK, *Selling Mrs. Consumer*, 1929

CHRISTINE FREDERICK'S OPTIMISTIC VIEW of business and her deep involvement in advertising, selling, and consumerism were a perfect reflection of
the nation's mood in the 1920s. Historians would later echo Christine's husband's label for the decade's remarkable increase in production: he called it
the "new industrial 'revolution.'"[1] Production almost doubled; by mid-decade,
Henry Ford could produce a car every ten seconds.

A Culture of Abundance

THE NATION was becoming a culture of abundance thanks to this mighty production force and the technological ability to distribute its goods. The organizational model that J. George praised in his books and articles created the need
for the managers, the sales people, and the engineers for whom he wrote.[2] The
business consolidation that he advocated was a *fait accompli*. Eight thousand
businesses disappeared through consolidation between 1919 and 1930. Herbert
Hoover, then secretary of commerce and a fierce defender of individual initiative, called for the coordination of transportation systems to facilitate distribution.[3] Christine found a way to relate these trends to the homemaker.

The 1920s was perhaps the most satisfying period of Christine Frederick's
career. In 1924, she spent a year developing an article for the scholarly journal *Annals of the American Academy of Political and Social Science* that amounted
to a position paper for the rest of her career as an advocate of consumption.[4]

"New Wealth, New Standards of Living and Changed Family Budgets" seemed to signal a seriousness of purpose in her work. This piece analyzed economic trends and explained her theory that future prosperity depended upon increased consumption. "The America of 1913 has been altered astonishingly," she wrote. Using statistics gathered from a variety of government reports and contemporary business journals, she reviewed the immense growth of the American economy. Although prices had risen, she did not believe that this should cause alarm, for wages had "outdistanced all price increases." Christine believed that the future held "*a vast broadening of the level of comfortable family budgets*" (Frederick's italics).[5] She wrote that it was "the soundest of national welfare policies that the standards of living be high among all classes, so that our increased manufacturing capacity may be used, and so that good wages be paid for competent productive labor."[6] Advertising to increase sales brought even greater prosperity, she argued, for when "artificial stimulations to consumption" were used, the American diet and standard of living improved. "Always the trend is toward something better." Poor families were now becoming "'regular American families'—capable of purchasing modern sanitary articles, a more varied and healthful diet, more and better clothes, and providing more schooling for their children."[7]

The Fredericks rarely mentioned the darker side of the business boom. Although Christine had paid lip service to the concerns of her contemporaries in the consumer leagues of the Progressive era who tried to improve workers' lives, her sympathies now lay with producers.[8] In fact, textile and garment industries still exploited labor through the subcontracting system, a proposed amendment to prohibit child labor was defeated in 1925, over 21 percent of the nation's families received incomes of less than one thousand dollars per year, and many suffered from substandard living and working conditions during the prosperous twenties.[9] But the Fredericks chose to focus on the higher standard of living enjoyed by most Americans, and they agreed that workers who were paid well enough to consume more were happy Americans.

By 1929, twenty-six million automobiles were on the road, Americans spent $852 million on radios, seventeen billion kilowatt-hours of electricity coursed through homes and businesses, and more and more American families were buying houses, furnishing them with electrical appliances, eating varied diets, and shopping at chain stores.[10]

Many people assumed that government should create a favorable environment for business prosperity. The *New York Times* urged that the government help the "disorganized selling and advertising machine" by telling the public to buy. Under President Calvin Coolidge, who succeeded to office upon Warren Harding's death in 1923, the federal government favored business even more than it had before. There were tax cuts for high-income earners and corporations, and conservative appointments to the Supreme Court led to antiunion decisions. When Herbert Hoover was elected president in 1928, the nation voted its satisfaction with the perceived prosperity that the favorable business climate of Republican administrations had brought.[11]

This was the climate that fostered the advertising boom of the twenties. "Without advertising," the *New York Times* warned, "large scale production is absolutely impossible and large scale production is the sine qua non of low prices."[12]

Advertising Comes of Age

WHEN THE FREDERICKS FOUNDED the women's advertising league in 1912, modern advertising was in its infancy. During the 1920s, it experienced phenomenal growth and dramatic change. In 1919 it was a $1,409 million industry; that figure had grown to $2,987 million by 1929. Magazines took in $200 million in advertising revenue that year, three times as much as they had earned in 1918. Makers of the antiseptic mouthwash Listerine increased their advertising spending from $100,000 in 1922 to $5,000,000 in 1929. Along with movies, comic strips, telephones, and automobiles, advertising became one of the decade's "new cultural forms."[13]

In the twenties, advertisers shifted from their earlier emphasis on "reason why" copy to focusing on personal, emotional appeals that sold the benefits of the product rather than the product itself. A New York advertising agency president George L. Dyer, who had been in the field for years, counseled advertisers to avoid emotional appeals that told "how the heroine wins a husband by the grace of her advertised footwear," whereas his younger competitor Bruce Barton touted the effectiveness of human-interest stories in advertising. Barton, argues Lears, was one of the "therapeutic ideologues" in the world of advertising and consumerism.[14]

The question of ethics in advertising gained urgency during the decade. Christine's relationship with manufacturers had not resulted in legal censure, but the president of the National Housewives' League faced legal charges when she promised an endorsement in return for a manufacturer's business in 1918.[15] A movement to promote truth in advertising was heralded by the opening speaker at the 1920 Associated Advertising Clubs of the World conference who spoke to thousands of advertisers about the group's National Vigilance Committee. J. George had helped establish the New York club's vigilance committee a few years earlier. The vigilance groups recognized the "bait and switch" deception—advertising one product at a low price and then substituting a product of lower quality—as a problem, and there was a significant campaign to stop it.[16] Some advertisers, like the writer Sherwood Anderson, who left the business, worried about "a dreadful decay of taste" in advertisements.[17]

Yet advertisers sometimes seemed to contradict these emerging standards. In 1925, J. George did not shrink from recommending strategies meant to fool the public, and he portrayed the relationship between advertiser and consumer as a military conflict. He wrote of "flank movement[s]," "frontal attack[s]," "feint moves," "wedge action[s]," and "time annihilation strategy."[18] Although they believed they were curtailing deception, advertisers honed persuasion to a fine art during the twenties, using new knowledge provided by psychologists.

When John B. Watson, the behaviorist, was forced to leave his post at Johns Hopkins University for "sexual misbehavior" in 1920, he turned to advertising and went to work for J. Walter Thompson, eventually becoming the firm's vice president. Watson showed advertisers how to mask their messages in ostensibly educational material.[19]

Walter Dill Scott and Harry Hollingworth had understood the role that psychology would play in advertising long before Watson entered the field, but it was the advertisers of the 1920s who made full use of it. One historian of advertising has written that the advertisers of the decade "had come to recognize a public demand for broad guidance—not just about product attributes, but about taste, social correctness, and psychological satisfactions." Advertisers came to see themselves as the experts who could provide that guidance. "People bought the car because they trusted the manufacturers," wrote one advertising executive in 1925. "And they trusted the manufacturers because of the suggestive copy in the advertising."[20]

Advertising became more and more important as the advance guard for business.[21] J. George Frederick had begun the decade by writing a book titled *The Great Game of Business*, an almost giddy celebration of business as "the greatest game left to man to play," a form of contest that would peacefully re-place war, a doctrine that would save the world. Bruce Barton believed that bus-iness was "the operation of Divine Purpose" and that "Jesus was . . . the great-est of all advertisers." Indeed, churches appropriated advertising techniques. The Associated Advertising Clubs of the World convention held a "Church Division" session in 1920, and one church told of raising $113 million through advertising.[22]

Christine's view of the relationship between business and the consumer de-veloped in tandem with her husband's. J. George Frederick was a visionary who wrote prolifically on business topics. His 1926 book on industrial consolidation sounded many of the themes Christine took up in her own work: he argued that increased consumption would alleviate overproduction and that advertising, refined by market research, would promote consumption.[23]

J. George's market research and publishing firm, the Business Bourse (relo-cated in the early twenties to 80 West 40th Street in the Beaux Arts Building overlooking Bryant Park), conducted industry investigations and market sur-veys and sold prepared reports and analyses. The vice president of the company reported to the Bureau of Vocational Information that the Business Bourse em-ployed a number of "statistical workers" in 1921.[24] He was suggesting that such work might be appropriate for women who wished to enter the field of adver-tising. The industry provided well-paid work for the few who were admitted into the field. Women copywriters could make one hundred dollars per week, and those at the top such as Dorothy Dignam could earn an annual salary of seventy-eight hundred dollars by the end of the decade. Still, the advertising field remained largely male through the 1920s; major agencies employed ten men to every woman, and the women were not in top executive positions; they were hired to help sell products to others of their sex.[25]

Marketing Consumption

FOR CHRISTINE FREDERICK, educating women in the art of buying became an even more compelling imperative than teaching them to be efficient; in-deed, she saw consumption as the only path to efficiency. After World War I, Christine told American women that the American home was "more badly in need of reconstruction than anything else." Appealing to those who feared for the home's survival, she spoke of saving the "separate family unit" by putting into every home "improved mechanical labor savers."[26] In 1929, she told her readers that she was "unusually and deeply interested in selling household equipment to Mrs. Consumer."[27] Equally important was teaching advertisers how to persuade women to purchase that equipment.

Christine now invited home economists and their students to come view the products that she tested at Applecroft. In 1921, for example, when she requested a refrigerator of a certain size and color from the McCray Refrigerator Company, she assured McCray's sales manager that five hundred women, including classes of domestic science students from Columbia's Teachers College, visited the kitchen and laundry room of her experiment station every year. She promised to distribute literature and write articles about the refrigerator while it was in use at her home. She asked the H. J. Smith Tool Company to send her a dish drainer and washer and promised publicity in two hundred newspapers. In another request she agreed to list a trial appliance in her *Shrine Magazine* "Tested Devices" column.[28] Her solicitations did not mention fees for these services. Presumably, she negotiated remuneration in person. In 1929 she expressed disgust with manufacturers that were surprised to learn from her that new products should be thoroughly tested and that she charged a fee for such tests.[29]

After 1920, the Applecroft brochures offered new services such as kitchen installation and photography. Christine's lectures were now divided into two categories: those offered to women's clubs and those appropriate for business groups, but by the end of the decade most of her services were offered not to housewives but to businesses. In an effort to compete with trained home economists who were, by then, routinely hired by large companies to train homemakers in the use of their new products, Christine advertised that she could develop home service departments for manufacturers.[30] A 1922 campaign that she developed to encourage the use of gas ranges for the People's Gas, Light and Coke Company in Chicago—a campaign that led to the establishment of a home service department—serves as an example.

People's Gas executives asked Christine to help them "bring Chicago housewives back to more home cooking," because, in their view, cafeterias and restaurants were keeping women away from their kitchens. "Up to that time," Christine wrote, "educational work by utilities had been largely perfunctory. I started and laid out the extensive plans on which this most successful home service is now run." She hired Anna I. Peterson, who, she believed, "had the 'market basket' point of view" necessary to conduct the campaign. Peterson, presumably with Christine's guidance, created a display kitchen and laundry for the company. The team printed leaflets, inserted recipes in gas bills, and designed an advertising campaign for Chicago newspapers. Tapping new technologies, they broadcast a weekly radio show, *Mrs. Peterson's "Radio Teas,"* and offered free telephone consultations. The campaign moved out into the neighborhoods with a demonstration kitchen on wheels staffed with assistance from the tearoom manager at Marshall Field's. Christine claimed that by 1928, well over two hundred thousand women attended the company's free lectures each year, and thousands of its canning and recipe booklets were in circulation. By 1929, the home service staff at People's Gas had grown to eighteen and the radio "teas" were broadcast daily.[31]

In the mid-1920s, Applecroft became the home testing station for *Shrine Magazine* and *Farm and Home Magazine*. Billed as a wife and mother whose laboratory was a warm home, Christine helped families find "the most desirable goods at the most favorable prices."[32] She had been contributing regularly to trade journals such as the *Hardware Dealers' Magazine*, *Hardware Age*, and *Wireless Age* for some time.[33] In 1923, she scolded hardware retailers for failing to show home appliances to farmers' wives. Posing as one herself, she wrote that rural women were sophisticated buyers who now wore stylish clothes and French perfume. They wanted fireless cookers and washing machines in their homes. In 1926, Christine suggested a "Begin Housekeeping All Over Again" campaign to induce women to buy new home products and modernize their homes.[34] Christine had become an "apostle of modernity," as the historian Roland Marchand has called the advertisers of the 1920s, one of those who brought new technologies, new styles, and modern conveniences to all Americans, urban dweller and farmer alike, promoting the idea that consumption was a democratic ideal.[35]

The historian T. J. Jackson Lears has suggested that the rise of consumption during this period was an aspect of the "therapeutic ethos" that developed in America's ruling middle class, a class "unsettled by the changes it was helping to promote." Others argue that consumption enabled female homemakers to participate fully in commercial relations. The Marxist critique of early-twentieth-century consumption holds that capitalism had promoted "false consciousness" through consumer goods.[36] At one level, Christine Frederick's enthusiastic endorsement of home consumption might be understood to conform to Lears's therapeutic model, for she saw the use of labor-saving devices (and later, the acquisition of as many consumer goods as one could afford) as a cure for many ills: the drudgery of housework, the threat to the single-family home, and the problem of overproduction, to name a few.

Acting As Broker

DURING THE TWENTIES Christine cultivated a wider audience among advertisers, promising to help them sell to Mrs. Consumer. In 1920, as "the first woman to address a general session" at the annual convention of the Associated Advertising Clubs of the World, she said that a woman's viewpoint was necessary to create advertising for home products. She also suggested that she could help advertisers "create good-will for advertising" among women.[37] In a similar speech that year, she warned that unless women understood why advertising was important to them, they were likely to blame advertisers for cost of living increases.[38]

Christine assured male advertisers that she knew women well, telling the New York Men's Advertising Club, "During the past five years I have lectured in thirty states among every type of woman's club and consumer league." She used statistics to illustrate the volume of merchandise purchased by women. She claimed to have helped the Columbia professor Harry Hollingworth compile figures that she used, unchanged, for many years. "'Even 34 per cent of the distinguished advertising fraternity I see before me is wearing clothes chosen and bought for them by women,'" she told the advertising clubs.[39] The club reported in its newsletter that she had provided "the soundest kind of practical advertising philosophy that has been heard by the members in many a day."[40]

A second appearance before the Associated Advertising Clubs of the World in 1921 earned her an invitation to Ohio. There, she spoke before the Advertisers' Club of Cincinnati, the *Ohio State Journal* Trade Show, and a joint meeting of the Women's Advertising Club of Toledo and the Toledo Woman's Club. A promotional piece billed her as an "economist" who made "brilliant, practical and illuminating talks on retail salesmanship, advertising and kindred topics, before business organizations the country over." Building on Christine's reputation as a broker between advertisers and women, the article promised that she could teach "men in business how to advertise 'in the feminine gender,' how to make their advertising . . . appeal to the average feminine mind, in short, how to sell to the American woman." She told the Toledo women, on the other side, that "advertising is more powerful than the vote." Women could acquire better homes and clothes by expressing "a consumer demand." Legislation, she said, would not do as much for the American woman as cooperation between consumer and advertiser. Every woman "'should have as many of the labor-saving devices as she can possibly secure.'"[41]

It was during this period that a large market for cosmetics was developed, but Christine did not believe that most women identified with glamour. Through-out the decade, she fought the use of the "Pretty Girl" as bait in advertising products for the home. The "'plain woman consumer'" wanted "'real facts and common sense,'" she said. The "eyebrow-shaved, massaged, short-skirted doll of anaemic New York life" appealed to men, not women. Those who used the "chicken type of girl in advertising" suffered from a "poverty of ideas."[42] She also railed against the "Pretty Girl" in advertising before female audiences. One such speech before the League of Advertising Women was published as a book-let. Castigating the "lurid," "chorustype of beauty" used as "bait" in advertising, Christine confidently predicted its demise because female buyers preferred the "reason why" approach that depicted "natural" women.[43] Christine failed to appreciate the growing appeal of advertisers' promotion of cosmetics, clothes, and glamour to create the sophisticated image of the flapper.[44]

Along with over twenty prominent advertising executives, Christine con-tributed to a book on writing advertising copy that J. George edited in 1925. Bruce Barton, the man who elevated advertising to a spiritual plane by trans-forming Jesus into a businessman in his best-selling book, *The Man Nobody Knows*, was just one of the well-known contributors.[45] In her essay, Christine revisited (as she would again and again) her caustic admonitions against using the "Pretty Girl" in advertisements aimed at women. This article also revealed a nasty tendency to belittle the American housewife, a recurring contradiction in Christine's writing. While she often told advertisers that they must appeal to the American woman with "reason why" advertising, she wrote here that ex-pensive advertising was often "pathetically over her pretty head." She portrayed women as childish and shallow, writing that most wanted to think themselves different from other women but liked to wear "what is 'the mode.'" The average woman tried to "imitate the 'best people'" and "accept[ed] authority readily." She was "not interested in mechanics or abstract ideas" and was not "alert to new ideas." Moreover, she could be "educated only slowly."[46]

Christine told advertisers that there were "not enough practically and theoretically trained women brought into consultation to dig out . . . broadening-out possibilities." She was presumably such a woman, a woman who could help manufacturers promote new uses for products already on the market. She recounted her successes in boosting the sales of a soup manufacturer by urging housewives to use canned soup in sauces and casseroles, and those of "a great California fruit-growing association" by encouraging women to bake home-made pies. Women consultants could educate housewives to use disinfectant in many new ways, she said. Besides sanitizing the garbage pail and toilet, they should be encouraged to use disinfectant in the icebox, the sick room, the bathtub, and the scrub bucket.[47] Such advice casts doubt on Christine's declarations of advocacy for the consuming housewife. If advertisers convinced women to use their products in these new ways, housekeeping would clearly require even more of their time and effort.

Still, large numbers of retailers listened to what Christine had to say. An audience of over one thousand heard her speech before the Louisville, Kentucky, Retail Institute. Her consulting business included helping "a new chain of food stores" organize a system for taking telephone orders. Solitaire Coffee quoted her on an advertising poster: "Mrs. Christine Frederick says: 'Any housewife can make good coffee every day with Solitaire,'" and the makers of Eskimo Pies used her photograph and testimonial, along with those of other "experts," in a 1929 advertisement.[48]

Promoting the Radio

ONE OF THE TECHNOLOGICAL MIRACLES that matured during the twenties was the radio, and Christine Frederick used her reputation as an expert to promote it. Both Fredericks were enthusiastic about the possibilities of radio; J. George wrote an article on its rapid growth in 1925.[49] In the beginning, Christine had responded to this new machine with skepticism. "I remember how I resented it when my husband first brought into the parlor the messy-looking box called a radio set, and how I was annoyed lest the acid from the battery spoil my rugs," she wrote in 1929.[50] But she soon overcame her distaste. "The youngsters and their father have been having a beautiful time with the radio phone," she told an interviewer. By the time the family had a "three-stage set," they all listened together in the living room.[51]

Early in 1922, Christine's ideas for a radio program were featured in the *Evening World*'s "Ten-Second News Movies" column. Under a series of eight photographs of her animated face, she announced plans to broadcast a household show from Applecroft to thousands of women, fifteen minutes of household tips every week to listeners within a five-hundred-mile radius of Greenlawn.[52] There is no evidence that the program was ever aired, but the idea demonstrated her grasp of radio's possibilities.

Christine promoted radio as an antidote to the housewife's loneliness and an educational tool for the whole family.[53] In 1922, when radio was "still a toy" according to the editor of the popular women's magazine *Good Housekeeping*, Christine wrote an article exploring its usefulness in the home. She thought that exercise drills broadcast between 6 and 7 o'clock in the morning would encourage the family to exercise together. Health talks and first-aid programs would promote hygiene. For children, programs on chemistry, electricity, and mechanical construction would further their education. She was most enthusiastic, however, about the radio's appeal to women. Like scientific management, the radio could make women happier in their prescribed role as homemaker: "The radio-telephone, it seems to me, is primarily an invention for the benefit of woman. . . . Housekeepers . . . as a class have felt that they were imprisoned within the four walls of the house, that they were 'tied down' to the monotony of household tasks, and that often they were deprived participation in cultural pleasures because they had to stay home and take care of young children."[54] Christine suggested regular programming for women, featuring physical education, talks on household topics and issues of social interest, cultural programs, and beauty advice. Radio, she believed, could relieve the housewife's loneliness.[55]

Christine's penchant for pedagogy and reform dictated her vision for radio: everything broadcast should be uplifting and educational. It was this sort of programming that gave birth to Washburn-Crosby's Betty Crocker cooking school, which Christine praised in 1924.[56] But in the beginning, Christine did not suggest direct advertising, and advertisers shied away from the medium as well. Newspapers objected to the competition, but advertising agencies were slow to develop radio expertise largely because they feared audience resentment. Still unsure of their ethical parameters, advertisers, like Christine, saw the radio as an educational opportunity. It was not until a year after Christine wrote the article for *Good Housekeeping* that advertisers began to sponsor radio programs.[57]

Advertising's slow start on radio did not prevent Christine from advertising the mechanism itself, and she wrote many articles for trade journals promoting the sale of radios. She advised hardware retailers to tidy up their stores, create inviting displays and listening alcoves, and emphasize the beauty of the new radio cabinets as furniture. She spent so much energy on promoting the radio that she once claimed to have made a career out of it. Christine's articles encouraging women to buy radios appeared in such Middle American newspapers as the *Toledo (Ohio) Times* and the *Dayton (Ohio) News*.[58]

To illustrate her pieces on the virtues of radio, Christine had dozens of photographs taken of the family and friends listening to radios in many different situations: camping, picnicking, exercising, resting in the sick bed, or relaxing before the fire.[59]

Christine's articles reflected some of the early problems electronic communication presented. In a 1922 article for a children's magazine, she wrote, "I am sure that readers of St. Nicholas will be glad to know that the chief reason why America leads the world to-day in radio progress is just because Uncle Sam is a wise old person and allows the radio amateurs to remain unmolested by hampering government restrictions." She went on to say that the boys of Europe had to hide their ham radio activities because "the French army owns the air!"[60] (Girls, apparently, were not interested in ham radio.) The scathing sarcasm aimed at potential government regulation of the airwaves illustrates once again that Christine's Progressivism was not of a piece. Although Christine was prepared to ask Congress's help in maintaining a manufacturer's right to fix prices, she found the threat of regulation in this particular instance to be oppressively un-American. Another piece written in 1924, however, suggested rules to limit the content of programs. Sectarian church services should be eliminated "in the interest of the greater good to the greater number," she wrote, although she would support a "radio church of general human appeal."[61]

Christine's enthusiasm for radio was yet another instance of her ability to perceive important trends and to capitalize upon them. Although her early, utilitarian vision for the radio failed to anticipate Americans' desire for pure entertainment, she understood that radio would become a significant cultural phenomenon and was one of the first to say so. But by 1929, the most popular programs were not the lectures and exercise sessions she had promoted. America listened to *Roxy and His Gang*, *The Ipana Troubadours*, and the *A&P Gypsies*. That year, millions of Americans tuned in every week to a new show called *Amos 'n' Andy*.[62]

Urging Europeans to Consume

HER INTEREST in radio enlarged the scope of Christine Frederick's influence and reputation. From 1927 to 1929 she received invitations to speak in England, France, Belgium, Holland, Germany, Switzerland, Italy, and Czechoslovakia.[63] The Women's Electrical Association of London, chaired by Lady Astor, invited Christine to give a series of lectures on modernizing the home. In February 1927, her portable typewriter in tow, she settled into Berner's Hotel, Oxford Street, London, for a three-month stay.[64] Despite a wall heater, a wood-burning fireplace (for which she had to pay), and layers of clothing, her teeth chattered in the cold. "No wonder," she wrote years later, "my women sponsors wanted me to present the advantages of central heating!"[65] During her stay in Great Britain, she lectured at King's College, the Publicity Club, and the Chamber of Commerce in London; Queen's College in Birmingham; and various groups in Lancashire, Liverpool, and Glasgow. She told British housewives how Americans had solved the servant problem by simplifying housekeeping through labor-saving devices. She gave the impression that most American homes had such conveniences and stated on one occasion that American women "simply will not move into an old-fashioned house or apartment until it has been brought . . . up to date."[66] She was astonished by the lack of efficiency in British establishments. The maids in her Brighton boardinghouse carried every dish up and down eighteen "narrow, ladder-like steps" from kitchen to dining room and back.[67]

Christine's reputation preceded her to France, where she had intended a restful sight-seeing tour of two weeks. Instead, Paulette Bernège, a French home expert who was promoting "*Taylorisme*" in France and who knew of Christine's work from her 1915 article in the *Revue de Metallurgie*, hastily organized a meeting of the League for Household Efficiency, the Association for Household Electric Appliances, and her own organization, Mon Chez Moi (My Home), presided over by the French minister of housing. On 22 April 1927, Christine addressed the group in passable French, reiterating her efficiency principles, her advocacy of labor-saving devices, and her views on the housewife's attitude. Bernège published the text in the May issue of her publication, *Mon Chez Moi*, and shared a full-page advertisement with Christine that promoted their joint efforts to teach household efficiency.[68] Christine and Paulette Bernège shared a mutual regard for one another. Christine wrote of Bernège's work, "In France a small but brave attempt is being made by my brilliant, self-sacrificing friend, Mlle. Paulette Bernège, who has sponsored and directs that unique home-management periodical, *Mon-Chez-Moi* which more than perhaps any other in Europe is attempting to educate the woman in modern scientific housekeeping."[69]

Christine left Paris in late April and traveled to Rotterdam, Berlin, and Czechoslovakia, where she spoke to groups of housewives. Returning to London in early May, she addressed the Publicity Club of London and the London Chamber of Commerce before returning to New York. To these last groups, Christine spoke of the woman buyer and how to approach her. She was hailed as a celebrated American expert by the European press. The *Birmingham Mail* called her the "mistress of the science of housewifery," the Edinburgh *Scotsman* reported that she was "one of America's greatest household efficiency experts," and the London *Chamber of Commerce Journal* was pleased to welcome the "well-known American lecturer and writer."[70]

In the fall of that year, Christine returned to Europe to speak before the International Home Economics Congress in Rome and the Home Exposition in Paris. While in France, she indulged in a bit of fun on a trip to Lyons, where she was the guest of Mlle. Bernège at an agricultural fair banquet. Christine wrote later that after she ate a special mushroom dish, she fell into a trance and kissed the chef. The "trance" was very likely the result of partaking in a ten-course extravaganza that included seven champagnes and ten other wines. The 99th Infantry Regiment offered a musical program, and Christine met the future French president Edouard Herriot.[71]

Christine was photographed with a far more notorious European leader when she went to Italy. The climax of a thirty-nine-nation home economics congress in Rome, where she exhibited a miniature efficiency kitchen equipped with doll figures and toy appliances, was a dinner attended by Benito Mussolini on the evening of 17 November 1927. Christine, along with eight other conferees, was photographed with *Il Duce*, who, despite a magnetic quality, she wrote years later, reminded her of "a head-waiter in an Italian restaurant on 45th Street, New York City."[72]

Christine returned to Europe in late spring, 1929, to speak to the British Housewife's Congress in Newcastle, the International Management Congress in Paris, and the International Advertising Clubs Convention in Berlin. The Fredericks' nineteen-year-old daughter, Jean, and J. George, who had a speaking engagement of his own in Paris, accompanied her on this trip. This time,

Christine took a "suitcase laundry," a model efficiency laundry room occupied by a doll laundress and fitted with toy washing machine, stationary tubs, and ironer. The point, Christine wrote, was to show European housewives how to make laundering efficient without servants. In Berlin, she helped German advertising women form their own league.[73]

The European engagements were but the most dramatic of the many accolades Christine Frederick received while building an international reputation as an expert on home efficiency, the economics of consumerism, and advertising. By the 1920s, she had sensed a significant development that resulted from the intersection of housekeeping and consumerism: to many advertisers of that decade, consumers were female. *Printers' Ink* told its readers in 1929 that "the proper study of markets is *woman*." As the decade progressed, advertisers came to think of female consumers, according to one historian, as "an emotional, feminized mass, characterized by mental lethargy, bad taste, and ignorance."[74] Christine's description of the "average" American woman reinforced this view and, in this case, placed her in the historical model that has capitalists manipulating women into serving as consumers. Whatever her niche in economic history, Christine Frederick saw herself as *the* Mrs. Consumer.

11 · *Private Life*

If ever I doubted that wifehood, motherhood and a successful career
could be happily combined, these doubts were all disspelled [*sic*] when I left the
home of Mrs. Christine Frederick.

UNIDENTIFIED REPORTER, "Expert on Labor Saving Devices Says Use Brains," 1925

A HOUSEHOLD WRITER who interviewed Christine Frederick in her home in 1925 reported that while she talked with the forty-two-year-old mother in the apple orchard, they heard "the merry laughter of the youngsters . . . through the trees." Christine told her that she had plenty of time for her husband and children because she worked efficiently. "Her home," the reporter marveled, "runs like a well-oiled machine." But she also noted that Christine spent at least six hours a day, five days a week, in the "well-ordered" office over the garage.[1]

Home Life

CHRISTINE HAD NEVER BELIEVED in hovering over her children, and indeed, with the schedule she kept, she could hardly have done so. In 1919 she had told an interviewer, "My babies are brought up on what a clever friend calls supervised neglect—that is, they are let alone, not fussed over, and their clothes kept very simple indeed—and yet it seems to agree with them."[2]

Christine was able to spend *some* time with her children. Despite her advice to manage the household with elaborate detail, she set priorities for herself: "I myself have always felt that every moment I spent in cooking or unnecessary work when I might be spending it with my husband and children was unfair to them as well as to myself."[3]

Her daughter remembers fun-filled trips to the city. Christine and the children, with perhaps one or two of their friends, would board the Long Island Railroad at Greenlawn and ride the forty miles to Pennsylvania Station on Thirty-fourth Street in Manhattan. They might shop at Macy's and meet friends at a Chinese restaurant around the corner. Sometimes the trip would include an expedition to the Lower East Side, where they would "load up on

136

vegetables [and] exotic fruits." Christine, ever conscious of nutrition, loved the fresh produce.[4]

Christine also continued to do much of the cooking at home. The wonderful mussels the family collected from Long Island Sound might go into a favorite dish that she christened "Wop and Consequence." (Even liberal thinkers like the Fredericks thoughtlessly used derogatory ethnic epithets in the 1920s.) She might treat the family to fancy desserts in "'company-like' . . . tall glasses thoroughly chilled." To save precious time with the family on Sundays, she and the housekeeper sometimes cooked and served "Sunday dinner" on Saturday night, preparing leftovers for a picnic the next day.[5]

In a charming article in which she compared the magic of radio to the magic of Christmas, Christine depicted a quaint holiday scene at Applecroft. As she and J. George decorated the tree on Christmas Eve, they listened to radio music as snow fell outside. To surprise the children, they rigged their radio to a speaker attached to the Santa Claus figure at the top of their tree. The speaking Santa was greeted with "wild excitement" on Christmas morning.[6]

The elder of Christine's two half-brothers, Crichton MacGaffey, often traveled from Chicago to spend part of his summer vacation with the Fredericks during the twenties. Christine was fond of Crichton, sometimes referring to him as her first baby since she was in her teens when he was born. He entertained the Frederick children on the piano and flute. "He just lit up the whole summer for us," Christine's daughter remembered. Christine was delighted to have Crichton visit, too, but at least partly for practical reasons: "[T]hen she could work uninterruptedly."[7]

Christine managed her household, as a consumer expert should, by shopping carefully. She did her "routine buying" in nearby Huntington and patronized local vendors from the farms around Greenlawn. She bought eggs, for example, from a Polish woman who raised chickens at a "humble farm home" in the vicinity. She frequented a specific chain store where she came to know the manager well enough that he gave her personal attention and remembered her "usual order" each time she shopped, even going so far as to send a clerk to a competitor if he lacked what she needed. Christine rewarded this special service by giving him fine Christmas gifts.[8]

Since her busy speaking schedule sometimes kept Christine away from her children for long periods of time, she tried to compensate by involving them in her work. "My own pet recipe for making friends early with my [children]," she wrote in 1928, ". . . is to have them share some of my work and enthusiasms as far as practicable. Children are very imitative, and there is no comradeship or friendship equal to that of doing things together."[9] When her eldest daughter was ten years old, she took her to a Fuller Brush banquet where the child sat next to a gentleman who was kind enough to help her choose the proper fork for the oyster course while her mother was busy giving the address. Christine created a fictional photography business for her second daughter, crediting the "Phyllis Frederick Photo Service" with many of the professional photographs that accompanied articles she wrote. Carol, the baby of the family, was included as coauthor of the children's cooking articles Christine wrote for *Designer Magazine*.[10]

The children took part in the Fredericks' social life, too. Their friend, the psychologist Leta Hollingworth, included the Frederick brood in a study of exceptional children, giving them IQ tests periodically. The older children were invited to attend the annual summer picnics of the Walt Whitman Society, of which J. George was a member. After eating in the Applecroft orchard, the club would troop to the Whitman house, just a few miles away. These folks were a "motley and interesting group for a kid to run into," the Fredericks' daughter remembered. For many years, there were annual Christmas parties when guests were invited from the city for a day in the country. There would be theatricals, turkey dinners, and walks in the countryside. The company was stimulating, usually made up of the writers, actors, and reformers that J. George knew in the city. Louis Brandeis's daughter Susan, the actor Beatrice Kaye, and the radio personality Mary Margaret McBride were among the guests who frequented these events.[11]

The Christmas parties led at least one neighboring family to view the Fredericks as rather "Bohemian." The parents of an adolescent friend of Phyllis disapproved of the Frederick household, although their daughter "was quite jealous" of the perceived freedom allowed the Frederick brood. Christine and J. George were not typical parents, this friend remembered, and she thought that the girls "sort of brought themselves up." But the Christmas parties were "fabulous," "absolutely unbelievable." For that very reason, perhaps, this girl's more conservative parents regarded the comings and goings at the Fredericks' with a wary eye.[12]

The children did not spend all their time at adult parties. Like many young American boys, David sold the *Saturday Evening Post* from door to door to earn spending money. And like many American families in the days before children could be immunized against most childhood diseases, the Fredericks knew the terrible anxiety of nursing a child through infantile paralysis. In 1923, J. George took thirteen-year-old Jean duck hunting on Long Island. When the dog failed to retrieve on command, Jean went after a felled duck and got very wet and chilled. The next morning, she could not rise from her bed. Their family doctor recognized the symptoms and prescribed exercise for the muscles, saltwater soaks, and massage. A woman was hired to move the leg regularly while Jean was still bedridden. The child walked again, but J. George was inconsolable and wept with guilt for endangering the "apple of his eye."[13]

Absent though she often was, Christine gave the impression that she was emotionally close to her children. In 1928, she wrote an article on the mother-daughter relationship for the *Christian Advocate*. She advised including children in their parents' activities at an early age and suggested turning a deaf ear to the teenage daughter's criticism. She disapproved of mothers who tried to be their daughters' "chums," but she heartily advocated sharing laughter and fun. As adults, at least two of her daughters remembered her as a good mother and inspiring role model.[14]

Outsiders sometimes saw a different picture. One of the daughters' childhood friends remembered a rather melancholy family, neither close nor happy. As a youngster, she had thought J. George egotistical and Christine unattractive and untidy. Neighbors gossiped about the state of the Fredericks' marriage, too, and it seemed to this visitor that both parents were away from the home so much that the children did not receive proper parental guidance.[15]

Yet others found Christine engaging. In 1925, a reporter described her as "a charming woman who looked as if she had just excused herself from a garden party. White-frocked, carrying colorful field flowers . . ., brown wavy hair and laughing brown eyes, exceedingly feminine."[16] Yet she was not a particularly social woman. Although she occasionally invited members of the Advertising Women of New York to Applecroft, she did not join many women's groups nor did she enlist in organized causes very often.[17] She was completely absorbed in her work, and her children provided a partial outlet for any need for intimacy she might have had.

Noyes School of Rhythm

CHRISTINE HAD ANOTHER OUTLET, too. Like Catharine Beecher, who re-paired to health spas whenever she had suffered a failure or felt overwhelmed by the work she had taken on, Christine found a refuge from the hectic pace of her professional life in a dance camp.[18] When she could, she would escape to the Connecticut countryside to spend two weeks during the summer at the Noyes School of Rhythm. "Although I never really 'shut shop,'" she once told Theresa Wolcott, "this year I hope to have August to myself."[19]

Florence Fleming Noyes held that rhythmic movement was a "medium of creative expression and release," and she taught dance as she imagined the ancient Greeks might have practiced it. She established the Noyes School of Rhythm summer school in a rural setting near Portland, Connecticut, in 1919. Noyes called her dance pavilion the Pavelon after the Parthenon, and she gave her students Greek names and had them choreograph "masques" representing the Greek myths. Campers slept in tents and made their own flowing costumes from cheesecloth that they dyed themselves and hung from the trees to dry. Christine adored the time spent at Noyes. The barefoot Greek dancing repre-sented liberation from corsets and from the demands of her work. She was also fascinated by the spiritual tenor of the camp: she painted the feet of the Buddha on stones outside her tent. After Jean had recovered sufficiently from her polio, Christine took her to the Noyes School for three summers after her fifteenth birthday. The girl worked for her tuition, helping to dye the cloth, carrying water, and incidentally building the strength in her weak leg.[20]

Christine made friends at Noyes School, and the school nurtured a part of her personality that rarely surfaced in her well-ordered, efficient, no-nonsense daily life. The mystical quality of the dance, Florence Noyes's spirituality, and the mystery of the association with ancient Greece appealed to Christine. Her household and consumer work did not reveal a fascination for mysticism, spirituality, even the occult that would surface later in her life. She remem-bered Noyes as "the one place to which I would like most to return (if that were possible)."[21]

If things ran smoothly at Applecroft, it was because Christine could leave the details to a full-time housekeeper when she was away. Since the days of "Nursie" when her older children were small, the Fredericks had continually employed a servant who lived at Applecroft. The faces changed, but there was always a housekeeper. In 1924, Christine employed "a rather lively young girl" as her "housekeeping assistant." The next year, she hired a woman who had a twelve-year-old son. In 1927, she explained to an audience in Paris, "As for me, completely absorbed in my professional work, I pay $100 a month to my house-keeper, and I provide board and room for her small child" (my translation).[22]

Family Finances

J. GEORGE'S FIRM, the Business Bourse, failed to provide a comfortable living for the Frederick family. The Fredericks' daughter's memories of a father who never made very much money, along with J. George's remarkably wide range of interests and activities, suggest that he did not apply enough of his boundless energy to the Business Bourse to make it succeed. And although he advised others on playing the stock market, he did not invest his own money successfully.[23]

Christine may have been thinking of J. George when she wrote in 1929: "[T]he American man . . . is not especially competent at personal or family purchasing. It is he, not his wife, who . . . gambles in Wall Street and loses like other lambs, and who buys cat-and-dog stocks and various other useless appendages which sap the family patrimony." Dissonance between them is revealed in J. George's views, written a year later: "Very few women should attempt to make their own investment analyses. It is not unfair to say that they have not the same coolness of judgment, as a rule, as men."[24]

If J. George was less than successful at accumulating personal wealth, he excelled at gaining access to New York's interesting artistic, intellectual, and literary communities.[25] But his own writing career, though he produced dozens of books over six decades, was not lucrative. In a 1928 volume, he used the introduction to ask readers to recommend the book to friends.[26]

Still, there was money enough to manage the housekeeper's salary in the busiest years of the twenties. And the Fredericks were able to make improvements to Applecroft. They electrified the entire house and office with their own electric plant so that Christine could operate the many appliances she tested.[27] As "streamlined" design came into fashion, Christine hired the New York decorative artist Russell Wright to help her renovate the Applecroft kitchen. They installed Monel metal counters, tables, and shelves that reflected the architectural vogue for curved lines and smooth surfaces.[28] In 1929, Christine bought four waterfront lots on Northport Bay, an inlet of Long Island Sound just northeast of Huntington. The lots were part of a private development, the Huntington Beach Community Association. The Fredericks had camped on the property for years, but they bought just months before the stock market crash of 1929 and were never able to build a summer cottage on it.[29]

Schooling for the Children

AS THE CHILDREN grew older, Christine and J. George decided that although country living had provided a wholesome atmosphere for small children, it was not satisfactory for maturing adolescents. Getting to Huntington High School involved a long train ride, and friends lived too far away.[30] In 1923, after two years at Huntington High, David was sent to the Peddie School in Hightstown, New Jersey, a college preparatory school for boys.[31] Boarding tuition during his tenure there approached one thousand dollars.[32] Two years later, Jean entered the Abbott Academy in Andover, Massachusetts, a distinguished girls' school that cost fourteen hundred dollars per year.[33] Phyllis, the Fredericks' third child, was sent to the Abbott Academy for the last two years of high school, too, but Carol, their youngest, whose high school career coincided with the Great Depression, graduated from Huntington High.[34] It was during the twenties, then, that the question of college for the two eldest children arose.

Christine was "absolutely committed to getting all three of [her] girls through college." She told her daughters that she could not allow them to go out into the world "without something that could earn [them their] place." The memory of her own young mother, obliged to depend upon a dictatorial father after leaving an abusive marriage, gave Christine a keen appreciation for female independence, at least where her own daughters were concerned. Paradoxically, J. George decided that college was not the appropriate course for their son, David. Although J. George encouraged Jean to become a lawyer, once purchasing a set of legal volumes for her, he stood firm in his refusal to fund David's education beyond preparatory school. David had been active at Peddie, editing the school's student directory, playing in the orchestra, and winning prizes for debates. In his senior year he had indicated a desire to attend Dartmouth. His marks, though good, were not outstanding, and when he graduated at eighteen years of age, J. George saw to it that he seek employment. After working briefly for two Boston advertising firms, David took a job with the *Boston Herald*.[35]

J. George's reasons for preventing his son from getting a college education are complex. On the one hand, he praised the young "university-trained men in business" who were "more appreciative of analytical thinking and research."[36] On the other, he took pride in being a self-made man himself and did not believe that college was necessary to success. Soon after David went to work for the *Herald*, J. George wrote an article titled "I'm Glad I'm Not a College Man." His protagonist claimed that even though he had been terribly disappointed when the lack of funds prevented him from going to college, he later came to appreciate the sales job he took instead. His father had not been able to pay his tuition, and when faced with earning the money himself, he cast about for a job. In the end, he realized that college was "not for a man of my temperament." It would have been wasted on him. He would have been "easily led" into becoming "a snob of the first water."[37] J. George, apparently, did not believe that his son was suited for higher education. Money, however, was certainly a consideration, too. For whatever reason, Christine did not insist that David be sent to college.

As her children entered expensive preparatory schools, Christine decided to establish contact with her biological father, William R. Campbell, hoping that he would help pay for his grandchildren's schooling. "She always greatly resented Campbell's failure to help with her education," her daughter recalled. Campbell did not believe in higher education for women. Although it hurt her mother, Christine publicly acknowledged her relationship to Campbell on occasion. In 1917, before her appearance at the Farmers' Institute in Streator, Illinois—where she shared a church podium with a minister—she identified herself as the "daughter of Rev. W. R. Campbell of Boston." And ten years later she told a reporter in her birth father's hometown that she was "the daughter of Rev. William R. Campbell of the Highland Congregational Church," hoping, perhaps, to win his favor. The Campbell family had no use for Mimie Mac-Gaffey, and not until the mid-1930s was William's sister Mary willing to speak to Christine. But when David and Jean were both in Boston, they were occasionally invited to dinner at their grandfather's home, and when he died, he left each of the Frederick children one thousand dollars.[38] That sum far exceeded their father's contribution to their education. In 1928 J. George gave Jean the only college money he would ever give her: fifty dollars. Jean attended Cornell University, New York State's federal land grant institution, where the tuition for certain courses of study was low. With further assistance from a state scholarship, she earned a bachelor of science degree in home economics in 1932.[39]

Christine tried to rationalize J. George's difficulty. In 1929, she wrote that the reason many women worked outside the home was that more families were trying to put their children through college. In a one-income family, the father "would need to strap himself to the wheel practically until old age, living in next-to-impossible economy to accumulate the thousands of dollars required for his children's college expenses."[40] Still, the disagreement about college caused tension between Christine and J. George. By the end of the twenties, there were other difficulties, too.

Cracks in the Domestic Picture

J. GEORGE SUPPORTED CHRISTINE in her work, even putting at her disposal the resources of the Business Bourse. But Christine's schedule, notwithstanding her protestations of making time for her family, did not allow much energy for the marriage. J. George sought the companionship of other women and used his city apartment as a hideaway to conduct extramarital affairs.[41] Christine pretended, at least in her writings, that the marriage was solid. She once told a reporter, indirectly admitting that her life did not match her model for other women, that one had "to be very careful in the selection of a husband, careful to get one in sympathy with his wife's work, if domestic harmony is to be maintained."[42] Later, she would intensify her campaign to encourage women to support their husbands' careers, suggesting, of course, that she supported J. George's work.

The Fredericks did often work together, but very early in the marriage, Christine put limits on intimacy; in *Household Engineering*, she advised that all family members, especially the hardworking housewife, should sleep in separate beds.[43] J. George's fictional description of a female character's distaste for the marriage bed may be telling: "To Phyllis the sexual *denouement* had been crude and undramatic—even noxious; and the injury to her imagination was considerable. She had found herself spent, exasperated, even nauseated; and finally unresponsive and petulant, yet realizing vaguely that there was more travail to endure as a matter of duty."[44] The Fredericks were familiar with the modern ideas expounded by Judge Ben B. Lindsey in his widely read *The Companionate Marriage* published in 1929.[45] Lindsey advocated legalized birth control and easier divorce and even suggested that married couples that agreed to have extramarital affairs could be happy. This thinking may have

freed J. George's conscience, but Christine denounced the "'companionate marriage' idea."[46]

Whatever the status of the Frederick marriage, Christine's career had become an international success story by 1929. That year, representing herself as
the American housewife's advocate, she gathered between the covers of a very
successful book her work of the decade. She wrote a manual for manufacturers
and advertisers titled *Selling Mrs. Consumer.*

12 · Selling Out Mrs. Consumer

Woman is of course powerful in buying largely because of
her secondary position to man. She is not man's equal in earning and doing and
building, therefore she gravitates toward the position of quartermaster
rather than general in their mutual organization. She takes charge of supplies
largely for the very reason that she can't lead the forces in the field.

CHRISTINE FREDERICK, *Selling Mrs. Consumer*, 1929

BY 1929 CHRISTINE FREDERICK had become intimately connected with business. *Selling Mrs. Consumer*, her third book, was the culmination of fifteen years of promoting advertising as the means by which the American home—and the homemaker's life within it—might be improved through consumerism. She frankly marketed the book as a manual for advertisers and manufacturers. Promotional literature billed Christine as "'the' Mrs. Consumer" and the book as "the great standard reference work for all who sell to consumers." Flyers claimed that "famous manufacturers" had "made a lot of money from her professional advice" and that others could "make money from what Mrs. Frederick discloses." The president of the International Advertising Association, the publisher of the *Chicago Daily News*, and the head of the home economics department at Cornell University provided testimonials regarding the book's sound advice and breadth of information.[1]

Christine had cast her lot with commercial interests. If she had ever aspired to scholarly investigation, as she seemed to do when she contributed the article on economics to the *Annals of the American Academy of Political and Social Science*'s issue on market distribution in 1924, she had forsaken that ambition. She was not included in the May 1929 issue of *Annals* devoted to "Women in the Modern World"; another writer contributed an article on her special field of expertise, "The Home Woman As Buyer and Controller of Consumption."[2] Instead, Christine had perceived and exploited advertisers' enormous interest in consumer research. *Selling Mrs. Consumer* was her magnum opus on the subject.

146

"Creative Waste"

THE IDEA of teaching advertisers how to tailor their appeals to the woman consumer was certainly not new when Christine wrote *Selling Mrs. Consumer*, and she merely anthologized her own previous advice. She had spoken out on the subject often, many of her ideas appearing in "Advertising and the So-Called Average Woman" in J. George's *Masters of Advertising Copy* in 1925. Others saw the need for the feminine viewpoint in advertising, too. A year before *Selling Mrs. Consumer* appeared, Carl Naether, a University of Southern California professor of business English, published *Advertising to Women*, in which he discussed specific copywriting styles based on a survey of three women's magazines. Naether was aware of Christine's work and quoted from her 1920 speech before the Associated Advertising Clubs of the World. He, too, used the figures from Harry Hollingworth's study of twenty-five New York families that Christine repeated so often, though Naether was more candid about the study's limitations. Naether called woman the "buyer-in-chief for the household," a variation on Christine's family "purchasing agent." But his manual was narrower in scope, concentrating on the writing of advertisements, pamphlets, and letters for clothing and toiletries manufacturers.[3] Christine's *Selling Mrs. Consumer* covered all kinds of merchandise and advertising advice.

Christine reiterated her view that the "trinity of consumer/distributor/producer" had helped raise the standard of living for all Americans, pointing out that increased consumption relieved America's industry of surplus goods. She praised advertising as a reliable source of information, comparing it to a movie that showed "all the good things that manufacturers make everywhere, set in a dramatic scenario." She devoted a chapter to her perennial cause, price maintenance, and encouraged loyal patronage to trademarked goods as a way to induce cost decreases through mass production.[4]

On occasion, Christine seemed to represent the consumer's interests by urging better products, better service, and better information from manufacturers and dealers. "[G]oods should more closely fit the market," she advised. The merchandiser who acted as "liaison officer between consumer and manufacturer" would influence the manufacture of products that consumers really needed.[5] She spoke out against the gradual shrinkage of product volume in standard can sizes and urged better, more complete labeling. Food packers, she wrote, should grade their products and display the grade on the label. Instruction booklets should be intelligible. And Christine pointed out that an important aspect of selling appliances was following up with good service and parts replacement. She had refused to recommend several otherwise satisfactory pieces of equipment because parts had to be sent for or service calls were too expensive.[6]

Christine's adherence to her standard arguments trapped her in several absurd contradictions in *Selling Mrs. Consumer*. She cited investigations by the Federal Trade Commission that showed that 72 percent of American consumers were against price maintenance, but she dismissed the figure by claiming that "it was folly to ask consumers such questions, for the average consumer is not familiar with economic terms and has no economic training and is misled by the term, 'maintaining price.'"[7] Although Christine was a champion of big business, she disapproved of the new chain stores on the grounds that they cut prices and threatened independent retailers. However, she reported that 71 percent of housewives responding to a survey believed they got better prices in the chains. The chain stores, she explained, "appealed to the poorer and lower middle classes who do not think very logically and who have always until recent years been short-sighted buyers." Some of Christine's supercilious conclusions were as class-conscious as they were sexist; she expressed the middle-class view that unschooled people were inferior to her educated peers. The emergence of chain stores was not the only new trend that Christine misjudged; she declared that installment buying had run its course and reiterated J. George's praise of Hoover's standardization campaign, which included reducing the varieties of manufactured items.[8]

True to her faith in manufacturers, Christine denounced the "big-business-hating" consumer clubs that sought to obtain better value by purchasing by specifications rather than by brand. She urged consumers to rely instead on the safeguards of "consumer voting power," magazine consumer services, the Federal Trade Commission, and the Better Business Bureaus. Although Christine had testified in favor of legislative measures to prevent price cutting, she abhorred political action in the marketplace if it countered her own cherished views. "The consumer's real hope is not political agitation, *but cooperation and consultation with manufacturers, plus the use of the purchasing vote,* instead of the political ballot," she wrote (Frederick's italics).[9]

Christine devoted much of the book to practical advice to the seller, including chapters on food, clothing, household equipment, and furniture. Along with consumer information, she discussed merchandising and distribution.[10] She proposed a plan for enabling young couples to increase their consumption by "capitalizing," or underwriting, the purchase of new homes for them. "'Industrial banking' corporations," she suggested, should make interest free loans "to be used in the financing of new homes." Such a plan would encourage home ownership and eliminate the "temptation to have the wife continue at work."[11]

Christine elaborated on her earlier descriptions of Mrs. Consumer, much of her rhetoric uncomplimentary and all of it intended to help the advertiser exploit Mrs. Consumer's vulnerability. She listed eighteen female "instincts" to which the advertiser might appeal. They included sex love, mother love, vanity, love of style, jealousy, and ostentation.[12] Christine classified Mrs. Consumer in various ways: by age, by economics, and by physical characteristics. Borrowing from Freud, she wrote that the "inferiority-superiority feelings, so prominent a part of modern psychoanalysis," were much stronger in women than in men, engendering in women "powerful social snobbery."[13] Repeating the observations she had made in *Masters of Advertising Copy,* she described the average female consumer as a poorly educated, emotionally and mentally immature housewife who could not remember seven digits and who probably did not brush her teeth. Yet this same Mrs. Consumer knew what she wanted, decided trends, and possessed both common sense and "selective thought processes." She was more alert, more sophisticated, and more powerful than previous generations of American women.[14]

Selling Mrs. Consumer was riddled with the same contradictions regarding women that Christine had exhibited throughout the decade. She declared in one instance that Mrs. Consumer would "probably 'blow herself' to a French face powder of identically the same chemical composition, at twice the price, because she wants the French trade name," yet she lectured advertisers in another that they "must realize that American women are not exactly morons, and that they have a most excellent record of intelligent buying."[15] These contrasting observations empowered women in the marketplace on the one hand and belittled them as helpless pawns of the advertiser on the other. Christine was unable to produce solid evidence for any of her pronouncements about women; to bolster some of her contentions, she drew from the sixteen-year-old findings of Harry Hollingworth.[16] Yet she ignored Hollingworth's warning that sex differences were not very large and that they were not true of everyone.

In fact, he had been careful to question "the popular notion that women are prone to react more strongly to emotional situations than men."[17]

Selling Mrs. Consumer's most surprising new contribution was the theory of consumer economics that Christine unveiled: "It is now time to assert and proclaim for the American family, on all levels above the Minimum Comfort Level, a bold new policy, already in existence, without fear of being called extravagant or wasteful. This is *the policy of creative waste in spending*" (Frederick's italics).[18] The year before, J. George had advocated "progressive obsolescence," a term he claimed to have coined. Americans must be taught to trade in or discard manufactured items "*when new or more attractive goods or models come out,*" he wrote (Frederick's italics). This was the key to solving manufacturers' problem of "securing more sales" and disposing of surplus.[19] Although Christine had urged readers to make 1928 "a saving year" just nine months before J. George wrote this piece, she took up and elaborated upon his theme in *Selling Mrs. Consumer,* sometimes borrowing material verbatim: "Mrs. Jones [or Mrs. Consumer] no longer takes pride in the great square ebony piano of excellent tone her mother handed down to her, but on the contrary, unsentimentally considers it a horror, and has perhaps bought several pianos of different shapes and woods in recent years." Christine took great delight in the "Consumer-Jones" family's progression through three homes, each more modern than the previous one because it "seemed obsolescent to this family so rapidly moving up on the social scale."[20] So enthusiastic was Christine over this concept that she claimed she would like to "burn up gradually a third of our houses!" Christine made a distinction between "real" waste (letting oranges rot in the crate) and "creative" waste (replacing an object before it was worn out with a new model). "There isn't the slightest reason in the world why materials which are inexhaustibly replenishable should not be creatively 'wasted,'" she exclaimed.[21]

Borrowing "[Thorstein] Veblen's excellent phrase," Christine condoned Americans' "conspicuous consumption" of clothing, furnishings, jewelry, automobiles, and houses. Christine misunderstood Veblen's indictment of the middle class's "emulation" of the wealthy and encouraged the practice because it would lead to everyone buying more household goods, an "important means of expressing the family's 'conspicuous consumption' or wealth."[22] She wrote disparagingly of the British woman who might wear one evening gown for five or ten years. To an American, she claimed, such frugality was "unheard of and preposterous." Mrs. Consumer was happiest when she consumed goods "at the same approximate rate of change and improvement that science and art and machinery can make possible." Christine did not completely forget the "93 millions who are too close to necessity to dispose of their purchases much before the last usage is out of them"; she claimed that progressive obsolescence would improve their lives, too, for they could buy the goods that more fortunate Americans traded in for new.[23] But her target was the prosperous middle-class American: "Mrs. Consumer has billions to spend. . . . She is having a gorgeous time spending it—and American industry, science, art, literature, invention is having the peak of its development catering to her quick appreciation, which does not hesitate to throw out of her house much that is still useful."[24]

The home economist Day Monroe, writing for the *Journal of Home Economics,* called *Selling Mrs. Consumer* a "guide for the manufacturer who wishes to sell his wares to Mrs. Consumer." Christine had based her conclusions, Monroe wrote, on her own point of view. Good, bad, and indifferent investigations were "quoted indiscriminately." She took umbrage at Christine's description of Mrs. Consumer as the creature that advertising copywriters wanted her to be: emotional, volatile, and suggestible: "We can only hope she is wrong in her diagnosis of Mrs. Consumer's characteristics." As for the advice, Monroe judged much of it unsound for any but the manufacturer.[25]

Other reviews were more enthusiastic. "[T]here is probably no one in this country," wrote the *New York Times* reviewer, "who has studied woman as a buyer and user of goods and as a factor in the economic life of the country as has Mrs. Frederick." Unlike Monroe, this reviewer found Christine's evidence sound. The *Saturday Review of Literature* called the book "a worthy exemplar of the new method of scrutinizing the characteristics of buyers and taking from them the cue as to how to find out what and how they will buy." The *Boston Transcript* reported that *Selling Mrs. Consumer* was sure to "attract attention on the part of efficient housewives," casting doubt on the care with which the reviewer read the book.[26]

Christine submitted *Selling Mrs. Consumer* to her publisher, J. George's Business Bourse, shortly after she returned from her European tour during the spring and summer of 1929. There had been nervous talk aboard ship of the rumblings from Wall Street. The first plunge in stock prices would come in early September. Christine seemed oblivious: "If the credit of the United States is the most solid credit in the world today, it must be because consumers make it so. The great bankers and great nations look to the American consumer for their money supply." On 29 October, the stock market crashed. During the next three years, the prosperity of the twenties would come apart at the seams as the value of the securities of many great corporations plummeted.[27]

Christine virtually ignored the Crash in her writing, and she paid scant attention to the ensuing Great Depression. If she referred to the crisis at all, it was to make oblique insinuations that the economic collapse had been exaggerated or that businesses were not trying hard enough to sell.[28] The publication of *Selling Mrs. Consumer* had secured her reputation as Mrs. Consumer's representative, and business groups were now more interested than ever in hearing what she had to say. For the next few years, she spoke in cities across the country on themes she had developed in the book.[29] A Columbus, Ohio, newspaper hailed her as a "nationally known analyst."[30] "Whether you think it or not," she would tell her audiences, "I am the most important woman in your lives. I am Mrs. Consumer." She continued to speak out for increased consumption. In the fall of 1930, she told the National Retail Institute in Columbus, Ohio, that the secret of American well-being was not mass production, but rather "industry's close alliance with the woman buyer," who drove the real engine of prosperity, "mass consumption."[31] Five months later in Chicago, Christine told the Home Service Conference of the National Electric Light Association, a group of home economists working in industry, that homes of the future would have many more electrical appliances and conveniences. Bankers were wrong, she said, to warn that the standard of living would fall. What electric companies must do was convince Mrs. Consumer to use more power. The following year, Christine again blamed businesses' poor consumer relations for the Depression in a speech before a fashion group.[32]

Christine was still using material from *Selling Mrs. Consumer* when she spoke before the New York Rotary Club nearly a decade later. Telling the Rotarians that she was "female, feminist, and Freudian," she entertained them with her list of Mrs. Consumer's foibles and called for more responsible advertising, better labeling, lower distribution costs, and closer contact between manufacturer and consumer. It was in this speech that she suggested that women should serve on the boards of corporations.[33]

Christine's lectures did not endear her to the group of women upon whose province she sometimes encroached. The home economist Anna L. Burdick of the Federal Board for Vocational Education wrote an irate letter to the head of the Bureau of Home Economics upon reading of Christine's speech to the National

Retail Institute. "Is Christine playing to the Gallery?" she asked. "Is she interested in Education or exploitation?"[34] *Selling Mrs. Consumer* appealed to its target audience, however. The business community accepted Christine's insights about the woman consumer as wisdom from an expert.

Twenties Sophisticate

WITH THE PUBLICATION of *Selling Mrs. Consumer*, Christine Frederick concluded two decades of exploiting the country's friendly mood toward business. She and J. George reflected the trends of the 1920s in other ways, too. Although some observers pronounced Progressivism dead after World War I, the passage of the Sheppard-Towner Act and the campaign to adopt protective legislation were signs that it had survived. The Fredericks were among those who still espoused some Progressive views. Christine put Woodrow Wilson at the top of her list of the twelve greatest American men in 1922, and at least once she told buyers to remember the "sisters in sweatshops" and pay fair prices to ensure that women workers "fare more humanely."[35]

The "national mania" for psychology engaged the attention of both Fredericks, and J. George took great interest in the Humanist movement, writing a book on the subject in 1930.[36] The Fredericks participated in the decade's "rapid accumulation of . . . new knowledge" and in the movement to popularize it. And if Christine was not strictly modern in the cultural sense of the word, she was certainly an apostle of modernization, heralding the possibilities of technology and advocating modern design. She wished to bring order to American middle-class life and cast out the trappings of Victorian material values.[37] The abandon with which she responded to Greek dance at the Noyes School suggests the influence of Isadora Duncan, who revolutionized the art with controversial performances in flowing, gossamer gowns and bare feet.[38]

In 1927, the journalist Walter Lippmann identified several issues in public life that divided the Americans of the twenties: prohibition, fears of immigration and Catholicism, the influence of the Ku Klux Klan, and the reactionary mood bred by religious fundamentalism. These anxieties arose, Lippmann wrote, "out of the great migration of the last fifty years, out of the growth of cities, and out of the spread of that rationalism and the deepening of that breach with tradition which invariably accompany the development of a metropolitan civilization." Lippmann saw prohibition, the Klan, fundamentalism, and xenophobia, all movements of considerable strength during the 1920s, as manifestations of the fear of the old "American village civilization making its last stand against" what looked "like an alien invasion."[39]

Christine Frederick, on balance, was with the invading forces. Even though she often portrayed herself as a country woman, her perspective was that of an urban American. In 1922, she wrote an article that condemned suburban living as "a snare and a delusion from almost any angle." For sophisticated Americans, she wrote, the suburbs were "the very apotheosis of standardization at its bitter worst." Quick to point out that her lifelong campaign to standardize was meant for the mechanics of life, she claimed that suburban living standardized things that people did not want standardized. She sneered with urban, middle-class disdain at the "neat little toy houses on their neat little patches of lawn and their neat colonial lives, to say nothing of the neat little housewives and their neat little children—all set in neat rows for all the world like children's blocks." This arrangement, she charged, was a "pretense of individualism" and country living. City apartments offered more privacy, and suburban planning wasted resources by requiring separate utilities. "Suburbiana" was bourgeois and appealed to social climbers. It was merely the re-creation of the small town where people practiced the "gossipy, prying standard of the village." Christine hoped that Sinclair Lewis, the novelist who satirized small-town America in *Main Street*, would expose the "naïveté" and "boobery" of the suburbs one day. Ignoring nearly all of rural America, she wrote that in the country—preferable to the suburbs—one could enjoy simplicity and privacy and still be within driving distance of a railway station where one could commute to the city. In one of her most stunning misapprehensions, Christine predicted the demise of "suburbiana."[40]

Christine and J. George were also aligned with the faction that inspired the fears of the fundamentalists. J. George wrote that the 1925 trial of John Scopes for teaching evolution in a Tennessee classroom dominated one of "the three great misguided periods" in American history, and criticized the prosecutor William Jennings Bryan for his defense of fundamentalism. "[T]he fundamentalist agitation," wrote J. George, was "fear of the vastly larger horizon which science gives to human knowledge." Bryan had served as a "mouthpiece for ignorant herd instincts." During the twenties, the Fredericks were not churchgoers nor did they adhere to any orthodoxy.[41]

J. George's wide circle of friends, many of them members of the intelligentsia, bore evidence of the Fredericks' acceptance of Americans of different backgrounds and religions. Some of the people who visited Applecroft from the city were Jewish, and several of the neighboring farmers from whom Christine bought produce and with whose children David and Jean romped were immigrants.[42] Still, both Fredericks accepted the stereotypes of the period. Christine wrote that one often encountered "a dirty, illiterate, short-sighted, half-Americanized foreigner" managing a store in 1929. J. George believed that people of American, Scots, English, or Jewish background were more likely to be geniuses than were Italians, Spaniards, or Germans. In an article about Tahiti, he described the native women as fat and silly, beguiled by "blousy" clothes and "glass beads."[43] But the Fredericks were not xenophobic. Christine genuinely wished to help immigrant women learn how to operate their homes with unfamiliar American technology.[44]

As for prohibition, Christine had been quite willing to circumvent laws banning alcohol in order to find whiskey for her Chautauquan colleague in 1918. During the twenties, however, she often wrote favorably of prohibition because it had freed billions of dollars for the consumption of manufactured goods.[45] J. George had been deeply influenced by the Women's Christian Temperance Union as a boy, and he showed strong disapproval of one of his daughter's college friends who prescribed gin for menstrual cramps. But as he became interested in cuisine and joined gourmet groups, he relaxed his standards and occasionally took wine with food.[46] The last of Lippmann's indicators of 1920s reaction, the Ku Klux Klan, enjoyed a significant following in Suffolk County, but it attracted scant attention from either Christine or J. George.[47]

Along with her celebration of the new, Christine also reflected a traditional component of 1920s America, particularly in her adherence to the nineteenth-century view of woman's role as a homemaker. Two of her heroes were Herbert Hoover and Edward Bok, both spokesmen for traditional values. Like Henry Ford, one of the giants of the decade, she defended the home, motherhood, hard work, and individualism.[48]

For his part, J. George recognized that the country must make adjustments in its methods of pursuing prosperity through business as the decade drew to a disastrous economic close. In a curiously ill-timed book written in 1929 and hastily edited to address changed conditions in 1930, he encouraged middle-class investors to buy common stock and condemned the rampant speculation of financiers that he believed had led to the debacle. The Crash, he told his readers, was "purely a state of mind." Like Christine, he was still convinced that "consumptionism" was the key to America's regaining its prosperity.[49]

The 1929 Crash plunged America into a calamitous depression that would take another decade and the economic stimulus of war to surmount, but the prosperity of the twenties had modernized the country irreversibly. Business triumphed, more Americans now lived in towns and cities than on farms, consumerism had become a way of life, and the automobile, the radio, and the movies all helped to transform Americans' daily existence. Christine Frederick had worked very hard to promote all these changes.[50]

She was, in many ways, a barometer of the 1920s. Christine celebrated the prosperity brought on by increased industrial production and enthusiastically joined in the move to develop the domestic market. She seized upon advertising and broke new ground with the advocacy of "creative waste." She advocated modernization in technology and design. Yet she also maintained her adherence to the nineteenth-century ideology that kept women at home and appropriated the reaction to prewar feminism to enforce it. Her modernity was gendered. As the twenties drew to a close, Christine had clearly taken an antifeminist position about how women should conduct their lives while she led an independent and satisfying life of her own. The publication of *Selling Mrs. Consumer* affirmed this contradiction.

13 · The Twilight of a Career

One of the happiest days of my life!
CHRISTINE FREDERICK, "At Auction," 1943

IN THE SPRING of 1935, Christine Frederick was honored at a dinner given by eighty of New York's business and professional clubs in the grand ballroom of the Hotel Astor. Chosen as one of the "thirty most successful Career Women of Greater New York," she shared the honor with cosmetics executive Elizabeth Arden, actor Ethel Barrymore, photographer Margaret Bourke-White, pilot Amelia Earhart, efficiency engineer Lillian Gilbreth, and artist Georgia O'Keeffe, among others. Writer Fannie Hurst and historian Mary Beard were two of the seven speakers at the event.[1] Christine received this tribute at the very time that her career was beginning its decline. Four years later, she would leave Applecroft.

Decline

DURING THE FIRST HALF OF THE DECADE that was marked by the Great Depression, Christine worked on momentum generated by the publication of *Selling Mrs. Consumer* in 1929, but she failed to stay abreast of the latest consumer information. In 1930, when a member of an audience asked her to name firms engaged in consumer research, a subject she constantly promoted, she could not tell him "offhand" and made vague references to "national organizations" and "public relations departments." In a 1938 speech before the New York Rotary Club, she claimed to have done "recent research," but the statistics she quoted were identical (as was much of the speech) to those that appeared in an address delivered eight years earlier.[2] Her consumer work was growing stale.

In addition to the lobbying efforts, lectures, and articles that sprang directly from *Selling,* Christine sometimes worked as an advertising consultant during the thirties, too. The organizing meeting of the Advertising Women of New York's speakers bureau took place at J. George's office on 40th Street in

1935, and Christine drafted the first speech the bureau would offer. The following year, she was invited to participate as a judge in a promotional contest conceived by the firm that handled the Colgate company's advertising. In 1938 she took part in a study that found that advertising cost the consumer only .036 of a cent for every can of soup sold and 1.5 cents for every three-dollar ham. That same year her speech on the history of women in advertising became an essay for a book edited by Dorothy Dignam.[3]

Christine continued to lobby for legislative measures she believed affected Mrs. Consumer. On 2 March 1932, she again testified on Capitol Hill in defense of a new price maintenance measure, the Capper-Kelly bill, and delivered the same message that she had taken to Washington in 1914 and 1919. "I am strongly opposed to all forms of trade deception," she told a reporter just prior to appearing before the Senate Committee on Interstate Commerce. "The present-day price cut shambles" caused confusion and "ill-will." In 1935 she joined a member of the Advertising Women of New York to attend subcommittee hearings on bills that would affect advertising.[4]

After the Supreme Court had ruled in 1937 that the National Labor Relations Act, more commonly known as the Wagner Act, was constitutional, Christine and J. George both took part in a radio discussion of the decision. The National Labor Relations Board's representative, Elinore Herrick, and James Bambrick, president of local 32B of the International Building Service Workers, were among the other panelists who explored the topic: "Are the Interests of Capital and Labor Identical?" All agreed that the Court's decision was good for both. A newspaper report of the program indicated that Christine sounded the only "belligerent" note of the evening. Arguing that the consumer had not enjoyed any benefits from increases in workers' pay but had, on the contrary, born "the brunt of recent price rises," she threatened that Mrs. Consumer would strike if prices kept going up.[5] Any inclination she might have had to join earlier Progressive attempts to induce consumers to support reforms for workers had vanished.

Christine continued to dispense household advice after the publication of *Selling Mrs. Consumer*, too. In 1932 a third book on housekeeping problems from table settings to buying a home appeared, and her column for the *American Weekly* supplement to the Hearst papers had run for nearly two decades. From 1937 to 1941 she also served as household editor for Fawcett Women's Group magazines. For several years, Christine prepared a household calendar with hints and recipes for a company in Coshocton, Ohio.[6]

In 1932, when her modern Monel metal kitchen was featured in *Home and Field*, Christine was identified as a specialist in kitchen planning, and that year she organized a home-building session for the Small House Forum sponsored by the American Institute of Steel Construction. Women must play a role in designing homes, she said, and she sent out one thousand questionnaires asking women what they wanted in a house. As a result of this exercise, Christine predicted that the house of the future would have no cellar, no attic, no dining room, and no porch. Air conditioning would enable builders to install stationary windows (a prediction that came true for commercial buildings if not for homes), and heating and cooling systems would be combined. These prophecies demonstrated Christine's grasp of modernization's continuing impact on the American home. Working for builders, Christine now exchanged the view that apartments were preferable to detached houses for the ideal that Hoover had promoted the year before. "Our problem now is to lure the woman out of the multiple dwelling with its identical shoebox apartments," she told a reporter. The detached home was "where family life really belong[ed]," she said, completely reversing the position she had taken four years earlier when she wrote the article on "suburbiana." Then she had extolled the "frank standardization" of city apartment buildings and harshly criticized suburban homes for their "neat rows, for all the world like children's blocks."[7] True to form, Christine embraced a trend; government and business had mounted a vigorous campaign during the twenties to increase home ownership in the United States, and she legitimized her claim to expertise by joining the effort.

Christine had always been interested in architecture and was familiar with current ideas about economic housing such as those proposed by the revolutionary European architect LeCorbusier.[8] Her attraction to architecture and planning led to a brief return to school. Phyllis, her second daughter, was ill during much of her youth. To be near her, Christine took an apartment in Ithaca, New York, where Phyllis was enrolled at Cornell University, and registered for two classes herself in the fall of 1935. She completed the fall semester of "Principles of City and Regional Planning" and a design seminar for which she submitted a report titled "Kitchen Design in Low Cost Housing," earning a grade of ninety in both courses.[9] Christine may already have begun to consider a change in her professional direction. Planning and design training would open new doors.

By 1937, although Christine was still asked to address business groups and still wrote regularly for the two syndicates, there were signs that her work was stagnating. An article featuring her career that year focused entirely on past accomplishments with no mention of current work or future plans. She worked less for manufacturers, because trained home economists had taken over the field of product testing. Christine did not have the scientific background to develop specifications such as those the home economist Margaret Mitchell designed for Wear-Ever's pots and pans in the 1930s.[10]

Yet Christine maintained the faith in progress that had been dashed for many of her contemporaries by the First World War and snuffed out completely during the dark years of the Depression for others. Her speeches optimistically encouraged business to target the housewife and watch sales climb. She predicted that the manufacturers of labor-saving devices and the providers of leisure activities would see a rise in profits during 1933. "If you would sell successfully in 1934," she told a Miami advertising group the next year, "you must understand women." That Christine virtually ignored the Depression was the result of her association with advertising. Advertisements changed very little in the thirties; copywriters chose not to portray the true state of affairs for the average American consumer.[11] Christine not only glossed over the Depression, she also increasingly enhanced her own accomplishments.

She told the interviewer who reported her association with the Fawcett Women's Group that she had "assistants in many parts of the country, who experiment[ed] with local recipes which [were] finally forwarded to the Applecroft Station for final testing."[12] These "assistants" were no doubt readers who shared recipes or food tips as a result of reading her syndicated columns. There is no evidence that Christine hired such people. In the thirties, she began to assert that she had attended the University of Chicago, a fabrication that she later embroidered when she claimed to have done "special work" at Chicago's Lewis Institute.[13]

Christine had always been willing to stretch the truth to make a point, but as she grew older the exaggerations took on a desperate tone as she sought to reaffirm her public stature. In 1942, for example, by which time it was highly unlikely that she could still afford a full-time secretary, she wrote to a reader, "As my good little secretary was answering some other letters of this type this morning, I decided to give you, too, a line in appreciation of comradeship." Still, accustomed to hard work and assertiveness, she never allowed her drive and determination to falter, and she continued to provide much of the family's income through the 1930s.[14]

Although J. George was writing prolifically, he was evidently not selling many books. Reviews of his work were mixed. The reviewer for the *Annals of the American Academy of Political and Social Science* praised his 1932 analysis of seventeen economic systems, *Readings in Economics,* as a "valuable source book" that was "refreshingly undogmatic." But the *International Journal of Ethics* called *Humanism As a Way of Life* "vague," "not wholly frank," and lacking in moral direction.[15] Christine's articles, lectures, and consulting jobs were paying for their daughters' college tuition. As their collaboration on the Wagner Act radio broadcast and the women advertisers' speakers bureau demonstrates, the Fredericks still sometimes worked together. Christine provided an introduction to J. George's 1930 edition of a book on cooking, and she used his office as her city address on Applecroft stationery.[16] The repetition of the piano story found in Christine's *Selling Mrs. Consumer* and J. George's article on progressive obsolescence was not an isolated instance; J. George borrowed language from *Selling* in a book on cooking, for example.[17] Still, an unhealthy element of competition was inevitable although Christine made attempts, at least publicly, to validate her husband's prominence. She told an Ohio reporter in 1937 that her "internationally famous" husband was an "illustrious author and advertising expert." Both he and she, Christine was careful to say, were included in *Who's Who in America.*[18] When she spoke before the Rotary Club in 1938, the notice to the Sales Managers' Club, in a rare instance, identified her as the "wife of J. George Fredericks [sic]."[19]

In fact, J. George Frederick conducted a virtually separate social life in New York. In the early 1930s, he served on the Board of Governors and as editor of the annual for the Artists and Writers Dinner Club, an illustrious group that included John Dewey, Edna Ferber, Sinclair Lewis, Walter Lippmann, and even the feminist Suzanne La Follette. As president of the Gourmet Society, a group he had helped found, he dined regularly with a sophisticated, privileged group of New Yorkers, and he continued membership in a number of business and advertising groups.[20] The city apartment served another aspect of his social life; it provided a place to conduct love affairs with other women.

In a chapter devoted to sex in his 1930 treatise on humanism, J. George wrote that the humanist philosophy called for "full complete, rhythmic sex expression, as free from self-consciousness and from the sin complex or fear as it was with the Greeks." Women, however, could not handle "casual" "sex relationships" as easily as men. Their "sensitivity to the character of any emotional relationship to a man," he wrote, made them prone to hysteria and insanity. Apparently full sexual expression was for men only: "The man who falls out of love, but not out of affection, with his wife, may debate very humanistically whether one hundred percent sincerity is called for. The basis of life cannot be changed with every wind of impulse. It would appear that moderation even in frankness may be a sounder philosophy of life, if the end sought is humanistically good, and if elemental sincerity is served."[21] This telltale passage might be read as J. George's defense of his extramarital affairs. Whatever Christine's reaction, she remained in the marriage for another nine years.

In spite of her advice to other women, however, Christine did not play the secondary role of helpmeet to J. George. Although she claimed to believe that women should subordinate themselves to their husbands, Christine's self-esteem was based upon her own work. She continued to impress many observers as "very human, gracious and understanding, full of life." But hers was a commanding presence, too. In 1937, an interviewer found that she emanated a "force of personality, intellect and abilities." Sometimes her forcefulness could seem curt and imperious. In response to a question from the floor after a speech, she might impatiently snap, "Why of course not!" or "Nothing so silly." A granddaughter found her "strong minded," "dominant," and even "arrogant." Her appearance reinforced this persona; by the end of the thirties, Christine had grown heavy and her hair was graying. She referred to herself in 1938 as a "stout, fat-legged lady."[22]

A year later she admitted to herself that her marriage was no longer the partnership she represented it to be. Christine turned her back on Applecroft at the age of fifty-six to pursue a new career and a new life. By that time, unfortunately, she was earning less money than she had during most of the decade. Hearst paid her $60.75 per week, and there were not so many other assignments as there had once been.[23]

Leaving Applecroft

"SOUVENIR! One of the happiest days of my life!" Christine scrawled across her copy of the auction notice that advertised the sale of the furnishings at Applecroft in 1943. The dining room, bedroom, and sitting room furniture was all for sale. Among the items listed, Christine's desk, her many filing cabinets, and her card files served as poignant reminders of her successful career in household efficiency. But she was selling everything; even the potbellied stove from her office over the garage went on the auction block.[24] The following year Christine sold the 1.6 acres of Applecroft to André and Mildred Fontaine for ten thousand dollars, just a year too early to profit from inflated postwar housing prices.[25] There is no evidence that J. George was party to this transaction.

Although she attempted to keep the experiment station operational, Christine had moved out of Applecroft five years earlier in 1939. Bitter and hurt by J. George's continued infidelity, she was finally leaving her thirty-two-year marriage, although neither she nor J. George talked of divorce, then or later.[26] It may have suited J. George to remain married to avoid inconvenient demands from other women. For her part, Christine undoubtedly harbored unpleasant memories of her parents' divorce, and in 1944, it was not entirely acceptable among middle-class families to end a marriage. In any case, they did not openly speak of their separation and at times pretended that the marriage was still viable. When Christine first moved to New York City, a local newspaper erroneously reported that she and J. George had taken an apartment together, and one of Christine's correspondents asked her to convey "kindest regards to Mr. Frederick" in 1944. A brief biography that accompanied an essay J. George wrote in 1952 noted that "other members of the busy Frederick family include his wife, Christine, who is a noted household editor." Still, rumors about J. George's infidelity circulated. When the Fontaines bought Applecroft from Christine in 1944, they had no contact with her husband but had heard that "he was a gay blade that kept another woman somewhere."[27]

By 1939 only the youngest daughter, Carol, was still in college, and she would graduate the following year. But Phyllis, still battling bouts of illness, needed to stay with her mother in New York from time to time. Since Christine's income was no longer what it had been, she asked J. George for support. He gave her only forty dollars per month for a short time after the separation. After she moved to New York and before the auction and sale of Applecroft, she sold some of her most prized personal possessions to make ends meet. Mimie's jewelry and a samovar brought from Russia fetched enough to help her survive.[28]

Christine took a small apartment at 6 Grove Court in Greenwich Village early in 1939. Three years later, in November 1942, she moved a few blocks north to a modern building at 55 West Eleventh Street where she would remain for the next eight years. She had Applecroft business cards printed with the new address and the words "Christine Frederick is staying in town! 'For the duration,'" implying that the move from Applecroft was only a temporary wartime relocation. She also continued to use Applecroft letterhead for the correspondence generated by her columns during the early 1940s. The banner still advertised food and appliance testing, household photographs, lectures, and home planning.[29] But there were few contracts for these services.

For the first five years that Christine lived in New York, her main occupation was writing the columns for Hearst's *American Weekly* and the Fawcett publications. The early *American Weekly* columns had covered a wide variety of subjects: insurance, automobiles, travel, and music in addition to the usual household advice. After 1941, however, the articles dealt almost exclusively with food and homemaking hints.[30] From that point on, Christine's work was clearly used by the magazine to court its advertisers.

In June 1941, the advertising manager of the American Molasses Company wrote Christine to thank her for an article titled "Try Molasses in Your Spring Diet." Later that year, a publicity agent sent her thanks for a story on spices and told Christine she had forwarded copies to all the members of the American Spice Trade Association. A December article that promoted cranberries prompted a thank-you letter from the director of advertising for Cranberry Canners, Inc. The following month, her boss at the *American Weekly* asked Christine to pass vitamin information along to the folks at Purity Stores because "the Purity Stores people are good friends of ours." To her credit, Christine responded to this request with indignation, not because of its commercial nature, but because she thought retailers were not qualified to dispense nutritional advice. "I turn thumbs down on the retailer himself, or any inexperienced dealers working [vitamin comparisons] out for themselves," she wrote. "[E]ven a good Home Economist is not able . . . to do this very technical job. I wouldn't do it myself!"[31]

But Christine was not averse to using her column to court advertisers. Indeed, doing so was part of her job. In the spring and summer of 1942, Christine participated in a conspiracy to induce Cranberry Canners, Inc. of Hanson, Massachusetts, to place its advertising with the *American Weekly*. The magazine's Boston manager wrote to Christine's boss suggesting that Christine ask the advertising director of Cranberry Canners for help on an upcoming article about cranberries. The letter from Boston referred to the plan as "scheming" and "skullduggery," but Christine's boss assured her that it was "according to Hoyle." Christine not only complied with the request, she took the advertiser to lunch and presented her with a gift. She shared the resulting thank-you note with her boss who wrote on it, "Many thanks. Your luncheon should be very helpful." The article appeared three months later and prompted another thank-you letter from the cranberry advertiser, who was grateful for the "nice things" Christine had written about "the all-important cranberry sauce and cranberry juice cocktail." Her gratitude was further demonstrated by the case of juice she sent to Christine. In the 1 November issue, an ad for Eatmor Cranberries appeared on the page following Christine's article, "Adding Zest to the Diet with Cranberries."[32] As soon as the article was out, Christine was prevailed upon to mention the recipes from a rival cranberry company as a hedge against losing *its* advertising.[33]

Christine still tried to generate product-testing work through her correspondence with manufacturers about whose products she wrote. The Will and Baumer Candle Company responded to such a solicitation with a free carton of candles, and an instrument company sent her two thermometers. But these were merely gifts in appreciation for articles that she had already written.[34] The *American Weekly* work generated only a few speaking engagements after 1940. In 1941 she spoke to a group connected with the California Dried Fruit Research Institute, and the next year she attended a meeting on nutrition sponsored by several big grocery chains.[35] She worked hard to please her employers, often suggesting products she might feature, timely topics for homemaking articles, and even booklets she hoped the *American Weekly* would publish. On one occasion, she proposed that the magazine underwrite her visits to manufacturers' laboratories. Admiring letters from readers suggest that her articles pleased the consumers.[36] But her hard work and long association with the Hearst chain could not stem the tide of change. In 1944, Christine lost this primary means of support.

Out of Work

ONLY TWO MONTHS before Christine was relieved of her household column for the *American Weekly*, a pleased advertiser had endorsed her good work to the editors.[37] The following month, however, the magazine launched a change in format that eliminated the food section. Alarmed, Christine arranged a meeting with one of the editors and a canned food advertiser, hoping perhaps that the advertiser would plead her case. Not two weeks later, she received notice that her services were no longer needed. The magazine explained that it was reducing its size, modernizing, and hiring a new staff member to handle women's issues. There would be no more "regular outside contributors." Christine was devastated. She scribbled across the notice that it severed a twenty-seven-year-long relationship and noted the exact time that she read it: "Recd Feb 16th/1944 Read at 8:45AM."[38]

Christine notified her children immediately, asking their advice. David wrote her the next day suggesting that she go see Mortimer Berkowitz, the Hearst editor for whom she had worked, but rejected her proposal that she write to Hearst himself.[39] After several exchanges with H. J. Carl, Christine was given a severance package of sorts. The *American Weekly* gave her "three months salary honorarium," which amounted to $60.75 per week from 1 May through 23 July 1944. In agreeing to this "honorarium," however, Carl made it clear that the magazine would expect weekly articles through April even though Christine had received word of the dismissal in February.[40]

David assured his mother that there were many things to which she might turn her hand. A letter from his wife suggests that Christine had begun to grow weary of household advice: "[I]t seems too bad not to capitalize on [your reputation] in some way—even though you'd prefer to disregard food and home forever!" But she echoed her husband's confidence that Christine would rebound: "We know that you will land on your feet with the dust of Mr. Hearst off them," she wrote. "You're a grand gal for sure, Muzzle, and not to be beat!"[41]

David's wife knew her mother-in-law well. Christine set about stemming the damage immediately. First, she wrote several letters of resignation to *American Weekly* executives to establish evidence, perhaps, that the relationship had ended upon her initiative. Then she launched a flurry of notes to companies with which she had worked over the years. She notified them that she had left the Hearst papers and requested that they send all promotional literature to her address on West Eleventh Street.[42] She tried to trade on the former relationship with Bruce Barton, whose advertising firm now operated out of ten offices from Boston to San Francisco. But she received only two noncommittal (if polite) notes from staff members.[43] The old contacts represented a phase of her life that was already over, and Christine would find new challenges in the pursuit of an entirely different career.

The courses at Cornell eight years earlier had whetted her interest in home interiors; Christine had always loved beautiful materials, color, and design.[44]

She found work as a teacher of advanced interior decoration and home design at the Ballard School of the Young Women's Christian Association, an institution that offered day and evening courses in tearoom management, household arts, practical nursing, and dressmaking. One of thirty-nine teachers, Christine taught classes at Ballard for the next five years, earning a share of the $12.50 tuition per student.[45] This work opened other doors; invitations to speak to the manufacturers of home decorating products led to decorating commissions. In 1949, for example, she redecorated a private vacation lodge in Shelter Island Heights, Long Island. She also claimed to have decorated "swank Park Avenue apartments" during this period.[46] And in addition to the courses she taught at Ballard, she offered private instruction. In 1949, she advertised an eight-session decorating course for a fee of fifteen dollars.[47]

Hoping for steady, full-time work, Christine applied for a job as an interior decorator in 1947. Her four-page cover letter informed the prospective employer that she had had "exceptional experience" as an interior decoration teacher and that her name appeared on the "accredited lists" of several wallpaper and fabric dealers. She wrote that, "as a speaker," she had "platform presence, wit, humor, and a flair" for helping her audience understand facts. The attached "personal record" highlighted her many achievements in advertising and speaking, but it revealed all too clearly that she had scant interior decorating experience. She claimed to be "in the mid-fifties." She was, in fact, just two months shy of sixty-five.[48]

Shortly after her birthday, Christine applied for Social Security, a frustrating and humiliating experience. She wrote letters to many of the editors for whom she had worked over the years at the *American Weekly* and Fawcett Publications asking for proof of employment only to be reminded that she had not been a permanent employee in either organization. The *American Weekly* confirmed the fact that she had contributed articles for twenty-seven years, but, they wrote, "we never considered you as an employee of American Weekly, Inc. because your work was not performed on the premises of American Weekly, Inc." Therefore, they had not withheld social security payments. Fawcett responded, "[W]e fail to find that you were ever an employee of Fawcett Publications, Inc.—your association with this organization being in the form of an editorial contributor."[49] Christine persisted, however. She sent the Social Security Administration copies of Fawcett letterhead that were printed with her name; an early letter from the *American Weekly* reflecting her fees in 1935; several letters from officials at the *American Weekly* who mentioned payments, assignments, or compliments, several from advertisers who expressed pleasure with her work; and even news clippings that identified her as *American Weekly*'s household editor. In 1949, she attempted to collect Social Security based on her employment at the Ballard School, sending as proof of employment a letter thanking her for her services.[50] Christine's busy and fulfilling career had never included full-time employment working for someone else; thus, she did not qualify.

Christine took advantage of New York's cultural offerings during the decade she spent in Greenwich Village. She developed a "coterie" of "distinguished" friends among the artists, actors, and writers who lived in the Village.[51] And she patronized concerts, galleries, and museums when she could. A complimentary letter to the pianist Olga Samaroff Stowkowski elicited a note of thanks in 1945.[52] Although Christine may have had financial difficulties of her own, she remembered her European friends during and after World War II. Emilie Van Waveren, whom the Fredericks had visited while in Holland in 1929, was profuse in her thanks for the sugar, bacon, rice, and roast beef Christine sent her in 1946. Christine had sent Mrs. Van Waveren her entire ration of sugar for the month. She stayed in touch with her old friend Paulette Bernège, too.[53]

Losses and Leave-takings

THE STRESS OF LIFE in the city began to take its toll by the end of the decade when she slipped and fell one icy winter and tore the cartilage in her knee, an injury that bothered her for the rest of her life. The constant financial worries, the weather, the proximity of J. George, and the personal tragedy of seeing her youngest daughter succumb to incurable mental illness combined to induce Christine to make a change. In 1949, one of her Greenwich Village friends, Betty MacMonnies, daughter of the sculptor Frederick MacMonnies, invited her along on a visit to California.[54]

As they grew to adulthood, all four of the Frederick children encountered domestic or emotional problems of their own. At midcentury each had weathered tragedy and sustained loss; their lives were very different than their mother, the home efficiency expert, must have imagined for them.

In 1942, Christine's youngest daughter, Carol, who had graduated from Drexel University in Philadelphia with a home economics degree in 1940, was diagnosed with juvenile schizophrenia and committed to King's Park Psychiatric Center, three miles east of Greenlawn. Her marriage of one year ended in divorce. Later, she was transferred to Pilgrim State Hospital at Brentwood, a short distance to the south. Thereafter her sister Jean and J. George visited Carol regularly, but Christine could neither endure the violent outbreaks nor admit the nature of Carol's illness. Eventually, she ceased to visit Carol at all.[55]

Christine's second daughter, Phyllis, an unusually gifted young woman, was not in good health either. After graduating from Abbott Academy in 1932, she embarked upon a sporadic and troubled college career, attending Cornell University, Traphagen School of Design, and Radcliffe College, never earning a degree. Phyllis was so ill during her third year at Cornell in 1935 that Christine had taken the Ithaca apartment to be near her. And during a protracted correspondence with Radcliffe about Phyllis's admission there, Christine had found it necessary to meet with college officials on her daughter's behalf.[56]

Phyllis's problems were emotional as well as physical. When she and Christine began consulting an astrologer who professed to have healing powers, Phyllis fell in love with him and briefly contemplated suicide when he left the country suddenly. The emotional collapse that followed required an extended period of bed rest.[57]

After leaving college in 1938, Phyllis found jobs writing and editing for a variety of publications and eventually became a toy designer for Mattel Toys, moving to southern California in 1960. There, as Filis Frederick, she continued her work as a devoted disciple of Meher Baba, the Indian mystic and spiritual leader whose followers believed him to be the manifestation of "God in human form."[58] From 1953 until her death, she edited *The Awakener*, a journal she conceived and dedicated to the mission of carrying Baba's "message of love and truth to the West."[59]

Christine's eldest daughter, Jean, graduated from Cornell in 1932 and demonstrated food products for a few months before landing a job with the Rochester, New York, *Times Union* as a food writer. Since Christine's Hearst column ran in Rochester's competing newspaper, it was decided that Jean should not use her own name. With her mother's help, she decided on Jean Joyce as her *nom de plume*. She left Rochester in 1936 and was an editor for the *New York Herald Tribune*'s Sunday magazine for the next eight years. While there, she collaborated with J. George on *The Long Island Seafood Cookbook*, a volume still in print.[60]

From the *Herald Tribune*, Jean moved to Washington, D.C., where she served on the staff of Chester Bowles, head of the Office of Price and Rent Controls. She later followed Bowles to subsequent posts in Connecticut and India. For the last decade of her successful career as a writer, she held a position in the State Department from which she retired in 1972.[61]

Like Filis, Jean had learned from the model her mother provided as an independent career woman, not from the rhetoric that promoted homemaking as a woman's highest calling. In Christine's later years, Jean provided some of her mother's support with monthly checks. And it was she who took the responsibility for Carol's well-being after she had fallen victim to schizophrenia.[62]

Christine's son, David, succeeded in spite of the fact that his parents had not helped him attend college. After several years of writing for the *Boston Herald* and the *Boston Traveler*, David moved back to New York to edit and then publish the advertising trade journal, *Tide*. In 1934, he married Beatrice Jennings and fathered Christine's first two grandchildren, Deborah and Peter. The marriage lasted only five years, and for a few weeks after the separation in 1939, David moved with the children out to Applecroft. Christine's grandchildren enjoyed playing in the Long Island countryside and dressing up in costumes their grandmother gave them.[63]

War provided a new opportunity, and in 1943, at age thirty-five, David applied for a position with the Treasury Department. He became the coordinator of domestic programs for the Office of War Information and moved his family to Washington, D.C., for the duration of World War II. It was from Washington that he wrote Christine upon her dismissal from the *American Weekly*.[64]

In 1949, David landed a job with *Harper's Magazine* as business manager, and here he prospered. The editor, Frederick Lewis Allen, credited him with "striking gain in the business showing of the magazine" and the foresight that made *Harper's* 1950 centennial number such a success.[65]

Christine was extremely proud of David's success at *Harper's,* although she characteristically stretched the truth when she told an interviewer in 1951 that her son was "publisher and general manager" of the magazine. But David was not to fulfill the promise of his early achievements at *Harper's.* On 2 January 1952, he collapsed and died of a heart attack. He was forty-two years old.[66] Thus within twelve years after leaving Applecroft, Christine had lost two of her children, one to mental illness, the other to death.

Christine knew her grandchildren only slightly. She had not had much contact with them until the summer of David's divorce. Occasionally she would

visit them in Connecticut after she moved to New York. Although she annoyed David's wife by interfering in the management of the household, she fascinated the children by telling them Sherlock Holmes stories. When Deborah,
the older granddaughter, was an adolescent, her grandmother would invite her
to visit at the Greenwich Village apartment from time to time. They went to
museums and art exhibits, and Christine encouraged the girl's artistic bent by
giving her a pair of artist's models to drape with fabric. When Christine moved
to California in 1950, however, the bond weakened, and after their father's
death, Christine's grandchildren did not see their grandmother.[67]

Ironically, on the eve of her journey, Christine told an interviewer, "[T]he
sense of permanence . . . is the essence of home."[68] Christine's home had not
been permanent after all. Her marriage had become untenable and she had left
the house in which she had reared her children, none of whom was to enjoy the
legacy of a happy home that their mother had promoted.

14 · Re-creation and Legacy

I believe that every writer is his own STAR, and must write or
produce the inner urge his personality, character, and above all,
his location and his 'age' provide him.
CHRISTINE FREDERICK, Laguna Library Book Day Speech, 1966

IN THE FALL OF 1949 it was clear that Christine Frederick's visit to California would be permanent. At midcentury, California led the way in creating a
new, postwar, suburban America. After a brief period of temporary shortages,
the two-decade-long prosperity that characterized the fifties and sixties encouraged enormous migration to the Golden State. California's population increased by more than half a million souls every year during this period, most
of them young working families. During the quarter century that followed
World War II, thirteen million new residents would need homes. The construction industry and the postwar tract developers that offered the economy
and speed of mass-produced developments did particularly well in places such
as Orange County. Such was the economic climate that greeted Christine
Frederick in 1949.[1]

Phoenix

CHRISTINE TOOK an apartment at 424 Glenneyre Street in Laguna Beach
and began writing a regular decorating column for the local newspaper. She
introduced herself to her new community as a well-known speaker and household expert and soon began lecturing to such groups as the Altrusa and Sorop-
timist Clubs.[2] But a weekly column in a small community newspaper and the
occasional lecture would not support her, so Christine set about finding a teaching post.

California's credential requirements were far more stringent than New York's,
and Christine had not had any formal design training beyond the courses she
had taken at Cornell fifteen years earlier. State officials would recognize neither Christine's past work in homemaking and consumerism nor her years at

Ballard School as adequate qualifications for a California adult teaching certificate, a fact that was "hard for her to swallow." Nevertheless, Orange Coast
Community College, located just eight miles up the coast from Laguna Beach,
hired Christine to teach a class in 1949 on the understanding that her credentials would be forthcoming. The college announcement introduced her as a
"nationally known interior decorator" and "authority on home management."[3]

She continued to teach for Orange Coast College, but by 1951 she had still
not convinced California education officials to certify her on the basis of her
past experience. Christine then took a course titled "Procedures and Methods
in Teaching Adults" at a University of California extension campus and finally
received her teaching credentials for interior decoration and home beautifica-
tion in 1953. She taught at Orange Coast Adult School from the fall of 1949
until the spring of 1957. Her employers were very pleased with her work; the
dean of the Evening College commended her after visiting one of her classes in
1950. But she was an hourly adjunct instructor and the job provided only part
of her income. Her September paycheck in 1952, for example, was $67.50, just
seven dollars more than the *weekly* pay she received from Hearst eight years
earlier.[4] Christine supplemented these meager earnings with extra teaching
outside the college; she offered interior decorating courses at the Laguna Beach
Woman's Clubhouse and through the City of Laguna Beach's summer recreation program.[5]

Christine also started her own decorating business in Laguna Beach. After
becoming certified as a member of the American Institute of Decorators, she
opened a business from her apartment—or "studio," as she called it—on
Glenneyre. Eventually, she was able to rent space in the Professional Building
in downtown Laguna Beach, but she did not remain there for long. Since she
did not drive after she moved to California, she had to rely on friends to take
her into Los Angeles, two hours away, for fabric and wallpaper samples.[6] These
friends provided business, too. One couple for whom she had decorated a home
in Laguna hired her to redecorate their new home when they moved to the
San Francisco Bay Area community of Los Altos. Christine's commissions included a few that earned substantial fees. In 1951, she decorated a living room
for $2,131.45. During the last years that Christine operated her decorating
business, she was affiliated with a shopping mall in the Pepper Tree Paseo in
Laguna Beach.[7]

Christine's various enterprises never completely supported even her simple life in California. And, too, her love of beautiful things induced her to spend extravagantly at times. Jean, sending monthly checks, chafed when her mother spent more than she could afford on luxuries; but Christine did not spend only for herself. She occasionally bought expensive books to give away as gifts. Sometimes she was forced to sell them instead; a cherished, beautifully illustrated book about the famous designer for the Ballets Russe, Leon Bakst, was offered to a friend for one hundred dollars. Eventually, her daughters and California friends hired an accountant to handle Christine's affairs.[8]

Christine re-created herself in Laguna Beach. As the resident older woman with experience, she attracted a "devoted following" of younger women who took her decorating classes, attended her lectures, and sought her advice on beautifying their new postwar homes. Several served as her chauffeurs, driving her to classes, to wholesale shops, and to meetings and social events. In return, Christine acted as surrogate mother and confidante to many of them. Like her children, they all called her "Muzz." These young women were struck by the multitude of her talents. "There was nothing that Christine did not know how to do," recalled one. She once entertained wounded Korean War servicemen from nearby Camp Pendleton by telling their fortunes and reading their horoscopes. Friends remember her as amusing, full of stories and anecdotes, yet always ready to listen to others.[9]

Although she had created a new life for herself, Christine often spoke of her accomplishments during the busy and exciting years in New York.[10] She remembered Russia, too. At Easter she would bake the traditional egg-shaped cake she had first eaten as a little girl in Saint Petersburg. On at least one occasion, her past association with Russia led to trouble in conservative Orange County during the "Second Red Scare" precipitated by Senator Joseph McCarthy of Wisconsin. She was fond of dressing in an elaborate Russian wedding costume her mother had brought to the United States so many years before and performing at fairs and festivals as a fortune-teller. The promotion for one such event promised that in her "colorful fortune telling booth," Christine would read horoscopes and "run the cards" while "wearing an heirloom European gypsy costume about 100 years old." An onlooker at one of the fairs, offended by the Russian regalia, accused her of Communist sympathies. Others she knew had been forced to leave Orange County because of rumors of their associations with Communist organizations. Fortunately, nothing so drastic came of Christine's unpleasant confrontation.[11]

After she moved to California, Christine took a serious interest in the occult, a pastime she had indulged only occasionally in busier days. The fortune-telling, which included tarot cards, palmistry, numerology, and astrology, was but a part of a larger quest for spiritual understanding. She sought out people who explored the supernatural, and soon after moving to California she sent to the women in her family drawings that she believed had been channeled through a living human from "Ferdinand, Spirit Artist." In the autobiographical notes she compiled in 1969, she wrote that "astrological experts" had proven that her birth occurred at exactly "4:13–32 A.M."[12]

The rector of a small chapel just down the street from her second Laguna Beach home soon attracted her attention. Lowell Paul Wadle was a bishop in the American Catholic Church, a denomination that had separated from the Roman Catholic Church in Chicago in 1915. Wadle located his headquarters in Laguna Beach and in 1933 oversaw the construction of a tiny chapel on Park Avenue. A Theosophist, Wadle looked to many different traditions and cultures for spiritual truth.[13] Christine was fascinated by his Wednesday night lectures during which he spoke of the secrets of the pyramids, mysticism, and reincarnation. She was drawn to the séances he occasionally held in the homes of parishioners, and she believed that Bishop Wadle enabled her to receive messages from beyond the grave.[14] In 1954 Christine was baptized in the Chapel of St. Francis-by-the-Sea at the age of seventy-one.[15]

Christine had left New York because she could no longer enjoy the fulfilling work and recognition she had once known there. But she was not forgotten. In 1951, she received the note from the New York architect Ferdinand Kramer, who told her that he had used her theories for years "in the development of modern housing." The next year, the Advertising Women of New York (AWNY) voted to name an annual award given to a student of advertising in the interior design field after her. In 1952, she was featured in a newsletter profile as AWNY's cofounder, and the historian of the club continued to keep track of Christine's whereabouts for its historical records. If Christine visited New York, as she did during the summer of 1957, AWNY would host a luncheon in her honor. In 1962, she was feted in grand fashion at AWNY's golden anniversary. The group's anniversary volume included a full-page tribute titled "Christine Frederick: Accolade to a First Lady." She was flown to New York to be honored at an anniversary dinner held at the St. Regis on 23 May 1962. Her dinner companion at the head table was co-honoree of the event, the journalist Mike Wallace.[16]

There were times, however, when she felt it necessary to remind people of her past achievements. When Northwestern University mistakenly sent a letter intended for her to J. George's New York apartment, she fired back a response that clearly demonstrated her chagrin. She was "astonished and surprised" to learn that Northwestern had not taken notice of her career since 1915. She wrote: "It is difficult to see how with all the unusual and worldwide development of certain ideas of which I was the originator and exponent, known in Europe and with books translated into seven languages—that my Alma Mater did not know this—nor had an address which was so widely known, to reach me correctly." Northwestern's alumni association rectified its error that very year by awarding Christine the Golden Reunion Certificate for sustaining "high standards of culture and service."[17]

Two years after the Advertising Women of New York had invited Christine to be a guest of honor at their golden anniversary celebration, J. George, cofounder of the organization, died of a heart attack in the apartment of one of the two women with whom he was then maintaining liaisons. She had been his mistress for over twenty years; the other was younger than his eldest daughter.[18] Since Christine's departure from Applecroft, J. George had continued to live in his Beaux Arts studio apartment in New York. Although he published over a dozen books between 1939 and 1957, fewer and fewer of his articles appeared in periodicals after 1940.[19] In 1952, however, Edward R. Murrow asked him to contribute a piece for a collection titled *This I Believe,* and in that endeavor, J. George joined such luminaries as Pearl Buck, Norman Cousins, Herbert Hoover, Margaret Mead, and Eleanor Roosevelt.[20] J. George never abandoned the goal of explaining and justifying the American economic system. At his death, family members found among his papers an uncompleted manuscript on the history of business.[21] As he grew older, his interest in food came to dominate his social life. He became an expert in Chinese and Indian cooking and often lectured on cuisine while dressed in the national costume of the featured cookery. In 1957, he coauthored a travel book that featured restaurants. Until his death, J. George wrote letters on Business Bourse letterhead that advertised "Practical Marketing Research, Statistics, Counsel, Surveys, Books."[22] But there was little work.

When J. George died in Queens "at the home of friends," as the *New York Times* reported, the woman in whose home he had collapsed called her fellow paramour, who then called the Fredericks' daughter Jean. J. George did not want a funeral; he had arranged for a simple interment among the Pennsylvania

Dutch relatives in Reading, Pennsylvania. Christine did not attend. Nor did she attend the tribute that the Advertising Women of New York paid to J. George three months after his death. But even then she could not bring herself to openly acknowledge the twenty-three-year estrangement. She responded to a sympathy letter from an old friend as if there had been nothing amiss in her marriage.[23]

Christine survived J. George by six years. In 1968, she was still active enough to throw herself an eighty-fifth birthday party in the little yellow house on Los Olivos Street into which she had moved some years earlier. She asked that only adults attend and promised music, fun, and friends.[24] But her health was deteriorating; in the late sixties, she developed breast cancer and underwent a mastectomy. During much of 1969, she used a walker or wheelchair.[25]

As she neared death, Christine efficiently sorted through all of her belongings and kept only those that she would need during her last months: a few books such as the beloved Sherlock Holmes stories, several articles of clothing, and necessary household items. She carefully marked the things that were to be given to family members. Lastly, she went through her papers and deliberately destroyed virtually all of her personal correspondence.[26] The only private letters she kept were those David and his wife had written after her dismissal from the *American Weekly*. On the papers she chose to preserve, Christine made notes to guide the biographers she knew would sift through them. She developed categories for her letters: some were marked "Praise!" some "Souvenir," and others "Career women." Into the "praise" file went any correspondence that commended Christine on her work, including that from pleased advertisers. On a memo about a speech she had given, she might write, "So many heard me[,] the emergence of the consumer." A photograph from one of her European trips was captioned in her own hand, "Paris Success Story!" She typed lists of complimentary comments from clients on statements and bills from her decorating business.[27]

Early in 1970, she suffered a series of small strokes and was forced to move into the Park Lido Convalescent Home in nearby Newport Beach. Organized and efficient to the end, Christine had already arranged for her own cremation. When she died of a heart attack on 6 April 1970 at age eighty-seven, she was given a memorial service at the little chapel she loved, St. Francis-by-the-Sea, and inurned at the beautiful and famous Forest Lawn Memorial Park in Glendale, just north of Los Angeles.[28] There were obituaries in the *New York Times*, the *Los Angeles Times*, and the *Laguna News-Post*. All mentioned Christine's distinguished career, noting her early writing and speaking campaigns to make homemaking more efficient. The two California papers reported erroneously that Christine had marched for the suffrage movement, and the Los Angeles Times called her an "ardent feminist."[29] Despite the financial problems Christine had had after leaving Applecroft, the accountant her daughters had hired in her later years had helped her to invest small sums from time to time, and she was able to leave four thousand dollars to each of her daughters and five hundred dollars to the Advertising Women of New York.[30]

Legacy of Courage

THE WORLD from which Christine Frederick departed was vastly different from the one in which her early career had emerged. She had adjusted with characteristic aplomb by changing not only her career, but also her life. Her sense of her own worth never diminished despite the vicissitudes that weakened the demand for her services. Her daughter described this remarkable adaptability well: "My own mother . . . who lived to be eighty-seven years was a good role model in presenting an interesting, alert and creative person in her older years. She actually took up a completely new profession at seventy years of age and became successful at it."[31] When she moved to California at the age of sixty-six, Christine expressed her own confidence in another way: "Let anyone drop in on me before my third cup of breakfast coffee, and he will mistake my lined sallow face for that of a character actress doing a 'bit part' in a waterfront cafe. But give me time to apply a cold cream base, pat my cheeks with rouge, add a smart smear of lipstick, and I may be mistaken for the glamour star herself."[32] She expected others to accept her on her own terms. Just as she had shaved ten years from her age in a 1947 job application, she misrepresented her birth date on health histories required by the California State Department of Education. She told Northwestern's alumni association that "for a considerable period, [she was] always list[ed] as one of the ten top women in professional life in America." In a 1966 speech, she told an audience that Mussolini had "pirated" her books and that she performed for Chautauqua "along with Wm. J. Bryan and gentlemen of his type."[33]

The boasts, though exaggerated, were based on solid achievement. When Christine claimed that she foresaw "the automatic washer-dryer and ironer," or that she saved the housewife's back by raising the kitchen sink, she was reminding her audiences that she had played an important role in promoting the technological changes that transformed household labor. If Christine claimed greater influence than she really exerted, as she did when she wrote that she had "pushed the whole Radio Idea so far over," she was trying to preserve the recognition that she had honestly earned in an earlier time.[34] She had hopes of publishing the autobiography she began at age eighty-six and confidently typed notes to the presumed publisher throughout. One such note, in reference to her grandparents' wedding on the wharf at Saint Louis, reads: "Note to Publisher: Very dramatic shot to be photographed for center spread in the book."[35]

Christine Frederick demonstrated remarkable courage and resolve when she struck out on an entirely new and hazardous enterprise at the age of sixty-six. She had endured the attrition of a brilliant career, the final collapse of a thirty-two-year marriage, and the shocks of watching a beautiful young daughter sink into a psychological abyss and of losing a beloved son in the prime of his life. Yet she succeeded in creating a new life for herself and enjoyed a measure of success by dint of her belief in her own abilities. As a young woman in the full flush of her success as a household expert, Christine had written:

> No matter how hard things were . . . I had that inward feeling that they would, and should, come right in the end. I felt that in spite of any difficulty or trying conditions, that I could master my house problems—that there were solutions, and that there was no such word as "fail" in the whole language of scientific management. I cannot express how much poise and determination came from this efficiency attitude—the attitude of being superior to conditions, of having faith in myself and in my work.[36]

She had, in the end, done what she had always advised others to do. Through a positive attitude about her circumstances, she had overcome unhappiness.

Legacy of Conflict

COURAGE AND PERSEVERANCE made Christine Frederick's life a far more liberating model for the women of her generation than her advice offered them. Her career as an adviser to American housewives began at a time when women's opportunities had expanded dramatically and crested during the decade when reaction to the consequences of that expansion caused a decline in the first wave of twentieth-century feminism. When Christine wrote the first installment of

"The New Housekeeping" series, feminists were questioning the view that all women were suited to the role of homemaker. Christine was not only aware of this new thinking, she profited from it by getting a college education and entering the public sphere. Yet she sensed that the vast majority of middle-class Americans would not respond favorably to radical changes in either women's role or the home. She herself was conflicted, yearning for public recognition while adhering to the nineteenth-century belief that women should be homemakers. She participated in the reaction to feminism during the 1920s by advising white middle-class Americans to maintain the status quo through the modernization of the home. She assured the women and men for whom she wrote that most women could be happier in the home than in the office, factory, or clubhouse.

Although the society into which Christine had been born was changing rapidly, it still embraced Catharine Beecher's prescription for women. In practical terms, the nineteenth-century doctrine of two spheres—the belief that women's place was in the home while men's was in the public arena—was an ideal that only affluent, middle-class white families had ever achieved; but most Americans accepted it as the model for proper gender roles. Christine grew to adulthood believing that women's highest duty was making the home "beautiful and sacred for husband and children," a sentiment that echoed perfectly Beecher's assertion that the home was "the place woman is appointed to fill by the dispensations of heaven."[37]

At the same time, Catharine Beecher's career as an educator had helped to give the women who followed her greater access to education. By the turn of the century, when Christine MacGaffey entered Northwestern University, a woman of her station could easily attain a college degree. Charlotte Perkins Gilman and others argued that women, like men, should pursue their individual talents in occupations to which they were best suited. The heady public discourse regarding women's suffrage, cooperative housekeeping, and women's entry into public occupations caused alarm in some quarters. As many Americans began to fear for the survival of the home itself, Christine faced a choice: she could use her education to enter the public sphere as the feminists were suggesting, or she could follow the more acceptable course dictated by her nineteenth-century upbringing. Her solution to the quandary was to do both, an approach that reflected her conflict. Christine married and bore four children. From the position of homemaker, then, she encouraged other women to embrace Beecher's ideology. But in doing so, she constructed a public career for herself.

Christine's talents led her into the traditionally male pursuits of technology, industry, business, advertising, and ultimately, consumerism. Counseling other women to apply the precepts of industrial efficiency to housekeeping, to purchase the labor-saving devices technology had produced, and to trade home production for purchased consumer goods, Christine took an active role in the public sphere while seeming to stay within the domestic. In fact, her advice to other women to enter the marketplace as consumers took them into the public sphere, too, but only as managers of homes. Like Beecher, who had led a very public life speaking about women's role as moral keeper of the home, Christine fashioned a public career by advising women to turn their homes into efficient, modern agents of consumption. Her advice exchanged the role of moral guardian for that of purchasing agent and manager, but it still assumed that the home was woman's sphere. Like the home economists, whose profession she sometimes claimed as her own, she instructed others in managing private homes even as she worked outside hers. This position allowed her to claim, as the home economists did, that her advice would help preserve the American single-family home.

Christine chose to ignore this contradiction; but, in fact, she often unwittingly exposed it as she did by her 1914 remark to the home economists that the career woman was their enemy. Later, as a consultant to advertisers, she not only argued that women should be homemakers, but she also worked to counteract their leaving the home for other occupations. Her campaign for the People's Gas, Light and Coke Company to bring "housewives back to more home cooking" was one example. *Selling Mrs. Consumer,* the manual that taught advertisers how to entice American housewives to buy consumer goods, was another.

Christine's life and work reflected many other contradictions, too, contradictions that peppered the larger society as it adjusted to the rapid changes of her time. The historian Alan Dawley has argued that nativism, nationalism, and Americanism were responses to conflict over change during the Progressive period.[38] The class-conscious, sexist deprecation of the "average" American housewife in *Selling Mrs. Consumer* exposed Christine Frederick's contempt for a large portion of the audience for which she wrote. By contrast, she often credited the woman consumer with great wisdom and good sense. As the dominant white, Protestant middle class of nineteenth-century America adjusted to a population changed by immigration and industrialization in the twentieth century, many of the Fredericks' peers revealed similar conflicts.

While Christine's own marriage suffered from J. George's infidelity and her own inattention, she wrote articles in which she blamed women for failed marriages because they did not support their husbands' professional development. Although her failure to sue for divorce was, in part, a reaction to unpleasant memories of her parents' ordeal, it was also a traditional response to the stigma of divorce. Yet she imbued her own daughters with the determination to become economically independent, and although two of them married, none ever managed a traditional home such as Christine espoused in her work. This contradiction also mirrored the general conflict. The debate over woman's rights versus her traditional duties was central to the first wave of feminism.

Talented and driven though she was, Christine Frederick never openly considered the radical change in fundamental beliefs about gender that was suggested by some of the feminists of her day. Nor did she ever entertain the possibility that men might share in the management of the home. Like Beecher, she preached that men should not be expected to assume housekeeping duties. Christine realized that most Americans, women and men alike, did not wish to make the radical changes necessary to achieve full gender equality. Her strong resistance to the cooperative housekeeping proposals of feminist reformers reflected this realization. She was successful because she offered modernization without radically modifying the separation of the spheres.

Christine Frederick participated fully in the shaping of one of the most significant cultural changes of her time: the rise of a consumer culture that was fueled by industry, commerce, and the development of modern advertising. She was thrilled by the progress she saw in technology, increased production, and consumerism. Her zeal kept pace with the changes themselves. When the popularity of home efficiency waned, she turned to advertising and consumerism. This shift not only followed naturally from her advice to make use of modern kitchen appliances and household products, it also reflected her enthusiasm for the expansion of American manufacturing and business. Christine chose to apply modernization to the home because she knew that it was only from the domestic sphere that a woman's voice would be heeded. Because she was the product of a society in which Catharine Beecher's ideology had prevailed, the application of her talents was circumscribed by her gender.

Though the fruits of the nineteenth-century women's movement enabled Christine to attend a university, discuss industrial technology with men, and speak in public before male audiences, she encouraged her peers to remain largely within the private sphere. Believing that she was reforming women's lives by showing them how to ease their housework, she rejected the substantial change in the female role of homemaker that industry might have facilitated. Thus when reaction to the first wave of feminism took hold in the 1920s, Christine was among those who reaffirmed the doctrine that women's proper place was in the home. She had spent the most effective years of her professional life promoting the idea that homemaking was the preferred occupation for most American women and thus helped to lessen the impact of twentieth-century feminism's first wave. At the end of her life, a new generation of women was beginning to question the assumption that Christine had so energetically defended, and when she died, a second wave of feminism was beginning to swell.

Epilogue

Man is not permitted to shirk his financial obligations. . . .
Neither is it fair, then, for women to pursue an unremunerative
career at the expense of the home.

CHRISTINE FREDERICK, "Shall the Housekeeper Have an Understudy?" 1924

AT THE TURN of the twenty-first century, American women have entered the public sphere to an unprecedented degree. Whether, in fact, there are still two clearly separate spheres represented by women in the home and men in the workplace is doubtful; in 2000, nearly 61 percent of all women over the age of sixteen were in the labor force, and increasingly, these have been mothers with young children. By 2000, 79 percent of mothers with children between six and seventeen worked for pay, and the Labor Department reported that 44 percent of all American workers were women. A sampling of the admissions to several prestigious law schools in 1998 suggests that women are approaching parity in achieving law degrees, and by 1996 "at least a dozen" medical schools had accepted more women applicants than men. In 1999, over 45 percent of all managers were women.[1] The list goes on and on.

Yet despite the advances, women workers have not reached parity with men. In 1999, employed American women, across the board, made seventy-six and one-half cents to every dollar earned by men. Although feminist writers early in the century had optimistically celebrated their belief that all occupations were opening to women, by 1999 most of the sixty-two million women who worked for pay were employed in technical, sales, or support positions. In the late 1990s, most female workers were still clustered in those lower-paying, female-dominated sectors: in 1999, the largest single occupation group was still "secretary." After 1963, to evade the Equal Pay Act and justify lower wages, many employers changed job titles for women without changing the work they did.[2]

Women have also entered the equally public, equally male arena of politics, and recent studies show that women candidates' chances for election to office have risen steadily. Yet more than eighty years after winning the franchise, women are markedly underrepresented in the United States Congress and in every statehouse in the land. In 2001, women comprised roughly 27 percent of state legislatures, and they fared even worse in Congress. As of October 2001, only 62 of the 435 seats in the U.S. House of Representatives were filled by women, and only 13 women were seated in the U.S. Senate.[3]

The reasons that women have failed to achieve complete equality in traditionally male enclaves are complex. But among them is the still-common notion that women, not men, are responsible for the care of home and children. Childbirth tends to interrupt a mother's career, but rarely a father's. When the first baby is born to a two-income, heterosexual couple, the mother often leaves full-time employment, at least temporarily. Because these childbearing women are "in and out of the job market," they do not earn the ever-increasing salaries of their male counterparts. The historian Elizabeth Fox-Genovese pointed out in 1991 that the "acceptance of conventional gender roles" was still widespread. "Culture encourages women and men . . . to internalize [the] prescriptions and practices" of those gender roles as "gender identity." Many who hold conservative views, Fox-Genovese argued, "persist in the illusion that traditional motherhood can be restored by fiat—primarily by eliminating supports for working women." But she, too, accepted the "prescription" that working *mothers* are the ones who need changes in our institutions. Working *women*, Fox-Genovese wrote, need community support so that they can both work and care for their families. The unspoken assumption is that the burden for child care rests not on the couple, but on the mother. The Southern Baptist Convention, the largest Protestant denomination in the United States, provided a clear illustration of motherhood by fiat when, in 1998, it adopted an amendment to its statement of beliefs that declared that woman should "submit herself graciously" to her husband's leadership.[4]

American society is still influenced by the nineteenth-century ideology of separate spheres because the road from Catharine Beecher's prescription for woman's role to the measure of equality enjoyed by twenty-first-century women has been a circuitous one. Early feminists who had sought to change women's role evoked a reactionary response that discouraged women from abandoning their traditional place as homemakers, a response in which Christine Frederick participated. After the retreat of feminist forces during the 1920s, there were few advocates for radically changing the American home or woman's place within it. During the 1940s a virulent antifeminism, based largely on Freudian teaching, was fueled by the recurring fear that the home was in peril when large numbers of women entered the workforce during the Second World War. A popular postwar psychological treatise was the most extreme example.

In 1947 the psychiatrist Marynia Farnham and the writer Ferdinand Lundberg published *Modern Woman: The Lost Sex*, a fierce indictment of feminism that resurrected the nineteenth-century view that women have "an infinitely complex psychology revolving around the reproductive function." Contemporary women, they argued, were "psychologically disordered" "in large numbers" due to the misguided teachings of feminism, a movement they compared to communism, racism, and Nazism as organized "around the principle of hatred, hostility and violence." They argued that women and men were not equal but complementary. What the "psychically ill" feminists wanted was masculinity: "*It was out of the disturbed libidinal organization of women that the ideology of feminism arose*" (authors' italics). Most women's organizations had been infected and were "thoroughly imbued with penis-envy," they claimed.[5]

After the war other commentators agreed with Lundberg and Farnham that women's place was in the home. Some blamed the psychological problems of returning soldiers on the independence their mothers had learned from the feminists of earlier decades. The historian of mechanization Siegfried Giedion wrote in 1948, "Woman shall rule in the household. She shall be educated for this, and to this she shall educate her children." Many women themselves embraced the role of homemaker enthusiastically as new suburbs that featured modern homes filled with household conveniences sprang up across the country. Thus, the postwar fifties, like Christine Frederick's postwar twenties, saw a return to the traditional nineteenth-century ideology that placed women in the home and men in the workplace. In 1962, Margaret Mead observed the regression and suggested that it reached even further back to the dawn of human existence: "Woman has gone back, each to her separate cave . . . almost totally unaware of any life outside her door. . . . In this retreat into fecundity, it is not the individual woman who is to blame. It is the climate of opinion that has developed in this country."[6]

Even highly educated women who grew to adulthood during the fifties often chose homemaking over careers. Six of the first eight women to graduate from the Harvard Business School in 1965, "faced with the conflict between a traditional woman's role and a career, chose the former." Most of them, in fact, did not receive any offers from America's still male-dominated corporations. Interviewed in 1994, three of these pioneering women reported that they had made the right decision by choosing marriage and children over careers, clearly revealing their belief that they had to choose.[7] Married women, they implied, were wholly responsible for the home.

Just two years before the Harvard Business School graduates made their choices, Betty Friedan electrified comfortable, suburban, middle-class America by identifying the female "problem that has no name" in the best-selling book that heralded the "second wave" of feminism, *The Feminine Mystique*. Friedan found a malaise that bordered on desperation among educated friends and interviewees who had forgone careers and become homemakers. Like Mead, she saw women isolated in their homes. "The feminine mystique has succeeded in burying millions of American women alive. There is no way for these women to break out of their comfortable concentration camps except by finally putting forth an effort . . . beyond the narrow walls of the home." Friedan identified consumerism and the advertisers who promoted it—the legacies of Christine Frederick and her fellow "apostles of modernity"—as major builders of these domestic "concentration camps."[8]

The housewife's role as consumer that Christine worked so hard to promote in the 1920s was even more important by midcentury. A vast array of consumer goods became available after World War II.[9] Like Christine, who had seen the housewife's self-esteem as critical to her happiness, advertising consultants tried to elevate the status of homemakers in order to sell their products. The Institute for Motivational Research, Croton-on-Hudson, New York, issued reports to assist advertisers from 1945 through the 1950s. One such report observed: "[P]rofessionalization [of homemaking] is a psychological defense of the housewife against being a general 'cleaner-upper' and menial servant for her family in a day and age of general work emancipation."[10] As Christine Frederick had done in *Selling Mrs. Consumer*, the Institute categorized female consumers into groups: the "True Housewife," the "Career Woman," and the "Balanced Homemaker." The ideal type, it advised, was the balanced homemaker because she accepted technology readily but did not expect it to change her life.[11]

If "properly manipulated," the Institute counseled, housewives could be "given a sense of identity, purpose, creativity . . . even the sexual joy they lack—by buying things." Like Christine, its reports recognized the housewife's isolation. She had suggested that radio could alleviate the loneliness;

modern consultants in the 1950s suggested that department stores exploit it. The suburban housewife, they wrote in 1957, had a "psychological compulsion to visit" the stores. Upon entering, she "suddenly" enjoyed the "feeling she knows what is going on in the world." Such language suggests that the writers of these reports understood the therapeutic character of consumerism that T. J. Jackson Lears has described. They also recognized, as had Christine, the important role consumerism played in the expression of social status. "We symbolize our social position by the objects with which we surround ourselves," the Institute reminded sellers.[12] Friedan blamed women's magazines for creating and promoting this image of the happy housewife as consumer. As they had done in the 1920s, editors courted the advertisers who urged women to go "back home" after the war. Magazines, Friedan believed, manipulated "the emotions of American women to serve the needs of business."[13]

Feminism lay dormant during the 1950s. Although the French writer Simone de Beauvoir's important work, The Second Sex—in which she argued that the secondary position of women was culturally imposed—was published in the United States in 1953, most American women took little notice at the time. The Ladies' Home Journal writer Dorothy Thompson complained that the earlier feminist movement had "never really faced up to" the fact that "the woman who is talented is torn between two functions."[14] The prevailing view from World War II until Friedan published The Feminine Mystique was the view held by Catharine Beecher and Christine Frederick: woman's place was in the home.

Thus the second wave of feminism raised the same questions that were current when Christine Frederick repudiated Charlotte Perkins Gilman's ideas. "Many of the issues of the contemporary women's liberation movement— from job discrimination, to sex-role conditioning, to marriage contracts, to birth control—were raised in the 1920s," wrote the English professor Elaine Showalter in her 1979 work on the women of that decade. Politically, the second women's movement of the twentieth century was symbolized by a new campaign to adopt an Equal Rights Amendment to the Constitution, a measure passed by both houses of Congress in the early 1970s. After a bitter struggle, the amendment fell short of ratification in 1982.[15] Fear about the consequences of a fundamental and far-reaching change in woman's traditional role was to blame.

Like the earlier feminists, proponents of the "women's liberation movement," as the second wave was initially called, attacked the middle-class, single-family house. A spate of critics in the 1980s pointed out that the suburban house responded to a nineteenth-century ideal, not to twentieth-century life. The single-family house, they argued, reflected the belief that the nuclear family with a full-time, homemaking mother was the best arrangement. Suburban houses, especially, support a division of labor by gender. "The home is so intimately tied to the definition of men's and women's roles," one commentator wrote, "that one might even say it exists as a cultural symbol primarily through these roles."[16] The architectural and social historian Dolores Hayden charged that the feminists of the second wave erred in accepting without question the "spatial design of the isolated home." She argued that it is the "least suitable housing imaginable for employed wives."[17]

These critics proposed housing that echoed the ideas of Charlotte Perkins Gilman and Henrietta Rodman who, in 1914, had planned a hotel with central services for working mothers. "Think about those dormitories with linen services and dining halls," wrote one. Another developed a proposal for "congregate housing" with collective services, and a third suggested multifamily housing especially designed for single parents who could share household management.[18]

Ideas for collective housing surfaced in the 1990s, too. A mid-decade commentary in the *Atlanta Journal-Constitution* urged Americans to rethink the 1950s ideal that spawned suburban developments of large single-family homes. Like the early feminists and the critics of the 1980s, this writer suggested clustered homes and community centers where cooks and child care providers could be hired to serve the entire community.[19] By 1998, at least 30 such "cohousing" communities were operative and 150 more were under construction. Most participants cite a desire for community as the motive for joining a cohousing project, but like Hayden's "material feminists," many women find the shared housework appealing, too.[20]

Still, as Christine Frederick pointed out in 1919, most Americans are fiercely individualistic in their attitudes about their homes. Cohousing advocates admit that few people are able to commit themselves to the communal style of living. Even those who are attracted to the community ideal fear the "loss of personal freedom." And neighbors are sometimes hostile; a Boston cohousing project met resistance because adjoining property owners thought it "odd" and "foreign." "Why do they want to live that way?" asked one neighbor. She questioned their sense of individuality, a value she obviously prized.[21] Such loyalty to the single-family home symbolizes not only American individualism, but also an acceptance of the traditional nuclear family with mother as home-maker. Women and men alike cherish this image.[22]

Notwithstanding the campaign to send women back to the kitchen when servicemen came home from World War II, the number of women in the work-force has been steadily rising since 1947. These employed women have also continued to be responsible for the work of managing their homes.[23] The jour-nalist Cookie Roberts noted in the spring of 1995 that married female political candidates are invariably asked who is minding their children. If they are single, they are often asked why they are not married. Such questions are rarely, if ever, asked of men.[24] The domestic sphere, it seems, is even now women's exclusive responsibility. The ideology still obtains.

Harvard Divinity School's Constance H. Buchanan argues: "Traditional be-liefs about public and private continue not only to restrict the public partici-pation of women, but to marginalize the daily unpaid labor of family and com-munity welfare associated with women preventing this labor from becoming a priority also of the public world."[25] There is still far less male participation in the labor of the domestic sphere than women's increasing share of earning might warrant. "[T]he expansion of women's family responsibilities to include 'breadwinning' represents a one-sided shift in the gender division of labor. . . . Men as a group are experiencing nothing like a corresponding redefinition and growth of their family duties."[26] A 1997 survey of 725 women by Lake Sosin Snell Perry and Associates suggested that of employed married women, a full 52 percent contributed one-half or more of their families' income.[27] Yet studies continue to show that women assume the lion's share of household chores.[28]

Christine Frederick valued housework, but neither she nor her predecessor Catharine Beecher believed that men should share it or that women should be paid salaries to do it. Several historians have argued that American soci-ety has never understood the value of housework because it has not been sep-arated from the domestic sphere.[29] In 1973, the feminist Robin Morgan turned Christine's 1914 speech to the American Home Economics Association on its head. Morgan told the same group: "[O]ne could say that I am here addressing the enemy." Home economics, she charged, reinforced marriage, family, and consumerism, institutions the radical women's movement was "out to destroy." Homemaking, she argued, should not be a "gender job." If home economics was to be required of high school students, it should be required of male students, too.[30]

In fact, more American men have begun doing housework according to the Americans' Use of Time project. In 2001, 43,089 of the 200,478 members of the Family, Career and Community Leaders of America (the former Future Homemakers of America) were male.[31] Still, Americans have remained ambivalent about gender's role in domestic labor; many have continued to behave as though it is primarily women's responsibility, an assumption that Christine Frederick helped perpetuate.

Constance Buchanan has observed that in recent years, "national concern about women's work outside the home has continued, generating . . . guilt in many employed mothers." Because of the "staying power" of the traditional ideology, efforts to achieve full equality in both private and public have been less than entirely successful. "[D]ivision of labor makes the private sphere the main arena of women's activity and the public sphere that of men's, giving authority in both spheres to men," she writes. Thus, women still lag behind in public participation.[32]

At a time when the first wave of feminism raised the possibility that women and men might share equally in conducting the business of the world, Christine Frederick embraced Catharine Beecher's ideology instead. She perpetuated the doctrine that bade women assume responsibility for the domestic sphere. Although the early feminists' hopes that women would enter all areas within the public sphere have been realized, equal representation in those areas has been curtailed by the division of labor by gender that Christine promoted; women cannot fully share the work of the public sphere until men fully share the work of the private. Christine Frederick did not single-handedly turn Americans away from the possibilities that her feminist contemporaries glimpsed. But her voice was among those who have made the feminist ideal more difficult to attain.

Appendix · Chronology
of Christine Frederick's Life

1883   Christine Isobel Campbell was born, Boston, Massachusetts, 6 February.

1885   Mimie Scott Campbell, Christine's mother, left her husband and took Christine to Russia.

1888   Mother and child returned to the United States when Christine's father, William R. Campbell, filed for divorce and custody of the child.

        Mimie Campbell was awarded custody by a Missouri court.

1889   A Massachusetts court granted custody of Christine to her father (a decision that was never implemented).

1888–94 Christine and her mother lived with her grandparents in Saint Louis, Missouri.

1894   They moved to Chicago with Mimie's new husband, Wyatt MacGaffey.

1902   Christine MacGaffey graduated from Northwestern Division High School, Chicago.

1902–6 She attended Northwestern University, Evanston, Illinois, and graduated Phi Beta Kappa.

1906–7 She moved to Ishpeming, Michigan, where she taught biology.

1907   Christine and Justus George Frederick were married in Irving Park, Chicago, and moved to an apartment at 1008 Simpson Street in the Bronx, New York.

1908   Their first child, David Mansfield, was born.

1910   J. George Frederick established the Business Bourse at 347 Fifth Avenue, New York City.

        The Fredericks' second child, Jean Olive, was born.

        The family moved to a second apartment in the Bronx at 830 Manida Street.

        Christine wrote a series of articles on trademarked goods in department stores for *Printers' Ink*.

1911   J. George and Christine bought Applecroft at Greenlawn, Long Island, New York, and moved the family to Port Washington while the house at Applecroft was remodeled.

1912   The family moved to Applecroft, where Christine established the Applecroft Experiment Station.

The Fredericks held the organizing meeting of the New York League of Advertising Women.

Christine published a series of four articles on scientific management in the *Ladies' Home Journal* and became the magazine's correspondent for housekeeping problems.

1913?   Christine gave birth to a stillborn baby boy.

1913   Her first book, *The New Housekeeping: Efficiency Studies in Home Management*, was published; she began writing columns for Wheeler Syndicate.

1914   Christine wrote her first advertising pamphlets and testified on price maintenance for the first time before the House Judiciary Committee.

1915   The Fredericks' second daughter, Phyllis Campbell, was born.

Christine published the short, 109-page *Household Engineering*.

1916   She lectured on household economics to the New York Bureau of Vocational Research and made a household efficiency movie at Applecroft.

1917   Christine testified on price maintenance before the House Interstate and Foreign Commerce Committee and the Federal Trade Commission, and she began writing a syndicated column for the Hearst papers.

Her fourth and last child, Carol Hope, was born.

1918   Christine spoke on the Redpath Chautauqua circuit.

1919   The American School of Home Economics published Christine's expanded *Household Engineering: Scientific Management in the Home*.

1922   Christine planned an advertising campaign for People's Gas, Light and Coke Company, Chicago.

She became interested in radio and developed a household program that she intended to broadcast from Applecroft.

1923   David was sent to Peddie School in Hightstown, New Jersey.

1924   Christine published "New Wealth, New Standards of Living and Changed Family Budgets" in the *Annals of the American Academy of Political and Social Science*.

1925	She wrote "Advertising and the So-Called Average Woman" for J. George's *Masters of Advertising Copy: Principles and Practice of Writing Copy by Its Leading Practitioners*.
	Jean was sent to Abbot Academy, Andover, Massachusetts.
1927	Christine toured Europe twice as a speaker on housekeeping.
1928	Daughter Jean began college at Cornell.
1929	Christine took her third speaking tour of Europe accompanied by J. George and daughter Jean.
	She bought beach property on Northport Bay.
	Selling Mrs. Consumer was published.
1929?	Applecroft Experiment Station was remodeled with Monel metal.
1930	Daughter Phyllis was sent to Abbott Academy.
1932	Christine testified on price maintenance before the Senate Committee on Interstate Commerce.
	Phyllis began college at Cornell.
1935	Christine was named one of thirty most successful career women in Greater New York.
	She took an apartment in Ithaca to be near Phyllis and enrolled in classes at Cornell.
1936	Daughter Carol began college at Drexel University.
1939	Christine moved from Applecroft to an apartment at 6 Grove Court in Greenwich Village, New York City.
1942	Carol was committed to King's Park Psychiatric Center.
	Christine moved to the apartment at 55 West Eleventh Street.
1943	Applecroft household goods were sold at auction.
1944	Hearst terminated Christine's employment.
	She took a job as interior decorating instructor at Ballard School, YWCA, New York City, and began a career as decorating consultant.
	Applecroft was sold.
1949	Christine moved to Laguna Beach, California.
1949–57	She taught interior decorating courses at Orange Coast College.

1952   Son David died of a heart attack at age forty-two.

1954   Christine was baptized in the St. Francis-by-the-Sea Chapel, Laguna Beach.

1962   She was honored as founder at the fiftieth anniversary celebration of the Advertising Women of New York.

1964   J. George Frederick died of a heart attack in New York, 23 March.

1968   Christine underwent a mastectomy.

1970   Christine Frederick died of a heart attack after a series of strokes, 6 April.

Notes

Works frequently cited have been identified by the following abbreviations:

AAAPSS   *Annals of the American Academy of Political and Social Science*
AJC   *Atlanta Journal-Constitution*
AWNY   Advertising Women of New York
BVI   Bureau of Vocational Information of New York City
JHE   *Journal of Home Economics*
LHJ   *Ladies' Home Journal*
NYT   *New York Times*
WEIU   Women's Educational and Industrial Union

Prologue

1. K. Sklar, *Catharine Beecher*, 3.

2. Ibid., 59, 107–80.

3. Welter, "Coming of Age in America," in *Dimity Convictions*, 4.

4. The term "true womanhood" was used by Barbara Welter in her groundbreaking 1966 essay on the subject. She identified this ideology in the prescriptive literature of the period. Welter, "The Cult of True Womanhood," in *Dimity Convictions*, 21.

5. *Mother's Magazine* advised in 1846 that "the true dignity and beauty of the female character seem to consist in a right understanding and faithful and cheerful performance of social and family duties." Welter, "Coming of Age in America," 8–16; "Cult of True Womanhood," 29, 31.

6. Many historians of the nineteenth century have discussed the reasons for the emergence of an ideology of the home or doctrine of two spheres. For specific reference to this doctrine with regard to the Beecher family, see Boydston, Kelley, and Margolis, eds., *Limits of Sisterhood*, 4–5, 13–14. For a view that challenges the thesis that "true womanhood" was defined in the nineteenth century and proposes instead that sixteenth-century Europe is the source of domestic sphere ideology, see Buchanan, *Choosing to Lead*.

7. Beecher, *Essay on Slavery*, 125, 128.

8. K. Sklar, *Catharine Beecher*, 113.

9. Beecher, "True Remedy," 139.

10. Edward Beecher to Catharine Beecher, 21 June, 25 August 1822, file folder 21, Beecher-Stowe Family Papers (hereafter cited as B-S Papers). Catharine was the eldest of the eight Beecher children born to Roxana, Lyman Beecher's first wife. As such, she

assumed the primary domestic role after her mother's death in 1816. Although Lyman remarried, Edward no doubt continued to depend upon Catharine for those domestic tasks usually performed by mothers. K. Sklar, *Catharine Beecher*, 19–22.

11. Beecher, *Treatise on Domestic Economy*, 152; Beecher and Stowe, *American Woman's Home*, 229; C. Frederick, *Household Engineering*, 384.

12. Beecher, *Essay on Slavery*, 100–102.

13. Beecher, *Treatise on Domestic Economy*, 4.

14. Ibid., 9; Beecher and Stowe, *American Woman's Home*, 214.

15. [Beecher], "Woman's Profession Dishonored," 768.

16. Beecher, "Address on Female Suffrage," 213. See Beecher and Stowe, *American Woman's Home*, 204, 451–52. Beecher did not follow her own advice. She never adopted children of her own. K. Sklar, *Catharine Beecher*, 186.

17. Beecher, of course, was aware that Stanton was in favor of divorce reform. Stanton had spoken out on other divorce cases in the 1860s and she always defended a woman's right to leave a bad marriage. In the McFarland-Richardson case, to which Beecher refers here, Abby Sage McFarland had divorced her dissolute husband and had begun to see another man, Albert Richardson. Daniel McFarland shot Richardson, who then married Abby on his deathbed. Ironically, Catharine's brother Henry Ward Beecher performed the nuptials. McFarland was acquitted on an insanity plea, and Abby was roundly criticized. Stanton wrote afterward, "I rejoice over every slave that escapes from a discordant marriage." Griffith, *In Her Own Right*, 159. Beecher's letter to Stanton, 16 May 1870, is in the Harper Collection, hm 10546.

18. Catharine Beecher to [Mary] Cogswell and Mary Weld, 29 May 1837, file folder 15, B-S Papers.

19. Catharine Beecher to Lyman Beecher, 1823, quoted in K. Sklar, *Catharine Beecher*, 52.

20. Catalogue of the Officers, Teachers, and Pupils of the Hartford Female Seminary, Summer 1828, pp. 7–11, 14, file folder 320, B-S Papers.

21. Beecher, *Treatise on Domestic Economy*, 45–46.

22. Beecher, "Woman's Profession Dishonored," 766–68; Beecher, "Address on Female Suffrage," 202; Beecher and Stowe, *American Woman's Home*, 313.

23. Beecher and Stowe, *American Woman's Home*, 220.

24. Beecher, "Address on Female Suffrage," 205.

25. Beecher and Stowe, *American Woman's Home*, 214; C. Frederick, *New Housekeeping*, 181–96.

26. Beecher, *Treatise on Domestic Economy*, 28.

27. Beecher, *Woman Suffrage and Woman's Profession*, 26, quoted in Fritschner, "Rise and Fall," 38.

28. Beecher, "Appeal to American Women," in *American Woman's Home*, 466–67.

29. K. Sklar, *Catharine Beecher*, 151–52, 263–64.

30. Handlin, *American Home*, 55.

31. Beecher, *Treatise on Domestic Economy*, 144–45, 148–51.
32. Ibid., 309–69.
33. Beecher and Stowe, *American Woman's Home*, 25–37.
34. Beecher, *Treatise on Domestic Economy*, 338.
35. Ibid., 178–81.
36. Beecher and Stowe, *American Woman's Home*, 287.
37. Beecher, *Treatise on Domestic Economy*, 252–62.
38. K. Sklar, *Catharine Beecher*, 186.
39. See Beecher's letters to Nathaniel Wright, a prominent Cincinnati leader during the 1830s, 1840s, and 1850s, for example. Catharine Beecher to Nathaniel Wright, 29 June 1835, box 19; 14 June 1839, box 23; April 1844, box 25; and 20 December 1859, box 34, Wright Family Papers.
40. K. Sklar, *Catharine Beecher*, 177.
41. See Beecher's "Appeal to American Women," 469, for evidence of her skill at selling.
42. Beecher and Stowe, *American Woman's Home*, 316–18.

Introduction

1. In a speech delivered before the American Society of Newspaper Editors on 17 January 1925, President Calvin Coolidge made this oft-quoted statement: "After all, the chief business of the American people is business. They are profoundly concerned with producing, buying, selling, investing, and prospering in the world." Sobel, *Coolidge*, 313.
2. Sochen, *New Woman*, 147.
3. Recent scholarship challenges this view of the consumer as female. See Lubar, "Men/Women/Production/Consumption," 7–37; Snyder, "Paradise of Bachelors," 247–84; Swiencicki, "Consuming Brotherhood," 774–808.
4. Sara Alpern et al., *The Challenge of Feminist Biography: Writing the Lives of Modern American Women*, quoted in Painter, "Writing Biographies of Women," 155.
5. Dawley, *Struggles for Justice*, 102.
6. Giedion, *Mechanization Takes Command*, 514–22; Haber, *Efficiency and Uplift*, 62–63.
7. Ewen, *Captains of Consciousness*, 134–36, 166; Wright, "Model Domestic Environment," 20; Handlin, *American Home*, 419–23.
8. Ehrenreich and English, *For Her Own Good*, 146–47, 181–83.
9. Banta, *Taylored Lives*, 4, 10, 235–36, 239–40.
10. Wright, "Model Domestic Environment," 20; Hayden, *Grand Domestic Revolution*, 285–86; Strasser, *Satisfaction Guaranteed*, 271; Marchand, *Advertising the American Dream*, 80, 159; Matthews, *"Just a Housewife,"* 170. For a recent challenge to Matthews's criticism of home economists, see Stage and Vincenti, eds., *Rethinking Home Economics*.
11. Goldstein, "Part of the Package," 274–75.

12. Scanlon, *Inarticulate Longings*, 61–71.

13. Marchand, *Advertising the American Dream*, 1.

14. Quoted in Fritschner, "Rise and Fall," 36.

15. Matthews, *"Just a Housewife,"* xvi.

16. Susman, *Culture As History*, 192.

1 · "Only a Girl"

1. [Christine Frederick], "Only a Girl," unpublished, incomplete autobiography, [1969], p. 1, file folder 9, Christine MacGaffey Frederick Papers (hereafter cited as Frederick Papers).

2. Existing records show Christine's middle name spelled variously as Isabel, Isabell, and Isobell, and Isobel. She used Isobel in her autobiography.

3. [C. Frederick], "Only a Girl," [6–9]; Joyce, interviews, 14–16 September 1994.

4. [C. Frederick], "Only a Girl," [9]; C. Frederick, *Selling Mrs. Consumer*, 318; Joyce, interview, 15 September 1994.

5. Christine Frederick, "Wait on Yourself!" *American Weekly*, 31 August 1919, 11.

6. *In the Matter of Christine Isabell Campbell*, no. 78051, "Decree remanding child to the custody of the mother," 27 December 1888, (photocopy), 10.

7. Joyce, interview, 15 September 1994; *In the Matter of Christine Isobel Campbell*, "Answer of Petitioner to Respondent Return," 18 December 1888, (photocopy), 2.

8. Christine Frederick, "What the New Housekeeping Means to the Farm Home," speech before the Farmers' Institute, Decatur, Illinois, [22 February 1916], p. 84, file folder 10, Frederick Papers; Joyce, interview, 15 September 1994.

9. Joyce, interview, 14 September 1994; *In the Matter of Christine Isobel Campbell*, "Answer of Petitioner," 2.

10. Marriage License, no. 2644, authorizing marriage between William R. Campbell and Mimie C. Scott, 14 March 1882 (Recorder of Deeds, Saint Louis, Missouri, photocopy).

11. Joyce, interview, 14 September 1994; [C. Frederick], "Only a Girl," 2.

12. [C. Frederick], "Only a Girl," 1, 3; Joyce, interview, 14 September 1994.

13. [C. Frederick], "Only a Girl," 1, 3; Joyce, interview, 14 September 1994; *In the Matter of Christine Isabell Campbell*, "Decree remanding child to custody of her mother," 7.

14. [C. Frederick], "Only a Girl," 1, 3; Joyce, interview, 14 September 1994; C. Frederick, *Selling Mrs. Consumer*, 354.

15. During the latter half of the nineteenth century, and until the Bolshevik revolution, many upper-class Russian families engaged English-speaking governesses. In the 1830s, a clearinghouse for English governesses was established in Moscow, so great was the demand. A Scots woman served as governess to Grand Duke Nicholas, son of Czar Nicholas I, in 1818, so the precedent for Scots governesses was well established by

the time the Brands sisters went to Russia in the 1870s. Pitcher, *When Miss Emmie Was in Russia*, 7–8, 33.

16. [C. Frederick], "Only a Girl," 4; Joyce, interview, 14 September 1995; *In the Matter of Christine Isabell Campbell*, "Decree remanding child to custody of the mother," 2.

17. [C. Frederick], "Only a Girl," [5], [34–35, 38].

18. The British governesses who worked for the Russian upper classes were treated far better in Moscow and Saint Petersburg than governesses were treated in England. They were accorded the same privileges as family members. Thus Christine's memories of a glittering social life in Saint Petersburg are plausible. Pitcher, *When Miss Emmie Was in Russia*, 35.

19. Pitcher refers to "tall Easter cakes" and a "special sweet cheese pyramid" in describing the special Easter foods served in Russia. Pitcher, *When Miss Emmie Was in Russia*, 81.

20. These details about Christine Frederick's childhood in Russia appear in her unpublished autobiographical notes written the year before her death after she had suffered several strokes. While the material must be viewed critically, many of the stories were repeated by her daughter, who had heard Christine recall the same events years earlier, and acquaintances from her later life remember her telling of them, too. Other than court records validating the trip and the dates, however, no corroborating written evidence remains. [C. Frederick], "Only a Girl," [32–38]; Joyce, interview, 14 September 1994; L. Arnold, telephone conversation.

21. Christine Frederick, "A Lesson from Norway," *American Weekly*, 16 November 1919, 10; [C. Frederick], "Only a Girl," 4.

22. *In the Matter of Christine Isabell Campbell*, no. 70851, 7–27 December 1888 (photocopies).

23. By the time Mimie Scott Campbell left her husband, one out of every fourteen to sixteen marriages in the United States ended in divorce. Between 1887 and 1906, there were a total of 798,672 divorces granted in the United States. Riley, *Divorce: An American Tradition*, 5, 52, 77–86, 124.

24. *William R. Campbell vs. Mimie Scott Campbell*, no. 75 (Superior Court, Suffolk County, Massachusetts, 28 November 1888, photocopy in Archives, Circuit Court, Missouri).

25. *In the Matter of Christine Isabell Campbell*, "Decree remanding child to the custody of the mother," 2–3.

26. *In the Matter of Christine Isobel Campbell*, "Petition for the Writ of Habeas Corpus," 7 December 1888; Id., "Return of Mimie Scott Campbell," 10 December 1888; Id., "Answer of petitioner," 18 December 1888. The matter of money raised the issue of William's reputation for parsimony. Mimie claimed in her return that he had told her before Christine's birth that if she could not provide clothes for the infant, they would have to depend on charity. Christine's daughter remembers that years later, William Campbell was so frugal that he kept accounts of the cost of every carrot in his kitchen

and that he sliced roast beef so thin that the slices were translucent. Joyce, interview, 14 September 1994.

27. *In the Matter of Christine Isabell Campbell*, subpoenaes, 14–17 December 1888. Although Christine had lived with her great-aunt Elizabeth, Isobel was particularly fond of the child and, according to Christine's daughter, left her niece "all she had" when she died. Joyce, interview, 16 September 1994.

28. *In the Matter of Christine Isabell Campbell*, "Decree remanding the child to the custody of the mother," 10–11.

29. Ibid., 8–10.

30. [C. Frederick], "Only a Girl," 36–37; Joyce, interview, 14 September 1994.

31. *William R. Campbell vs. Mimie S. Campbell*, transcript summary (Suffolk County Superior Court (photocopy), 133.

32. M. Keller, *Affairs of State*, 371; Wiebe, *Search for Order*, 11–12, 24–26; Leach, *Land of Desire*, 17–18.

33. Strasser, *Never Done*, 68–94.

34. Wiebe, *Search for Order*, 14–19; Handlin, *American Home*, 89.

35. Wiebe, *Search for Order*, 104–12; Leach, *Land of Desire*, 17–18; Strasser, *Never Done*, 259; Mowry, *Era of Theodore Roosevelt*, 53.

36. Leach, *Land of Desire*, 177–79; Wiebe, *Search for Order*, 92.

37. Leach, *Land of Desire*, 160, 161–62, 165–70.

38. See Kerber, "Separate Spheres," 9–39, for a discussion of the historiographical development of the doctrine of two spheres.

39. Berch, *Endless Day*, 32–43.

40. Quoted in Clark, *American Family Home*, 104.

41. Kerber, "Separate Spheres," 15; Matthews, *"Just a Housewife,"* 19, 43–44.

42. Quoted in Matthews, *"Just a Housewife,"* 125.

43. Brown, *Setting a Course*, 35; Matthews, *"Just a Housewife,"* 125–28.

44. See Flexner and Fitzpatrick, *Century of Struggle*. This new, enlarged edition of Flexner's pioneering monograph provides a thorough account of the nineteenth-century woman's movement. For details regarding suffrage, see chapters 10–12, 16, 17, and 19–21.

45. Horowitz, *Alma Mater*, 28.

46. Rossiter, *Women Scientists in America*, 31, 91. Ellen Swallow Richards had studied chemistry at Vassar and the Massachusetts Institute of Technology. She had wanted to teach, but there were no chemistry positions open to women in 1873, so she helped to develop a new science that eventually became known as home economics. See Ehrenreich and English, *For Her Own Good*, 136–40. Home economics is treated more thoroughly in chapter 3.

47. Tidball et al., *Taking Women Seriously*, 72–74; Horowitz, *Alma Mater*, 117–18.

48. Howells, *Hazard of New Fortunes*, 310.

49. Matthews, *"Just a Housewife,"* 82–85.

50. Ibid., 90–91; Cott, *Grounding of Modern Feminism*, 19–21; Kraditor, *Ideas of the Woman Suffrage Movement*, 44–53.

51. Stage points out that many Americans viewed the home as "a physical space presided over by a woman helpmeet yet firmly under the control of male authority." "Ellen Richards and the Social Significance of Home Economics," in *Rethinking Home Economics*, 30, 31.

52. Handlin, *American Home*, 69–76.

53. Ibid., 54.

54. Mark Twain to Burton Parker Twitchell, 19 January 1897, quoted in K. Andrews, *Nook Farm*, 232.

55. Handlin, *American Home*, 265.

56. Keller, *Affairs of State*, 373.

57. Strasser, *Never Done*, 29.

58. C. Frederick, *Selling Mrs. Consumer*, 119–20.

59. Cromley, *Alone Together*, 200.

60. "Over the Drafting Board, Opinions Official and Unofficial," *Architectural Record* 13 (January 1903): 91, quoted in Hayden, *Grand Domestic Revolution*, 194.

61. Crane, *Maggie, a Girl of the Streets*, 47, 55.

62. Riis, *How the Other Half Lives*.

63. The Saint Louis city directories list a "Minnie S. Campbell, bkpr, H. Watson" for the years 1891 through 1893. The residence listed is the Scotts' address: 1116 St. Ange Avenue. *Gould's*, 1891, pp. 270, 1254; 1892, pp. 293, 1392; 1893, pp. 282, 1279 (photocopies).

64. [C. Frederick], "Only a Girl," [9, 10].

65. Joyce, interview, 14 September 1994; C. Frederick, *Selling Mrs. Consumer*, 119–20.

66. Joyce, interview, 14 September 1994. In 1994 Christine's daughter Jean Joyce claimed to have the letters Mimie wrote MacGaffey from Russia, but they were not available at the time of the interviews nor were they made accessible to the author in spite of several subsequent requests.

67. Marriage certificate of Wyatt McGaffey and Mimie S. Campbell, 7 August 1894, file folder 14, Frederick Papers. This spelling of MacGaffey is a variation. Christine used both McGaffey and MacGaffey.

68. "Northwestern University College of Liberal Arts Entrance Statistics," entry form, 2 September 1902, series 51/12, box 18, Alumni Biographical Files.

69. Joyce, interview, 14 September 1994.

70. *The Review*, May 1901, p. 7, clipping, file folder 14, Frederick Papers.

71. "Gifted Girl the Champion Orator," [*Chicago American*, 29 May 1901], file folder 14, Frederick Papers.

72. Christine wrote in her autobiography that Grandpa Robbie's only son, "Gentleman Bob," a "handsome man" with a "deep interest in both ladies and horses," took over the business when her grandfather died and that the "tun of gold" that had been promised her then disappeared. Her daughter does not remember this mysterious uncle, but there is a "Robert L. Scott" listed in the Saint Louis directories during the period

Christine lived with her grandparents. From 1887 until 1894, he, too, was living at the Scotts' residence, 1116 St. Ange Avenue. [C. Frederick], "Only a Girl," [10]; *Gould's*, 1883–94.

73. [C. Frederick], "Only a Girl," [11].

74. Joyce, interview, 16 September 1994.

75. "Northwestern Entrance Statistics"; *The Syllabus*, 1906 (photocopy), 187.

76. "Miss MacGaffey," calling card, file folder 14, Frederick Papers.

77. [C. Frederick], "Only a Girl," [11–14].

78. *The Syllabus*, 1906, 187.

79. "Christine MacGaffey," transcript, series 51/12, box 18, Alumni Biographical Files (photocopy).

80. Ibid.; Patrick M. Quinn to the author, 31 August 1994; Mr. Quinn, an archivist at Northwestern University, supplied the author with a list of professors who taught the courses listed in Christine MacGaffey's transcript for the years 1902 through 1906. Scott did not teach advertising courses at this time, but rather instructed Christine in psychology, the new science he so skillfully applied to advertising in his writings.

81. Joyce, interview, 15 September 1994.

82. [C. Frederick], "Only a Girl," [15].

83. *The Syllabus*, 1905, pp. 187, 222; 1906, pp. 205, 218, 229; 1907, pp. 235 (photocopies).

84. [C. Frederick], "Only a Girl," [14].

85. *The Syllabus*, 1905, 225; 1906, 187 (photocopies).

86. There are many photographs of Christine Frederick in the Frederick Papers at the Schlesinger Library, folders 20–38. Her image appears in the Northwestern University yearbook, *The Syllabus*, several times from 1902 to 1907. Photographs accompany many newspaper and magazine articles by or about Frederick from the 1910s through the 1960s.

87. "Christine MacGaffey," transcript; "Phi Beta Kappa Notice of Election," 25 May 1906, file folder 14, Frederick Papers; Joyce, interview, 15 September 1994.

88. [C. Frederick], "Only a Girl," 14; Edouard P. Baillot, letter of recommendation, 6 April, 1906; J. S. Clark, letter of recommendation, n.d.; Harold Goddard to Whom It May Concern, n.d.; Solon C. Bronson, letter of recommendation, 9 April 1906, file folder 14; Walter Dill Scott to J. George Frederick, 5 August 1929, file folder 3, Frederick Papers.

89. MacGaffey, "The Genius of Woman," 1–3, 10.

90. Ibid., 3.

91. Ibid., 4–5.

92. Ibid., 5–6, 8.

2 · "Drudgifying Housework"

1. Joyce, interview, 15 September 1994; Photograph mc 261-20-5; "Personalities in the Village," *[Villager]*, 9 March 1939, clipping, microfilm M-107, Frederick Papers.

2. Joyce, interview, 15 September 1994.

3. Wedding announcement, Christine Isobel McGaffey to Justus George Frederick, 29 June 1907; Marriage license, Justus George Frederick and Christine Isobel Mac-Gaffey, 27 June 1907, Cook County, Illinois, file folder 14, Frederick Papers.

4. Joyce, interview, 15 September 1994.

5. Christine Frederick, "Getting the Most out of Country Living," speech before Farmers' Institute, Streator, Illinois, [1917], p. 80, file folder 10, Frederick Papers.

6. The activist and New York teacher Henrietta Rodman fought this policy through her radical organization, the Feminist Alliance, and saw it overturned in 1914 after Christine had successfully launched a very different career. Sochen, *Movers and Shakers*, 41–43.

7. Jean Joyce to author, 15 January 1995.

8. Deed Liber 762 at p. 251, Suffolk County Deed Liber Books (photocopy).

9. J. G. Frederick, *Two Women*, 116.

10. Ibid., 194, 196.

11. Ibid., 326.

12. Joyce, interview, 15 September 1994; N. Frederick, telephone conversation; J. G. Frederick, "Play Confessions," 563.

13. Howells, *Hazard of New Fortunes*, 190.

14. For a discussion of the process of expanding markets in the early years of the twentieth century, see Strasser, *Satisfaction Guaranteed*, 126–46.

15. J. G. Frederick, ed., *Masters of Advertising Copy*, 40.

16. Presbrey, *History and Development of Advertising*, 261, 303–4, 319–21, 350–51.

17. Ibid., 542; Strasser, *Satisfaction Guaranteed*, 93.

18. Strasser, *Satisfaction Guaranteed*, 148; Scott, *Theory and Practice of Advertising*; Id., "Psychology of Advertising."

19. Pope, *Making of Modern Advertising*, 239–40.

20. Scott, "Psychology of Advertising," 30; Tebbel and Zuckerman, *Magazine in America*, 68.

21. Strasser, *Satisfaction Guaranteed*, 94–95, 150–55. For a detailed account of one of the most famous examples of these early campaigns, see Strasser's discussion of J. Walter Thompson's development of Procter and Gamble's Crisco campaign between 1905 and 1912, pp. 9–14.

22. Scott, "Psychology of Advertising," 30.

23. J. G. Frederick, *Masters of Advertising Copy*, 32.

24. Joyce, interview, 15 September 1994; *Who Was Who in America with World Notables*, vol. 9 (Wilmette, Ill.: Marquis Who's Who, Macmillan Directory Division, 1990), 125.

In 1902, J. George had published a small volume that had originated as a tale for the *Review of Reviews*. *Breezy* was the story of a young grocery clerk who rose to the position of advertising manager because of his boundless energy, hard work, and aggressive sales ideas. Four years later J. George sold a short story to the *American Magazine*. J. George Frederick, *Breezy*; Id., "Tie That Binds," 435–43.

25. In his 1930 work, *Humanism As a Way of Life*, J. George drew upon an eclectic knowledge of authors from Dickens to Aldous Huxley to Schopenhauer. These authors are mentioned merely as examples; Frederick refers to literally dozens of works. J. G. Frederick, *Humanism*, 138, 192, 263.

26. Joyce, interview, 16 September 1994.

27. J. G. Frederick, *Masters of Advertising Copy*, 23–24.

28. Strasser, *Satisfaction Guaranteed*, 156–57.

29. Harold J. Swart to Dorothy Dignam, 29 February 1952, carton 2, file folder 4, AWNY Papers. J. George wrote an admiring article in 1913, for example, about Crisco's marketing techniques. Strasser, *Satisfaction Guaranteed*, 14.

30. J. G. Frederick claimed to have helped the publishers of *Judicious Advertising* revolutionize copywriting by introducing "reason why" copywriting while still in Chicago. J. G. Frederick, *Masters of Advertising Copy*, 25.

31. Park Mathewson to Beatrice Doerschuk, 2 April 1921, carton 7, file folder 347, BVI Records. The Business Bourse would allow J. George the luxury of seeing all his future works published.

32. Allen L. Beatty, Council of Better Business Bureaus, Inc., to the author, 16 May 1994. Some sources, J. G. Frederick's obituary in the *New York Times*, for example, stated erroneously that J. George was founder of the Better Business Bureau of New York. "J. G. Frederick, 82, a Writer, Is Dead," *NYT*, 24 March 1964, p. 33, col. 1. In fact, he was a member of this early vigilance committee, a movement that eventually led to the establishment of Better Business Bureaus. See also Pope, *Making of Modern Advertising*, 208.

33. *Who Was Who in America*, 125.

34. Ibid., 125; J. G. Frederick, *Modern Sales Management*.

35. Pope, *Making of Modern Advertising*, 241; Strasser, *Satisfaction Guaranteed*, 156; J. G. Frederick, *What Is Your Emotional Age?* ix.

36. J. G. Frederick, *Two Women*, 170–72.

37. Joyce, interview, 16 September 1994.

38. Ibid.; D. Frederick, telephone conversations, 20 February 1996, 7 September 1996.

39. Joyce, interview, 15 September 1994. Her daughter remembered vividly the stories of these early years, and her description of Christine's feeling about her new life are corroborated by Christine's own writings.

40. C. Frederick, *Household Engineering*, 7.

41. Examples of the pervasiveness of the old doctrine abound. The year before the Fredericks married, the Atlanta Woman's Club published the following statement: "The home is the center of the universe, and the mistress is the center of the home." "Eleventh Annual Announcement of the Atlanta Woman's Club," 1905–6, box 1, Atlanta Woman's Club Papers. Even those who advised women to take part in public activities subscribed to this ideology. University of Chicago educators wrote, "'The woman's place is in the home' is an old saying to which all subscribe, perhaps with varying appreciation of its significance." Talbot and Breckinridge, *Modern Household*, 84.

42. J. G. Frederick, *Two Women*, 195.

43. C. Frederick, *New Housekeeping*, vii–viii.

44. Joyce, interview, 15 September 1994.

45. Kerber, "Separate Spheres," 27.

46. Sochen, *The New Woman*, ix.

47. Muncy, *Creating a Female Dominion*, 18, 38. Muncy's book offers evidence for her argument that women seized monopoly of government agencies responsible for child welfare policy as they created new professions that would serve the needs of educated women reformers.

48. Rickert, "Women's Clubs," 12.

49. A large number of these brochures for the years 1911 and 1912 can be found in box 1, file folder 4, WEIU Records.

50. There were many such conferences for women during the 1910s and 1920s. Early ones were held at the University of Wisconsin in 1912 and Oberlin College in 1916. See carton 4, file folders 221, 226, BVI Records.

51. Quoted in Hall, *Revolt against Chivalry*, 30.

52. "The Girl on the Fence," *LHJ*, September 1915, 30.

53. Friedman and Shade, eds., *Our American Sisters*, 163–64.

54. Schwarz, *Radical Feminists of Heterodoxy*, 25.

55. "The Woman Suffrage Crisis," *NYT*, 7 February 1915, sec. 3, p. 2, col. 1.

56. "Should Women Vote in New York State?" *NYT*, 14 February 1915, sec. 8, pp. 1–7.

57. *LHJ*, September 1914, 6.

58. Three months before Bok issued his warning, J. George Frederick had attended an Associated Advertising Clubs convention where several members of the New York Club signed a petition in favor of a woman's suffrage amendment to New York's state constitution. J. George's name was not listed among the signatories. "Advertising Clubs Widen Their Scope," *NYT*, 23 June 1914, p. 6, col. 4.

59. "Career Chronology of Mrs. Christine Frederick," p. 1, carton 2, file folder 4, AWNY Papers; Joyce, interviews, 15–16 September 1994.

60. Nancy Cott suggests that the term was first used in the American press in a 1906 article in the *Review of Reviews*. See *Grounding of Modern Feminism*, 14.

61. "Talk on Feminism Stirs Great Crowd," *NYT*, 18 February 1914, p. 2, col. 4; "Feminists Ask for Equal Chance," *NYT*, 21 February 1914, p. 18, col. 1.

62. Hapgood, *Victorian in the Modern World*, 332.

63. The meaning of the term feminism has undergone many permutations since it was first used in America. As historians turned their attention to women's history in the 1960s, it became clear that women's movements have never been monolithic. Feminism, then, had to be explained, modified. Some feminists have wanted radical reform, while others have worked for moderate change within the existing system. The term has continued to inspire emotional debate, as illustrated by the heated exchanges between the National Organization of Women president Patricia Ireland and the writer Camille Paglia on *CNN and Company*'s "The New Face of Feminism," 24 June 1998. For an

excellent, if somewhat dated, discussion of the usages and modifications of the term feminism, see Cott, "What's in a Name?" 809–28. The object here is simply to note that the concept arose around 1910, when Christine Frederick was a young bride facing decisions about her place in the world as a woman.

64. Schwarz, *Radical Feminists of Heterodoxy*, 19, 120; Joyce, interview, 15 September 1994.

65. Talley, "Cooperative Kitchen," 373.

66. Hayden, *Grand Domestic Revolution*, 197–202, 239–48, 207–8.

67. Christine's views on cooperative living will be discussed in a later chapter. See *Household Engineering*, 405–8.

68. The ideal of the single-family home would soon be bolstered by government policy. A National Conference on Housing, the purpose of which was to increase home ownership, had been held as early as 1911. Wright, *Building the Dream*, 175–76.

69. Talbot and Breckinridge, *Modern Household*, 2, 10. For a challenge to the view that production had moved out of the home, see Ruth Schwartz Cowan's *More Work for Mother*. She argues that even though many work processes did move out of the home, others moved in and created new work for the homemaker.

70. Bruère, "The New Home-Making," 595; Talbot and Breckinridge, *Modern Household*, 4–5, 21–24.

71. Talbot and Breckinridge, *Modern Household*, 6–8, 79.

72. "Fourteenth Annual Announcement of the Atlanta Woman's Club," 1908–9, pp. 7, 8, box 1, Atlanta Woman's Club Papers.

73. "Mrs. Dodge Says Women Are a Privileged Sex Now—Not Willing to Renounce Their Privilege," *NYT*, 14 February 1915, sec. 8, p. 1, col. 4.

74. Editorial, *LHJ*, May 1914, 5.

75. Talbot and Breckinridge, *Modern Household*, 68, 20.

76. "A World of Woman's Work," *(Atlanta) City Builder*, May 1916, 13.

77. Margaret Deland, "The Change in the Feminine Ideal," *Atlantic*, (March 1910): 290–91, quoted in Lasch, "Woman As Alien," 168.

78. C. Frederick, *New Housekeeping*, ix.

79. "World of Woman's Work," 14.

3 · The Rise of Home Economics and Scientific Management

1. "Christine MacGaffey," transcript.

2. Chemistry was linked to the new field of home economics as early as the 1890s. Ellen Swallow Richards, a pioneer in the field, was a chemist by training. See Ehrenreich and English, *For Her Own Good*, 141–43.

3. For a study of the growth of home economics as a curriculum in the land grant colleges established by the Morrill Acts of 1862 and 1890, see Fritschner, "Rise and Fall."

4. The term "home economics" will be used throughout this discussion, but it should be noted that the organized study of the home arts underwent several name changes before the founding of the American Home Economics Association in 1909.

Throughout the late nineteenth and early twentieth centuries, it was variously called "domestic economy," "domestic science," "home economics," and "euthenics." Selection of the appropriate name for the discipline was a "primary order of business" at the first Lake Placid Conference in 1899 according to the historian Sarah Stage, who provides an interpretation of the implications of the various terms under consideration in "Introduction: Home Economics: What's in a Name?" in *Rethinking Home Economics*, 5–6. The 1904 Lake Placid Conference decided to call it "handiwork" in the elementary schools, "domestic science" in the secondary schools, "home economics" in the normal schools, and "euthenics" in colleges and universities. See also Ehrenreich and English, *For Her Own Good*, 140, and Matthews, *"Just a Housewife,"* 145.

5. Richards, "Social Significance," 118.

6. The School of Housekeeping offered four courses its first year: Development of Domestic Service, House Sanitation, Philosophy of Cleaning, and Practical Side of Housekeeping. By 1900 it boarded its students and offered a certificate of completion after a course of cooking, chamber work, and parlor work. There were two curricula: one for young women studying housework "as a trade" and one "designed to meet the needs of young college women and others who wish to fit themselves to manage a household on the best economic and hygienic basis." "Women's Educational and Industrial Union," leaflet; "The School of Housekeeping Course for House-Workers, 1900–1901," brochure, box 1, file folder 9, WEIU Records; "School of Housekeeping, Course for Employees, 1899–1900," circular; "School of Housekeeping, Spring Quarter, April 1900," brochure, p. 6, box 1, file folder 9, WEIU Records.

7. "The School of Housekeeping Course for House-Workers," brochure.

8. *Journal of American Medical Association* 32 (1899), quoted in Ehrenreich and English, *For Her Own Good*, 141.

9. Handlin, *American Home*, 409–10.

10. Matthews, *"Just a Housewife,"* 145; Handlin, *American Home*, 410.

11. "School of Housekeeping," unpaginated page from journal, box 1, file folder 9, WEIU Records.

12. Handlin, *American Home*, 410.

13. Richards, "Outlook in Home Economics," 17.

14. "Domestic Training Courses Conducted by State," *Union News Item*, November 1912, p. 8, box 1, file folder 3, WEIU Records.

15. "19th Year Book of the Atlanta Woman's Club," 1913–14, pp. 22–23, box 1, Atlanta Woman's Club Papers.

16. Fritschner, "Rise and Fall," 57, 59, 62, 63; Strasser, *Never Done*, 206.

17. Several writers have discussed this paradox. See Handlin, *American Home*, 412–14; Strasser, *Never Done*, 203; and Matthews, *"Just a Housewife,"* 108–10, for example. Newer studies on home economics emphasize the fact that home economics provided women with an avenue to professionalism. See, for example, Stage and Vincente, *Rethinking Home Economics*.

18. "Proceedings of the 1902 Lake Placid Conference," quoted in Strasser, *Never Done*, 210.

19. "School of Housekeeping, Spring Quarter, April 1900," brochure, box 1, file folder 9, WEIU Records.

20. "School of Housekeeping," [1899], brochure, pp. 4–8, box 1, file folder 9, WEIU Records.

21. Strasser, *Never Done*, 207–8.

22. "Proceedings of the Fourth Annual Conference on Home Economics," Lake Placid, N.Y., 1902, quoted in Ehrenreich and English, *For Her Own Good*, 141.

23. For a discussion of Peirce's career, see Hayden, *Grand Domestic Revolution*, 67–89.

24. Bellamy, *Looking Backward*; Handlin, *American Home*, 394–98. See also Hayden, *Grand Domestic Revolution*, chap. 8.

25. Gilman, *The Home*, 38.

26. For Gilman's own discussion of this particular theory, see Gilman, *The Man-Made World*.

27. Hill, *Charlotte Perkins Gilman*, 185.

28. Allen, *Building Domestic Liberty*, 32–33.

29. Gilman, foreword to *The Living of Charlotte Perkins Gilman: An Autobiography* (1935; reprint, New York: Arno Press, 1972), quoted in Allen, *Building Domestic Liberty*, 30.

30. Allen, *Building Domestic Liberty*, 37–42.

31. Ibid., 42–45; Hayden, *Grand Domestic Revolution*, 186.

32. Gilman, *The Home*, 53, 58, 60. See chapter 3 for Gilman's full critique of "domestic mythology."

33. Ibid., 70, 90–101.

34. Ibid., 133, 136.

35. Ibid., 193, 273, 277.

36. Ibid., 311–15, 326–34, 342–47.

37. Hayden, *Grand Domestic Revolution*, 189.

38. Ibid., 202.

39. A. E. Knapp and Charlotte Perkins Stetson to members of PCWPA, July 1892; "Constitution and By-Laws of the Pacific Coast Women's Press Association," n.d.; "An Evening with Charlotte Perkins Stetson," invitation, 10 April 1891, box 1, file folder 13, Calbreath Family Collection.

40. Hayden, *Grand Domestic Revolution*, 205.

41. Gilman, *The Home*, 101.

42. MacGaffey, "The Genius of Woman," 6–7.

43. See Haber, *Efficiency and Uplift*, 51–55, for a description of the Eastern Rate Case in which shippers protested a railroad rate hike.

44. F. Taylor, *Principles of Scientific Management*, 39, 40–59, 85.

45. Haber, *Efficiency and Uplift*, 32–33.

46. Ibid., 72–74, 37–41.

47. F. Taylor, *Principles of Scientific Management*, 77–81; Haber, *Efficiency and Uplift*, 37–39; Giedion, *Mechanization Takes Command*, 101.

48. Gilbreth, *Quest of the One Best Way*, 28, 54.

49. *LHJ*, October 1912, 5.

50. *LHJ*, January 1901, 16.

51. "Standardization of Housework," *JHE* 2 (November 1910): 475.

52. Richards, "Social Significance," 122–23.

53. Guernsey, "Scientific Management," 821–25.

54. Talbot and Breckinridge, *Modern Household*, 47.

4 · Conceiving a Career

1. C. Frederick, *New Housekeeping*, viii, 4; Id., *Household Engineering*, 7–9.

2. C. Frederick, *Household Engineering*, 8.

3. See Ibid., 9–12 for an account of Emerson, fictionalized as "Watson," describing his principles to her.

4. C. Frederick, *New Housekeeping*, 14.

5. Ibid., viii, ix.

6. Ibid., 3–9.

7. C. Frederick, *Household Engineering*, 8.

8. C. Frederick, *New Housekeeping*, 10. Emerson's twelve principles of efficiency, the components he believed necessary in an efficient manufacturing system, were 1. ideals, 2. common sense and judgment, 3. competent counsel, 4. discipline, 5. the fair deal, 6. reliable, immediate, and accurate records, 7. planning and despatching, 8. standards and schedules, 9. standardized conditions, 10. standardized operations, 11. written standard-practice instructions, and 12. efficiency reward. Emerson, *Twelve Principles of Efficiency*, xiv–xvii. Christine repeated the principles in *New Housekeeping*, 14 and *Household Engineering*, 9.

9. C. Frederick, *New Housekeeping*, 17.

10. Taylor, *Twelve Principles of Efficiency*, 144.

11. C. Frederick, *Household Engineering*, 12–14.

12. Lears, "From Salvation to Self-Realization," 4.

13. Tebbel and Zuckerman, *Magazine in America*, 93, 181, 195. See also Scanlon's profile of the magazine in *Inarticulate Longings*, 1–48.

14. S. L. Laciar to Christine McGaffey Frederick, 29 January 1912; Karl Edwin Harriman to Frederick, 7 March 1912, file folder 1, Frederick Papers. Cyrus Curtis, owner of the *LHJ*, had built an imposing new building bounded by Walnut, Sixth, Seventh, and Sansom Streets in 1911. Bok, *Man from Maine*, 121.

15. Quoted in Scanlon, *Inarticulate Longings*, 64.

16. Bok to Frederick, 18 March 1912, 1 April 1912; Karl Edwin Harriman to Frederick, 16 April 1912, file folder 1, Frederick Papers.

17. Harriman to Frederick, 16 April 1912.

18. William E. Walter to Frederick, 20 June 1912, file folder 1, Frederick Papers.

19. C. Frederick, "Country Kitchen," 20; Harriman to Frederick, 4 November 1912, file folder 1, Frederick Papers.

20. Harriman to Frederick, 4 November 1912.

21. C. Frederick, "Woman Who Buys Wisely," 95.

22. Bok to Frederick, 13 January 1914, file folder 1, Frederick Papers; Scanlon, *Inarticulate Longings*, 50.

23. Notes on envelope dated 28 April 1913; Lists, "How Can I Run My Home More Easily?" file folder 1, Frederick Papers.

24. Joyce, interview, 15 September 1994; C. Frederick, *Household Engineering*, 418, 437.

25. The author has not been able to find evidence of this organization's existence, but Christine signed her work as the "National Secretary" of this group until 1915. She mentioned attending alternate Thursday meetings in her second "New Housekeeping" article, October 1912, 20.

26. See the first four articles in the *LHJ*, September 1912, 13; October 1912, 20; November 1912, 20; December 1912, 16.

27. C. Frederick, "The New Housekeeping," October 1912, 100.

28. See, for example, "The New Housekeeping: How It Helps the Woman Who Does Her Own Work," September 1912, 13.

29. C. Frederick, "The New Housekeeping," September 1912, 13, 70–71.

30. C. Frederick, "The New Housekeeping," September 1912, 13, 70–71.

31. Victoria de Grazia, "Establishing the Consumer Household," in *Sex of Things*, 51.

32. C. Frederick, "The New Housekeeping," *LHJ*, October 1912, 20; Id., "The New Housekeeping," *LHJ*, November 1912, 19.

33. C. Frederick, "The New Housekeeping," *LHJ*, December 1912, 16. Christine's views on servants is treated in depth in chapter 7.

34. J. G. Frederick, "Efficiency Movement," 11.

35. J. George bought the house and property in March 1911. Deed Liber 762 at pp. 251–53.

36. Joyce, interview, 15 September 1994; "Applecroft 'shack' before remodeling into home," photograph MC261-23-1, Frederick Papers; "The Experiment Station Itself," photograph in "Household Expert Has Experiment Station," clipping, Springfield, Massachusetts, *Republican*, 18 February 1923, microfilm M-107, Frederick Papers.

37. Joyce, interview, 15 September 1994.

38. Ibid.; Photograph MC261-23-3, Frederick Papers.

39. Joyce, interview, 15 September 1994.

40. The early fireless cooker was an insulated, airtight metal box fitted with wells that held removable covered pots. Preheated food was cooked by radiation from preheated soapstone disks placed in the bottom of the wells. See C. Frederick, *Meals That Cook Themselves*, 17–18.

41. Photograph MC261-23-10, Frederick Papers; C. Frederick, *New Housekeeping*, 249–55.

42. Christine wrote that she needed a sink that was at least thirty-one inches high. According to her working surface height charts, a five-foot, six-inch woman required a sink thirty-one inches high. C. Frederick, "Putting the American Woman," 202; Id., "Country Kitchen," 20; Id., *Household Engineering*, 54.

43. Beecher and Stowe, *American Woman's Home*, 371.

44. C. Frederick, *New Housekeeping*, 250–51.

45. Joyce, interview, 15 September 1994.

46. Ibid.

47. C. Frederick, *Household Engineering*, 326.

48. Joyce, interview, 15 September 1994.

49. Ibid.

50. C. Frederick, *Household Engineering*, 440. The commute by rail from New York City to Greenlawn took one and a quarter hours, and, except for the rush hours, trains were none too frequent when the Frederick children were small. Jean Joyce to author, 17 September 1996.

51. Joyce, interview, 15 September 1994.

52. C. Frederick, *Household Engineering*, 437.

53. Ibid., 391.

54. "The Woman Who Invented Scientific Housekeeping," *NYT*, 6 July 1913, sec. 7, p. 10.

55. Mary B. Mullett, "Who's Who Among Women," n.p., n.d., clipping, microfilm M-107, Frederick Papers.

56. C. Frederick, *Household Engineering*, 489–90; Joyce, interview, 15 September 1994.

57. C. Frederick, "The New Housekeeping," *LHJ*, October 1912, 20.

58. C. Frederick, *Household Engineering*, 198.

59. C. Frederick, "The New Housekeeping," *LHJ*, November 1912, 20; Jean Joyce to the author, 14 June 1995.

60. J. G. Frederick, "Play Confessions," 564–65.

61. C. Frederick, "Equipping an Orchard," 108.

62. C. Frederick, "Making a Tennis Court," 66; Joyce, interview, 15 September 1994.

63. Joyce, interview, 15 September 1994; Christine Frederick, Laguna Library Book Day Speech, 22 November 1966, file folder 10, Frederick Papers.

64. Joyce to author, 15 January 1995.

65. C. Frederick, *Household Engineering*, 383–84; Id., "A Health Room," *American Weekly*, 9 May 1920, 14.

66. C. Frederick, "The New Housekeeping," *LHJ*, November 1912, 20.

67. Joyce to author, 15 January 1995; [David Frederick] to Christine Frederick, 17 February 1944, file folder 5, Frederick Papers.

68. Joyce, interview, 15 September 1994; Schwarz, *Radical Feminists of Heterodoxy*, 67.

69. J. G. Frederick, *Two Women*, 210; C. Frederick, *Household Engineering*, 503; Joyce, interview, 16 September 1994.

70. Joyce, interview, 15 September 1994; Falk, telephone conversation.

71. C. Frederick, "The New Housekeeping," *LHJ*, October 1912, 100.

72. Cowan, *More Work for Mother*, 158. Harry Hollingworth, for example, earned an annual salary of one thousand dollars as a professor at Columbia. Schwarz, *Radical*

Feminists of Heterodoxy, 57. For a description of the many "poor" homes in which Americans lived in 1912, see Cowan, 160–72. Women in these circumstances had difficulty keeping houses and bodies clean and providing sufficient food for their families; they could not begin to think about introducing scientific management into their households.

73. C. Frederick, *Household Engineering*, 366.

74. Joyce, interview, 15 September 1994.

75. Bok, *Man From Maine*, 199–201; Bok to Frederick, 17 March 1913; Harriman to Frederick, 16 April 1913; Harriman to Frederick, 28 April 1913, file folder 1, Frederick Papers.

76. "Devices Tested by Shrine Service," *Shrine Magazine*, n.d., microfilm M-107, Frederick Papers; C. Frederick, *Selling Mrs. Consumer*, 224–25; "Greetings from the Applecroft Home Experiment Station," [1928?], brochure, file 15, Frederick Papers.

77. Beecher, *Treatise on Domestic Economy*, quoted in C. Frederick, *New Housekeeping*, 240.

78. C. Frederick, *New Housekeeping*, 183–86.

79. Harrington Emerson, foreword to C. Frederick, *Household Engineering*, [2–3].

80. See Ruth Cowan's discussion of the increased labor necessitated by indoor plumbing in *More Work for Mother*, 86–89.

81. C. Frederick, *Household Engineering*, 147–48.

82. Ibid., 82, 173, 389, 484.

83. A study of sixty "comfortable" New York families from 1912 to 1914 revealed that the housewives in these homes spent an average of fifty-six hours a week on housework. John B. Leeds, "The Household Budget: With a Special Inquiry into the Amount and Value of Household Work" (Ph.D. diss., Columbia University, 1917) cited in Cowan, *More Work for Mother*, 245 n. 1.

84. C. Frederick, "Putting the American Woman," 206.

85. C. Frederick, "How I Save Money," *LHJ*, January 1914, 38.

86. C. Frederick, "Putting the American Woman," 208.

87. C. Frederick, "Points in Efficiency," 280.

88. C. Frederick, *Household Engineering*, 68–72, 198.

89. C. Frederick, *New Housekeeping*, 190.

90. F. Taylor, *Principles of Scientific Management*, 70.

91. Ibid., 43, 123.

92. Arnold, "Fundamental Conceptions," *JHE*, 6 (December 1914): 423, 429.

93. "Housekeeping Old Style," *NYT*, 1 June 1915, p. 14, col. 6.

5 · Promoting Industry to Save the Home

1. Women in Industry Lecture no. 1, 1.

2. C. Frederick, "Household Economics," 16–21.

3. C. Frederick, "Points in Efficiency," 280.

4. "Housekeepers to Learn to Save 1,000 Steps a Day," *New York Tribune*, 12 March 1914, clipping, microfilm M-107, Frederick Papers.

5. C. Frederick, *Selling Mrs. Consumer*, 167.

6. "An Experiment Station for Making Housekeeping Easy," *NYT*, 7 May 1911, sec. 5, p. 13.

7. "Experiment Station to Solve Housekeepers' Problems," *NYT*, 26 March 1911, sec. 5, p. 4; Pattison, "Scientific Management in Home-Making," 96–98.

8. C. Frederick, *New Housekeeping*, 248, 250.

9. C. Frederick, "Putting the American Woman," 201, 252.

10. "Applecroft Experiment Station," billing statement, 30 November 1914, file folder 1, Frederick Papers.

11. Christine often stretched the truth. On a later letterhead, to add extra "staff" to the Applecroft enterprise, she used the name Isobel Brands, the name of one of the great aunts who served as governesses in Russia. She also wrote under that name occasionally. Sometimes Christine invented the names of other businesses. On the backs of various photographs promoting her activities, she stamped "Phyllis Frederick Photo Service," a "made-up name to sound businesslike," according to her daughter. Christine Frederick to Mr. W. E. Loucks, 3 April 1919, file folder 2, Frederick Papers; Photograph M261-23-2, Frederick Papers; Jean Joyce to author, 15 January 1995.

12. C. Frederick, *Household Engineering*, 16; Joyce, interview, 15 September 1994. Copies of the bulletin can be seen in file folder 12, and an example of a food wheel, "Mrs. Christine Frederick's Housekeepers' Food Guide," in file folder 16 of the Frederick Papers.

13. Bruère, "The New Home-Making," 594.

14. "Laundry Washing Brings Leisure Hours," calendar cover sheet, n.d., oversize file folder 1, Frederick Papers.

15. For a discussion of how the manufacture of washing machines brought laundry back into the home even after it had appeared to move to the commercial laundry, see Strasser, *Never Done*, 109–13, 121–24. Siegfried Giedion provides an interesting account of the early development of the home washing machine in *Mechanization Takes Command*, 560–70.

16. See chapter 6, "The Practical Laundry: Methods and Tools," in C. Frederick, *Household Engineering*, 211–64.

17. C. Frederick, *You and Your Laundry*, 26–28.

18. Christine Frederick, "How America Simplifies Housekeeping," the *Daily Mail*, 22 February 1927, microfilm M-107, Frederick Papers.

19. Christine Frederick, "What the Customer Needs," speech before the National Electric Light Association, 25 March 1931, p. 4, file folder 10, Frederick Papers.

20. "Motion Picture Dancing Lessons at Home! With the Pathoscope," *NYT*, 9 August 1914, picture sec., p. 9.

21. Marion Glenn, "Films Make Markets," *Forbes Magazine*, 4 May 1918, pp. 63–64, carton 7, file folder 356, BVI Records.

Camilla Donworth, "the only woman advertisement screen expert" and president of Films of Business Corporation, produced sales films for American companies that showed how fast their workers could move through the entire manufacturing process. One of Donworth's tactics was to get her industrial films screened in local movie houses. "Is There Room at the Top?" *Woman Citizen*, [15 March 1919], clipping, carton 7, file folder 356, BVI Records.

22. "Motion Pictures of Old and New . . . Methods Are the Latest Thing in the . . .," [2 November 1916], fragmentary clipping, microfilm M-107, Frederick Papers.

23. Karl Edwin Harriman to Christine Frederick, 15 August 1916, file folder 1, Frederick Papers.

24. C. Frederick, "The New Housekeeping," *LHJ*, September 1912, 13, 70–71.

25. C. Frederick, *New Housekeeping*, 256–57.

26. See note 52 of this chapter.

27. Bruère, "The New Home-Making," 592–93.

28. C. Frederick, *Household Engineering*, 391–92.

29. Dawley, *Struggles for Justice*, 74.

30. Cowan, *More Work for Mother*, 90–95.

31. C. Frederick, *Household Engineering*, 127–29, 242, 370.

32. C. Frederick, "Country Kitchen," 20.

33. C. Frederick, *New Housekeeping*, 253–54.

34. Orelup, "For Scientists and Artists," 40; Photograph 261-23-16, Frederick Papers.

35. *The Efficient Kitchen and Laundry*, 1914, pamphlet, file folder 12, Frederick Papers.

36. C. Frederick, *Household Engineering*, 16.

37. Ibid., 116, 135, 203, 240–41. The pamphlet was *Meals That Cook Themselves*.

38. C. Frederick, *Household Engineering*, 173–75.

39. Ibid., 117–24, 244–49.

40. Ibid., 100–108.

41. Christine Frederick, "Push Button Cookery," [1916], clipping, microfilm M-107, Frederick Papers.

42. C. Frederick, *Household Engineering*, 199, 111–16.

43. Wiseman, "Christine Frederick," 17.

44. Christine Frederick, "Mrs. Consumer Speaks Up," speech before the New York Rotary, 10 March 1938, p. 4, file folder 10, Frederick Papers.

45. Goldstein, "Part of the Package," 288; Theresa H. Wolcott to C. Frederick, 16 September 1915, file folder 1, Frederick Papers; L. M. Robinson, "Safeguarded by Your Refrigerator," 253; Ronald R. Kline, "Agents of Modernity: Home Economists and Rural Electrification, 1925–1950," in *Rethinking Home Economics*, ed. Stage and Vincenti, 241.

46. J. George Frederick to Jo Foxworth, 3 March 1964, file folder 8, Frederick Papers. There are also references to these early articles in C. Frederick, "Mrs. Consumer Speaks Up," 4, and "Career Chronology."

47. J. G. Frederick, *Masters of Advertising Copy*, 29.

48. Strasser, *Satisfaction Guaranteed*, 165–66.

49. C. Frederick, *You and Your Kitchen;* "Housekeepers to Learn to Save 1,000 Steps a Day."

50. The following pamphlets either written by or referring to testing done by Christine Frederick can be found in file folder 12 of the Frederick Papers: *The Efficient Kitchen and Laundry* (New York: Efficiency Society, 1914); *How to Plan and Equip the Efficient Kitchen* (Philadelphia: *Ladies' Home Journal,* n.d.); *You and Your Laundry* (New York: Hurley Machine Company, 1920); *Woman As Bait in Advertising* (New York: League of Advertising Women of New York, 1921); *Come into My Kitchen* (Sheboygan, Wis.: Vollrath Company, 1922); *Tested and Recommended Household Equipment* (Springfield, Mass.: *Farm and Home Magazine,* n.d.); *Seald Sweet Cook Book* (Tampa, Fla.: Florida Citrus Exchange, n.d.); *Parties All the Year Round* (New York: *Shrine Magazine,* 1928); *Frankfurters As You Like Them* (New York: Stahl-Meyer, Inc., 1931); *Hershey's Favorite Recipes* (Hershey, Pa.: Hershey Chocolate Corporation, 1937); *Let's Bring the Kitchen Up-to-Date* (New York: International Nickel Company, n.d.). Other promotional publications include *Meals That Cook Themselves* and *The Ignoramus Book of Housekeeping*.

One pamphlet commissioned by *Farm and Home Magazine* features a variety of household appliances, and a booklet published by the *Ladies' Home Journal* advises on equipping a kitchen.

51. WEIU, *Advertising As a Vocation for Women,* 1911, booklet, box 1, file folder 9, WEIU Records.

52. "Business Advertising," Women in Industry Lecture no. 12, 4 January 1916, pp. 43–45, carton 1, file folder 13, BVI Records.

53. "Vocational Conference," 22–24 February 1917, Vassar College, program, carton 4, file folder 225, BVI Records.

54. "Vocational Conference," 11 April 1919, University of Pittsburgh, program, carton 4, file folder 221, BVI Records.

55. Dorothy Dignam, "More Women in Advertising Now Than in World War I," *Printers' Ink,* 29 May 1942, p. 16, clipping, carton 3, file folder 18, Dorothy Dignam Papers.

56. "Women in the Field of Advertising," [10 April 1919], pp. 1–3, typescript, carton 2, file folder 75, BVI Records.

57. Cott, *Grounding of Modern Feminism,* 230. The American Medical Association's standards made it difficult for women to practice medicine, so female physicians organized the Medical Women's National Association in 1915. Because there was no female equivalent to the all-male Chamber of Commerce, businesswomen established the National Federation of Business and Professional Women's Clubs three years later. Lemons, *Woman Citizen,* 42–44.

58. "Organizations of Advertising Women," 3 September 1919, typescript, carton 2, file folder 74, BVI Records.

59. This version of AWNY's beginnings was synthesized from the following sources: "Beginnings—Formation of the League," n.d., typescript; J. George Frederick, "Notes on the Formation of the Advertising Women's Club of New York," October 1961,

typescript; "Founders' Section," n.d., typescript; "History of Club," n.d., typescript, carton 2, file folder 1, AWNY Papers; Wiseman, "Christine Frederick," 17; Oakley, "AWNY," 60; Dorothy Dignam, "Some Women Have Made Good in Advertising, But As to Other—," *Printers' Ink*, 27 April 1939, p. 18, clipping, carton 3, file folder 18; "History of Advertising Women of New York, Inc., Chronological Record of the Year 1958," carton 3, file folder 17, Dignam Papers. Twenty years after she had repeated this account, Christine changed her own version of the story, claiming that she was the one who asked to attend the men's league. She wrote that J. George had replied that she could attend only if she wanted to sit "in the boxes above, behind the curtains—in kind of a purdah." Angry, she decided to form the women's group. Since this version, written in the 1950s, is quite different from the one she told in a 1938 speech, it must be viewed with suspicion. "Excerpts from a letter from Christine Frederick," [1951], carton 2, file folder 4, AWNY Papers.

60. Excerpt from a letter from Christine Frederick to Sally [Martin], November 1951, carton 2, file folder 1, AWNY Papers.

61. "Advertising Women of New York Golden Anniversary Dinner and Installation," 23 May 1962, invitation, file folder 17, Frederick Papers.

62. Nadine Miller to Christine Frederick, 9 June 1952, file folder 8, Frederick Papers; "Founders' Section," n.d., 7–8; Oakley, "AWNY."

63. "Dazzling Styles Bewilder Diners," *NYT*, 13 March 1914, p. 11, col. 3.

64. "Briliant [sic] Banquet Planned for Dr. Wiley," *Lancaster Morning Journal*, 30 January 1915, clipping, microfilm M-107, Frederick Papers.

65. Photograph MC261-22-1, Frederick Papers.

66. J. G. Frederick, *Masters of Advertising Copy*, 33–34, 39.

67. C. Frederick, *Household Engineering*, 357.

68. Ibid.

69. Gilman, "Advertising Nuisance," 327.

70. Leach, *Land of Desire*, 67–68.

71. C. M. Robinson, "Abuses of Public Advertising," 289–92.

72. Lears, "From Salvation to Self Realization," 20.

73. C. Frederick, *Household Engineering*, 357. Christine's views on the common interests of manufacturers, advertisers, and consumers is treated in depth below.

74. Lears, "From Salvation to Self Realization," 18.

75. C. Frederick, "Household Economics," 4, 11–12.

76. Gilman, "Women and Vocations," 27, 30, 33.

77. Ohmann, *Selling Culture*, 271.

6 · Expounding the Business Ethic

1. The Online Computer Library Center (hereafter cited as OCLC) lists five separate publication years: 1913, 1914, 1918, 1919, and 1926. Christine at one time claimed that the book was translated into "French, German, Polish, Scandinavian, and

Japanese." In a speech given three years before she died, she added Italian, Czechoslovakian, and Dutch to the list. The 1914 printing included the copyright notice: "All rights reserved, including that of translation into Foreign Languages, including the Scandinavian." OCLC lists a German translation published in 1921 and a Polish one in 1926. An undated *New Housekeeping* book jacket in Christine's papers is imprinted, "Seventh Large Printing," file folder 11, Frederick Papers. C. Frederick, "Advertising Copy," 223; C. Frederick, Laguna Library Book Day Speech; C. Frederick, *New Housekeeping*, iv.

2. "The New Housekeeping," a review of *New Housekeeping*, 336–37.

3. "Chronicle and Comment," a review of *New Housekeeping*, 3.

4. "The New Housekeeping," [12 June 1913], clipping; "Servant Question Solved," n.d., clipping; Marguerite Mooers Marshall, "American Housewives Losing $1,000,000 a Day by Domestic Inefficiency," [1913], clipping, microfilm M-107, Frederick Papers.

5. "A Corner for Local Housewives," *The Summit Herald*, 18 July [1913], clipping, microfilm M-107, Frederick Papers.

6. "The Woman Who Invented Scientific Housekeeping."

7. C. Frederick, *Selling Mrs. Consumer*, 166; "Career Chronology."

8. C. Frederick, *New Housekeeping*, 242–43.

9. The bibliography of *The New Housekeeping* lists several works about the home economics movement, including Ellen Richards, *The Art of Right Living* and Isabel Bevier and Susannah Usher, *The Home Economics Movement*, 260. Historians of the home economics movement hasten to distance their subjects from Christine. Carolyn Goldstein has pointed out that Christine was not a member of the home economists' community because she lacked formal training in the discipline. Furthermore, Goldstein asserts, the home economists were uncomfortable with her association with advertising. On Christine's part, she sometimes privately referred to home economists as "lima beans" and considered her own work to be based on "broader" thinking than theirs. She criticized their emphasis on training teachers instead of homemakers. Goldstein, "Part of the Package," 5; Joyce, interview, 15 September 1994; C. Frederick, *New Housekeeping*, 235–36.

10. Quoted in Bevier and Usher, *Home Economics Movement*, 40.

11. Some of the home economics textbooks mentioned by Talbot and Breckinridge in 1912 were Bertha Terrill, *Household Management*; T. M. Clark, *Care of the House*; Isabel Bevier, *The House*; S. Maria Elliot, *Household Hygiene*; Caroline L. Hunt, *Home Problems from a New Standpoint*; Maria Parloa, *Home Economics*; Ellen Richards, *Euthenics*; and Helen Campbell, *Household Economics*. *Modern Household*, 27–28, 36, 81.

12. Homer L. Patterson, comp. and ed., *Patterson's American Educational Directory*, vol. 43 (Chicago: American Educational Company, 1946), 781; Thomas Kennelly, director of Independent Studies, American School, telephone conversation. Advertisements for American School courses appeared in *The Craftsman* (see February 1908, xvii), and Martha Bruère mentioned the American School of Home Economics in her *Outlook* articles, 7 September 1912, 30; and 6 July 1912, 540.

13. "Our New Courses," American School of Home Economics Bulletin, n.d., series 1, no. 56, pp. 1–5, file folder 11, Frederick Papers.

14. The debut of *Household Engineering* was as a Bulletin of the American School of Home Economics, series 1, no. 39. *National Union Catalog: Pre-1956 Imprints*, vol. 183 (n.p.: Mansell, 1971), 602. OCLC lists editions of the expanded book in 1919, 1920, 1923, and 1925. The 1925 edition is listed as the sixth in Mary Burnham and Ida M. Lynns, eds., *The Cumulative Book Index* (New York: H. W. Wilson Company, 1927), 461.

15. C. Frederick, *Household Engineering*, [1].

16. Frank Gilbreth, preface to *Household Engineering*, [4].

17. Harrington Emerson, foreword to *Household Engineering*, [2–3].

18. Ibid., [3].

19. C. Frederick, *Household Engineering*, 17.

20. See *Ibid.*, 325, 336, 337, 339, and 347 for reference to specific numbers.

21. Ibid., 15–16.

22. "Household Engineering," review of *Household Engineering: Scientific Management in the Home*, by Christine Frederick, *Impressions: A Magazine of Character*, [1915], 48, clipping, microfilm M-107, Frederick Papers.

23. C. Frederick, *Household Engineering*, 124–27, 170–75, 212–21.

24. Ibid., 169–70, 331–33, 481–503; Beecher, *Treatise on Domestic Economy*, 47–70.

25. C. Frederick, *Household Engineering*, 45–46, 59, 224, 373–76. Monel metal, a corrosion-resistant alloy of nickel and copper, was developed in 1905 by Robert C. Stanley, an employee of International Nickel Company who named the alloy for the company's president, Ambrose Monell. Zahner, *Architectural Metals*, 285–90.

26. "Household Engineering," *Impressions*, 48. The *Journal of Home Economics* praised the book as a stimulus that would encourage homemakers "to try new methods of housekeeping." The American Library Association's *Booklist* wrote that Christine had "excellent ideas, well presented." *Book Review Digest: Fifteenth Annual Cumulation* (New York: H. W. Wilson Company, 1920), 183.

27. Mary Koll Heiner to Christine Frederick, 28 February 1947, file folder 6, Frederick Papers.

28. Ferdinand Kramer to Christine Frederick, 10 December 1951, file folder 8, Frederick Papers.

29. "Household Engineering," *Impressions*, 48.

30. Examples are Christine Frederick, "Have a Step-Saving Kitchen," *Delineator*, July 1914, 23–24; Isobel Brands, "Household Devices Which Save Time and Labor," [*Priscilla*], n.d., clipping, microfilm M-107, Frederick Papers.

31. C. Frederick, "Equipping an Orchard," 108.

32. C. Frederick, "La Tenue Scientifique," with an introduction by M. Henry Le Chatelier, 348–82.

33. C. Frederick, Laguna Library Book Day Speech; "New Series of Daily Articles, Entitled: 'The Business of Homemaking,'" newspaper advertisement, [April 1919], oversized folder 1, Frederick Papers. For information about John Neville Wheeler's New

York syndicate, see *Who's Who in America,* vol. 12 (Chicago: A. N. Marquis and Company, 1912), 3266.

34. Christine told an audience in 1966 that she had written for the Hearst papers for twenty-nine years, which would have meant that she began in 1915. But in a typed note she attached to a 1942 letter, she wrote that she had begun a "syndicate for Am. Weekly in 1917." Her first article appeared on 14 January 1917. Laguna Library Book Day Speech; Christine Frederick to Portus Baxter, 12 May 1942, file folder 4, Frederick Papers; Christine Frederick, "How Long Does It Take Your Wife to Dress?" *American Weekly,* 14 January 1917, 10.

35. Tebbel, *Compact History,* 238–39.

36. Scanlon, *Inarticulate Longings,* 51.

37. Applecroft Experiment Station statement to Curtis Publishing Company, 30 November 1914, file folder 1, Frederick Papers.

38. Christine Frederick, ed., "The New Housekeeping," *LHJ,* December 1915, 47.

39. Karl Harriman asked Christine to have a talk with a disgruntled correspondent who apparently felt Christine had used a plan he had devised in a *Journal* article. "It is possible that it may have been exploited by us without his knowledge . . . You, of course could tell him that at once," Harriman wrote. K. E. Harriman to Christine Frederick, 13 July 1914, file folder 1, Frederick Papers.

40. K. E. Harriman to Christine Frederick, 3 March 1916, file folder 1; W. E. Loucks to Curtis Publishing Company, 27 February 1919; [Christine Frederick] to W. E. Loucks, 3 April 1919, file folder 2, Frederick Papers.

41. Harriman to Frederick, 22 September 1915; Theresa H. Wolcott to Christine Frederick, 16 January 1918, file folder 1, Frederick Papers.

42. See, for example, Christine Frederick, "The Housewife's Tools," *LHJ,* November 1915, 66.

43. Harriman to Frederick, 9 March 1914; 28 May 1914; 23 June 1914; 13 July 1914; 23 July 1914; A. M. East to Frederick, 12 February 1916, file folder 1, Frederick Papers.

44. See, for example, C. Frederick, ed., "The New Housekeeping," *LHJ,* September 1915, 21; and December 1915, 47.

45. C. Frederick, "The New Housekeeping," *LHJ,* January 1916, 41; Id., "Preserving Your Wood Floors and Woodwork," *LHJ,* March 1916, 67; Id., "What You Should Know about the Can You Buy," *LHJ,* October 1916, 54; "Ask the *Ladies' Home Journal,*" *LHJ,* March 1916, 61.

46. Theresa H. Wolcott to Christine Frederick, 8 September 1915; 16 September 1915; Anna M. East to Frederick, 20 October 1915; 12 February 1916, file folder 1, Frederick Papers.

47. Virginia E. Kift to Christine Frederick, 30 July 1917; Theresa H. Wolcott to Frederick, 16 January 1918, file folder 1, Frederick Papers.

48. Theresa H. Wolcott to Christine Frederick, 21 June 1917; 12 July 1917, file folder 1, Frederick Papers.

49. Karl E. Harriman to Christine Frederick, 13 December 1917, file folder 1, Frederick Papers.

50. [Theresa Wolcott] to Christine Frederick, 28 May 1919, file folder 2, Frederick Papers.

51. Theresa H. Wolcott to Christine Frederick, 27 August 1919, file folder 2, Frederick Papers.

52. Theresa H. Wolcott to Christine Frederick, 19 December 1919, file folder 2, Frederick Papers.

53. Theresa H. Wolcott to Christine Frederick, 29 December 1919; 2 April 1920; 22 May 1920; 3 June 1920; 24 September 1920; 25 October 1920, file folder 2, Frederick Papers.

54. Helen Ormsbee to Christine Frederick, 22 April 1920; Theresa H. Wolcott to Christine Frederick, 12 March 1920; 30 March 1920; 16 June 1920, file folder 2, Frederick Papers.

55. Norman Hapgood, "Journalism for Women," *Art Life*, February 1915, clipping, p. 1, carton 7, file folder 352, BVI Records.

56. Guernsey, "Scientific Management," 821–22.

57. Richards, "Social Significance," 117, 124.

58. Talbot and Breckinridge, *Modern Household*, 15–19.

59. C. Frederick, "Woman Who Buys Wisely," 95.

60. Susan Porter Benson, "Living on the Margin," 212, 222; Lears, "From Salvation to Self-Realization," 7–9, 12–13.

61. C. Frederick, *New Housekeeping*, 205–10.

62. Ibid., 211–14, 217, 218–19.

63. Ibid., 223–24.

64. See C. Frederick, "Woman Who Buys Wisely," 95.

65. C Frederick, *Household Engineering*, 315, 318–20.

66. Ibid., 320–23, 353. Congress passed an updated version of the trademark statute in 1905. At that time, companies could register their trademark to protect ownership. See Strasser, *Satisfaction Guaranteed*, 45.

67. C. Frederick, *Household Engineering*, 355–56.

68. Ibid., 358.

69. J. G. Frederick, "Patented Articles," 501. The Fredericks' daughter believed that J. George bore "major responsibility for his wife's emphasis on consumerism" and that Christine's interest in business and advertising stemmed from his "strong pro-business" and "strong pro-advertising" beliefs. Jean Joyce to the author, 17 September 1996.

70. For a thorough discussion of this struggle and the reasons behind it, see Strasser, *Satisfaction Guaranteed*, especially 37–43, 81–88, 194–206, 224–84.

71. House Committee on the Judiciary, *Hearings before the Committee on the Judiciary on Trust Legislation*, 63rd Cong., 2nd sess., 18 February 1914, 725–33.

72. Strasser, *Satisfaction Guaranteed*, 272–73.

73. "Women Will Rout Crooked Tradesmen," *NYT*, 18 December 1911, p. 5, col. 3;

Mrs. Julian Heath, "Work of the Housewives' League," *AAAPSS* 48 (July 1913): 125; "Women Watch Prices," *NYT*, 7 August 1914, p. 13, col. 3.

74. House Committee on the Judiciary, *Trust Legislation*, 725–28.

75. Ibid., 728–33.

76. "Quell Unfair Competition Is Plea of Housewives," [*Baltimore Star*, 23 February 1914], clipping, microfilm M-107, Frederick Papers; "Hits at Bargain Follies," *NYT*, 19 February 1914, p. 11, col. 2.

77. "Price Maintenance Again," *NYT*, 8 April 1917, sec. 2, p. 8, col. 1; "Woman Expert in Home Efficiency for Stephens Bill," n.d., clipping; "Brands Needed by Consumer," 29 October 1917, clipping, microfilm M-107, Frederick Papers.

78. "Brands Needed by Consumer."

79. Since the commission found that "unrestricted price cutting" was "not in the public interest," manufacturers should be able to apply to "an agency designated by Congress" that would review "terms of resale contracts." A manufacturer, the commission advised, should be able to fix prices only by negotiating such a contract agreed upon by all parties, for price fixing by any other means was restraining trade. House, *Report on Resale Price Maintenance*, 66th Cong., 1st sess., 1919, H. Doc. 145, serial 7644, pp. [1]–3.

80. Price maintenance was a very complex issue that encompassed relationships between government and corporations, regulatory debates, trust legislation, and the discourse concerning competition versus controlled monopoly. Disputes from the 1880s well into the twentieth century often focused on price setting as a restraint of trade. Thorough exploration of these matters is well beyond the scope of this work. The intention here is simply to disclose Christine Frederick's involvement in the issue of manufacturer-controlled price setting insofar as she understood it to affect consumers. Whether she understood that her position favored the producer over the consumer is difficult to assess from the arguments that survive. For a comprehensive discussion and thoughtful analysis of the larger questions surrounding standardized pricing, see M. Sklar, *Corporate Reconstruction*.

7 · Accommodating Progressivism

1. Mowry, *Era of Theodore Roosevelt*, 38, 48, 85–100, 209; Wiebe, *Search for Order*, 236; Rosenstone, "Reform and Radicalism," 135; Susman, *Culture As History*, 88–95; M. Sklar, *Corporate Reconstruction*, 431–34; Galambos, "Emerging Organizational Synthesis," 281.

2. For an analysis of the efficiency movement as Progressive reform, see Haber, *Efficiency and Uplift*.

3. See, for example, "What Causes Slips of the Tongue? Why Do We Forget?" *NYT*, 18 October 1914, sec. 5, p. 10, col. 1.

4. See M. Sklar's discussion of the transformation of capitalism from a proprietary-competitive model to a corporate-administered one during this period, *Corporate Reconstruction*, 1–11.

5. C. Frederick, "What the New Housekeeping Means to the Farm Home," 85.

6. Lebovitz, "Home and the Machine," 143–45.

7. C. Frederick, "What the New Housekeeping Means to the Farm Home," 91.

8. Bowers, *Country Life Movement*, 24–27, 34–36, 129; Cremin, *Transformation of the School*, 54–55, 83–84; True, "Home Economics"; "Application of Smith-Lever Funds," *JHE* 7 (August-September 1915): 355, 357–58.

9. C. Frederick, "Getting the Most out of Country Living," 71, 79.

10. C. Frederick, "The 'Professional Grandma,'" 102.

11. C. Frederick, "What the New Housekeeping Means to the Farm Home," 93.

12. C. Frederick, "The 'Professional Grandma,'" 102.

13. Talbot and Breckinridge, *Modern Household*, 41.

14. C. Frederick, *New Housekeeping*, 226–28.

15. "Suggested Articles for Journal, for Sept. And Following Months," n.d., typescript, file folder 1, Frederick Papers.

16. C. Frederick, *Household Engineering*, 339–40.

17. C. Frederick, "Rousing the Small Town," 22–23.

18. C. Frederick, "What the New Housekeeping Means to the Farm Home," 91.

19. Hechtlinger, *Patent Medicines*, 11, 122. In Ruth Suckow's novel about Iowan farm families during the years before and after World War I, August Kaetterhenry, who had been told by the Mayo Clinic that he had high blood pressure, was advised by a neighbor, "Them places makes a big noise, but there's some stuff right down here at the drug-store that me and the missus always takes when we got anything the matter with us, and it does the business." And when August's daughter had become ill with seizures, "August and Emma bought her large bottles of 'nerve tonic' at the drug-store, but that didn't seem to help." Suckow, *Country People*, 174.

20. C. Frederick, *New Housekeeping*, 10–12.

21. Quoted from the 1901 Lake Placid Conference in Ehrenreich and English, *For Her Own Good*, 159.

22. Purcell, "Home Economics," 9–15; Washington, "Dorothy Hall," 200–206.

23. District Agent to Tuskegee Institute, 26 June 1920; J. T. Blair Buck, "Extension Work," n.d., typescript, Laura Randolph Daly file folder, Home Economics Materials Collection, Political History Division, National Museum of American History, Washington, D.C. (hereafter cited as Home Economics Materials).

24. Washington, "Dorothy Hall," 200–204.

25. Purcell, "Home Economics," 13–14; Washington, "Dorothy Hall," 202.

26. Beecher, *Treatise on Domestic Economy*, 206.

27. Beecher and Stowe, *American Woman's Home*, 324–25.

28. I. M. Rubinow, "Household Service As Labor Problem," *JHE* 3 (April 1911): 132–34. See also Lebovitz, "Home and the Machine," 141, and Talbot and Breckinridge, *Modern Household*, 57–58.

29. Helen Calbreath, born and reared in rural Oregon, wrote to her mother from Europe in 1909: "I think you should have the orphan girl to wash dishes and sweep . . . Of course one doesn't expect a maid—old or young—to eat with them. That is easily reg-

ulated from the first. Someone has to wait on the table . . . It isn't a question of 'equality.' It is a question of service." Helen Calbreath to Dr. and Mrs. Calbreath, 2 May 1909, box 3, file folder 4, Calbreath Family Collection.

30. Gilman, "Waste of Private Housekeeping," 91.

31. C. Frederick, *New Housekeeping,* 13.

32. Talbot and Breckinridge, *Modern Household,* 57.

33. "Domestic Reform League, Form of Contract," [August 1907], box 1, file folder 5, WEIU Records.

34. Talbot and Breckinridge, *Modern Household,* 58–63.

35. C. Frederick, "The New Housekeeping," *LHJ,* December 1912, 16. Christine often used the fictitious name "Katy" when discussing servants. This reflected the fact that in the years prior to World War I, Irish women comprised nearly one-third of the servant population in the United States. Fritschner, "Rise and Fall," 53.

36. C. Frederick, "The New Housekeeping," *LHJ,* December 1912, 16, 79.

37. Edward Bok to Christine Frederick, 25 May 1914, file folder 1, Frederick Papers.

38. C. Frederick, "Suppose Our Servants," 102.

39. Ibid.

40. Beecher and Stowe, *American Woman's Home,* 324; C. Frederick, "Suppose Our Servants," 102.

41. C. Frederick, "Why Should Our Servants," 47.

42. C. Frederick, *Household Engineering,* 441.

43. Ibid., 422–23.

44. Ibid., 393, 437.

45. Ibid.

46. Committee on Household Assistants, "The Seven Weeks Experiment," [1919], typescript, carton 2, file folder 126, BVI Records; "Eight Hour Service," *JHE,* December 1920, 9, (carton 2, file folder 129, BVI Records, photocopy).

47. C. Frederick, "Putting the American Woman," 200, 205–6.

8 · "A World Wide Lecturer"

1. "Annual Meeting of the American Home Economics Association—June 27–July 4, Cornell University, Ithaca, New York," *JHE* 5 (January 1913): 289–90.

2. C. Frederick, "Points in Efficiency," 280.

3. Ibid.

4. "Lectures by Mrs. Christine Frederick," brochure, [1914]; "Mrs. Christine Frederick, Author and Lecturer," brochure, [1916], file folder 15, Frederick Papers. There are dozens of Applecroft brochures in this file. Some promote Christine's books as well as her lectures.

5. "The New Housekeeping," 18 January 1914, clipping, microfilm M-107, Frederick Papers; "Dazzling Styles Bewilder Diners"; House Committee on the Judiciary, *Trust Legislation.*

6. Christine's daughter remembered that when "Mother would go off . . . Nursie was

a very good mother to us and homemaker, house-keeper. Very, very nice woman." Joyce, interview, 15 September 1994.

7. "Briliant [*sic*] Banquet Planned for Dr. Wiley."

8. "Indiana Home Economics Association Third Annual Convention," 13 January 1916, program, microfilm M-107, Frederick Papers.

9. "Mrs. Christine Frederick," untitled typescript, file folder 15, Frederick Papers.

10. Gilman, "Women and Vocations," 33.

11. "Outline of Course: Women in Industry: Her Opportunities in Business To [Day]," typescript, carton 1, file folder 2; Fay Kellogg, "Women's Work: Her Opportunities To-Day: Architecture," 7 December 1915, typescript, carton 1, file folder 10, BVI Records.

12. C. Frederick, "Household Economics," 4–6.

13. "Farmers Will Meet at Streator," n.p., [February 1917], clipping; "Urges Women to Be 'Kitchen Soldiers,'" *Louisville Herald*, [1917], clipping, microfilm M-107, Frederick Papers; "Price Maintenance Again"; "Brands Needed by Consumer."

14. "Urges Women to Be 'Kitchen Soldiers.'"

15. "Ad Club Will Hear Interesting Address," *Virginian-Pilot*, n.d., clipping, microfilm M-107, Frederick Papers.

16. C. Frederick, "Getting the Most Out of Country Living," 74.

17. C. Frederick, "What the New Housekeeping Means to the Farm Home," 86.

18. "Mrs. Consumer Speaks Her Mind," speech, 20 October 1930, [p. 1], file folder 10, Frederick Papers.

19. C. Frederick, "Getting the Most Out of Country Living," 74; League of Advertising Women, "Advertising Women Minus Blue Spectacles," 1921, [p. 7], carton 1, file folder 2, AWNY Papers.

20. "Urges Advertisers to Tell the Truth," *NYT*, 10 June 1920, p. 16, col. 2.

21. "Household Expert Has Experiment Station."

22. "Brands Needed by Consumer."

23. Joyce, interview, 15 September 1994.

24. "May Yohe, $2-a-Day Janitress, Is Happy at Last," 26 January 1919, 3; "The Hope Diamond Mystery," *American Weekly*, 24 October 1920, 9.

25. "Miss Aluminum: Mrs. Christine Frederick," n.p., 13 November 1924, clipping, microfilm M-107, Frederick Papers.

26. "Aluminum Company Declared Monopoly in Federal Report," *NYT*, 6 October 1924, p. 1, col. 8.

27. "Ad Club Will Hear Interesting Address"; Joyce, interview, 16 September 1994; Photograph MC261-34-1, Frederick Papers.

28. [C. Frederick], "Only a Girl," 22–29.

29. The Redpath Chautauqua circuits, named for James Redpath, who had begun a lecture bureau in Boston in 1867, were organized by Keith Vawter in 1904. Other promoters established their own circuits and soon twenty-two separate Chautauqua circuits traveled around the United States. Those who wanted to use the Redpath name paid a royalty to the Redpath Lyceum Bureau in Boston. In 1912, Redpath split, and the

Redpath-Chicago circuit concentrated on the states of Illinois, Indiana, Ohio, Michigan, and Kentucky. Harrison, *Culture under Canvas*, 30–38, 53, 81–83; Gould, *Chautauqua Movement*, 78–79.

30. Harrison, *Culture Under Canvas*, 90, 211.

31. Ibid., 208.

32. Ibid., 91–96, 158; Gould, *Chautauqua Movement*, 81.

33. Harrison, *Culture under Canvas*, 181–82, 191, 224; [C. Frederick], "Only a Girl," [22].

34. C. Frederick, Laguna Library Book Day Speech; "Career Chronology," 2.

35. "Career Chronology," 2; "Consumer Work," typescript, p. 2, carton 1, file folder 15, Dignam Papers.

36. Harrison, *Culture under Canvas*, 212.

37. Ibid., 199; "Take Your Vacation at the Big Redpath Chautauqua," n.d., poster, Frederick Papers (filed in map case, drawer 4, Schlesinger Library); "Redpath Chautauqua Program DeLuxe," 10 August [1918], flyer, microfilm M-107, Frederick Papers.

38. [C. Frederick], "Only a Girl," [22]. Bryan delivered his "Cross of Gold" speech many times during the 1896 presidential campaign when he was promoting free silver. It was the "Prince of Peace" speech that he gave thirty-four times for Chautauqua in 1912. Harrison, *Culture under Canvas*, 91–92.

39. "Consumer Work," 2.

40. "Mrs. Frederick Shows How to Put Home on Conservative Basis," *Fayetteville Observer*, 4 July 1918, clipping, microfilm M-107, Frederick Papers.

41. Ibid.

42. "Turn Energy Wrong Way," [1918], clipping, microfilm M-107, Frederick Papers.

43. "Urges Women to Be 'Kitchen Soldiers.'"

44. F. La Follette, "Suffragetting," 27; Harrison, *Culture under Canvas*, 110, 225.

45. C. Frederick, "Your Health Depends," 53.

46. F. La Follette, "Suffragetting," 27.

47. Harrison, *Culture under Canvas*, 107.

48. [C. Frederick], "Only a Girl," [27–28].

49. Leuchtenburg, *Perils of Prosperity*, 213–14.

50. [C. Frederick], "Only a Girl," [24–26].

51. Suckow, *Country People*, 115.

52. C. Frederick, ed., "The New Housekeeping," *LHJ*, September 1915, 21; October 1915, 45.

53. Marshall, "American Housewives Losing $1,000,000 a Day."

54. C. Frederick, *Household Engineering*, 406–8. Christine would advocate apartment dwelling over "suburbiana" in later writings. See chapter 12.

55. "How Can a Family of Five Live on $1,000 a Year?" article reprinted in newspaper advertisement [1919], oversized file folder 1, Frederick Papers.

56. Fox-Genovese, *Feminism without Illusions*, 63.

57. C. Frederick, *Household Engineering*, 384.

58. C. Frederick, *New Housekeeping*, 189–90.

59. C. Frederick, *Household Engineering*, 384.

60. C. Frederick, "What the New Housekeeping Means to the Farm Home," 93.

61. C. Frederick, *New Housekeeping*, 233.

62. "The Woman Who Invented Scientific Housekeeping."

63. Gilman, "Waste of Private Housekeeping," 91. This assumption was not unique to the United States; from the mid–nineteenth century, European statisticians had omitted consideration of female household labor in computing family income. Victoria de Grazia, "Changing Consumption Regimes," in *Sex of Things*, 16.

64. C. Frederick, "How I Save Money."

65. C. Frederick, "Woman Who Buys Wisely," 95.

66. Lemons, *Woman Citizen*, 17–22, 27–30; "Banking for Women," *News-Bulletin of the Bureau of Vocational Information*, 1 November 1922, p. 2, carton 1, file folder 29, BVI Records; Christine Frederick, "Help for the Farmer's Wife, Too," *NYT*, 10 June 1917, sec. 2, p. 2, col. 7.

67. Charlotte Perkins Gilman, "Mrs. Tarbell's 'Uneasy Woman,'" *Forerunner*, February 1912, 39.

68. [Charlotte Perkins Gilman], "The Work before Us," *Forerunner*, January 1912, 7; Christine Frederick, "Women, Politics, and Radio," October 1924, clipping, microfilm M-107, Frederick Papers.

69. "How Can a Family of Five Live on $1,000 a Year?"

70. Joyce, interview, 15 September 1994.

9 · Reframing Women's Role in the Twenties

1. L. Hollingworth, "New Woman in the Making," 15–18; Bruère, "Highway to Women's Happiness," 28; Lears, "From Salvation to Self-Realization," 27. For a discussion of the retreat of feminism, see Sochen, *New Woman*, 126–29.

2. Parsons, *Woman's Dilemma*, 5–6, 7–11, 55, 79–80, 201; S. La Follette, *Concerning Women*, 4–5, 10, 20–21, 33–34, 36, 46, 95.

3. Beard, *On Understanding Women*, 17–22.

4. Cott, *Grounding of Modern Feminism*, 120–29; "Mrs. Gilman Urges Hired Mother Idea," *NYT*, 23 September 1919, p. 36, col. 1; "Charlotte Perkins Gilman, Author and Lecturer," flyer, file folder 49, Gilman Papers, Addendum; Degler, "Charlotte Perkins Gilman," 213; Gilman, "Woman's Achievements," 9.

5. Gilbert, "Why I Hate My Independence," 139.

6. Symes, "Still a Man's Game," 681–86.

7. Most men did not vote that year either. According to statistics reported by the League of Women Voters, only 49 percent of the voting public, male and female, voted in the 1920 presidential election. League of Women Voters, "Report on the 1924 Get Out the Vote Campaign," quoted in Stuhler, *For the Public Record*, 115. Statisticians who compile information about past elections point out that a "pre-

cise breakdown that shows which groups of voters (such as blacks or women) have higher turnout rates have never been possible." *Congressional Quarterly's Guide to U. S. Elections*, 324.

8. Lemons, *Woman Citizen*, 51, 103; Lape, "What Do Women Want," 91; Rapp and Ross, "Twenties Backlash," 93.

9. Lemons, *Woman Citizen*, 184–87; Cott, *Grounding of Modern Feminism*, 255–57, 263–64.

10. Brown, *Setting a Course*, 54; Lemons, *Woman Citizen*, 65–68; Connecticut representative quoted on 71.

11. "O'Connell Deplores 'Sinister Feminism,'" *NYT*, 9 March 1920, p. 8, col. 2; McMenamin, "Evils of Woman's Revolt," 32; Lemons, *Woman Citizen*, 22–23; Beard, *On Understanding Women*, 28–29.

12. Massachusetts Civics Alliance quoted in Lemons, *Woman Citizen*, 171; Cott, *Grounding of Modern Feminism*, 242, 249–50; "Sees Menace to Country," *NYT*, 10 December 1924, p. 30, col. 6.

13. Cott, *Grounding of Modern Feminism*, 254–55, 257–59.

14. "Proposed Plan for an Institute of Economic Relations," [11 November 1927], typescript, carton 7, file folder 365, BVI Records; C. Frederick, *Selling Mrs. Consumer*, 396, 397; "The Readers Write," [Scribner's-Commentator], n.d., clipping, microfilm M-107, Frederick Papers.

15. Bent, "Woman's Place," 209; Martin, "Women and 'Their' Magazines," 92; Cott, *Grounding of Modern Feminism*, 163; Gregg, "What Women Are Thinking," 301.

16. C. Frederick, *Selling Mrs. Consumer*, 47; "Housewife's Face Is International—Expression the Same in All Lands," n.p., 1927, clipping, microfilm M-107, Frederick Papers.

17. C. Frederick, *Selling Mrs. Consumer*, 355–56. Frederick's emphasis.

18. Wright, *Building the Dream*, 197; "'Own Your Own Home' Show," *NYT*, 28 October 1923, sec. 10, p. 2, col. 6; "Sixth Annual 'Own Your Home' Show," *NYT*, 13 April 1924, sec. 11, p. 2, col. 8; "To Show Gas Units," *NYT*, 21 December 1924, sec. 10, p. 2, col. 3; "Building Booms Started to Order," *NYT*, 22 December 1924, p. 33, col. 1; Brown, *Setting a Course*, 71; Herbert H. Hoover, "Address of President Hoover," 1.

19. Hildegarde Kneeland to Beatrice Doerschuk, 12 June 1925, carton 2, file folder 126, BVI Records.

20. Horowitz, *Alma Mater*, 56, 281–84, 295–97.

21. University of Minnesota, "Training Courses for Occupations for Women," leaflet, 5–8 March 1924, carton 4, file folder 195; Helen W. Atwater to Beatrice Doerschuk, 30 March 1925, carton 2, file folder 126; *Vocational Education News Notes*, June 1926, p. 15, carton 2, file folder 127; "Careers for Women in Gas Companies," *Utility Bulletin*, 11 May 1925, clipping, carton 2, file folder 131, BVI Records; Baltimore Gas and Electric Company, *The Culinary Courier*, May 1928 (Home Economics Materials Collection, photocopy).

22. Laura V. Clark, "A Study of Occupations, Other Than Home-Making, Open to

Women Trained in Home Economics," *Vocational Education News Notes*, n.d., pp. 10–11, carton 2, file folder 127, BVI Records; Goldstein, "Part of the Package," 276–80, 282; "Consumer Work."

23. Gregg, "What Women Are Thinking," 302; Perfume advertisement quoted in Ewen, *Captains of Consciousness*, 182; Lillian G. Genn, "Business Unfits Girls for Matrimony Says Dr. John B. Watson," *Record Weekly*, n.d., clipping, box 2, Watson Papers.

24. Parsons, *Woman's Dilemma*, 101–2; Brown, *Setting a Course*, 142–43. See Cott's discussion of this paradox in *Grounding of Modern Feminism*, 150–58.

25. Naether, *Advertising to Women*, 245, 81; "American Beauty Hand Made in America," *NYT*, 6 March 1921, sec. 3, p. 11; Beard, *On Understanding Women*, 9.

26. C. Frederick, *Selling Mrs. Consumer*, 27–28.

27. "Urges Advertisers to Tell the Truth."

28. "Mrs. Frederick Scores a Hit," *Advertising Club News*, 8 November 1920, [3], microfilm M-107, Frederick Papers; C. Frederick, *You and Your Laundry*, 31.

29. "Is the Advertiser Over-Playing the Color Appeal?" *Advertising and Selling*, 2 May 1928, 66.

30. C. Frederick, "What the Customer Needs," 5.

31. C. Frederick, *You and Your Laundry*, 30; Id., "Every Woman Her Own Repairman," *Designer*, March 1925, clipping, microfilm M-107, Frederick Papers.

32. Christine Frederick, "Housewives Who Fail: The 'Scourer'"; "Housewives Who Fail: The 'Slacker,'" 1922, *Evening World*, clippings, microfilm M-107, Frederick Papers.

33. Christine Frederick, "Keeping Men Fit," *American Weekly*, 8 February 1920, 11.

34. "Shall the Housekeeper Have an Understudy?" *New York Evening World*, [13 May 1922], clipping, microfilm M-107, Frederick Papers.

35. C. Frederick, "New View of 'Home,'" 145.

36. "Ask Mrs. Frederick," *Shrine Magazine*, December 1927, 54–55, clipping; Christine Frederick, "The Modern Wife Faces a Problem," *Designer*, July 1924, 2, microfilm M-107, Frederick Papers.

37. C. Frederick, "Man's Business," 189.

38. Ibid., 169, 188; C. Frederick, "Modern Wife."

39. C. Frederick, "Man's Business," 169, 189.

40. Ibid., 168–69.

41. C. Frederick, "Shall the Housekeeper Have an Understudy?"

42. "Calls Frying Pan the U.S. Emblem," clipping; "Nothing in the World Is More in Need of Reconstruction Than the American Home, Says Expert in Household Engineering," *Evening Sun*, 18 April 1919, microfilm M-107, Frederick Papers.

43. C. Frederick, "Twelve Supermen," p. 18, col. 8.

44. C. Frederick, *Selling Mrs. Consumer*, 241–42.

45. Ibid., 59.

46. C. Frederick, "Mrs. Consumer Speaks Up," 16.

47. C. Frederick, "New View of Home"; "Nothing in the World Is More in Need"; C. Frederick, *Selling Mrs. Consumer*, 168.

48. C. Frederick, "Advertising Copy," 232; Women's Bureau quoted in S. La Follette, *Concerning Women*, 165; Cott, *Grounding of Modern Feminism*, 129–30. Not all historians agree that middle-class women who worked for pay felt that they had to do so. See Cowan, *More Work for Mother*, 188; Lemons, *Woman Citizen*, 141.

49. Christine's daughter told the author that her mother had never discussed the "feminism problem" with her; she believed that her mother was more interested in what she was doing to make housework efficient than in any other women's issue. Joyce, interview, 15 September 1994.

50. C. Frederick, *Selling Mrs. Consumer*, 189, 190, 191, 25.

51. Helen Woodward, *Through Many Windows*, 314, quoted in Ewen, *Captains of Consciousness*, 147; L. G. Genn, "Business Unfits Girls."

10 · Becoming Mrs. Consumer

1. J. G. Frederick, *Modern Industrial Consolidation*, 211. William Leuchtenburg dubbed the twenties the "Second Industrial Revolution" in *Perils of Prosperity*, 178.

2. Leuchtenburg, *Perils of Prosperity*, 179–80; Susman, *Culture As History*, xx–xxii.

3. Leuchtenburg, *Perils of Prosperity*, 190; Herbert Hoover, "Nationalized Power," 319.

4. "Expert on Labor Saving Devices Says Use Brains, Forget Nerves," [17 August 1925], clipping, microfilm M-107, Frederick Papers; C. Frederick, "New Wealth," 74–82. A copy of this article in booklet form is in file folder 10, Frederick Papers.

5. C. Frederick, "New Wealth," 74–75, 82.

6. Ibid., 81.

7. Ibid., 78, 82.

8. For a discussion of the consumers league movement and the founding of the National Consumers' League in 1898, see K. Sklar, *Florence Kelley*, chapters 7 and 12.

9. Leach, *Land of Desire*, 94; Lemons, *Woman Citizen*, 146; Noggle, "Configurations of the Twenties," 476.

10. Leuchtenburg, *Perils of Prosperity*, 180–96.

11. "Time for People to Learn to Buy," *NYT*, 16 March 1919, sec. 3, p. 5, col. 3; Leuchtenburg, *Perils of Prosperity*, 96–99; Noggle, "Configurations of the Twenties," 467.

12. "Urges Advertising As Church Benefit," *NYT*, 8 June 1920, p. 10, col. 8.

13. Pope, *Making of Modern Advertising*, 29; Strasser, *Never Done*, 253; Marchand, *Advertising the American Dream*, 20; Susman, *Culture As History*, xxvi.

14. Marchand, *Advertising the American Dream*, 10; Dyer, "Advertising Writer"; Barton, "Human Appeals in Copy," 55, 60, 65–66; Lears, "From Salvation to Self-Realization," 31–34.

15. "Advertising Clubs Meet in Indianapolis," *NYT*, 7 June 1920, p. 15, col. 3; Allen L. Beatty to author, 16 May 1994; *Who Was Who in America*, 125; "Question Mrs. Heath," *NYT*, 4 January 1918, p. 9, col. 2.

16. See, for example, "'Bait' Advertising Imperils Consumer Confidence," *Trade*

Service Bulletin of the National Vigilance Committee, Associated Advertising Clubs of the World, 17 July 1925; "More Bait Advertising," 18 March 1926; "Facts Then Action."

17. Sherwood Anderson, *Letters*, 135, quoted in Ewen, *Captains of Consciousness*, 66. During the twenties, civic groups such as the League of Women Voters, the General Federation of Women's Clubs, and the Federated Garden Clubs supported an organization called the National Committee for the Restriction of Outdoor Advertising, a movement that suggests reformers' concern about the aesthetics of advertising, too. "Consumer Work," 3.

18. J. G. Frederick, "The Research Basis of Copy," in *Masters of Advertising Copy*, 170–72.

19. Strasser, *Satisfaction Guaranteed*, 155–56; J. B. Watson, "Just a Piece of Key Copy," *J. Walter Thompson News Bulletin*, August 1929, box 2, John Broadus Watson Papers. In 1923, Watson colluded with the manufacturer of Pebeco toothpaste to repeat the language from their magazine advertisements in his radio talk, "Glands in the Human Body." He told the readers of the company bulletin, "This talk illustrates fairly well the technique of commercial advertising by radio . . . The speaker does not have to say anything about the product being advertised—scientific men would not in general be willing to speak if the product had to be mentioned in the body of the talk." J. B. Watson, "Advertising by Radio," *J. Walter Thompson News Bulletin*, May 1923, box 1, Watson Papers.

20. Marchand, *Advertising the American Dream*, 347. MacManus, "Underlying Principles," 81.

21. Not all successful manufacturers agreed in the beginning. Henry Ford disapproved of advertising and, in 1926, decided not to advertise at all. But even he recapitulated the following year and launched a big campaign to sell the Model A. Marchand, *Advertising the American Dream*, 7.

22. J. G. Frederick, *Great Game of Business*, vi–viii; Barton, "Human Appeals in Copy," 71, 73; "Urges Advertisers to Tell the Truth"; Schmidt, *Consumer Rites*, 8, 14.

23. J. G. Frederick, *Modern Industrial Consolidation*, 212–17.

24. "J. G. Frederick, 82, A Writer, Is Dead"; J. George Frederick, form letter attached to letter from Park Mathewson to Beatrice Doerschuk, 2 April 1921, carton 7, file folder 347, BVI Records.

25. "Women in Advertising," *News Bulletin of the Bureau of Vocational Information*, 1 April 1924, p. 51, carton 1, file folder 30, BVI Records; Marchand, *Advertising the American Dream*, 33, 34.

26. "Nothing in the World Is More in Need of Reconstruction Than the American Home, Says Expert in Household Engineering," *Evening Sun*, 18 April 1919, clipping, microfilm M-107, Frederick Papers.

27. C. Frederick, *Selling Mrs. Consumer*, 168.

28. Christine Frederick to Sales or Advertising Manager, McCray Refrigerator Company, 7 July 1921, file folder 2; Director of Applecroft Experiment Station to the H. J. Smith Tool Company, 15 April 1921, file folder 2; Director, Shrine Home Service to Dear Sir, n.d., file folder 8, Frederick Papers.

29. C. Frederick, *Selling Mrs. Consumer*, 224–25.

30. "Applecroft Home Experiment Station," [1928], brochure, file folder 15, Frederick Papers; Stage and Vincenti, *Rethinking Home Economics*, 235–36.

31. C. Frederick, *Selling Mrs. Consumer*, 281–82.

32. "Shrine Service Departments," *Shrine Magazine*, March 1927, clipping; "Household Expert Has Experiment Station," microfilm M-107; *Tested and Recommended Household Equipment* (Springfield, Mass.: *Farm and Home Magazine*, n.d.), booklet, file folder 12, Frederick Papers.

33. See, for example, Christine Frederick, "A Woman's Advice on How to Sell Kitchen Utensils," *Hardware Age*, 1 April 1920, 93–96; "Pink Paint," *Hardware Dealers' Magazine*, June 1923, 33–35; "The Night before Xmas," *Wireless Age*, December 1924, 36, microfilm M-107, Frederick Papers.

34. Christine Frederick, "The 'Hick' Housekeeper," *Hardware Dealers' Magazine*, August 1923, 20–23; "If I Could Begin Housekeeping All Over Again," *Hardware Dealers' Magazine*, September 1926, 62–63, microfilm M-107, Frederick Papers.

35. Marchand, *Advertising the American Dream*, 1–2, 9, 68.

36. Lears, "From Salvation to Self-Realization," 16; Victoria de Grazia, "Empowering Women As Citizen-Consumers," in *The Sex of Things*, 281, 278.

37. "Urges Advertisers to Tell the Truth."

38. "Mrs. Frederick Scores a Hit," [1, 3].

39. "Urges Advertisers to Tell the Truth." Christine arrived at the 34 percent by adding the 11 percent of men's clothing found to be purchased by women and the 23 percent found to be purchased by men and women together in a survey of twenty-five New York families in 1912. H. Hollingworth, *Advertising and Selling*, 290. The claim to have assisted in this research appears in *Selling Mrs. Consumer*, 54.

40. "Mrs. Frederick Scores a Hit," [1].

41. "Ad-vance," *The Advertisers' Club of Cincinnati*, 19 November 1921, clipping; "They 'Learned about Women from Her,'" *The Ohio Woman's Magazine*, November 1921, 38; "Calls Frying Pan the U.S. Emblem," n.d., clipping, microfilm M-107, Frederick Papers.

42. "Urges Advertisers to Tell the Truth"; "Mrs. Frederick Scores a Hit," [3].

43. C. Frederick, *Woman As Bait*, 7, 17.

44. For a discussion of the impact of cosmetic marketing on women and changing attitudes about women's appearance as the consumer culture matured, see Peiss, "Making Up, Making Over," 311–36.

45. Barton, "Human Appeals in Copy," 65–73. See Bruce Barton, *The Man Nobody Knows: A Discovery of Jesus* (Indianapolis: Bobbs-Merrill Company, 1925).

46. C. Frederick, "Advertising Copy," 227–28, 233, 241.

47. Ibid., 238, 240–43.

48. "Merchandising Is Topic of Address at Institute," *Louisville Courier-Journal*, n.d., clipping, microfilm M-107, Frederick Papers; C. Frederick, *Selling Mrs. Consumer*, 312; "Mrs. Christine Frederick Says," poster, oversize folder 1; "What Do the Experts Say?" advertisement, microfilm M-107, Frederick Papers.

49. "Topics of the Times," *NYT*, 29 January 1925, p. 18, col. 7.

50. C. Frederick, *Selling Mrs. Consumer*, 50.

51. Marguerite Mooers Marshall, "Radio-Phone Homekeeping Will Relieve Housewife's Monotony, Simplify Labors," n.d., clipping; Christine Frederick, "Wireless Receiving Outfits for the Home," *Hardware Dealers' Magazine*, n.d., clipping, microfilm M-107, Frederick Papers. Christine's reference to a "three-stage set" indicates the number of "stages" of radio frequency her family's set could receive. See reprinted advertisements in Douglas, *Radio Manufacturers*, 238, 256.

52. "Mrs. Christine Frederick, Household Efficiency Expert, Will Hook Up Radio to Thousands of Kitchens," *Evening World*, 3 February 1922, clipping, carton 2, file folder 4, AWNY Papers; Marshall, "Radio-Phone Homekeeping"; "Household Expert Has Experiment Station."

53. Christine Frederick, "Enter Radio—Exit Loneliness: Radiophone Banishes Isolation from Farm Home," [*Farm and Home*, June 1922], clipping, microfilm M-107, Frederick Papers.

54. C. Frederick, "Real Use," 77.

55. Elsie Jean, "What Radio Features Do Women Like Best?" [*Radio Review*, 24 November 1923], 3, clipping; E. Jean, "Mrs. Christine Frederick Looks Ahead," *Evening Mail Radio Review*, 27 October 1923, 6, clipping, microfilm M-107, Frederick Papers.

56. "Women Won to Better Cooking by Radio; Nation's Health Is Given a Decided Boost," [*Toledo (Ohio) Times*, 23 November 1924], clipping, microfilm M-107, Frederick Papers.

57. Marchand, *Advertising the American Dream*, 90–94.

58. C. Frederick, "Wireless Receiving Outfits," 706; Id., "Ten Suggestions to Help Dealers Sell Radio to Women," *Radio Industry*, January 1925, 11–12; Id., "How I Made a Career out of Home and Radio," *Home and Radio*, August 1924, 34–35; Id., "Listening-in As a Stimulus to Hard Work," [*Dayton (Ohio) News*], 9 November 1924], 2–3, clipping, microfilm M-107, Frederick Papers; "Women Won to Better Cooking by Radio."

59. There are four folders (file folders 26–29) that contain forty-seven photographs of the Frederick family, their friends, neighbors, and employees in scenes illustrating daily life lived to the sound of the radio in the Frederick Papers. For examples of the articles in which Christine used these photographs, see E. Jean, "Mrs. Christine Frederick Looks Ahead" and C. Frederick, "Real Use."

60. Christine Frederick, "Radio—The New Aladdin's Lamp," *St. Nicholas*, [November 1922], microfilm M-107, Frederick Papers.

61. Christine Frederick, "What Should Radio Bring on Sunday?" *Telegram and Evening Mail Radio*, 25 October 1924, microfilm M-107, Frederick Papers.

62. Leuchtenburg, *Perils of Prosperity*, 196–97.

63. "Housewife's Face Is International." Christine claimed to have gone to France in 1924 as well, but there is no other evidence that she did so. *Selling Mrs. Consumer*, 355.

64. Although Christine's oldest daughter claims that Christine was a "hands-on"

mother, Christine's two youngest daughters might have had rather different memories. They had been toddlers when their mother traveled so many months with Chautauqua, and they were ten and twelve years old when she went to Europe for this extended stay. During their youth, she made many shorter trips.

65. "Chronology of Mrs. Christine Frederick," 2; [C. Frederick], "Only a Girl," [18].

66. "Household Economy Expert Sails on Home Mission to Foreign Port," [February 1927], n.p., clipping; "How Women Shop," *Daily Telegraph*, 16 June 1927, clipping; "Chambers of Commerce at Work," *Chamber of Commerce Journal*, 6 May 1927, clipping; "Housewife's Face Is International"; "Electricity and the Home," *Wolverhampton Express*, 22 February 1927, clipping, microfilm M-107, Frederick Papers.

67. [C. Frederick], "Only a Girl," [19].

68. "American Home Economist in Paris after Lecturing English Housewives," n.p., n.d.; "Mrs. Christine Frederick," *Mon Chez Moi*, May 1927, 345–49; "Le ménage sans fatigue en deux fois moins de temps," *Mon Chez Moi*, May 1927, 350, file folder 15, Frederick Papers; "Housewife's Face Is International."

69. C. Frederick, *Selling Mrs. Consumer*, 284–85.

70. "American Home Economist in Paris"; "Mrs. Christine Frederick"; "Chambers of Commerce at Work"; "How Women Shop"; "Electricity and the Home"; "Labour Saving in America," *The (Edinburgh) Scotsman*, 21 February 1927, clipping, microfilm M-107, Frederick Papers.

71. C. Frederick, *Selling Mrs. Consumer*, 335; "Journée gastronomique," 10 November 1927, program menu, file folder 17, Frederick Papers; [C. Frederick], "Only a Girl," [43–44].

72. Photographs MC261-32-1, MC261-32-2, and MC261-32-3, Frederick Papers; [C. Frederick], "Only a Girl," [42].

73. C. Frederick, *Selling Mrs. Consumer*, 80; Joyce, interview, 15 September 1994; Christine Frederick, "An American Laundry Abroad," *New York Herald Tribune*, 26 May 1929, 23; "Bostonian Founder of Advertising League of Berlin Women," [*Boston Sunday Post*, 13 October 1929], clipping, microfilm M-107, Frederick Papers.

74. *Printers' Ink*, 7 November 1929, 133, quoted in Marchand, *Advertising the American Dream*, 66, 69.

11 · Private Life

1. "Expert on Labor Saving Devices Says Use Brains."

2. "Nothing in the World Is More in Need of Reconstruction Than the American Home."

3. C. Frederick, "Cooking Sunday's Dinner," 117.

4. Joyce, interview, 16 September 1994.

5. Ibid.; C. Frederick, "Your Health Depends," 53; C. Frederick, "Cooking Sunday's Dinner," 117.

6. C. Frederick, "The Night before Xmas," 36, 87–88.

7. Joyce, interview, 14 September 1994.

8. C. Frederick, *Selling Mrs. Consumer,* 124–25, 304–6.

9. Christine Frederick, "How Can Mothers and Daughters Be Friends?" *The Christine Advocate,* 15 November 1928, 1394–95, microfilm M-107, Frederick Papers.

10. Joyce, interview, 15 September 1994; Photograph MC261-22-4, Frederick Papers; The Phyllis Frederick credit appears on the back of many of the photographs in the Frederick Papers and on the photograph of Christine as "Miss Aluminum" at the New York Advertising Club Ball; C. Frederick, "The Children's Cooking Corner—Lesson Three," *Designer,* [March], n.d., microfilm M-107, Frederick Papers.

11. Schwarz, *Radical Feminists of Heterodoxy,* 20; Joyce, interviews, 15–16 September 1994; "An Invitation," 26 December 1926, file folder 15, Frederick Papers; "General Program," 30 December 1928, Christine Frederick Collection, Huntington Historical Society.

12. Falk, telephone conversation.

13. Joyce, interview, 16 September 1994; Christine Frederick, "Putting Happiness into Housework," *Hardware Dealers' Magazine,* March 1925, clipping, microfilm M-107.

14. C. Frederick, "Mothers and Daughters," 1394–95; Joyce, interview, 16 September 1994; F. Frederick, "The Older Woman," interview by Wolkin.

15. Falk, telephone conversation.

16. "Expert on Labor Saving Devices Says Use Brains."

17. Dorothy Dignam to Christine Frederick, 4 October 1951, file folder 8, Frederick Papers; Joyce, interview, 15 September 1994.

18. K. Sklar, *Catharine Beecher,* 184.

19. Christine Frederick to Theresa Wolcott, 19 June 1920, file folder 2, Frederick Papers.

20. Joyce, interview, 15 September 1994; *Noyes Rhythm, Past, Present, Future,* n.d., booklet, 1–5, 6–7, 9; Christine Frederick to Valerie Ladd, 11 September 1969; Christine Frederick to Thetis, 24 September 1969, file folder 8, Frederick Papers.

21. Joyce, interview, 15 September 1994; C. Frederick to Thetis.

22. C. Frederick, "Listening-in," 2; C. Frederick, "Putting Happiness into Housework"; "Mrs. Christine Frederick," 346.

23. Joyce, interview, 15 September 1994.

24. C. Frederick, *Selling Mrs. Consumer,* 14; J. George Frederick, *Common Stocks,* 289.

25. In 1928, J. George Frederick described himself as "a sophisticated New Yorker" and implied that his friends were "the most sophisticated, blasé habitués of literary circles." As secretary to the Society of Arts and Sciences, he was on familiar terms with popular authors of the day. In 1923, J. George wrote a teasing letter to the humorist Ellis Parker Butler, who was slated to speak to the Society. In reference to one of Butler's popular works, he addressed him as "Dear Pigs Is Pigsy." J. G. Frederick, *What Is Your Emotional Age?* viii; J. George Frederick to Ellis Parker Butler, 31 March 1923, Manuscript Letters Collection (photocopy); Ellis Parker Butler, *Pigs Is Pigs* (New York: McClure, Phillips and Company, 1906).

26. J. G. Frederick, *What Is Your Emotional Age?* xii. J. George's one attempt at fiction was not a success. *Two Women*, written in 1942, received a scathing review from the *New York Times*. "Just what J. George Frederick intended to prove in 'Two Women,'" wrote the reviewer, "is hard to discover." It was "daring," no doubt, but "poor writing" weakened it. His portrayal of Phyllis, the "blue-stocking," was "unconvincing," and his climactic scene in which the four unconventional protagonists meet was "abysmal." His theme—that one man could love two women "if he can get away with it"—required far more delicate writing than J. George could manage. "Latest Fiction," review of *Two Women*, by J. George Frederick, *NYT*, 10 February 1924, sec. 3, p. 22, col. 1.

27. C. Frederick, *Selling Mrs. Consumer*, 167–68.

28. Joyce, interview, 15 September 1994; Photographs 261-24-1 through 261-24-6, Frederick Papers. For a discussion of streamlined design, see Giedion, *Mechanization Takes Command*, 607–8.

29. Deed Liber 1657 at p. 9353.45, Suffolk County Deed Liber Books (photocopy); *Huntington Beach Community Association: 60th Anniversary, 1928–1988*, booklet, Greenlawn-Centerport Historical Association; Jean Joyce to author, 23 September 1995.

30. Joyce, interview, 16 September 1994; C. Frederick, "Suburban Living," 313.

31. Joyce, interview, 16 September 1994; *Old Gold and Blue*, 1924, 57.

32. *A Handbook of Private Schools for American Boys and Girls: An Annual Survey* (Boston: Porter Sargent, 1928), 299.

33. Joyce, interview, 16 September 1994; *Abbott Circle*, 1928, 14; *Handbook of Private Schools*, 1928, 905.

34. *Abbott Circle*, 1932, 20; Joyce, interview, 16 September 1994.

35. Joyce, interviews, 15–16 September 1994; *Old Gold and Blue*, 1925, 39; "Frederick, David Mansfield," grade cards (the Peddie School, photocopy); "David Frederick of Harper's Dead," *NYT*, 3 January 1952, p. 46, col. 2.

36. J. G. Frederick, *Modern Industrial Consolidation*, 203–4.

37. J. G. Frederick, "College Man," 20–21.

38. Joyce, interviews, 14, 16 September 1994; "Farmers Will Meet at Streator"; "Bostonian Founder of Advertising League."

39. Joyce, interview, 15 September 1994; David S. Yeh, Assistant Vice President and University Registrar, Cornell University, to author, 11 January 1995; Jean Joyce to author, 17 September 1996.

40. C. Frederick, *Selling Mrs. Consumer*, 398.

41. Joyce, interview, 16 September 1994.

42. "Turn Energy Wrong Way."

43. C. Frederick, *Household Engineering*, 485.

44. J. G. Frederick, *Two Women*, 115.

45. Lindsey and Evans, *Companionate Marriage*, v, 21–31.

46. Christine referred to "Judge Ben Lindsey's 'companionate marriage' idea" in *Selling Mrs. Consumer*, 388. She called it a "myth" in "Man's Business" 188.

12 · Selling Out Mrs. Consumer

1. "Selling Mrs. Consumer," n.d., flyer, file folder 11, Frederick Papers.

2. See Andrews, "Home Woman," *AAAPSS* 143 (May 1929): 41–48.

3. Naether, *Advertising to Women*, v, 4–5, 7–9, 12, 53.

4. C. Frederick, *Selling Mrs. Consumer*, 3–7, 334–37, 369–78.

5. Ibid., 223.

6. Ibid., 157–60, 185–87.

7. Ibid., 378.

8. Ibid., 225, 308, 377, 381–82. J. George had advocated reducing styles of collars from over one hundred to fewer than fifty and kinds of pocketknives from over one thousand to under five hundred. Christine wrote that "the more shapes and sizes and items offered the housewife, the more difficult her choice." J. G. Frederick, "Standardization," 50; [C. Frederick, *Hardware Dealers' Magazine*, September 1926], 64, clipping, microfilm M-107, Frederick Papers.

9. C. Frederick, *Selling Mrs. Consumer*, 320, 331.

10. C. Frederick, *Selling Mrs. Consumer*, chapters 13 through 22, 115–230.

11. Ibid., 392–95.

12. Ibid., 45.

13. Ibid., 23–27, 48.

14. Ibid., 8, 19–23.

15. Ibid., 29, 326, 384.

16. For example, Hollingworth found that women disagree on advertising "appeals made to the instincts and impulses underlying social solidarity, such as the recommendation, the reputation of the firm, family affection, guarantee, union made, sympathy, growth of the business, etc." *Advertising and Selling*, 296. Christine changed this to "Women are . . . less prone than men to be influenced by appeals to social solidarity such as guarantee, union made, sympathy, recommendation of others, etc." *Selling Mrs. Consumer*, 51.

17. H. Hollingworth, *Advertising and Selling*, 299–300.

18. C. Frederick, *Selling Mrs. Consumer*, 79.

19. J. G. Frederick, "Progressive Obsolescence," 19–20.

20. Ibid., 44, and C. Frederick, *Selling Mrs. Consumer*, 252–53.

21. C. Frederick, *Selling Mrs. Consumer*, 81–83.

22. Ibid., 120–21, 169. Veblen, in fact, scorned the middle-class wife's absorption in "vicarious" consumption, writing that her daily routines showed "that she does not occupy herself with anything that is gainful or that is of substantial use." Veblen, *Theory of the Leisure Class*, 66–69.

23. C. Frederick, *Selling Mrs. Consumer*, 249–51, 253–54.

24. Ibid., 251.

25. Monroe, "New Books," review of *Selling Mrs. Consumer*, 856–57.

26. "Woman's Hand in the Market Place," *NYT*, 25 August 1929, sec. 4, p. 26, col. 2;

Tead, "The New Consumer," review of *Selling Mrs. Consumer*, 338; *Book Review Digest*, 1930 ed., 332.

27. Joyce, interview, 15 September 1994; Leuchtenburg, *Perils of Prosperity*, 244–45; C. Frederick, *Selling Mrs. Consumer*, 379.

28. An example of Christine's apparent disregard of the reality of the crisis is her 1930 response to a question about the 40 percent business failure over the past year. The failures, she claimed, were due to "misleading, exaggerated statements" and the "inefficiency of clerks." "Mrs. Consumer Speaks Her Mind," [8].

29. "Mrs. Christine Frederick, Internationally Famous Home Economics Authority Will Speak on 'Selling Mrs. Consumer,'" [Minneapolis, 16 November 1929], clipping; "Find U.S. Women Spend $350,000 a Minute," *Chicago American*, 29 January 1930, clipping; "Mrs. Frederick Hit at Institute," *Retail Advertising Institute Bulletin*, 30 January 1930, clipping; David Brickman, "You May Think Your Children Are Bad but Their Youngsters Will 'Explode' If You Don't Watch Out—Should Marry When Young, Claims Mrs. Frederick," n.p., [1930], clipping; *Adcrafter*, 27 January 1931, clipping; "Mrs. Frederick to Speak at Retail Institute Tuesday Night," *Louisville (Ky.) Courier-Journal*, [22 February 1931], clipping; "Mrs. Frederick to Speak Here," [*Cincinnati Post*, 19 February 1931], clipping; "'Selling Mrs. Consumer,'" *Spokes*, 24 January 1933, clipping; "Selling to Women Outlined by Editor," *Miami Herald Telephone*, 9 February 1934, clipping, microfilm M-107; O. A. Bursiel, memo to Members of the New England Division of the National Electric Light Association, 7 February 1931, file folder 3; "Boston Conference on Retail Distribution," 22–24 September 1930, program, file folder 17, Frederick Papers.

30. "Urges Study of Feminine Buyers," clipping attached to letter from Anna Burdick to Louise Stanley, 21 October 1930, box 564, file folder "Federal Board for Vocational Edu., 1929–32," Records of the Bureau of Human Nutrition and Home Economics (Record Group 176), General Records, Correspondence with Other Government Departments and Bureaus, 1923–37.

31. C. Frederick, "Mrs. Consumer Speaks Her Mind," [2].

32. C. Frederick, "What the Customer Needs"; "Urges Consumer Study," *NYT*, 28 October 1932, p. 37, col. 1.

33. C. Frederick, "Mrs. Consumer Speaks Up," 6, 12.

34. Anna Burdick to Louise Stanley.

35. C. Frederick, "Twelve Supermen"; Id., *Selling Mrs. Consumer*, 266.

36. Leuchtenburg wrote that "psychology became a national mania" in *Perils of Prosperity*, 164; Roderick Nash discussed the Humanist movement in *Nervous Generation*, 104–7; see J. G. Frederick, *Humanism*.

37. Susman, *Culture As History*, 106, 118. See Singal, "Definition of American Modernism," 7–8, for a discussion of the difference between modernism and modernization.

38. There are many sources on Isadora Duncan and her work; for a discussion of her innovations in movement and costume, see Loewenthal, *Search for Isadora*, 9–19.

39. Lippmann, "Political Indifference," 261–67. For two discussions of Lippmann's

assessment, see Noggle, "Configurations of the Twenties," and Eagles, "Urban-Rural Conflict," 26–48.

40. C. Frederick, "Suburban Living," 290–91, 313.

41. J. G. Frederick, *Modern Industrial Consolidation*, 27; Joyce, interview, 16 September 1994. For a description of the Scopes trial, see Leuchtenburg, *Perils of Prosperity*, 222–23.

42. Joyce, interview, 16 September 1994.

43. C. Frederick, *Selling Mrs. Consumer*, 306; J. G. Frederick, *What Is Your Emotional Age?* 215; Id., "Tahiti Has a Traffic Cop," sec. 4, p. 14.

44. C. Frederick, "What the Customer Needs," 3.

45. C. Frederick, "New Wealth," 7; Id., *Selling Mrs. Consumer*, 270.

46. Joyce, interview, 16 September 1994.

47. Klan lecturers sponsored by Protestant churches built a considerable base of support in the county during the twenties. See Jane Gombieski, "Klokards, Kleagles, Kludds, and Kluxers: The Ku Klux Klan in Suffolk County, 1915–1928," *Long Island Historical Journal* 6, no. 1 (1993): 41–62.

48. Brown, *Setting a Course*, 210. For a commentary on traditional values during the 1920s, see Nash, *Nervous Generation*, especially 61–77, 155–56.

49. J. G. Frederick, *Common Stocks*, 18–23.

50. For discussions of these changes, see Cott, *Grounding of Modern Feminism*, 145–47, and Evans, *Born for Liberty*, 185.

13 · The Twilight of a Career

1. Emma Dot Partridge to [Christine] Frederick, 3 March [1935] and 19 March 1935, file folder 3; "In Celebration of National Woman's Week," invitation, March 1935; "In Honor of Career Women of New York City Tribute Dinner," program, 22 March 1935, file folder 17, Frederick Papers.

2. C. Frederick, "Mrs. Consumer Speaks Her Mind," 2, 3, [6]; "Mrs. Consumer Speaks Up," 3, 7, 8–10.

3. "Speakers' Bureau Carries Consumer Message," typescript, carton 1, file folder 15, Dignam Papers; Helen Strauss to Christine Frederick, telegram, 4 June 1936, file folder 3; "Advertising Cost Really a Saving," *New York Journal and American*, [9 February 1938], clipping, microfilm M-107, Frederick Papers; Christine Frederick, "The Rise of Advertising Women," speech before Advertising Women of Philadelphia, September 1938, carton 2, file folder 4; "Rosy-Hued Futures," *New York Herald Tribune*, 23 July 1939, clipping, carton 2, file folder 2, AWNY Papers.

4. "Woman Editor Fights for Fair Trade Bill," *Washington Herald*, 2 March 1932, clipping; "'Fair Trade' Bill Urged to Restrict Cutting of Prices," *United States Daily*, 3 March 1932, clipping, microfilm M-107, Frederick Papers; Oakley, "AWNY," 63, 96; "Speakers' Bureau Carries Consumer Message"; "Chronological Record for the Year 1935," typescript, carton 3, file folder 17, Dignam Papers.

5. "Wagner Ruling Hailed As Aid to Labor, Capital," n.p., [1937], clipping, microfilm M-107, Frederick Papers.

6. C. Frederick, *Ignoramus Book of Housekeeping*, 174–75; "Christine Frederick Joins Fawcett Women's Group As Household Editor," *Southern Advertising and Publishing*, February 1937, clipping, microfilm M-107; Christine Frederick to *New York Times*, 6 December 1947, file folder 6; S. V. Cox, "Noted Household Authority Sees Growth of 'Civic Housekeeping,'" [*Coshocton (Ohio) Tribune*, 11 February 1937], clipping, microfilm M-107, Frederick Papers.

7. Phyllis Carroll, "Two Kitchens Assume Modern Attire," *Home and Field*, August 1932, 22; "Farewell Cellar, Attic," *New York Evening Post*, 23 May 1932, clipping, microfilm M-107, Frederick Papers; C. Frederick, "Suburban Living," 290.

8. LeCorbusier's paper, "*Economie domestique et construction economique*," delivered at the Fourth International Congress of the Organization of Scientific Work in 1929, is among the papers in file folder 15, Frederick Papers.

9. Joyce, interview, 15 September 1994; E. D. Partridge to C. Frederick, 27 February, 6 April 1936, file folder 3; Thomas W. Mackesey to Christine Frederick, 29 September 1949, file folder 7, Frederick Papers. Mackesey was responding to Christine's request for proof of enrollment, but he indicated that he could find no record of her registration. He found her name and scores in the roll books of the courses mentioned.

10. "The Latest Jazz Model Kitchen of 10 Years Ago," n.p., 24 September 1937, clipping, microfilm M-107, Frederick Papers; Goldstein, "Part of the Package," 290–91.

11. "Mrs. Frederick to Speak Here," [*Cincinnati Post*, 19 February 1931], clipping; "'Selling Mrs. Consumer,'" *Spokes*, 24 January 1933, 4; "Selling to Women Outlined by Editor," *Miami Herald Telephone*, 9 February 1934, clipping, microfilm M-107, Frederick Papers; Marchand, *Advertising the American Dream*, xvi.

12. "Christine Frederick Joins Fawcett Women's Group."

13. "Personalities in the Village," *The Villager*, 9 March 1939, clipping, microfilm M-107, Frederick Papers; C. Frederick, "Personal Record," attachment to C. Frederick to *New York Times*, 6 December 1947, file folder 6, Frederick Papers. Christine's daughter stated that, to her knowledge, her mother never attended the University of Chicago, and the university has no record of her. Joyce, interview, 15 September 1994; Maxine Hunsinger Sullivan to author, 15 March 1995.

14. Christine Frederick to Portus Baxter, 12 May 1942, file folder 4, Frederick Papers. The Fredericks' daughter told the author that Christine was "the large or sole support of" the family, and other informants who knew Christine had the same impression. Joyce, interview, 15 September 1994; L. Arnold, telephone conversation.

15. Mallery, "Book Department," review of *Readings in Economics* 224; Smith, "Book Reviews," review of *Humanism As a Way of Life*, 409–10.

16. Christine Frederick, introduction to *Cooking As Men Like It* by J. George Frederick, [xv]; Christine Frederick to Bernice Cronkhite, 1 October 1936, Phyllis Frederick student file (Radcliffe College Archives, photocopy).

17. Christine wrote, "Woman has always been judged for what she *is* or *seems, personally;* while men are judged by what they *do.*" *Selling Mrs. Consumer,* 191. J. George wrote, "At the same time, men are judged by what they *do,* while women are more definitely judged by what they *are.*" *Cooking As Men Like It,* 9–10.

18. Cox, "Noted Household Authority Sees Growth."

19. Elon G. Pratt to Members of the New York Sales Managers' Club, 2 March 1938, file folder 3, Frederick Papers.

20. J. George Frederick to Evelyn Light, 23 November 1933, file folder 273, Theodore Dreiser Papers (photocopy); *Who Was Who in America,* 125.

21. J. G. Frederick, *Humanism,* 254, 249–50, 252.

22. "Personalities in the Village"; "Mrs. Frederick's Career Started by Edward Bok," [1937?], clipping, microfilm M-107, Frederick Papers; C. Frederick, "Mrs. Consumer Speaks Her Mind," 7, 8; D. Frederick, telephone conversation, 20 February 1996; C. Frederick, "Mrs. Consumer Speaks Up," 15.

23. A. Merritt to Whom It May Concern, 25 October 1935; H. J. Carl to Christine Frederick, 3 March 1944, file folder 7, Frederick Papers.

24. "At Auction."

25. Deed Liber 2394 at p. 91, Suffolk County Deed Liber Books (photocopy); Krusa, telephone conversation; Joyce, interview, 15 September 1994.

26. Although Christine left no evidence that she acknowledged J. George's infidelity, all informants confirmed it. Their daughter, their granddaughter, Christine's California friends, friends of a deceased daughter, and even the daughter of the couple who bought Applecroft from Christine all reported that J. George had affairs with other women.

27. "Personalities in the Village"; Dorothy B. Marsh to Christine Frederick, 7 April 1944, file folder 5, Frederick Papers; J. G. Frederick, "Law of the Heart," 56; Krusa, telephone conversation.

28. Joyce to author, 17 September 1996; Joyce, interview, 16 September 1994.

29. Christine Frederick to Mortimer Berkowitz, 16 January 1942; Ellen Stillman to Christine Frederick, 2 November 1942; Richard Shapira to Christine Frederick, 9 November 1942, file folder 4, Frederick Papers; Joyce, interview, 16 September 1994; "Christine Frederick Is Staying in Town!" [1942], business card, file folder 15, Frederick Papers; Christine Frederick to Portus Baxter, 12 May 1942, file folder 4, Frederick Papers.

30. [Christine Frederick], "American Weekly Household Articles, 1934–1943," lists, file folder 13, Frederick Papers.

31. John Godston to Christine Frederick, 13 June 1941; Amy Vanderbilt to Christine Frederick, 6 November 1941; E. Stillman to C. Frederick, 12 December 1941; Mortimer Berkowitz to Christine Frederick, 12 January 1942; Christine Frederick to Mortimer Berkowitz, 16 January 1942, file folder 4, Frederick Papers. File folders 4, 5, and 13 in the Frederick Papers contain many more thank-you letters from manufacturers about whose products Christine wrote articles between 1941 and 1943.

32. Leon W. Stetson to Mortimer Berkowitz, 27 May 1942; Mortimer Berkowitz to Christine Frederick, 28 May 1942; Ellen Stillman to Christine Frederick, 2 July 1942, 20 July 1942; Whitney Payne to Christine Frederick, 20 October 1942, file folder 4, Frederick Papers; Christine Frederick, "Adding Zest to the Diet with Cranberries"; "Eat-mor Cranberries," advertisement, *American Weekly*, 1 November 1942, 23, 24.

33. Whitney Payne to Christine Frederick, 2 November 1942, file folder 4, Frederick Papers.

34. Leo Nerenberg to Christine Frederick, 16 December 1941; W. W. Lockwood to Christine Frederick, 28 November 1941, file folder 4, Frederick Papers.

35. L. B. Williams to Coulter McKeever, 27 November 1941; [Christine Frederick] to A. Merritt, 23 April 1942, file folder 4, Frederick Papers.

36. Richard S. Shapira to Christine Frederick, 9 July 1942, file folder 5; Christine Frederick to [Mortimer] Berkowitz, January 1943, file folder 13; J. A. Beauparlant to Christine Frederick, 17 November 1941; Mrs. C. Van deVelde to Christine Frederick, 21 July 1942; Portus Baxter to Christine Frederick, 19 December 1942, file folder 4, Frederick Papers.

37. Happer Payne to Whitney Payne, 17 December 1943; Whitney Payne to Kennedy and [Mortimer] Berkowitz, 20 December 1943, file folder 5, Frederick Papers.

38. [Christine Frederick] to E[mile] C. Shermacher [*sic*], 15 January 1944; Emile C. Schnurmacher to Christine Frederick, 17 January 1944; Whitney Payne to Christine Frederick, 29 January 1944, file folder 5; Harry J. Carl to Christine Frederick, 14 February 1944, file folder 7, Frederick Papers.

39. David [Frederick] to [Christine Frederick], [17 February 1944], file folder 5, Frederick Papers.

40. H. J. Carl to Christine Frederick, 3 March 1944, file folder 7, Frederick Papers.

41. David [Frederick] to [Christine Frederick], [17 February 1944]; [Barbara Bement Frederick] to [Christine Frederick], n.d., file folder 5, Frederick Papers.

42. James B. Meigs to Christine Frederick, 9 March 1944; Franklin S. Allen to Christine Frederick, 28 March 1944; Coulter McKeever to Christine Frederick, 7 April 1944; Arthur H. Anson to Christine Frederick, 16 March 1944, file folder 5, Frederick Papers. This file contains twenty-five responses to Christine's solicitation letters of 1944. They include letters from many food and household products manufacturers and at least two advertising agencies, including Bruce Barton's Batten, Barton, Durstine and Osborn.

43. Grace M. White to Christine Frederick, 29 March 1944; Jean Wade Rindlaub to Christine Frederick, 29 March 1944, file folder 5, Frederick Papers.

44. Joyce, interview, 16 September 1994.

45. *Handbook of Private Schools*, 1944, 383; "Christine Frederick, Here for Visit, Won National Attention with Work to Improve Efficiency of Kitchens," [*South Coast News*, 22 September 1949], clipping, microfilm M-107; "Save Money!—Regrets! The New House," flyer, n.d., file folder 17, Frederick Papers; Mrs. Julia Elsen to Whom It May Concern, 6 January 1949, file folder 8, Frederick Papers.

46. "Women Buy Dreams—Not Techniques," n.p., [1947], clipping, microfilm M-107; Clarissa P. Edson to Christine Frederick, 30 March 1949, 18 May 1949, 17 January 1950; "Christine Frederick, Here for Visit."

47. "Are You Happy With . . .," [*Villager*, 10 February 1949], advertisement, microfilm M-107, Frederick Papers.

48. C. Frederick to *New York Times*; Id., "Personal Record."

49. J. E. Fontana to Christine Frederick, 26 February 1948; Donald M. Vanderbilt to Christine Frederick, 2 March 1948, file folder 7, Frederick Papers.

50. "Fawcett Women's Group," letterhead; A. Merritt to Whom It May Concern; Mortimer Berkowitz to Christine Frederick, 18 July 1941; A. Merritt to Christine Frederick, 27 April 1942; H. J. Carl to Christine Frederick, 7 May 1942; Arthur H. Anson to Christine Frederick, 3 December 1942; "Leading Food Editors Attend AIB's Wartime Cake Luncheon," *Bakers' Weekly*, 19 October 1942, clipping, file folder 7; Julia Elsen to Christine Frederick, 13 June 1947, file folder 6, Frederick Papers.
Christine labeled this group of documents "Prepared for Social Security Administration, 42 Bdw'y NYC" and affixed a note to each explaining how it proved that she was considered a regular employee by her editors. The last letter was stamped "Received Sept. 27, 1949, Accounting Office" by the Social Security Administration. There is no evidence of the administration's response.

51. Joyce, interview, 16 September 1994; D. Frederick, telephone conversation, 20 February 1996.

52. D. Frederick, telephone conversation, 20 February 1996; Olga Samaroff Stokowski to Christine Frederick, 3 March 1945, file folder 6, Frederick Papers.

53. Emilie Van Waveren to Christine Frederick, 17 September 1946, file folder 6; Paulette [Bernège] to Dorothy [Dignam], 9 December 1946, file folder 8, Frederick Papers.

54. Joyce, interview, 16 September 1994.

55. Ibid., 15 September 1994; Preston M. Moretz to author, 15 December 1994; "Home Economics," Drexel yearbook, 1940, 83; Joyce to author, 15 January 1995; Wolkin, telephone conversation. The institutions in which Carol Frederick Herman was treated declined to respond to requests for confirmation of her residence with them, but all informants agreed that she had been committed to two hospitals on Long Island between 1942 and 1955. Four years after her daughter was committed to King's Park, Christine wrote to Emilie Van Waveren that Carol's marriage had failed, but apparently she did not mention the reason. Years later, she barely spoke of Carol, and in 1962 Christine described her to an interviewer simply as "a nice homemaker who married young." Even when a drug that controlled Carol's schizophrenic behavior was discovered in the mid-1950s and she was transferred from the psychiatric center to a supervised home facility, Christine found visits too painful to continue. It fell to Jean to manage Carol's affairs for the rest of her long life. Carol died on 19 October 1993 at the age of seventy-six. Emilie Van Waveren to Christine Frederick, 17 September 1946, file folder 6, Frederick Papers; L. Arnold, telephone conversation, interview; "Career Chronology of

Mrs. Christine Frederick"; Joyce, interview, 15 September 1994; D. Frederick, telephone conversation, 20 February 1996.

56. Joyce, interview, 15 September 1994; Jane Knowles to author, 15 December 1994; David Yeh to author, 11 January 1995; Phyllis Frederick to Radcliffe College, 1 July 1936; "Application for Admissions to Advanced Standing," 14 July 1936; Phyllis Frederick to [Bernice] Cronkhite, 14 July, 16 August, 27 August, 1 October 1936; Phyllis Frederick to [Mildred P.] Sherman, 8 November 1936; Christine Frederick to Mildred P. Sherman, 2 August 1937; Phyllis Frederick to Radcliffe Appointment Bureau, 24 August 1938, Phyllis Frederick student file; Untitled transcript for [Phyllis Frederick], 1936–37, 1937–38, (Radcliffe College Archives, photocopies).

57. Wolkin, telephone conversation; Justin, interview; F. Frederick, "Older Woman."

58. F. Frederick, *Design and Sell Toys*, [167]; Phyllis Frederick, *Jiffy Fashions* (New York: Arco Publishing Company, 1949); F. Frederick, " City of Lost Angels"; Stevens, introduction to *Discourses*, xiii–xiv.

59. F. Frederick, foreword to *Path of Love*, iii; Wolkin, interview. The author saw the complete run of *The Awakener* in Ojai, California, at the home of Peter Justin. In the early 1940s, Phyllis Frederick became acquainted with disciples of Meher Baba and became a convert immediately. She helped establish a center in Myrtle Beach, South Carolina, where she first met the spiritual leader in 1952. Baba had ceased speaking in 1925 and communicated by pointing to letters on an alphabet board. When he was introduced to Phyllis, he quickly repeated her name on his board as "F-I-L-I-S," a spelling that she adopted. As Baba's disciple, Filis vowed to remain celibate and devote her life to his ministry. She continued teaching, writing, and speaking on Baba's behalf until, greatly esteemed by his followers, she was nursed through her last illness by the Los Angeles faithful. Filis died of breast cancer on 19 March 1987 at the age of seventy-two. Wolkin, telephone conversation, interview; [Filis Frederick], "A Short Biography of Meher Baba," foreword to *The Path of Love*, [v–vi]; Id., "Memories of '52," 4–5; Stevens, introduction to *Discourses*, xiv; F. Frederick, "Older Woman"; Id., "Darshan III," 32–37; Joyce, interview, 15 September 1994; D. Frederick, telephone conversation, 20 February 1996.

60. Yeh to author, 11 January 1995; Joyce, interview, 14 September 1994; "Personalities in the Village"; J. G. Frederick, *Long Island Seafood Cookbook*.

61. Joyce, interview, 14 September 1994; Wolkin, telephone conversation; J. G. Frederick, "Law of the Heart," 56; "Mrs. Frederick on Trip to Eastern Cities," [16 May 1950], clipping, microfilm M-107, Frederick Papers. Jean entered into a brief and unhappy marriage in 1936, but she had divorced her husband by the time she was offered the position as Bowles's ghostwriter. In 1948 she followed Bowles to Connecticut to work on his successful gubernatorial campaign and remained on his staff in Hartford until 1950, when he lost his bid for reelection. When President Truman appointed him ambassador to India, he once again invited Jean to join his staff. She worked as an attaché writing speeches and editing the bimonthly tabloid the *American Reporter* in the New Delhi embassy for the next two years. When Bowles tendered his resignation to the new

Republican administration in 1953, Jean stayed in India as a writer for the Ford Foundation until 1961. After a decade abroad, she returned to the United States to take the job with the State Department, where she was senior editor in the Bureau of Education and Cultural Affairs. This account of Jean's career is based almost entirely on the author's interviews with her during September 1994 and subsequent correspondence through 1996. Other family members and acquaintances—Deborah Frederick, Adele Wolkin, and Louise Arnold, for example—also have contributed information through interviews. For an account of Bowles's career, see Bowles, *Promises to Keep*. Jean is mentioned on 180 and 191. Jean worked for the Ford Foundation's community development program, established in New Delhi in 1951. See MacDonald, *Ford Foundation*, 60. Jean died in Washington, D.C., in 1998 according to a telephone conversation with personnel at Georgetown Retirement Residence on 3 March 2002.

62. Joyce, interview, 15 September 1994.

63. This interlude was very brief; it occurred just before Christine left Applecroft, and after David's divorce, Beatrice attempted to make a home for the children in Newbury, Massachusetts. She was not successful, and they were soon returned to their father, who married again in 1941 and sent little Deborah and Peter to the Bement School, a boarding school for small children operated in Deerfield, Massachusetts, by his new mother-in-law. Jean Joyce to the author, 2 April 1996, 17 September 1996; "David Frederick of Harper's Dead," *NYT*, 3 January 1952, p. 46, col. 2; D. Frederick, telephone conversation, 7 September 1996.

64. David F. Kenny to Peddie School, 25 August 1943, (Peddie Archives, Highstown, N.J., photocopy); *Publishers' Weekly*, 19 January 1952, 233.

65. After the war, David Frederick had had trouble finding the right job. He moved to suburban Connecticut and bounced from assistant to the president of *Parents' Magazine* to director of sales and advertising for the Columbia Broadcasting System and finally to a job in market research. This was a difficult period for him financially, and he was forced to move his family, which had increased by another child born to his second wife, into a smaller house. Thus, the job at *Harper's* was an extremely fortuitous opportunity, and he made the best of it. "David Frederick of Harper's Dead"; D. Frederick, telephone conversation, 20 February 1996; *Harper's Magazine*, February 1952, 104.

66. L. Arnold, interview; "Publisher of Harper's Is Laguna Visitor," *South Coast News*, 10 May 1951, clipping, microfilm M-107, Frederick Papers; "David Frederick of Harper's Dead"; Joyce, interview, 14 September 1994.

67. D. Frederick, telephone conversation, 20 February 1996.

68. "Sense of Permanence Is Essence of Home, Mrs. Frederick Declares," n.p. [31 January 1949], clipping, microfilm M-107, Frederick Papers.

14 · Re-creation and Legacy

1. Caughey with Hundley, *California*, 376–77.

2. "Christine Frederick, Here for Visit"; Christine Frederick, "You and Your Home,"

18 October 1949; "You and Your Home," 25 October 1949; "Wallpaper Adds Warmth and Individuality," 1 November 1949, *South Coast News*; C. Frederick, "Design for Better Living," speech before Altrusa Club, Laguna Beach, Calif., 28 November 1949, p. 2, file folder 10, Frederick Papers; "Women Should Be Taught Interior Decoration, Laguna Expert Says," *Santa Ana Register*, 4 December 1949, 10C; "Christine Frederick Tells Altrusans of Decorating," *South Coast News*, 1 December 1949, 8; "Mrs. Frederick Tells Soroptomists of Role of Decorator in Home," 19 January 1950, clippings, microfilm M-107, Frederick Papers.

3. Joyce, interview, 16 September 1994; Bill J. Priest to Commission on Credentials, 11 July 1951, file folder 8; *Orange Coast Evening College News*, January 1950, clipping, microfilm M-107, Frederick Papers.

4. "Credit Certificate" for Christine Frederick, 1951, University Extension, University of California; California State Board of Education Adult Education Credential, 26 May 1953, file folder 14, Frederick Papers; Kathleen A. Woodward to author, 27 April 1994; B. J. Priest to Christine Frederick, [summer 1950], file folder 8, Frederick Papers; Renley, telephone conversation.

5. "Mrs. Frederick to Give Special Course Here," n.d., clipping; "Join Now! Spring Shortcourse," n.d., advertisement; "Christine Fredericks [sic] Starts Lecture Series," *Laguna Beach Post*, 7 July 1955, 7, clipping, microfilm M-107, Frederick Papers.

6. George St. Aubin to Christine Frederick, 8 November 1951, file folder 8, Frederick Papers; Joyce, interview, 16 September 1994; "Christine Frederick, Professional Building, Laguna Beach, 4—1937," letterhead, Alumni Biographical Files (photocopy); L. Arnold, interview.

7. Carolyn S. Baer to Christine Frederick, 4 November 1951, file folder 8; Helen Smith to Christine Frederick, 11 April 1951, file folder 18; Ivy Deibel Browne, "This Is Your Neighbor," *Laguna Beach Post*, 5 April 1956, clipping; "Fiesta Day at the Pepper Tree Shops," n.d., clipping; "Christine Frederick Responsible for 'Face-Lifting' Newly Remodeled, Strikingly Decorated Landmark Gift Shop," n.d., clipping; "Decorator's Jumble Sale," n.d., clipping, microfilm M-107, Frederick Papers.

8. Joyce, interview, 16 September 1994; L. Arnold, interview; Lang, telephone conversation.

9. Joyce, interview, 16 September 1994; L. Arnold, telephone conversation, interview; Barbara Baer, telephone conversation; Lang, telephone conversation; "T. F. Baers Entertain Five Patients from Margie Hospital," *South Coast News*, [1950], clipping, microfilm M-107, Frederick Papers.

10. In the speech Christine gave for the Laguna Library Book Day in 1966, for example, she talked of her work in publishing, radio, and Chautauqua. She also had copies of her books available for the audience to examine.

11. L. Arnold, telephone conversation; Baer, telephone conversation; Lang, telephone conversation; Joyce, interview, 16 September 1994; "To Tell Fortunes at Ebell Festival," *Newport-Balboa Press*, 17 April 1952, clipping, microfilm M-107, Frederick Papers. For a discussion of McCarthyism, see Diggins, *Proud Decades*, 110—17.

12. Wolkin, telephone conversation; L. Arnold, telephone conversation; Lang, telephone conversation; Joyce, interview, 16 September 1994; D. Frederick, telephone conversation, 20 February 1996; [C. Frederick], "Only a Girl," 1.

13. *The American Catholic Church*, n.d., leaflet; "Retrofitting Completed at St. Francis by the Sea," *Laguna Coastline News*, 2 December 1994, clipping; "Bishop Lowell Paul Wadle—1901–1965: In Memoriam," [April 1965], typescript, St. Francis-by-the-Sea Archives. The scholar Eugene Taylor defines theosophy as "a set of teachings that . . . drew upon ancient and modern religions, philosophies, and sciences in order to investigate the unexplained laws of nature and the physical powers latent in all human beings." *Shadow Culture*, 141.

14. L. Arnold, telephone conversation, interview; Tsalarczyk, interview. Christine's granddaughter reports seeing a letter to Christine from her son, David, dated after his death in papers now in the possession of a family member. According to this informant, the collection also contains other letters from the dead, one warning Christine to stay away from Carol. The author has not been able to see these papers. D. Frederick, telephone conversation, 7 September 1996.

15. "The American Catholic Church," 10 January 1954, certificate of baptism for Christine Frederick, St. Francis-by-the-Sea Archives.

16. Ferdinand Kramer to Christine Frederick, 10 December 1951; Nadine Miller to Christine Frederick, 9 June 1952, file folder 8, Frederick Papers; "History of Advertising Women of New York, Inc, Chronological Record of the Year 1952" and "Chronological Record of the Year 1960," carton 3, file folder 17, Dignam Papers; Dorothy Dignam to Harriet Raymond, 6 August 1957; "Chronology of Mrs. Christine Frederick," carton 2, file folder 4, AWNY Papers; Wiseman, "Christine Frederick," 17; "Advertising Women of New York Golden Anniversary Dinner and Installation," 23 May 1962, invitation, file folder 17; Photograph MC261-22-10, Frederick Papers.

17. Christine Frederick to editor of Northwestern Alumni Bulletin, 25 August 1956, Alumni Files, (Northwestern, photocopy); "Golden Reunion Certificate," Northwestern University Alumni Association, 1956, file folder 14, Frederick Papers.

18. "'Founding Father' Passes," n.d., typescript, carton 2, file folder 4, AWNY Papers; Joyce, interview, 16 September 1994; Joyce to author, 17 September 1996. According to the report in the AWNY Papers, J. George had also attended the AWNY dinner but was dangerously ill at the time.

19. This information derives from a survey of the *Cumulative Book Index, 1912–1960* and *The Readers' Guide to Periodic Literature*, 1912–64.

20. J. G. Frederick, "Law of the Heart," 55–56.

21. Joyce to author, 17 September 1996.

22. "J. G. Frederick, 82, A Writer, Is Dead"; Field and Frederick, *1000 Pleasure Spots*; J. George Frederick to Jo Foxworth, 3 March 1964, carton 2, file folder 1, AWNY Papers.

23. Joyce, interview, 16 September 1994; Joyce to author, 17 September 1996; Christine Frederick to Emma Stock, 27 June 1964, carton 2, file folder 4, AWNY Papers.

24. "Open House," 11 February [1968], invitation, St. Francis-by-the-Sea Archives.

25. Christine Frederick to Valerie Ladd, 11 September 1969.

26. Joyce to author, 4 May 1994; Joyce, interview, 16 September 1994.

27. Emma Dot Partridge to Christine Frederick, 4 March [1935], 6 March 1936, file folder 3; Ray Fowler to Richard S. Shapira, 29 July 1942, file folder 4; Memo to Members of the New England Division of the National Electric Light Association, 7 February 1931, file folder 3; "Memo on Peacock Installation," typescript; "'So now we can all relax,'" typescript; "Peacock Building Now in Process of Remodeling," n.p., [31 January 1952], clipping, file folder 18; Photograph MC261-33-3, Frederick Papers.

28. Joyce, interview, 16 September 1994; L. Arnold, interview; "Certificate of Death, Christine Frederick," 6 April 1970, box 36, Christine Frederick file, Notable American Women Records (photocopy); "AWNY Founder 1883–1970, Early Women's Lib!" [*Ad Libber*, spring 1970], clipping; "Christine Frederick Dies," *Laguna News-Post*, 8 April 1970, clipping, file folder 19, Frederick Papers.

29. "Mrs. Christine Frederick Dies; Home Economist and Author, 87," *NYT*, 8 April 1970, p. 43, col. 2; "Christine Frederick Dies"; "Feminist from Earlier Era," sec. 3, p. 1, col. 3.

30. Joyce, interview, 16 September 1994; Paul A. Hanna to Advertising Women of New York, 9 June 1972, carton 2, file folder 4, AWNY Papers.

31. F. Frederick, "Older Woman."

32. C. Frederick, "You and Your Home."

33. C. Frederick, "Personal Record"; "Health History," California State Department of Education, 13 September 1951 and 25 May 1953, file folder 14, Frederick Papers; C. Frederick to Editor, Northwestern Alumni Bulletin, 25 August 1956; C. Frederick, Laguna Library Book Day Speech.

34. "Career Chronology of Mrs. Christine Frederick"; Handwritten note on clipping, "Mrs. Christine Frederick, Household Efficiency Expert, Will Hook Up Radio Telephone to Thousands of Kitchens," carton 2, file folder 4, AWNY Papers.

35. Christine even chose the publishing house: "Possible Publisher: Simon and Schuster," "Only a Girl," 3, [40].

36. C. Frederick, *Household Engineering*, 15.

37. C. MacGaffey, "Genius of Woman," 5; Beecher, *Essay on Slavery*, 97.

38. Dawley, *Struggles for Justice*, 109–15.

Epilogue

1. U.S. Department of Labor, Civilian Labor Force Participation Rates; Labor Force Participation Rates of Women; Civilian Labor Force for Selected Demographic Groups; Lammert-Reeves, *Law School Admissions Advisor*; Wear, ed., *Women in Medical Education*, 5; U.S. Department of Labor, Women's Bureau, "Women at the Millenium," 5.

2. U.S. Department of Labor, Women's Bureau, *Wage Gap*; Id., *20 Leading Occupations*; Berch, *Endless Day*, 122.

3. Newman, interview by Neary; *Percentage of Women in State Legislatures; Current Congressional Profile*.

4. Carrie Teegardin in "You've Come a Long Way," *AJC*, 27 March 1994, p. A1; Fox-Genovese, *Feminism without Illusions*, 138, 120, 24, 244; Gustav Niebuhr, "Southern Baptists Declare Wife Should 'Submit' to Her Husband," *NYT*, 10 June 1998, A1.

5. Lundberg and Farnham, *Modern Woman*, v, 3, 25, 143–45, 162, 173, 371.

6. Friedan, *Feminine Mystique*, 180–81; Giedion, *Mechanization Takes Command*, 513; Sochen, *Movers and Shakers*, 189–90; Mead, "Return of the Cave Woman," 6, 8.

7. Linden, "Class of '65," 92, 93–95.

8. Friedan, *Feminine Mystique*, 11, 15–16, 24–27, 325.

9. Ehrenreich and English, *For Her Own Good*, 163–64.

10. Quoted in Friedan, *Feminine Mystique*, 205.

11. Ibid., 199–200.

12. Quoted in Ibid., 199, 210, 214.

13. Ibid., 32, 198.

14. Simone de Beauvoir, *The Second Sex*, trans. H. M. Parshley (New York: Alfred A. Knopf, 1953); Thompson is quoted in Sochen, *Movers and Shakers*, 188.

15. Showalter, ed., *These Modern Women*, 26; Mansbridge, *Why We Lost the ERA*, ix, 11–12. The early feminist suffragist Alice Paul headed the first effort to add an equal rights amendment to the Constitution in 1920. It and subsequent attempts failed, partly because women's groups opposed it. See Mansbridge, 8–10.

16. Hayden, *Redesigning the American Dream*, 14–15; Sherry Ahrentzen, introduction to Franck and Ahrentzen, eds., *New Households, New Housing*, xii; Susan Saegert and Gary Winkel, "The Home," 41; Keller, introduction to *Building for Women*, x.

17. Hayden, *Grand Domestic Revolution*, 294; Id., *Redesigning the American Dream*, 50.

18. Berch, *Endless Day*, 103; Leavitt, "Two Prototypical Designs," 164; Ahrentzen, introduction to *New Households, New Housing*, xiii.

19. Marilyn Geewax, "Houses and Highways Should Fit the Future, Not the Past," *AJC*, 28 January 1996, G3.

20. In 1988, the architects Kathryn McCamant and Charles Durrett had coined the term "cohousing" to describe such cluster communities; they, too, suggested a common center where residents would share cooking, dining, child care, and laundry. McCamant and Durrett agreed that "traditional forms of housing no longer address[ed] the needs of many" Americans. McCamant and Durrett, *Cohousing*, 7; Jennifer Peck, "Cohousing Gains Ground but Some Eye Shared Living with Suspicion," *Boston Globe*, 30 November 1997, WKW1; "New Tumwater Project Builds a Neighborhood: Meals, Ideas May Be Shared in Planned Community," *Tacoma News Tribune*, 23 July 1998, 1.

21. Nelson, "Neighborhood for the '90s," 28–29; Fromm, *Collaborative Communities*, 91; Peck, "Cohousing Gains Ground."

22. For commentaries on Americans' entrenched attitudes about the home, see Saegert and Winkel, "The Home," 46–51; Hayden, *Redesigning the American Dream*, 67; Cowan, *More Work for Mother*, 101.

23. Berch, *Endless Day*, 4–5, 149–50. See also Hochschild, *Second Shift*.

24. Miriam Longino, "Strong Will, Southern Ways," AJC, 3 May 1995, p. B1, col. 2.

25. Buchanan, *Choosing to Lead*, 198.

26. Ibid., 26.

27. Tamar Lewin, "Equal Pay Top Concern of Working Women, Study Shows," *Spokane Spokesman-Review*, 5 September 1997, A4.

28. Time-diary data gathered from 1965 to 1985 in the Americans' Use of Time Project funded by the National Science Foundation show that in 1985, women were still doing 80 percent of child care, 40 percent more shopping than men, and in general, almost twice as much of the "core" housework (cleaning, cooking, laundry) than their male partners. Robinson and Godbey, *Time for Life*, 100, 104–5.

29. See Berch, *Endless Day*, 91; Hayden, *Redesigning the American Home*, 91, 149; Vanek, "Time Spent in Housework," 119–20.

30. "What Robin Morgan Said," *JHE* 65 (January 1973): 13. In 1972, amendments to the Education Acts of 1965 paved the way for equality between the sexes in virtually all public school activities, and by the 1980s *some* boys were taking home economics just as *some* girls were enjoying increased funding to participate in sports. *Title IX of the Education Amendments of 1972*.

31. Robinson and Godbey, *Time for Life*, 104; *Family Career and Community Leaders of America Membership Map*.

32. Buchanan, *Choosing to Lead*, 6, 7, 19.

Bibliography

Works by Christine Frederick

Many of the articles and speeches by Christine Frederick that are cited in this book are located in the Christine MacGaffey Frederick Papers at the Arthur and Elizabeth Schlesinger Library on the History of Women in America, Radcliffe Institute, Harvard University. They are not listed separately in this bibliography.

1912

"The New Housekeeping." *Ladies' Home Journal*, September, 13, 70–71.
"The New Housekeeping." *Ladies' Home Journal*, October, 20, 100.
"The New Housekeeping." *Ladies' Home Journal*, November, 19–20.
"The New Housekeeping." *Ladies' Home Journal*, December, 16, 79.

1913

"How I Made My Country Kitchen Efficient." *Ladies' Home Journal*, July, 20.
"Rousing the Small Town." *Collier's*, 11 October, 22–24.
"The Woman Who Buys Wisely." *Ladies' Home Journal*, November, 95.

1914

"How I Save Money in My Home." *Ladies' Home Journal*, January, 38.
"Putting the American Woman and Her Home on a Business Basis." *American Review of Reviews*, February, 199–208.
"Points in Efficiency." *Journal of Home Economics* 6 (June): 278–80.
"Have a Step-Saving Kitchen." *Delineator*, July, 23–24.
"Suppose Our Servants Didn't Live with Us?" *Ladies' Home Journal*, October, 102.
The New Housekeeping: Efficiency Studies in Home Management. Garden City, N.Y.: Doubleday, Page and Company.
You and Your Kitchen. New Castle, Ind.: Hoosier Manufacturing Company.

1915

"La tenue scientifique de la maison." *Revue de metallurgie* (Paris) 12 (April): 348–82.
"Why Should Our Servants Live with Us?" *Ladies' Home Journal*, October, 47.
"The Housewife's Tools." *Ladies' Home Journal*, November, 66.
Meals That Cook Themselves and Cut the Costs. New Haven, Conn.: The Sentinel Manufacturing Co.

1916
"Preserving Your Wood Floors and Woodwork." *Ladies' Home Journal*, March, 67.
"What You Should Know about the Can You Buy." *Ladies' Home Journal*, October, 54.

1917
"Equipping an Orchard As a Living Room." *New Country Life*, March, 108.
"The 'Professional Grandma.'" *Ladies' Home Journal*, April, 102–3.
"Help for the Farmer's Wife, Too." *New York Times*, 10 June, sec. 2, p. 2, col 7.
"No-Waste Dinners." *Ladies' Home Journal*, September, 34.
"When Your Board Goes Up." *Ladies' Home Journal*, October, 52.
"How I Learned Food Values As Told by a Farmer's Wife." *Ladies' Home Journal*,
    November, 56.

1919
"What Is a Safe Amount of Food?" *Ladies' Home Journal*, February, 108.
"Your Health Depends upon Your Eating." *Ladies' Home Journal*, February, 53.
"The College Graduate's New View of 'Home.'" *Ladies' Home Journal*, June, 145.
"My Morning of Intensive Baking." *Ladies' Home Journal*, June, 98.
"A Handy Chart for Home Canning by the Cold-Pack Method." *Ladies' Home Journal*,
    July, 77.
"Will the Eight-Hour Home-Assistant Plan Work Out?" *Ladies' Home Journal*, Sep-
    tember, 47.
"Cooking Sunday's Dinner on Saturday." *Ladies' Home Journal*, November, 117.
Household Engineering: Scientific Management in the Home. Chicago: American School of
    Home Economics.

1920
"The Most Important Kitchen Tool." *Ladies' Home Journal*, March, 186.
"If Your Laundress Retires." *Ladies' Home Journal*, September, 106.

1921
"The Economic Strike of the American Housewife." *Current Opinion*, June, 750–52.
"Practical Points for the Pantry." *New Country Life*, November, 66–67.

1922
"A Real Use for the Radio." *Good Housekeeping*, July, 77, 144–46.
"Twelve Supermen." *New York Times*, 5 July.
You and Your Laundry. New York: The Hurley Machine Company.

1924
"New Wealth, New Standards of Living and Changed Family Budgets." *Annals of the
    American Academy of Political and Social Science* 115 (September): 74–82.

"Advertising Copy and the So-Called Average Woman." In *Masters of Advertising Copy*, ed. Frederick, 225–46.

1925
Efficient Housekeeping or Household Engineering: Scientific Management in the Home. Chicago: American School of Home Economics.

1927
"Making a Tennis Court." *New Country Life*, May, 66.

1928
"Man's Business and the Woman's." *Outlook*, 1 February, 168.
"Is Suburban Living a Delusion?" *Outlook*, 22 February, 290.
"Is the Advertiser Over-Playing the Color Appeal?" *Advertising and Selling*, 2 May, 23, 66–70.
"Grown-up Accessories for Small People." *The American Home*, December, 227.

1929
Selling Mrs. Consumer. New York: Business Bourse.

1932
The Ignoramus Book of Housekeeping. New York: Sears Publishing Company.

Work Edited by Christine Frederick

"The New Housekeeping." *Ladies' Home Journal*, December 1915, 47.

Other Printed Works

Abbott, Charles F. Preface to *Modern Salesmanagement: A Practical Handbook Practical Handbook and Guide*, by J. George Frederick. New York: D. Appleton and Company, 1923.
The Abbott Circle. Yearbook, Abbott Academy, 1928, 1932. Phillips Academy Archives, Andover, Mass. Photocopies.
Advertising Women of New York Golden Salute to Advertising. New York: Advertising Women of New York Foundation, 1962.
Allen, Polly Wynn. *Building Domestic Liberty: Charlotte Perkins Gilman's Architectural Feminism*. Amherst: University of Massachusetts Press, 1988.
The American Weekly, 1917–44.
Andrews, Benjamin R. "The Home Woman As Buyer and Controller of Consumption." *Annals of the American Academy of Political and Social Science* 143 (May 1929): 41–48.

Andrews, Kenneth R. *Nook Farm: Mark Twain's Hartford Circle*. Cambridge: Harvard University Press, 1950.

"Annual Meeting of the American Home Economics Association—June 27–July 4, Cornell University, Ithaca, New York." *Journal of Home Economics* 5 (January 1913): 289–90.

"Application of Smith-Lever Funds." *Journal of Home Economics* 7 (August–September 1915): 355–58.

Arnold, Sarah Louise. "Fundamental Conceptions of Home Economics." *Journal of Home Economics* 6 (December 1914): 423, 429.

Association of American Medical Colleges. *Enhancing the Environment for Women in Academic Medicine: Resources and Pathways*. Washington, D.C.: Association of American Medical Colleges, 1996.

Atlanta Journal-Constitution, 1993–96.

"'Bait' Advertising Imperils Consumer Confidence." *Trade Service Bulletin*. National Vigilance Committee Associated Advertising Clubs of the World, 17 July 1925.

Banta, Martha. *Taylored Lives: Narrative Productions in the Age of Taylor, Veblen, and Ford*. Chicago: University of Chicago Press, 1993.

Barton, Bruce. "Human Appeals in Copy." In *Masters of Advertising Copy*, ed. Frederick, 65–73.

Beard, Mary. *On Understanding Women*. London: Longmans, Green and Company, 1931.

Beecher, Catharine E. *Essay on Slavery and Abolitionism: With Reference to the Duty of American Females*. 1837. Reprint, Salem, N.H.: Ayer Company, Publishers, 1988.
———. *A Treatise on Domestic Economy*. 1841. Reprint, New York: Source Book Press, 1970.
———. "Woman's Profession Dishonored." *Harper's* 29 (November 1864): 766–68.
———. "An Address on Female Suffrage." In *Pioneers in Women's Education in the United States*, ed. Goodsell, 1931, 189–214. Reprint, New York: AMS Press, 1970.
———. "The True Remedy for the Wrongs of Women." In *Limits of Sisterhood*, eds. Boydston, Kelley, and Margolis, 138–42.

Beecher, Catharine E., and Harriet Beecher Stowe. *The American Woman's Home: or, Principles of Domestic Science Being a Guide to the Formation and Maintenance of Economical, Healthful, Beautiful, and Christian Homes*. 1869. Reprint, American Education: Its Men, Ideas, and Institutions Series, New York: Arno Press, 1971.

Bellamy, Edward. *Looking Backward, 2000–1887*. New York: Grosset and Dunlap, 1888.

Benson, Susan Porter. "Living on the Margin." In *Sex of Things*, ed. de Grazia with Furlough, 212–43.

Bent, Silas. "A Woman's Place Is in the Home." *Century Magazine* 116 (June 1928): 204–13.

Berch, Bettina. *The Endless Day: The Political Economy of Women and Work*. New York: Harcourt Brace Jovanovich, 1982.

Bevier, Isabel, and Susannah Usher. *The Home Economics Movement, Part I*. Boston: Whitcomb and Barrows, 1906.

Blau, Francine D., and Ronald G. Ehrenberg, eds. *Gender and Family Issues in the Workplace*. New York: Russell Sage Foundation, 1997.

Bok, Edward W. *A Man from Maine*. New York: Charles Scribner's Sons, 1923.

"Book Department," review of *Humanism As a Way of Life*, by J. George Frederick. *Annals of the American Academy of Political and Social Science* 166 (March 1933): 224.

Boston Globe, 1997.

Bothwell, Bessie Bishop. "Visiting Housekeeping Work in Detroit." *Journal of Home Economics* 6 (February 1914): 8.

Bowers, William L. *The Country Life Movement in America, 1900–1920*. Port Washington, N.Y.: Kennikat Press, 1974.

Bowles, Chester. *Promises to Keep: My Years in Public Life, 1941–1969*. New York: Harper and Row, 1971.

Boydston, Jeanne, Mary Kelley, and Anne Margolis, eds. *The Limits of Sisterhood: The Beecher Sisters on Women's Rights and Woman's Sphere*. Chapel Hill: University of North Carolina Press, 1988.

Brown, Dorothy. *Setting a Course: American Women in the 1920s*. Boston: Twain Publishers, 1987.

Bruère, Martha Bensley. "The New Home-making." *Outlook*, 16 March 1912, 591–95.

———. "The Highway to Woman's Happiness." *Current History*, October 1927, 26–29.

Buchanan, Constance H. *Choosing to Lead: Women and the Crisis of American Values*. Boston: Beacon Press, 1996.

Caughey, John W., with Norris Hundley Jr. *California: History of a Remarkable State*. 4th ed. Englewood Cliffs, N.J.: Prentice-Hall, Inc., 1982.

"Charlotte Perkins Gilman's Dynamic Social Philosophy." *Current Literature*, July 1911, 67–70.

Chase, Stuart, and F. J. Schlink. *Your Money's Worth: A Study in the Waste of the Consumer's Dollar*. New York: Macmillan, 1927.

"Chronicle and Comment." Review of *The New Housekeeping: Efficiency Studies in Home Management*, by Christine Frederick. *The Bookman*, September 1913, 3.

Clark, Clifford Edward, Jr. *The American Family Home, 1660–1960*. Chapel Hill: University of North Carolina Press, 1986.

Congressional Quarterly's Guide to U.S. Elections. 2d ed. Washington, D.C.: Congressional Quarterly, Inc., 1985.

Cott, Nancy. *The Grounding of Modern Feminism*. New Haven: Yale University Press, 1987.

———. "What's in a Name: The Limits of 'Social Feminism'; or Expanding the Vocabulary of Women's History." *Journal of American History* 76 (December 1989): 809–29.

Cowan, Ruth Schwartz. *More Work for Mother: The Ironies of Household Technology from the Open Hearth to the Microwave*. New York: Basic Books, 1983.

Crane, Stephen. *Maggie, a Girl of the Streets: A Story of New York.* 1893. Reprint, with an introduction by Joseph Katz, Gainesville, Fla.: Scholars' Facsimiles and Reprints, 1966.

Cremin, Lawrence A. *The Transformation of the School: Progressivism in American Education, 1876–1957.* New York: Alfred A. Knopf, 1961.

Cromley, Elizabeth Collins. *Alone Together: A History of New York's Early Apartments.* Ithaca: Cornell University Press, 1990.

Culligan, Matthew J. *The Curtis-Culligan Story: From Cyrus to Horace to Joe.* New York: Crown Publishers, 1970.

"David Frederick." *Harper's Magazine,* February 1952, 104.

Dawley, Alan. *Struggles for Justice: Social Responsibility and the Liberal State.* Cambridge: Harvard University Press, Belknap Press, 1991.

de Grazia, Victoria, with Ellen Furlough, eds. *The Sex of Things: Gender and Consumption in Historical Perspective.* Berkeley: University of California Press, 1996.

Degler, Carl N. "Charlotte Perkins Gilman on the Theory and Practice of Feminism." In *Our American Sisters,* ed. Friedman and Shade, 197–218.

Diggins, John Patrick. *The Proud Decades: America in War and Peace, 1941–1960.* New York: W. W. Norton and Company, 1988.

Douglas, Alan. *Radio Manufacturers of the 1920s.* Vestal, N.Y.: Vestal Press, Ltd., 1989.

Drexel University Year Book, 1940, 83. Photocopy.

Dyer, George L. "The Advertising Writer Who Is Bigger than His Ad." In *Masters of Advertising Copy,* ed. J. G. Frederick, 55–65.

Eagles, Charles W. "Urban-Rural Conflict in the 1920s: A Historiographical Assessment." *The Historian* 49 (November 1986): 26–48.

Ehrenreich, Barbara, and Deirdre English. *For Her Own Good: 150 Years of the Experts' Advice to Women.* Garden City, N.Y.: Anchor Press/Doubleday, 1978.

Emerson, Harrington. *The Twelve Principles of Efficiency.* New York: The Engineering Magazine Company, 1913.

Evans, Sara M. *Born for Liberty: A History of Women in America.* New York: Free Press, 1989.

Ewen, Stuart. *Captains of Consciousness: Advertising and the Social Roots of the Consumer Culture.* New York: McGraw-Hill Book Company, 1976.

"Facts Then Action: A Merchandise Report, 1925–1930." *Better Business Bureau of Metropolitan New York,* 1922–1932.

"Feminist from Earlier Era Dies at 87." *Los Angeles Times,* 8 April 1970, sec. 3, p. 1, col. 3.

Field, Marilyn, and J. George Frederick. *1000 Pleasure Spots in Beautiful America.* New York: Business Bourse, 1957.

Flexner, Eleanor, and Ellen Fitzpatrick. *Century of Struggle: The Woman's Rights Movement in the United States.* Enlarged ed. Cambridge: Harvard University Press, Belknap Press, 1996.

The Forerunner, 1909–16. *Radical Periodicals in the United States, 1890–1960.* New York: Greenwood Reprint Corporation, 1968. Microfilm.

Fox-Genovese, Elizabeth. *Feminism without Illusions: A Critique of Individualism*. Chapel Hill: University of North Carolina Press, 1991.

Franck, Karen, and Sherry Arhentzen, eds. *New Households, New Housing*. New York: Van Nostrand Reinhold, 1989.

Frederick, Filis. *Design and Sell Toys, Games, and Crafts*. Radnor, Pa.: Chilton Book Company, 1977.

———. Foreword to *The Path of Love*, by Meher Baba. 2d ed. Hermosa Beach, Calif.: Awakener Press, 1986.

———. "Darshan III: A Time for Lovers." *The Awakener* 13, nos. 1 and 2 (n.d.): 32–69.

———. "Memories of '52." *The Awakener* 14, no. 2 (n.d.): 4–5.

———. "Reminiscences of the City of Lost Angels." Photocopy.

Frederick, J. George. "The Tie That Binds." *American Magazine*, August 1906, 435–43.

———. "The Play Confessions of a Busy Man." *Craftsman*, February 1908, 563–66.

———. *Breezy*. N.p.: Doubleday, Page and Company for *The Review of Reviews*, 1909.

———. "Is It Right to Maintain Prices on Patented Articles?" *Scientific American* 106 (1 June 1912): 501.

———. "The Efficiency Movement." *Harper's Weekly*, 2 November 1912, 11.

———. *Modern Sales Management*. New York: Appleton, 1919.

———. *The Great Game of Business: Its Rules, Its Fascination, Its Services and Rewards*. New York: D. Appleton and Company, 1920.

———. "Tahiti Has a Traffic Cop." *New York Times*, 12 October 1924, sec. 4, p. 14.

———. *Two Women*. New York: Brown, N. L., 1924.

———. *Modern Industrial Consolidation*. New York: Frank-Maurice, 1926.

———. "Standardization—Bane or Blessing?" *Outlook*, 12 January 1927, 50–51.

———. "I'm Glad I'm Not a College Man." *Outlook*, 4 January 1928, 20–21.

———. "Is Progressive Obsolescence the Path toward Increased Consumption?" *Advertising and Selling*, 5 September 1928, 19–20, 44–46.

———. *What Is Your Emotional Age? And 65 Other Mental Tests*. New York: Business Bourse, 1928.

———. *Common Stocks and the Average Man*. New York: Business Bourse, 1930.

———. *Cooking As Men Like It*. With a foreword by Christine Frederick. New York: Business Bourse, 1930.

———. *Humanism As a Way of Life*. New York: Business Bourse, 1930.

———. *The Long Island Seafood Cookbook*. Recipes edited by Jean Joyce, 1939. Reprint, New York: Dover Publications, 1971.

———. *How to Understand a Man, Emotionally and Temperamentally and How to Understand a Woman, Emotionally and Temperamentally*. New York: Business Bourse, 1941.

———. "The Law of the Heart." In *This I Believe: The Living Philosophies of One Hundred Thoughtful Men and Women in All Walks of Life — As Written for and with a Foreword by Edward R. Murrow*, ed. Edward P. Morgan, 55–56. New York: Simon and Schuster, 1952.

————, ed. *Masters of Advertising Copy: Principles and Practice of Copy Writing According to Its Leading Practitioners*. New York: Business Bourse, 1925.

Friedan, Betty. *The Feminine Mystique*. New York: W. W. Norton and Company, 1963; New York: Dell Publishing Company, 1964.

Friedman, Jean E., and William G. Shade, eds. *Our American Sisters: Women in American Life and Thought*. Boston: Allyn and Bacon, 1974.

Fritschner, Linda Marie. "The Rise and Fall of Home Economics: A Study with Implications for Women, Education, and Change." Ph.D. diss., University of California, Davis, 1973. Ann Arbor, Mich.: University Microfilms International, 1978.

Fromm, Dorit. *Collaborative Communities: Cohousing, Central Living, and Other New Forms of Housing with Shared Facilities*. New York: Van Nostrand Reinhold, 1991.

Galambos, Louis. "The Emerging Organizational Synthesis in Modern American History." *Business History Review* 44 (autumn 1970): 279–90.

Giedion, Siegfried. *Mechanization Takes Command: A Contribution to Anonymous History*. New York: Oxford Press, 1948.

Gilbert, Eleanor. "Why I Hate My Independence." *Ladies' Home Journal*, March 1920, 139–40.

Gilbreth, Lillian Moller. *The Quest of the One Best Way: A Sketch of the Life of Frank Bunker Gilbreth*. New York: Society of Women Engineers, n.d.

Gilman, Charlotte Perkins. *The Home: Its Work and Influence*. 1903. Reprint, New York: Source Book Press, 1970.

————. "The Work before Us." *Forerunner*, January 1912, 7.

————. "The End of the Advertising Nuisance." *Forerunner*, December 1912, 327.

————. "The Waste of Private Housekeeping." *Annals of the American Academy of Political and Social Science* 48 (July 1913): 91–95.

————. "Is Feminism Really So Dreadful?" *Delineator*, August, 1914, 6.

————. *The Man-Made World or, Our Androcentric Culture*. New York: Charlton Company, 1914.

————. "Women and Vocations," Women in Industry Lecture no. 1, [4 October 1915], pp. 23–41, carton 1, file folder 3, BVI Records.

————. "Woman's Achievements Since the Franchise." *Current History*, October 1927, 7–14.

Goldstein, Carolyn. "Part of the Package: Home Economists in the Consumer Products Industries, 1920–1940." In *Rethinking Home Economics*, ed. Stage and Vincenti, 271–96.

Gould, Joseph E. *The Chautauqua Movement: An Episode in the Continuing American Revolution*. N.p.: State University of New York, 1961.

Gould's St. Louis Directory. St. Louis: David B. Gould, Publisher, 1891–94.

Gregg, Mrs. Abel J. "What Women Are Thinking: The Y.M.C.A. Talks It Over." *Survey*, 1 June 1929, 300–303.

Griffith, Elizabeth. *In Her Own Right: The Life of Elizabeth Cady Stanton*. New York: Oxford University Press, 1984.

Grimké, A[ngelina] E. *Letters to Catharine E. Beecher in Reply to an Essay on Slavery and Abolition*. 1838. Reprint, Freeport, N.Y.: Books for Libraries Press, 1971.

Guernsey, John B. "Scientific Management in the Home." *Outlook,* 13 April 1912, 821–25.

Haber, Samuel. *Efficiency and Uplift: Scientific Management in the Progressive Era, 1890–1920*. Chicago: University of Chicago Press, 1964.

Hall, Jacquelyn Dowd. *Revolt against Chivalry: Jessie Daniel Ames and the Women's Campaign against Lynching*. New York: Columbia University Press, 1979.

Handlin, David. *The American Home: Architecture and Society, 1815–1915*. Boston: Little, Brown, 1979.

Hapgood, Hutchins. *A Victorian in the Modern World*. New York: Harcourt, Brace, and Company, 1939.

"The Harm My Education Did Me." *Outlook,* 30 November 1927, 396–97, 405.

Harrison, Harry P., as told to Karl Detzer. *Culture under Canvas: The Story of Tent Chautauqua*. New York: Hastings House, Publishers, 1958.

Hayden, Dolores, *The Grand Domestic Revolution: A History of Feminist Designs for American Homes, Neighborhoods, and Cities*. First MIT Paperback Edition. Cambridge, Mass.: MIT Press, 1982.

———. *Redesigning the American Dream: The Future of Housing, Work, and Family Life*. New York: W. W. Norton and Company, 1984.

Heath, Mrs. Julian. "Work of the Housewives' League." *Annals of the American Academy of Political and Social Science* 48 (July 1913): 121–26.

Hechtlinger, Adelaide. *The Great Era of Patent Medicines*. New York: Galahad Books, 1970.

Hill, Mary A. *Charlotte Perkins Gilman: The Making of a Radical Feminist, 1860–1896*. Philadelphia: Temple University Press, 1980.

Hochschild, Arlie, with Anne Machung. *The Second Shift: Working Parents and the Revolution at Home*. New York: Viking, 1989.

Hollingworth, Harry L. *Advertising and Selling: Principles of Appeal and Response*. New York: D. Appleton and Company, 1918.

Hollingworth, Leta S. "The New Woman in the Making." *Current History,* October 1927, 15–20.

"Home Efficiency." *Outlook,* 2 December 1911, 807.

Hoover, Herbert. "Nationalized Power." *The Nation,* 18 September 1920, 318–19.

Hoover, Herbert H. "Address of President Hoover." In *Housing Objectives and Programs*. Vol. 11 of *Publications of the President's Conference on Home Building and Home Ownership*. Washington, D.C.: [GPO], 1932.

Horowitz, Helen Lefkowitz. *Alma Mater: Design and Experience in the Women's Colleges from Their Nineteenth-Century Beginnings to the 1930s*. New York: Alfred A. Knopf, 1984.

Howells, William Dean. *A Hazard of New Fortunes*. 1890. Reprint, New York: New American Library/Signet Classics, 1965.

Katchmer, George A. *Eighty Silent Film Stars: Biographies and Filmographies of the Obscure to the Well Known.* Jefferson, N.C.: McFarland and Company, 1991.

Keller, Morton. *Affairs of State: Public Life in Late Nineteenth Century America.* Cambridge: Harvard University Press, Belknap Press, 1977.

Keller, Suzanne, ed. *Building for Women.* Lexington, Mass.: Lexington Books, 1981.

Kerber, Linda K. *Women of the Republic: Intellect and Ideology in Revolutionary America.* Chapel Hill: University of North Carolina Press, 1980.

————. "Separate Spheres, Female Worlds, Woman's Place: The Rhetoric of Women's History." *The Journal of American History* 75 (June 1988): 9–39.

Kneeland, Hildegarde. "Is the Modern Housewife a Lady of Leisure?" *Survey,* 1 June 1929, 301–36.

Kraditor, Aileen. *The Ideas of the Woman Suffrage Movement, 1890–1920.* 2d ed. New York: W. W. Norton and Company, 1981.

La Follette, Fola. "Suffragetting on the Chautauqua Circuit." *Ladies' Home Journal,* January 1916, 27.

La Follette, Suzanne. *Concerning Women.* 1926. Reprint, New York: Arno Press, 1972.

The Ladies' Home Journal, 1901–30.

"Lake Placid Conference on Home Economics, 1899–1908." *JHE* 1 (February 1909): 4.

Lammert-Reeves, Ruth. *Law School Admissions Advisor.* New York: Simon and Schuster, 1999.

Lape, Esther Everett, "What Do Women Want with the Vote?" *Ladies' Home Journal,* March 1920, 39.

Lasch, Christopher. "Woman As Alien." In *Our American Sisters,* ed. Friedman and Shade, 168–86.

Leach, William. *Land of Desire: Merchants, Power, and the Rise of a New American Culture.* New York: Pantheon Books, 1993.

Lears, T. J. Jackson. "From Salvation to Self-Realization: Advertising and the Therapeutic Roots of the Consumer Culture, 1880–1930." In *The Culture of Consumption: Critical Essays in American History, 1880–1980,* ed. Richard Wightman Fox and T. J. Jackson Lears, 1–38. New York: Pantheon Books, 1983.

Leavitt, Jacqueline. "Two Prototypical Designs for Single Parents." In *New Households, New Housing,* ed. Franck and Arhentzen, 161–86.

Lebovitz, J. "The Home and the Machine." *Journal of Home Economics* 3 (April 1911): 141–48.

Lemons, J. Stanley. *The Woman Citizen: Social Feminism in the 1920s.* Urbana: University of Illinois Press, 1973.

Leuchtenburg, William E. *The Perils of Prosperity, 1914–1932.* The Chicago History of American Civilization Series. Chicago: The University of Chicago Press, 1958.

Linden, Dana Wechsler. "The Class of '65." *Forbes Magazine,* 4 July 1994, 92–98.

Lindsey, Ben B., and Wainwright Evans. *The Companionate Marriage.* Garden City, N.Y.: Garden City Publishing Company, 1929.

Lippmann, Walter. "The Causes of Political Indifference To-Day." *Atlantic Monthly*, January 1927, 261–68.

Lockley, Lawrence C. "Notes on the History of Marketing Research." *Journal of Marketing* 14 (April 1950): 733–36.

Loewenthal, Lillian. *The Search for Isadora: The Legend and Legacy of Isadora Duncan*. Pennington, N.J.: Princeton Book Company, 1993.

Lubar, Steven. "Men/Women/Production/Consumption." In *His and Hers: Gender, Consumption, and Technology*, ed. Roger Horowitz and Arwen Mohun, 7–37. Charlottesville: University Press of Virginia, 1998.

Lundberg, Ferdinand, and Marynia F. Farnham. *Modern Woman: The Lost Sex*. New York: Harper and Brothers, 1947.

MacDonald, Dwight. *The Ford Foundation: The Men and the Millions*. New York: Reynal and Company, 1956.

MacManus, Theodore F. "The Underlying Principles of Good Copy." In *Masters of Advertising Copy*, ed. J. G. Frederick, 77–92. New York: Business Bourse, 1925.

Mallery, Otto T. "Book Department," review of *Readings in Economics*, by J. George Frederick. *Annals of the American Academy of Political and Social Science* 166 (March 1933): 224.

Mansbridge, Jane J. *Why We Lost the ERA*. Chicago: University of Chicago Press, 1986.

Marchand, Roland. *Advertising the American Dream: Making Way for Modernity, 1920–1940*. Berkeley: University of California Press, 1985.

Martin, Anne. "Women and 'Their' Magazines." *New Republic*, 20 September 1922, 91–93.

Matthews, Glenna. *"Just a Housewife": The Rise and Fall of Domesticity in America*. New York: Oxford University Press, 1987.

McCamant, Kathryn, and Charles Durrett. *Cohousing: A Contemporary Approach to Housing Ourselves*. Berkeley: Habitat Press, 1988.

McMenamin, Hugh L. "Evils of Woman's Revolt against the Old Standards." *Current History*, October 1927, 30–32.

Mead, Margaret. "Return of the Cave Woman." *Saturday Evening Post*, 3 March 1962, 6–8.

Monroe, Day. "New Books." Review of *Selling Mrs. Consumer*, by Christine Frederick. *Journal of Home Economics* 21 (November 1929): 856–57.

"More Bait Advertising." *National Better Business Bureau of the Associated Advertising Clubs of the World*, 18 March 1926.

Mowry, George E. *The Era of Theodore Roosevelt and the Birth of Modern America, 1900–1912*. New York: Harper and Brothers, 1958; Harper Torchbook, 1962.

"Mrs. Christine Frederick." *Mon Chez Moi* (Paris), May 1927.

Muncy, Robyn. *Creating a Female Dominion in American Reform, 1890–1935*. New York: Oxford University Press, 1991.

Nadworny, Milton J. "Frederick Taylor and Frank Gilbreth: Competition in Scientific Management." *Business History Review* 31 (spring 1957): 23–34.

Naether, Carl A. *Advertising to Women*. New York: Prentice-Hall, 1928.

Nash, Roderick. *The Nervous Generation: American Thought, 1917–1930*. Chicago: Rand McNally, 1970; Elephant Paperback, 1970.

Nelson, Andrew. "A Neighborhood for the '90s." *Special Report*, January/February 1993, 28–31.

"The New Housekeeping." Review of *The New Housekeeping: Efficiency Studies in Home Management*, by Christine Frederick. *Journal of Home Economics* 5 (October 1913): 336–37.

The New York Times, 1913–98.

Noggle, Burl L. "Configurations of the Twenties." In *The Reinterpretation of American History and Culture*, ed. William H. Cartwright and Richard L. Watson Jr., 465–90. Washington, D.C.: National Council for the Social Studies, 1973.

Oakley, Helen Peffer. "AWNY—An Informal History, 1912–1962." In *Advertising Women of New York Golden Salute to Advertising*. New York: Advertising Women of New York Foundation, 1962.

Ohmann, Richard. *Selling Culture: Magazines, Markets, and Class at the Turn of the Century*. London: Verso, 1996.

The Old Gold and Blue. Yearbook, Peddie School, 1924. Peddie School Archives, Hightstown, N.J. Photocopy.

Orelup, Margaret Anne. "For Scientists and Artists: Model Kitchens, 1912–1935." Master's thesis, George Washington University, 1981.

Painter, Nell Irvin. "Writing Biographies of Women." *Journal of Women's History* 9 (summer 1997): 154–63.

Parsons, Alice Beal. *Woman's Dilemma*. New York: Thomas Y. Crowell, 1926.

Pattison, Mrs. Frank A. "Scientific Management in Home-Making." *Annals of the American Academy of Political and Social Science* 48 (July 1913): 96–103.

Peiss, Kathy. "Making Up, Making Over: Cosmetics, Consumer Culture, and Women's Identity." In *Sex of Things*, ed. de Grazia, with Furlough, 311–36.

Pitcher, Harvey. *When Miss Emmie Was in Russia: English Governesses before, during and after the October Revolution*. London: John Murray (Publishers) Ltd., 1977.

Pope, Daniel. *The Making of Modern Advertising*. New York: Basic Books, 1983.

Presbrey, Frank. *The History and Development of Advertising*. Garden City, N.Y.: Doubleday, Doran and Company, 1929.

Publishers' Weekly, 19 January 1952, 233.

Purcell, Blanche W. "Home Economics at Hampton Institute." *Southern Workman*, LIV (January–December 1925): 9–15.

Rapp, Rayna, and Ellen Ross. "The Twenties Backlash: Compulsory Heterosexuality, the Consumer Family, and the Waning of Feminism." In *Class, Race and Sex*, ed. Amy Swerdlow and Hanna Lessinger, 93–107. Boston: Barnard College Women's Center, G. K. Hall and Company, 1983.

"Revelations about the 'Vice Trust.'" *Current Opinion*, January 1913, 5.

Richards, Ellen H. "The Outlook in Home Economics." *Journal of Home Economics* 2 (February 1910): 17–19.

————. "The Social Significance of the Home Economics Movement." *Journal of Home Economics* 3 (April 1911): 117–25.

Rickert, Edith. "What Women's Clubs Have Really Done." *Ladies' Home Journal,* October 1912, 12.

Riis, Jacob. *How the Other Half Lives: Studies among the Tenements of New York.* 1890. Reprint, New York: Dover Publications, 1971.

Riley, Glenda. *Divorce: An American Tradition.* New York: Oxford University Press, 1991.

Robinson, Charles Mulford. "Abuses of Public Advertising." *Atlantic Monthly,* March 1904, 289–99.

Robinson, John P., and Geoffrey Godbey. *Time for Life: The Surprising Ways Americans Use Their Time.* University Park: Pennsylvania State University Press, 1997.

Robinson, Lisa Mae. "Safeguarded by Your Refrigerator: Mary Engle Pennington's Struggle with the National Association of Ice Industries." In *Rethinking Home Economics,* ed. Stage and Vincenti, 253–70.

Rosenstone, Robert A. "Reform and Radicalism: John Reed and the Limits of Reform." In *Reform and Reformers in the Progressive Era,* ed. David R. Colburn and George E. Possetta, 133–51. Westport, Conn.: Greenwood Press, 1983.

Rossiter, Margaret W. *Women Scientists in America: Struggles and Strategies to 1940.* Baltimore: Johns Hopkins University Press, 1982.

Rubinow, I. M. "Household Service As a Labor Problem." *Journal of Home Economics* 3 (April 1911): 131–40.

Saegert, Susan, and Gary Winkel. "The Home: A Critical Problem for Changing Sex Roles." In *New Space for Women,* ed. Gerda R. Wekerle, Rebecca Peterson, and David Morley, 41–64.

Scanlon, Jennifer. *Inarticulate Longings: The Ladies' Home Journal, Gender, and the Promises of Consumer Culture.* New York: Routledge, 1995.

Schmidt, Leigh Eric. *Consumer Rites: The Buying and Selling of American Holidays.* Princeton: Princeton University Press, 1995.

Schwarz, Judith. *The Radical Feminists of Heterodoxy: Greenwich Village, 1912–1940.* Rev. ed. Norwich, Vt.: New Victoria Publisher, 1986.

Scott, Walter D. *The Theory and Practice of Advertising: A Simple Exposition of the Principles of Psychology in Their Relation to Successful Advertising.* Boston: Small, Maynard and Company, [1903].

————. "The Psychology of Advertising." *Atlantic Monthly,* January 1904, 29–36.

Showalter, Elaine, ed. *These Modern Women: Autobiographical Essays from the Twenties.* Rev. ed. New York: The Feminist Press, 1989.

Singal, Daniel Joseph. "Towards a Definition of American Modernism." *American Quarterly* 39 (spring 1987): 7–26.

Sklar, Kathryn Kish. *Catharine Beecher: A Study in American Domesticity.* New Haven: Yale University Press, 1973.

————. *Florence Kelley and the Nation's Work: The Rise of Women's Political Culture, 1830–1900.* New Haven: Yale University Press, 1995.

Sklar, Martin J. *The Corporate Reconstruction of American Capitalism, 1890–1916: The Market, the Law, and Politics.* Cambridge: Cambridge University Press, 1988.

Smith, T. V. "Book Reviews." Review of *Humanism As a Way of Life,* by J. George Frederick. *International Journal of Ethics* 41 (April 1931): 409–10.

Snyder, Katherine. "A Paradise of Bachelors: Remodeling Domesticity and Masculinity in the Turn-of-the-Century New York Bachelor Apartment." *Prospects* 23 (1998): 247–84.

Sobel, Robert. *Coolidge: An American Enigma.* Washington, D.C.: Regnery Publishing, 1998.

Sochen, June. *The New Woman: Feminism in Greenwich Village, 1910–1920.* New York: Quadrangle Books, 1972.

———. *Movers and Shakers: American Women Thinkers and Activists, 1900–1970.* New York: Quadrangle Books, 1973.

Stage, Sarah. "Introduction: What's in a Name?" In *Rethinking Home Economics,* ed. Stage and Vincenti, 1–13.

Stage, Sarah, and Virginia B. Vincenti, eds. *Rethinking Home Economics: Women and the History of a Profession.* Ithaca, N.Y.: Cornell University Press, 1997.

"Standardization of Housework." *Journal of Home Economics* 2 (November 1910): 475.

Stegelin, Dolores A., and Judith Frankel. "Families of Employed Mothers in the United States." In *Families of Employed Mothers: An International Perspective,* ed. Judith Frankel, 237–61. New York: Garland Publishing, 1997.

Stevens, Don E. *Man's Search for Certainty.* New York: Dodd, Mead and Company, 1980.

———. Introduction to *Discourses,* by Meher Baba. Reprint (3 vols. in 1), with a foreword by Eruch Jessawala, J. Flagg Kris, and Bal Natu. N.p.: Sheriar Press, 1987.

Strasser, Susan. *Never Done: A History of American Housework.* New York: Pantheon Books, 1982.

———. *Satisfaction Guaranteed: The Making of the American Mass Market.* New York: Pantheon Books, 1989.

Stuhler, Barbara. *For the Public Record: A Documentary History of the League of Women Voters.* Westport, Conn.: Greenwood Press, 2000.

Suckow, Ruth. *Country People.* 1924. Reprint, Rediscovered Fiction by American Women Series. With an introduction by Elizabeth Hardwick. New York: Arno Press, 1977.

Susman, Warren I. *Culture As History: The Transformation of American Society in the Twentieth Century.* New York: Pantheon Books, 1984.

Swiencicki, Mark. "Consuming Brotherhood: Men's Culture, Style and Recreation as Consumer Culture, 1880–1930." *Journal of Social History* 31 (summer 1998): 774–808.

The Syllabus. Evanston, Ill.: Northwestern University, 1905–7.

Symes, Lillian. "Still a Man's Game: Reflections of a Slightly Tired Feminist." *Harper's,* May 1929, 678–86.

Tacoma News Tribune, 1998.

Talbot, Marion, and Sophonisba Preston Breckinridge. *The Modern Household*. Boston: Whitcomb and Barrows, 1912.

Talley, Charlotte. "A Cooperative Kitchen That Is Meeting a Need in Its Community." *Journal of Home Economics* 7 (August-September 1915): 373–75.

Taylor, Eugene. *Shadow Culture: Psychology and Spirituality in America*. Washington, D.C.: Counterpoint, 1999.

Taylor, Frederick Winslow. *The Principles of Scientific Management*. New York: Harper and Brothers, 1913.

Tead, Ordway. "The New Consumer." Review of *Selling Mrs. Consumer*, by Christine Frederick. *Saturday Review of Literature*, 2 November 1929, 338.

Tebbel, John. *The Compact History of the American Newspaper*. Rev. ed. New York: Hawthorn Books, 1969.

Tebbel, John, and Mary Ellen Zuckerman. *The Magazine in America, 1741–1990*. New York: Oxford University Press, 1991.

Tidball, M. Elizabeth, Daryl G. Smith, Charles S. Tidball, and Lisa E. Wolf-Wendel. *Taking Women Seriously: Lessons and Legacies for Educating the Majority*. Phoenix: The American Council on Education and the Onyx Press, 1999.

Title IX of the Education Amendments of 1972. *U.S. Code*. Vol. 20, secs. 1681–88 (1972).

True, A. C. "Home Economics Work under the Smith-Lever Act." *Journal of Home Economics* 7 (August-September 1915): 353–55.

U.S. Department of Commerce. Building and Housing Division, Standards Bureau. *How to Own Your Own Home: A Handbook for Prospective Homeowners*, by John M. Gries and James S. Taylor. Washington, D.C.: Government Printing Office, 1925.

―――. *Present Home Financing Methods*, by John M. Gries and Thomas M. Curran. Washington, D.C.: Government Printing Office, 1928.

U.S. Department of Labor, Women's Bureau. "Women at the Millenium, Accomplishments and Challenges Ahead." *Facts on Working Women*, no. 00–02 (March 2000): 5.

U.S. House Committee on the Judiciary. *Hearings before the Committee on the Judiciary on Trust Legislation*. 63rd Cong., 2d sess., 18 February 1914.

U.S. House of Representatives. *Report on Resale Price Maintenance*. 66th Cong., 1st sess., 1919. H. Doc. 145. Serial 7644.

Van Buskirk, Ursula. "Filis." *Meher Baba Center of No. Ca. Inc. Quarterly Newsletter*, summer 1987.

Vanek, Joann. "Time Spent in Housework." *Scientific American* 231 (November 1974): 116–20.

Veblen, Thorstein. *The Theory of the Leisure Class*. 1899. Reprint, with an introduction by C. Wright Mills, New York: New American Library, 1953.

Washington, Margaret J. "Dorothy Hall." *Southern Workman*, LIV (January–December 1925): 200–206.

Wear, Delese, ed. *Women in Medical Education: An Anthology of Experience*. Albany: State University of New York Press, 1996.

Wekerle, Gerda R., Rebecca Peterson, and David Morley, eds. *New Space for Women.* Boulder, Colo.: Westview Press, 1980.

Welter, Barbara. *Dimity Convictions: The American Woman in the Nineteenth Century.* Athens: Ohio University Press, 1976. Reprint, 1977.

"What Robin Morgan Said at Denver." *Journal of Home Economics* 65 (January 1973): 13.

"Where Are the Pre-War Radicals?" *Survey*, February 1926, 556–66.

Wiebe, Robert. *The Search for Order, 1877–1920.* New York: Hill and Wang, 1967.

Wiseman, Eileen Barry. "Christine Frederick: Accolade to a First Lady." In *Advertising Women of New York Golden Salute to Advertising.*

"A World of Woman's Work." *Atlanta City Builder*, May 1916, 13–14.

Wright, Gwendolyn. "The Model Domestic Environment: Icon or Option?" In *Women in American Architecture: A Historic and Contemporary Perspective*, ed. Susana Torre, 18–31. New York: Whitney Library of Design, 1977.

———. *Building the Dream: A Social History of Housing in America.* Cambridge, Mass.: MIT Press, 1983.

Zahner, L. William. *Architectural Metals: A Guide to Selection, Specification, and Performance.* New York: Wiley and Sons, 1995.

Manuscript Sources

Advertising Women of New York. Papers. Arthur and Elizabeth Schlesinger Library on the History of Women in America, Radcliffe Institute, Harvard University, Cambridge, Mass.

Alumni Biographical Files. Northwestern University Archives, Evanston, Ill.

Atlanta Woman's Club Papers. Atlanta History Center, Atlanta, Ga.

Beecher, Catharine, to Elizabeth Cady Stanton, 16 May 1870. Harper Collection. Henry E. Huntington Library and Art Gallery, San Marino, Calif. Photocopy.

Beecher-Stowe Family Papers. Schlesinger Library, Radcliffe Institute, Harvard University.

Burdick, Anna, to Louise Stanley, 21 October 1930. Records of the Bureau of Human Nutrition and Home Economics. Record Group 176. General Records. National Archives Branch Depository, College Park, Md.

Bureau of Vocational Information of New York City. Records. Schlesinger Library, Radcliffe Institute, Harvard University. Microfilm, Strozier Library, Florida State University, Tallahassee, Fla.

Calbreath Family Collection. Special Collections. Knight Library, University of Oregon, Eugene.

Campbell, Christine Isobel, In the Matter of. No. 78051. Archives Department, Circuit Court, City of St. Louis, Mo.

Dignam, Dorothy. Papers. Schlesinger Library, Radcliffe Institute, Harvard University.

Frederick, Christine. File. Huntington Historical Society, Huntington, N.Y.

Frederick, Christine MacGaffey. Papers. Schlesinger Library, Radcliffe Institute, Harvard University.

Frederick Collection. Greenlawn-Centerport Historical Association, Greenlawn, N.Y.

Frederick, David. Grade cards. Peddie School Archives, Hightstown, N.J.

Frederick, J. George, to Ellis Parker Butler, 31 March 1923. Manuscript Letters Collection. Special Collection Department. University of Iowa Libraries, Iowa City. Photocopy.

Frederick, J. George, to Evelyn Light, 23 November 1993. Theodore Dreiser Papers. Special Collections. Van Pelt-Dietrich Library Center, University of Pennsylvania, Philadelphia. Photocopy.

Frederick, Phyllis. Student file. Radcliffe College Archives, Cambridge, Mass.

Gilman, Charlotte Perkins. Papers. Library of Congress.

Gilman, Charlotte Perkins. Papers. Schlesinger Library, Radcliffe Institute, Harvard University.

Harper Collection. HM10546. Henry E. Huntington Library and Art Gallery, San Marino, Calif.

Home Economic Materials Collection. Political History Division. National History Museum, Washington, D.C.

Notable American Women. Records. Radcliffe College Archives.

St. Francis-by-the-Sea Archives. St. Francis-by-the-Sea Chapel, Laguna Beach, Calif.

St. Louis, Mo., City of. Recorder of Deeds.

Suffolk County Deed Liber Books. Suffolk County Clerk's Office, Riverhead, N.Y.

Suffolk County Superior Court, Department for Civil Business. Record Book, Divorces, 1890. Boston, Mass.

Watson, John Broadus. Papers. Library of Congress.

Women's Educational and Industrial Union. Records. Schlesinger Library, Radcliffe Institute, Harvard University.

Wright, Nathaniel Family. Papers. Library of Congress.

Interviews

Arnold, Louise. Telephone conversation with author. Tape recording. 13 March 1994.

———. Interview by author. Tape recording. Laguna Beach, Calif., 6 September 1995.

Baer, Barbara. Telephone conversation with author, 9 April 1994.

Falk, Barbara. Telephone conversation with author, 9 August 1998.

Frederick, Deborah. Telephone conversations with author, 20 February, 7 September 1996.

Frederick, Filis. "The Older Woman." Interview by Adele Wolkin. Typescript, Redondo Beach, Calif., 10 May 1982.

———. *Holding On to Baba's Damaan*. Produced by Wendell Brustman. Los Angeles, May 1986. Videocassette.

Frederick, Nan. Telephone conversation with author, 18 September 1996.

Joyce, Jean. Interviews by author. Tape recordings. Washington, D.C., 14–16 September 1994.

Justin, Peter. Interview by author. Tape recording. Ojai, Calif., 10 September 1995.

Kennelly, Thomas. Telephone conversation with author, 22 August 1995.

Krusa, Renée. Telephone conversation with author. Tape recording. 15 August 1994.

Lang, Fred. Telephone conversation with author. Tape recording. 3 June 1994.

Newman, Jody. Interview by Lynn Neary. *Morning Edition.* National Public Radio, 14 October 1994.

Renley, John. Telephone conversation with author, 13 March 1994.

Tsalarczyk, Bishop Simon. Interview by author. Laguna Beach, Calif., 6 September 1995.

Wolkin, Adele. Telephone conversation with author. Tape recording. 22 June 1995.

———. Interview by author. Redondo Beach, Calif., 6 September 1995.

Electronic and Media Sources

Current Congressional Profile. Available [on-line]: <http://clerkweb.house.gov/> Path: Members and Committees/House Member Information/Current Congressional Profile of the 107th Congress. [30 October 2001].

Family Career and Community Leaders of American Membership Map. Available [on-line]: <http://www.fhahero.org/> Path: Membership/Membership Map/Totals [30 April 2001].

Percentage of Women in State Legislatures. Available [on-line]: <http://www.stateaction.org/index.cfm> Path: State of States/Percentage of Women in State Legislatures [30 April 2001].

Senators of the 107th Congress. Available [on-line]: <http://www.senate.gov/senator/senators/index.cfm> [30 April 2001].

Tillotson, Mary. "The New Face of Feminism." *CNN and Company,* 24 June 1998.

U.S. Department of Labor. Civilian Labor Force for Selected Demographic Groups. Available [on-line]: <http://www.dol.gov/> [18 October 2001].

———. Civilian Labor Force Participation Rates. Available [on-line]: <http://www.dol.gov/> [18 October 2001].

———. Labor Force Participation Rates of Women. Available [on-line]: <http://www.dol.gov/> [18 October 2001].

U.S. Department of Labor, Women's Bureau. *20 Leading Occupations of Employed Women.* Available [on-line]: <http://www.dol.gov/dol/wb/> Path: Statistics and Data/20 Leading Occupations [30 April 2001].

———. *The Wage Gap between Women and Men.* Available [on-line]: <http://www.dol.gov/wb/> Path: Library/Facts on Working Women/20 Facts on Working Women [30 April 2001].

Index